ROMAN EPIC

ROMAN EPIC

Edited by

A. J. Boyle

London and New York

First published 1993
First published in paperback 1996
by Routledge
11 New Fetter Lane, London EC4P 4EE

Simultaneously published in the USA and Canada
by Routledge
29 West 35th Street, New York, NY 10001

Routledge is an International Thomson Publishing company I(T)P

Typeset in 10/12pt Baskerville by
Ponting-Green Publishing Services, Sunninghill, Berkshire
Printed and bound in Great Britain by
T.J. Press (Padstow) Ltd, Padstow, Cornwall

British Library Cataloguing in Publication Data
Roman Epic
I. Boyle, A.J.
873.009

Library of Congress Cataloguing in Publication Data
Roman epic / edited by A.J. Boyle.
p. cm.
Includes bibliographical references.
1. Epic poetry, Latin-History and criticism. 2. Epic poetry - Roman
influences. 3. Rome in literature. I. Boyle, A.J. (Anthony James)
PA6054.R65 1993
873.009-dc20
92-25458

ISBN 0-415-14357-8

FOR JOHN SULLIVAN

CONTENTS

Preface   xi

I   INTRODUCTION: THE ROMAN SONG   1
A. J. Boyle

II   SATURNIAN EPIC: LIVIUS AND NAEVIUS   19
Sander M. Goldberg

III   FROM GREECE TO ROME: ENNIUS' *ANNALES*   37
William J. Dominik

IV   NEOTERIC EPIC: CATULLUS 64   59
David Konstan

V   THE CANONIC TEXT: VIRGIL'S *AENEID*   79
A. J. Boyle

VI   FORM CHANGED: OVID'S *METAMORPHOSES*   108
William S. Anderson

VII   FORM EMPOWERED: LUCAN'S *PHARSALIA*   125
Frederick Ahl

VIII   FORM OPPOSED: ELEGY, EPIGRAM, SATIRE   143
J. P. Sullivan

IX   FORM REMADE/STATIUS' *THEBAID*   162
John Henderson

X   FLAVIAN VARIANT: MYTH. VALERIUS' *ARGONAUTICA*   192
Martha A. Malamud and Donald T. McGuire, jr

XI   FLAVIAN VARIANT: HISTORY. SILIUS' *PUNICA*   218
Marcus Wilson

XII   EPIC IN MIND: CLAUDIAN'S *DE RAPTU PROSERPINAE*   237
Peter Connor

CONTENTS

XIII AFTER ROME: MEDIEVAL EPIC   261
      John O. Ward

XIV AFTER ROME: RENAISSANCE EPIC   294
      Philip Hardie

      References   314
      General index   327
      Index of main passages discussed   334

CONTRIBUTORS

Frederick Ahl   Professor of Classics, Cornell University.

William S. Anderson   Professor of Classics, University of California, Berkeley.

A. J. Boyle   Professor of Classics, University of Southern California.

Peter Connor   Senior Lecturer in Classics, University of Melbourne.

William J. Dominik   Lecturer in Classics, University of Natal.

Sander M. Goldberg   Professor of Classics, University of California, Los Angeles.

Philip Hardie   Lecturer in Classics and Fellow of New Hall, Cambridge.

John Henderson   Lecturer in Classics and Fellow of King's College, Cambridge.

David Konstan   Professor of Classics, Brown University.

Donald T. McGuire jr   Adjunct Professor of Classics, State University of New York, Buffalo.

Martha A. Malamud   Associate Professor of Classics, State University of New York, Buffalo.

J. P. Sullivan   Professor of Classics, University of California, Santa Barbara.

John O. Ward   Senior Lecturer in History, University of Sydney.

Marcus Wilson   Lecturer in Classics, University of Auckland.

PREFACE

In the early 1960s Routledge published two volumes of *Critical Essays on Roman Literature*, edited by J. P. Sullivan: *Elegy and Lyric* (1962) and *Satire* (1963). Both volumes had a seminal impact on the teaching and literary investigation of Latin authors, especially Latin poets, and contributed substantially to the critical revolution in Latin studies which began to manifest itself (not always at the same pace or with the same clarity) in the English-speaking world at that time. Much has changed in classical literary studies since those 'heady' days. The battle of scholar versus critic which fuelled the pages of journals such as *Arion* and gave birth to *Ramus* is today effectively dead – in its place a plurality of questions, approaches, methods and perspectives now applied to literary works and their contexts. What has not changed has been the need for close scrutiny of particular texts in their active engagement with each other and with the generic and literary tradition to which they belong and respond, and which they transform through that response. In the present and laudable preoccupation with 'theory', critical practice has sometimes been disproportionately ignored, and nowhere more unfairly and paradoxically, it seems to me, than in the case of the quintessentially Roman verse-form, epic. Hence the present volume, a collection of specially commissioned, critically and methodologically distinct essays, focusing on particular practitioners of this Roman art and their reaction to, influence on and rewriting of each other. The result, I hope, is a book demonstrating not only the (largely unknown) poetic sophistication and (underused) political and social import of Roman epic but the undying moral and intellectual force of perhaps Europe's prime literary form.

The book began in the brain of J. P. Sullivan, who on a cold summer's day in London urged me to this task, and I was encouraged from the start by Richard Stoneman, who both at Croom Helm and most especially at Routledge has done so much to enliven classics. Neither of these two scholars is responsible for any deficiencies in what follows, although to both of them I am grateful. Other colleagues who assisted me in various ways include John Henderson, David Konstan, Frances Muecke, John Penwill and Marcus Wilson, to whom I should add all the energetic participants in the Pacific Rim Roman Literature Seminar, held at USC in September 1991, especially its co-director Donald McGuire. Al Lim provided much-needed word-processing expertise and labour. My daughter Kathy helped with the preparation of the final copy for the publisher. Faye Nennig helped most of all.

A.J.B.

USC, Los Angeles
April 1992

I

INTRODUCTION:
THE ROMAN SONG

A. J. Boyle

As Rome herself, by long unwearied toil,
Glean'd the fair produce of each foreign soil;
From all her wide Dominion's various parts
Borrow'd their laws, their usages, their arts;
Imported knowledge from each adverse zone,
And made the wisdom of the world her own:
Thy patient spirit thus, from every Bard
Whose mental riches won thy just regard,
Drew various treasure; which thy skill refin'd,
And in the fabric of thy Verse combin'd.
(William Hayley, *An Essay on Epic Poetry* (1782))

Hayley's homage to Virgil constitutes an appropriate epitaph not only
for Virgil but for Roman epic itself. From Livius' 'translation' of *Odyssey*
1.1 onwards Roman epic defined itself as a palimpsestic genre, deriving
much of its meaning and significance from its relationship to and
rewriting of other, especially Greek but increasingly, as Rome's literature developed, Roman texts. As in its architecture, its sculpture, its
painting, as throughout its entire political, social and cultural system,
Rome in its literature, most especially in epic, created forms which
unceasingly *re*formed earlier achievements. Most important here was
Ennius, a wide-ranging and ambitious poet, whose overt, creative and
extensive use in his *Annales* not only of Homer, Hesiod and Callimachus
but of his Latin predecessors, Livius and Naevius, became the model for
Roman epicists to come. What Ennius did (and here he built upon what
was latent in Livius' *Odussia*) was to establish the notion of sub-text(s)
as essential to the reading of Roman epic. Inevitably this palimpsestic
dimension of the genre could be (and was) handled with varying
degrees of subtlety and richness by the poets of Rome; but it gave to the
great Roman epics a profundity and semantic allusiveness exceeding
the Greek texts which the poets rewrote. The paradigm and canonic
case was Virgil, whose exploitation of the semantic properties of literary

1

allusion set the standard which the imperial epicists and later the poets
of the European Renaissance, including Milton, endeavoured to attain.
One of the injustices done to the early imperial epicists by nineteenth-
and twentieth-century scholarship has been precisely to confuse functional allusion and rewriting with slavish, uncreative imitation. *Imitatio*
was a goal of ancient writers because (*inter alia*) it gave textual layers to
their work. Far from being slavish, it was (in the hands of the major
practitioners) an instrument of great creative power. It is not simply, as
Eliot observed over seventy years ago, that

> No poet, no artist of any art, has his complete meaning alone. His
> significance, his appreciation is the appreciation of his relation to
> the dead poets and artists.[1]

Nor is it merely a matter of poetic 'memory', if construed as the
inevitable reuse of poetic language, codes and conventions, or the
similarly inevitable recall of the style and mannerisms of earlier poets.
What has to be recognized (and this is something the present volume
sets out to show) is that this relationship to 'dead poets and artists', and
to living ones too, was something the Roman poets actively and
creatively exploited, not only at the level of formal or stylistic similarities
and inherited generic codes, but at the more important and profound
levels of political, social and moral meaning and poetic ideology. As the
twenty-first century draws near, the Romantic prejudice in favour of
'pure originality' (whatever that may be) is at last fading from the work
of contemporary classical scholarship. The time is right for a revaluation of the Roman epic's achievement.

One of the primary tasks demanded of such a revaluation is a
clarification of both the 'norms' of Roman epic (in Conte's sense) and
(ideally) the complexity of the individual instantiation of those norms.
It should be stated at the outset that the Roman epic we are concerned with is what contemporary writers referred to as *carmen heroum*,[2]
large-scale, narrative, 'heroic' poetry, concerned with the deeds of
heroes and/or the history of a nation – in Virgil's early, pregnant
phrase, *reges et proelia* ('kings and battles', *Eclogue* 6.3; cf. Horace, *Ars
Poetica* 74). In Rome as opposed to Greece *carmen heroum* was from first
to last primarily a political genre; it was almost aggressively the *Roman*
song. Indeed one of the most lasting achievements of the early Roman
epicists, influenced by but substantially transforming the contemporary
Greek predilection for panegyrical historical epics on Hellenistic
monarchs,[3] was the establishment of Rome, its history, values and
destiny as the main subject matter of Latin epic; in the words of one of
its most recent critics, they 'made a hero out of a nation'.[4] The term
'national epic' is often used in this connection,[5] but its implied
assumptions of jingoism and panegyric in several cases (most notori-

ously that of Virgil) mislead. The term 'politico-historical epic', though more clumsy, is also perhaps more to the point. Certainly both Naevius' *Bellum Punicum* and Ennius' *Annales* set the ground-rules here and inaugurated a mainstream Roman tradition of what seems to have been mainly panegyrical historical epic. Hostius' *Bellum Histricum* (late second century), Furius Antias' *Annales* (c. 100 BCE), Volusius' *Annales* and Cicero's *Marius, De Consulatu Suo* and *De Temporibus Suis* (mid-first century, the former 'On His Consulship' of 63 BCE, the latter on his exile of 58–57 BCE and subsequent return), Varro Atacinus' *Bellum Sequanicum* (on Caesar's Gallic campaign in 58 BCE) and Furius Bibaculus' *Bellum Gallicum* (mid-fifties BCE), Cornelius Severus' *Res Romanae* or *Bellum Siculum* (early Augustan), together with the Augustan civil war epics of Gaius Rabirius and Sextilius Ena and the Herculaneum remnants of a *Bellum Actiacum* index the generic norm and its contract of (reader) expectations.[6] These epics survive only in fragments. Individual differences between them in their realization of political or panegyrical goals can in most cases not even be conjectured. Ennius' case, however, suggests that, even before Virgil, this was sometimes more complex than is often believed. He seems no simple *poeta cliens*. Bakhtin's view of the non-polyphonic nature of epic is simply false – and not only in the case of Virgil.[7] The impetus towards epic form could sometimes be, and after Virgil increasingly was, an impetus to *re*form the implicitly celebratory values of the form itself.

There were divergences from the politico-historical mode, but before Virgil surprisingly few. Apart from various translations of Homer's *Iliad* or adaptations of the Trojan cycle the only pre-Augustan mythological epic attested is Varro Atacinus' *Argonautae*, an Alexandrianizing *tour de force*, written against the backdrop of the neoteric mythological epyllion. After 30 BCE the names and works multiply: Ponticus' *Thebaid*, Carus' *Heracleid*, Domitius Marsus' *Amazonis*, Largus' epic on Antenor, Camerinus' on Hercules, Iulus Antonius' *Diomedea*, Lynceus' *Thebaid* and *Heracleid*, Arbronius Silo's epic on the Trojan war, Macer's and Lupus' epics on the Trojan cycle. All this before Ovid was dead – and without mentioning the greatest post-Virgilian, Augustan mythological epic, Ovid's own *Metamorphoses*. Virgil seems in fact to have changed the genre's primary modes through the force of his own achievement. But while he extended the genre to embrace fully mythological epic, he reinforced the genre's political and historical focus. By overtly using mythical discourse *as* political discourse in what was primarily a political form, he made it more difficult in the Roman context for mythological epic to be apolitical. Although the general point holds that 'the function of the genre persists beyond its historical modifications as a lasting awareness of its primitive origins'[8] (in Roman epic's case politico-historical origins), Virgil's extension of that function and awareness to the mythological mode was itself authoritative. Indeed, as the cases of Statius and Valerius Flaccus show, the effect of his transformation of the genre was to bequeath to the politically repressed years which followed an epic language and mode in which contemporary political, social and moral concerns could be articulated and explored. It is not accidental that the primary myths chosen for that exploration (the Theban cycle: Ponticus, Lynceus, Statius; the Argonautic expedition, Valerius Flaccus) had profound social and political resonance for early imperial Rome.

Thus what needs to be realized for an adequate understanding of Roman epic is that the decision to write epic (even mythological epic) was in most cases never simply a poetic one. Listen to Virgil describe an alleged forthcoming poem on the victor of Actium (which he did not write):[9]

> mox tamen ardentis accingar dicere pugnas
> Caesaris et nomen fama tot ferre per annos,
> Tithoni prima quot abest ab origine Caesar.
>
> (*Georgic* 3.46–8)

> Soon I'll arm myself to tell Caesar's burning battles
> And bear his name in glory for as many years
> As separate Tithonus' distant birth from Caesar.

Compare Propertius' advance description of Virgil's *Aeneid* (2.34. 59ff.),[10] and observe his (2.1, 3.3, 3.9), Horace's (*Odes* 1.6, 2.12, 4.2, 4.15, *Epistles* 2.1.250ff.) and Ovid's (*Amores* 1.1) refusals to write epic. What is often forgotten is that the neoteric aversion to epic was political as much as it was aesthetic. And, when a generation later Augustus appropriated the god of poetry Apollo as his own political guardian, joining the imperial residence to the great temple to Apollo he built on the Palatine, placing images of Apollo *Cithaerodus* on his coins, all poetic choices became political (and potentially dangerous) ones. Ovid's debate with Cupid in *Amores* 1.1 is a political debate as much as it is a poetic one. His banishment to Tomis shows how overtly political all poetry had become.[11]

Epic, however, remained the prime political form. It was the prime poetic form too. Roman readers and writers had no difficulty recognizing what it was.[12] It was narrative poetry, but narrative poetry 'great' (*magnum, grande*) in both scale and subject; it was 'serious', 'weighty', 'important' (*grave*); it was 'sturdy', 'enduring', 'adamantine' (*durum*); it was 'soaring', 'lofty', 'elevated' (*altum*); it affected a 'public' (prior to Lucan) 'non-personal' stance; it was 'heroic' verse (*carmen heroum*); and

– after Ennius replaced Livius' and Naevius' Saturnians with the Homeric verse-form – it was written in hexameters.[13] Other poetic genres defined themselves in relation to epic.[14] Pastoral was 'lowly' (*gracile*) and 'thin' (*tenue, gracile*); elegy was 'soft' (*molle*), 'light' (*leve*), 'puny' (*parvum, exiguum*), 'playful' (*iocosum*), occasionally *risqué* (*lascivum*), and adopted a 'private', 'personal stance'; lyric, similarly, though aspiring sometimes to 'vatic' stature, was declared 'delicate', 'effeminate' (*molle*), 'puny' (*parvum*), 'thin' or 'slight' (*tenue, leve*), even – in Catullus' notoriously ironic phrase – 'trash' (*nugae*). As the new genre 'satire' started to emerge, that too proclaimed itself in comparison with epic as closer to prose (*sermoni propriora*) than to poetry (Horace, *Satires* 1.4.39ff.); and when epigram with Martial laid claim to the status of a genre, of which it regarded Catullus as the founder (Martial *Epigrams* 1, Preface), it yet placed itself self-consciously at the bottom of a hierarchy crowned by epic (Martial, *Epigrams* 12.94). Nearly all such descriptions of these genres by their practitioners are at least in part ironic (Catullus, the pastoral Virgil and Propertius were in Callimachean revolt against epic bombast), but they serve to clarify conventional (contemporary) assumptions and expectations. The Augustan *recusatio* is particularly helpful here. 'Too slight for such important matters' (*tenues grandia*, *Odes* 1.6.9), claims Horace; 'lacking the ability for adamantine verse' (*durus versus*, 2.1.41), claims Propertius. In comparison with epic, pastoral and elegy especially were sometimes proclaimed mere 'play', *lusus* (e.g. Virgil, *Eclogue* 6.1, Ovid, *Fasti* 2.6, Pliny, *Epistle* 7.9ff.). Its only rivals for poetic primacy were non-narrative, didactic hexameter verse (Lucretius' *De Rerum Natura*, Virgil's *Georgics*, Manilius' *Astronomica*), regarded by the ancients as a form of *epos*,[15] and tragedy. Tragedy received similarly elevating epithets to those showered upon epic: 'stern' (*severa*), 'great', 'important' (*grandis*). But for the Romans epic remained supreme. It was what ambitious politicians sought to be associated with; it shaped both poetic expectation and poetic practice. When Quintilian conducts his evaluation of Roman poets, he begins with the writers of epic (*Inst.* 10.1.85ff.).[16]

What is often not recognized (even by the ancient critics themselves) is that, though the highest of the genres, Roman epic admitted of a variety of styles, incorporating features of other 'genres' within itself. 'Generic mixture', *Kreuzung der Gattungen*, was in fact a thoroughly Roman poetic practice (highlighted in the essays on Catullus and Ovid below), and defined late republican and early imperial Latin verse as it did Hellenistic verse, whose poetics the Roman poets absorbed and transformed. A work such as Virgil's *Aeneid* or Lucan's *Bellum Civile* (more popularly known as *Pharsalia*) employed styles ranging from high Ennian or declamatory or tragic to elegiac, satiric, lyric, pastoral or even scientific/philosophical didactic. A glance at the juxtaposition in *Bellum Civile* 5 of the 'lowly' scene at the fisherman's hut with the verbal pyrotechnics of the storm scene (5.504–677), or the contrast in *Aeneid* 8 between the erotic scene between Venus and Vulcan at the centre of the book (8.370–406) and the great ecphrasis with which the book concludes (8.608–731) shows both how effective and essential such stylistic variety was. Even the fragments of an early epicist such as Naevius reveal considerable stylistic variety.[17] The allocation of a consistently 'high' style to epic is the product of ancient, medieval and Renaissance theorizing, much of it originating both from the battle of the genres and from the attention given to the Aristotelian and Horatian concept of 'decorum' (the 'appropriateness' of style to subject).[18] Much of it originated too from Virgil's own tripartite career and a concern to associate with that tripartition the ancient doctrine of the three styles ('high', 'middle' and 'low') set out for rhetoricians in the pseudo-Ciceronian *Ad Herennium*. The medieval concept of 'Virgil's Wheel' is a telling embodiment of this error.[19] Ironically Agrippa, who disliked Virgil's style, classified it as an affected 'middle' style (*Vita Verg. Donati* 44).

Stylistic range was in fact a feature of the ambitious scale of epic and the demands made of it by an increasingly sophisticated readership or audience (the public *recitatio* of Roman epic being particularly common, especially in the imperial period – to the chagrin of Juvenal).[20] More surprising perhaps – and quintessentially Roman – is its self-consciousness. Listen to Ennius proclaim his own relationship to the (relatively) recent Roman epic tradition:

> scripsere alii rem
> vorsibus quos olim Faunei vatesque canebant
> nec dicti studiosus [quisquam erat] ante hunc . . .
> nos ausi reserare . . .
>
> (Annales, 7 frr. 1–1a)[21]

> Others wrote of the subject
> In verses which long ago Fauns and seers sang . . .
> No one was concerned with style before this man [= me] . . .
> I dared to unseal . . .

Or to Virgil announce his rivalry with Homer and his own native epic tradition by transforming the first line of *Odyssey* and of Latin literature into the opening line and title of his work:

> arma virumque cano, Troiae qui primus ab oris . . .
>
> (Aeneid 1.1)

> Arms I sing and a man, who first from Troy's shores . . .

Compare Livius' version:

> virom mihei, Camena, insece vorsutum.
>
> > (*Odussia* 1.1)

> A man well versed speak to me, Camena.

Livius' opening word, *virom*, translates the opening word of Homer's *Odyssey*. Note how Virgil places this word second, commencing with a word, *arma*, which sonally recalls Homer's opening word, *andra*, even as it signals the subject matter of Homer's other epic, the *Iliad*. Virgil's epic is neither an *Iliad* nor an *Odyssey*; it is both. It is also a reformation of Roman literature's first text. There are echoes too of the Homeric tag *klea andrōn* ('glorious deeds of men' = *arma virum*), of the opening line of Apollonius Rhodius' *Argonautica* (*klea phōtōn*), and possibly of Ennius' *Annales*.[22] Worthy of notice is how Virgil indicates his difference from Homer, Apollonius, Livius and (possibly) Ennius by postponing the conventional request for inspiration by the Muses until his own role and control have been proclaimed. In three highly self-conscious words Virgil precisely locates his own individual position in the Graeco-Roman epic tradition.

Virgil's example was not ignored. Ovid's complex and overt exploitation of the *Aeneid* is apparent throughout the *Metamorphoses* (discussed by Anderson in chapter VI below); while his self-conscious use of Ennius even extends to the quotation of a whole line from the *Annales* in both the *Metamorphoses* (14.814) and *Fasti* (2.487).[23] Lucan cannot wait to signal his relationship to the *Aeneid* (and distance from it), emulating Virgil's use of the poem's opening as the site for poetic declaration:[24]

> *bella* per Emathios plus quam civilia campos
> iusque datum sceleri *canimus* . . .
>
> > (*Bellum Civile* 1.1)

> *Wars* worse than civil, waged on Emathia's plains,
> And justice given to crime *we sing* . . .

Bella replaces *arma*; the plural *canimus* ('we sing') replaces the singular *cano* ('I sing'). Lucan's subject is not a man, and the realization/vitiation of his ideals in violence but a specific cultural dismemberment, the moral, linguistic and carnal dissolution caused by Rome's internal wars. Nor is his voice a lone Virgilian one; it is communal and public. Lucan's concerns are themselves echoed by Statius, whose opening words self-consciously pick up the phrase *cognatasque acies* ('and kindred battlelines') from the beginning of the fourth line of Lucan's Proem, and transform it:

fraternas acies alternaque regna profanis
decertata odiis sontesque evolvere Thebas,
Pierius menti calor incidit.

(*Thebaid* 1.1–3)

Fraternal battlelines and alternate reign
Fought out with sacrilegious hate and guilty Thebes
Pierian fire touches my mind to recount.

As with Lucan, 'wars worse than civil' are his subject; but Statius is concerned initially to camouflage his voice with the conventions and rhetoric of the tradition rather than to focus upon it. Not so at the ending of the work, when he exhorts his epic to live and be read, and to take its proper place in the Roman tradition *behind* Virgil's canonic text:

vive, precor; nec tu divinam Aeneida tempta,
sed longe sequere et vestigia semper adora.

(*Thebaid* 12.816–17)

Live, I implore – but not to rival the divine *Aeneid*;
Follow in the distance and ever worship its footsteps.

Signalling itself as a *post* and *propter Lucanum* remaking of the Virgilian politico-historical mythological epic, the *Thebaid* not only indicates its main sub-texts but the continuing self-consciousness of the Roman epic tradition. The opening two words of Silius' *Punica* – *ordior arma* ('I begin the arms') – with their programmatic allusion to Virgil's *Aeneid* and the opening four lines of Valerius' *Argonautica* with their allusions to Lucan, Catullus and Seneca[25] (Virgil too: *Argonautica*'s first words, *prima deum*, recall by similarity and difference *arma virum*) further testify to the Flavian – and Roman – epic mode.

Much of this self-consciousness derives from the self-consciousness of most Roman art. The Hellenizing of Rome that took place between 250 and 100 BCE gave Rome a new cultural and intellectual image as the inheritor and transformer of the Greek artistic achievement.

Graecia capta ferum victorem cepit et artis
intulit agresti Latio.

(Horace *Epistles* 2.1.156–7)

Captive Greece captured her savage conqueror
And brought culture to rustic Latium.

In late republican and early imperial architecture and sculpture especially, this self-consciousness proclaimed itself. The marriage of the Greek trabeated system and orders with the Roman arcuated system in Sulla's Tabularium (78 BCE),[26] the allusions to the Parthenon's

Panathenaic procession on the Augustan Ara Pacis (9 BCE), and the *re*formation of Polyclitus' Spearbearer as the Augustus of Prima Porta (19 BCE) are conspicuous examples of the self-conscious historicism of Roman art. In Roman epic this self-consciousness sometimes extended to detailed self-reflection and self-critique. The main ecphrases of the *Aeneid* and *Metamorphoses*, the proem to the *Bellum Civile* and the Delphic Sibyl section of Book 5 are but the more famous passages where this extended self-reflection takes place. Roman epic, especially from the *Aeneid* onwards, is a complex intellectual form admitting the play of many voices in a dynamic of semiotics, which critically places the many voices and the values they imply or express. It is in the hands of its greatest masters a form of human expression which generates meaning as complex (and important) as the form itself.

Not that all periods of Rome's literary history were equally fertile in the production of epic. Though patronage was in many cases not essential, it is no accident that the main periods of productivity coincide with the main periods of republican and imperial patronage of the arts. The middle republic (240–160 BCE: Livius, Naevius, Ennius), the late republic (Cicero, Furius Bibaculus, Varro Atacinus), the Augustan period (Virgil, Ovid, Ponticus, Macer, Rabirius, Ena etc.), the Neronian/Flavian era (Lucan, Serranus, Saleius Bassus, Statius, Valerius, Silius, etc.), the late fourth century (Claudian, Prudentius) – and in the Middle Ages the Carolingian Renaissance, later the European Renaissance itself – were periods of extensive political patronage of literature. Public figures such as the Claudii Marcelli, Marcus Fulvius Nobilior, Scipio Aemilianus, Julius Caesar, Messala Corvinus, Maecenas/ Augustus, the early emperors and Honorius' chief minister Stilicho sought to promote themselves, their images and their policies through association with, even representation in, the works of the greatest contemporary poets. In the cases of Nero and Domitian the patron-emperors had poetic pretensions themselves. However, patronage, which Romans would have called *amicitia* even if it involved social unequals, was a complex relationship, and one which served to enhance the prestige of both parties as well as the financial status of the poets concerned, who were nearly always men of reasonable means (i.e. equestrians) to begin with.[27] The system also provided poets with a much-needed audience and/or readership. But no poet needed patronage simply to survive or even to live moderately well, and not all epic poets had patrons. Ovid certainly did not; nor did Silius nor (possibly) Valerius Flaccus. And even those who did (in a sense) have patrons, such as Ennius, Virgil and Statius, created works which are ideologically far more complex than the concept 'commissioned work' (with its associations of bootlicking) implies. The best text for the clarification of the concept 'commissioned work' as understood by the practising

Roman epicist is Virgil's *Aeneid*, which contains within it two images of commissioned works to be compared with itself. The self-consciousness and self-reflection characteristic of Roman epic are there brought to bear precisely upon the problem of whether the values of a work of art are delimited by the imperatives of its production. In the examination of this issue below (chapter V) Virgil's answer is presented as emphatically negative.[28] Neo-Marxist beliefs in text as determined product find little verification even in the area where most would choose unthinkingly to find it, Roman literature's most public form, epic. As it reveals itself as both index and critique of the foundational culture of the western world, and as demonstrably (through its transmutation into medieval and Renaissance Latin epic and their vernacular generic and non-generic successors) one of Europe's most persistent and determinant poetic modes, Roman epic lays claim to being western civilization's prime literary form.

The following thirteen previously unpublished essays outline some of the basis for this claim. They were all commissioned for the book. They represent – intentionally – a variety of methodologies and approaches, but share a common focus. Each essay concentrates on the contributions to the genre of an individual epicist or epic (or, in the case of the 'After Rome' chapters, two epicists and epics), drawing especial attention to the epic's relationship to, differences from and rewriting of its predecessors. There is an attempt throughout to relate these differences to differences in historical context, to the different poetic, political, social, moral or even religious issues which define the poem's and poet's historical *locus* and which each epic is designed in part to address.

The first three essays (chapters II–IV) examine pre-Virgilian epic. Sander Goldberg's important study is a long-awaited aesthetic analysis of the fragmentary verses of Rome's first epicists, Livius Andronicus and Naevius. He examines their radical employment of the native Italian metre, the 'Saturnian', for epic poetry, their use of word-order, cola structure, metaphor, 'layered' epithets, verse stops and other techniques to reveal a concern with epic decorum, narrative integration and structure, and a pronounced sensitivity to style. William Dominik's contribution on Ennius places a new and distinct focus on Ennius' poetic self-consciousness and his fruitful mingling of individual, 'Homeric', and inherited Roman mannerisms and techniques to produce a powerful, if sometimes primitive, style well suited to the epic's primary purpose. This purpose Dominik sees as the glorification of the emerging Roman nation rather than the partisan political eulogy of particular historical figures. Dominik does not subscribe to the ingratiating *poeta cliens* view of Ennius fashionable in the last two decades.[29] David Konstan addresses himself to the literary form which the neoterics chose on the whole to exploit in preference to epic proper, namely the 'epyllion' or miniature epic, which – despite the silence of the ancient critics on the matter – Konstan (in my view correctly) views as a genuine literary category. The essay is a detailed critical commentary on Catullus' *Peleus and Thetis*, with attention to its mannered, allusive, self-consciously artful quality, and its exploitation of 'intricate structure, density of texture and generic variety . . . to represent multiple themes and perspectives' and to mediate its own 'ethical critique'. The poem's deployment of Hellenistic conventions for 'an engagement with immediate social issues' paved the path to Virgil.

The second triad of essays (chapters V–VII) treat those whom many would regard as the three major (extant) epicists of the Roman literary tradition: Virgil, Ovid and Lucan. I and others would want to add Statius to this distinguished group. My own essay on Virgil concerns the *Aeneid*'s radical nature and attempts to clarify certain features of the work central to its transformation of the genre and to its status as a canonic text. It highlights the poem's recuperability, moral meaning, stylistic power, formal intricacy, its palimpsestic strategies, and self-reflexive nature. W. S. Anderson's perceptive paper on Ovid discusses both the formal and thematic originality of Ovid's masterwork, the *Metamorphoses*, opposing generic simplifications (what Croce called the 'Generic Fallacy') and drawing attention to the rich mixture of epic and elegy in the poem. The essay focuses on Ovid's complex use of Virgil's *Aeneid*, which Anderson sees as serving not to create 'anti-*Aeneids*', as has been recently argued, but to enrich and enlarge the narrative of what is essentially a 'humane epic', a 'searching study of changed humanity'. Frederick Ahl's contribution on Lucan is a *bravura* attempt to instil in the reader the literary, political, moral and historical importance of Lucan's great work, which he proclaims to be as much a 'political act' as a 'political poem'. Presenting the *Bellum Civile* or *Pharsalia* as a sharply focused work historically and ideologically, and more self-contained than Virgil's *Aeneid*, Ahl locates the prime significance of Lucan in what he says rather than in how he says it. Lucan's authorial voice adopts a consistent *persona* which saturates the *Pharsalia* with an unrelieved resistance to autocracy, shaping 'history into an ideological sword ready to plunge into the tyrant-dominated present or future'. The displacement of epic's gods is itself a protest against history's 'morality'. The rhetoric of liberty and opposition structuring the epic 'threatens all absolutist systems, ideological as well as secular', and to it are indebted not only political theorists such as de Battaglia writing in the 1930s but the rhetoric of the French and American revolutions.

Roman epic, however, had its opponents, many of them among the

finest poets and writers. J. P. Sullivan's essay (chapter VIII) on the
enemies of epic traces the ideological and poetic opposition to epic
from Catullus, through the elegists Propertius and Ovid, the fabulists
Phaedrus and Babrius, to the satirists Persius, Petronius, Martial and
Juvenal. His study focuses on their (failed) attempt to subvert the
traditionally high status of epic through the generic elevation of elegiac
and pastoral love poetry, moral fable, satire and epigram, and through
the criticism of epic as irrelevant to the social and moral problems of
contemporary Rome. Sullivan's essay is followed by three studies in
Flavian epic (chapters IX–XI). John Henderson's explosive essay on
Statius' *Thebaid* investigates the semiotics of the Theban myth in
Graeco-Roman culture and the poem's potential to mean within the
Flavian cosmos. Special attention is drawn to the epic's scopic horror.
Henderson's incisive, detailed discussion of the language and narra-
tology of Statius' epic, its 'combinatorial imitation' and remaking of its
epic predecessors, its promotion of the Woman's Voice, its challenge to
Virgil, yields a view of the poem as a desecration of war and its
categories (especially the category Manhood, *virtus*), a tragedization of
epic, and a '"strong" rereading of the *Aeneid* as itself a text *about to
turn*, for ever, towards a plaintive critique of the militarism of its
narrative of action'. Henderson's essay joins with the work of other
recent critics to underscore the importance and poetic stature of
Statius' *Thebaid*. It precedes Martha Malamud's and Donald McGuire's
study of Valerius Flaccus and Marcus Wilson's contribution on Silius.
Malamud and McGuire examine how the *Argonautica* generates meaning
through Valerius' engagement with his predecessors, his rewriting of
Homer, Apollonius, Theocritus, Propertius, Virgil and Ovid, and his
readers' awareness of that engagement and rewriting. In an intricate
analysis of the poem's treatment of the abduction of Hylas they argue
for Valerius' 'refusal to create a seamless, univocal account', his overt
allusions to earlier treatments of the myth serving both to collapse the
myth, denying it authoritative force, and to create from his handling of
the myth a reflection of his own 'reflective text'. Wilson in a forceful
essay presents Silius' *Punica* as an 'uncompromisingly anti-historical'
epic, in which the narrative exploits – pervasively – the discrepancy
between epic and history in respect of their implicit assumptions about
time, cause and effect, ensuring that 'the epic imagination is everywhere victorious over historical probability'. *Punica*'s focus on aetiological explanation, divine instigation and purpose, heroic *aristeiai*,
incredible forms of death, glory and its quest, the connection between
mortal and immortal, and the projection of time through dreams,
omens, prophecies and works of art, is illustrated by Wilson in telling
detail. Recent commentators have seen Silius' insistent dialogue with
Lucan's *Bellum Civile/ Civil War* and Virgil's *Aeneid* as index of a concern

to create from the three poems 'an epic trilogy on the history of Rome – from its mythic foundation (*Aeneid*) through its republican zenith (*Punica*) to Rome's dismemberment by Caesar (*Civil War*)'[30] – bearing strongly on the conditions of Silius' world. Wilson argues that Silius' 'perspective' is not that of 'Augustan or even Flavian Rome', but of the 'eternity' of the epic imagination.

The Flavian period was one of the great, productive periods for epic in ancient Rome. In addition to the three epicists discussed in this volume we know of Cordus' *Theseid*, pilloried by Juvenal, *Satire* 1.2, Julius Cerialis' *Gigantomachia*, mentioned by Martial (*Epigrams* 11.52.17), the prize-winning poet Carus (Martial, *Epigrams* 9.23 and 24), Saleius Bassus and Serranus (Quintilian, *Inst. Orat.* 10.1.90, Martial, *Epigrams* 4.37, Tacitus, *Dialogus* 5.2, etc., Juvenal, *Satire* 7.80), Statius' friend Manilius Vopiscus (*Silvae* 1.3) and his own father (who wrote an epic on the civil fighting of 69 CE and was planning one on the eruption of Vesuvius in 79 CE, *Silvae* 5.3.195ff.), and Domitian himself, perhaps the author of as many as three historical epics on his own military exploits.[31] After the early second century CE (because in part of changing social conditions and tastes – among which were a decline in imperial patronage and a paradoxical increase in both sterile anti-quarianism and illiteracy)[32] the writing of epic virtually disappears from ancient Rome (Apuleius' friend Clemens may have written an *Alexandriad* in the middle of the second century and Nemesianus states an 'intention' to write an epic on the triumphs of the sons of Carus at the end of the third century)[33] until its conversion into biblical Latin epic in the *Evangeliorum Libri IV* of the New Testament Constantinian poet Juvencus (c. 330 CE). After Juvencus we witness a late reflowering of the genre in the work of the Christian poet Prudentius (*Psychomachia*) and the pagan epicist Claudian at the end of the fourth century and in that of the north African epicist Corippus (*Iohannis* – a historical epic in eight books) in the middle of the sixth.[34] In the fourth century too there occurs for the first time since Ovid a revival of the epyllion (Reposianus, Claudian), which was to climax at the end of the following century in the four epyllia of Dracontius from Vandal Africa and the anonymous *Aegritudo Perdicae*.[35] Many of these developments lie outside the scope of this volume. Some await full investigation, while others are well described elsewhere. The important development, for example, of biblical Latin epic in the Old and New Testament poets of the fifth and sixth centuries (Sedulius 'the Christian Virgil', the author of *Hepta-teuchos* [Cyprianus Gallus (?)], Claudius Marius Victorius, Avitus, Arator) and their success in transforming (primarily) Virgilian epic language into a new Christian poetic idiom are well expounded in a comprehensive recent study.[36]

The final triad of essays (chapters XII–XIV) directs itself initially to

Claudian, and thence to the reflowering of the Roman epic tradition in the Latin epics of the Middle Ages and the Italian Renaissance. Several critics have now drawn attention to the implicit poetics of the writers of late antiquity, especially to their penchant for virtuoso descriptive passages in which principles of regularity, brilliance and *variatio* may be combined in what Roberts calls a 'jewelled style', and to their 'logocentrism', their elevation of the verbal world over the material.[37] Peter Connor's essay on Claudian examines intricately the poet's descriptive and narrative modes in several episodes of *De Raptu Proserpinae* and underlines the poet's mastery of a baroque, gothic style, his fusion of epic and non-epic, the power of his (occasional) narrative restraint, and the visually impressive quality of his epic tableaux. Indeed Connor sees Claudian's epic ambition as resting 'unequivocally on a strong desire to produce impressive examples of epic episodes'. Much of this is to be explained in terms of the new aesthetic of the late antique, but Connor regards *De Raptu* as 'one amongst many classicizing artefacts' of this period which must also be judged in relation to its classical forebears. And from that perspective the poem's lack of thematic and narrative consonance, narrower stylistic range (though 'well mastered and well sustained'), predilection for speeches and 'episodes', and the predominantly 'unselective', 'all-embracing lushness' of its narrative and descriptive style (which Connor sees as the product of Claudian's attempt to compete with his great predecessors through *amplificatio*) perhaps detract from the epic's force.

Medieval Latin epic could receive a volume of essays in its own right. The late Carolingian *Waltharius* (in the manner of Virgil and Statius) and *De Rebus Gestis Ludovici Pii* (of Ermold the Black: in praise of Charlemagne's successor Louis 'the Pious'), the mid-tenth-century *Gesta Ottonis* by the Gandersheim canoness and first female German poet Hrotsvit, the eleventh-century *Ruodlieb* (in 'leonine' hexameters) and *De Hastingae Proelio* (of Gui d'Amiens), the twelfth-century *Ysengrimus* (of Nivardus of Ghent), the *De Bello Troiano* (of Joseph of Exeter: eight books) and *Alexandreis* (of Gautier de Chatillon: ten books) are just a selection of the works that merit detailed analysis and attention. For, though these poets sometimes resort to the language of Roman elegy and lyric (*ludere, levis*) to defend their choices of ostensibly non-Christian subjects,[38] it is clear that they took their epic poetry very seriously indeed. John Ward shows how seriously. He refutes the idea that medieval epic was simply a 'product of the schools', emphasizing the numerous sources that fed medieval epic, the variety of its modes (vatic, satiric, celebratory, carnivalistic) and its close link with the literary and political worlds in which the epicists lived and wrote. His detailed analysis of *Waltharius* examines its sophisticated handling of the classical, especially Virgilian tradition, but construes its purpose as being to transform Germanic legend not only into 'a pleasurable and entertaining form suited to the new Latin reading classes of the Carolingian empire' but into a form too which underscored the new attitudes to marriage, to male–female relationships, and to women as a whole expounded by the Carolingian clergy. Ward concludes his challenging essay with a brief survey of the only 'female' epic addressed in this volume, *Gesta Ottonis*, which he sees as concerned to undermine the conventional acceptance of female fragility and inferiority and to celebrate female heroism. The model for this celebration according to Ward is *Waltharius*.

The volume concludes with Philip Hardie's informed account of two Renaissance Latin epics: Petrarch's *Africa*, product of the Italian *quattrocento*, and Vida's *Christiad*, a six-book epic on the life of Christ published in 1535. Hardie presents Petrarch as a self-conscious epicist, overtly utilizing his Roman predecessors, Livy, Cicero, Lucan, Virgil and Ennius himself, whom he uses as an image of his own poetic self. Vida's fusion of antique form and Christian content is examined with attention to Vida's creative imitation of Virgil and transvaluation and inversion of Virgilian themes for Christian purposes. As Hardie's essay shows, the synthesis of the classical and the Christian, which was one of the hallmarks of late antique biblical epic,[39] could be revivified success-fully and with sophistication in the emerging 'modern' world. What Hardie's essay also shows is that, even as the Roman/Latin epic tradition was shedding itself of its Latinity and beginning to generate in the evolving European literatures vernacular forms of epic verse (Dante's *Divina Commedia* preceded Petrarch's *Africa* by some thirty years), it still retained the capacity to reuse the language of Livius, Ennius and Virgil creatively for contemporary cultural and poetic concerns. The opening lines of *Africa* –

> et mihi conspicuum meritis belloque tremendum,
> Musa, virum referes

> Also to me will you recount of outstanding merit,
> Muse, and fearful in war a man

– pick up without Petrarch's realization the opening line of Latin literature and reformulate it palimpsestically for a new task and a new age.

But despite the plethora of Latin epic (especially panegyrical epic) written in the Renaissance, the future lay elsewhere. Increasingly the great writers of the new age, including Petrarch himself, were to seek inspiration in their own languages rather than in the language of Roman epic. The primacy of Virgil and of Latin epic, however, as an educative and cultural force remained to inform these very departures from the language of ancient Rome, most noticeably in the modern 'golden age' of European epic, stretching from the late sixteenth to the early eighteenth century, which witnessed such works as Camoens' *Os Lusiadas* (1572), Tasso's *Gerusalemme Liberata* (1575), Spenser's *Fairie Queene* (1590–6), Cowley's *Davideis* (1656), and of course Milton's glorious, if genre-consumptive,[40] masterwork, *Paradise Lost* (2nd edn, 1674). In the gap vacated by epic new literary and (later) visual forms emerged and flourished, but the mark of their epic forebears was as ineradicable as it was conspicuous. From Wordsworth's *Prelude* (1805), Byron's *Childe Harold* (1811–17), Tolstoy's *War and Peace* (1863–9), Browning's *Ring and the Book* (1868), through Joyce's *Ulysses* (1922), Pound's *Cantos* (1925–5), Durrell's *Alexandria Quartet* (1957–60), to Eisenstein's *Battleship Potemkin* (1925), Bergman's *Seventh Seal* (1956), Visconti's *Gattopardo* (1963), Bertolucci's *Novecento* (1976) and Costner's *Dances With Wolves* (1990) the great Roman epic tradition echoed and echoes dynamically word and image without end. Lucretius was right: 'Ennius . . . perEnni fronde' (*DRN* 1.117–18). Rome's prime literary form would itself transform perEnnially to index, to shape and to locate critically the western world's hegemonic culture.

NOTES

1 Eliot 1919: 15.
2 See, e.g., Propertius 3.3.16; Ovid, *Tristia* 4.10.47; Quintilian 1.8.5, 10.1.88; Tacitus, *Dialogus* 10.4 (*heroicum*). Similarly Renaissance writers referred to epic as 'heroic' or 'heroical' poetry: see Sidney's *Defense of Poesie* (1583) *passim*, and Tasso, *Discorsi sul poema eroico* (1584).
3 On Greek historical epic see Feeney 1991: 264–7.
4 Hainsworth 1991: 146 (of Ennius).
5 The phrase occurs in 'modern' critics as diverse and chronologically distant as Page 1894: xvi and Hainsworth 1991: 77ff.
6 On 'generic contracts' see Dubrow 1982: 31ff. and Hirsch 1967: 93 (cited by Dubrow): 'A genre is less like a game than like a code of social behavior.'
7 Bakhtin 1981: 35, 'The epic world knows only a single and unified world view.' For qualifications to the conventional view of Ennius as panegyrist see Goldberg 1989.
8 Conte 1986: 79. Conte, however, seems not to appreciate the force of his own observations in respect to early imperial epic, which he seems to regard as 'manneristic composition' (74 n. 43).
9 See below, pp. 80f.
10 Quoted below, p. 79 (see also pp. 147f.).
11 Poetry was not alone. The works of the orator and historian Titus Labienus were publicly burned in 6 CE (Seneca, *Controversiae* 10, Preface 4–8) and probably also about this time those of Cassius Severus (Suetonius, *Caligula* 16.1). Ovid's books were also removed from public libraries. Under Tiberius the historian Cremutius Cordus (25 CE) and the orator and tragedian Aemilius Scaurus (34 CE) had their works burned and their lives terminated (Seneca, *Controversiae* 10.3, Tacitus, *Annals* 4.34–5, 6.29). Others

met similar fates (Tacitus, *Annals* 3.49ff., Dio 57.22.5). Under the early empire writing was a dangerous activity.

12 Modern readers also have few difficulties in recognizing ancient epics, despite the many difficulties raised by the attempt to define the epic (or any other) genre. Criteria such as metre, subject matter, style, length, scope, voice, tone, effect, function, etc. are all relevant to generic classification. What is also relevant is Wittgenstein's theory of 'family resemblances', which enables similarities and differences between various instances of the genre to be accommodated. Like most interesting concepts that of 'genre' is (to use Wittgenstein's words) 'a concept with blurred edges' and indefinable. The pursuit of a verbal definition seems a will o' the wisp. See Wittgenstein 1958: Sect. 66ff.

13 Sometimes taken as the prime ancient criterion for epic. But note that one of epic's principal literary antagonists, satire, was written in hexameters, as were pastoral and didactic.

14 For a recent restatement of the existence and importance of the hierarchy of genres in Roman poetry, see Lyne 1989: 14f.

15 *Epos*, though used primarily of 'epic', covers most forms of hexameter poetry, especially didactic, but includes at times even pastoral. Quintilian groups Hesiod, Aratus and Theocritus with Homer, Antimachus and Apollonius Rhodius, and Lucretius with Virgil, Lucan and Valerius (*Inst. Orat.* 10.1.52ff., 87ff.). His classification is based essentially on metre and derives from the Alexandrian (primarily metrical) classification of pre-Alexandrian Greek poetry: see Zetzel 1983: 97ff. *Epos*, because of its primary use in relation to epic, often in fact means 'epic'; but because of the complexity of its field of reference and meaning, I have avoided the term. Northrop Frye's use of *epos* to 'describe works [both prose and verse] in which the radical of presentation is oral address' (Frye 1971: 248) corresponds to no ancient usage.

16 The Roman generic hierarchy thus inverts Aristotle's preference for tragedy over epic (*Poetics* 1461b26–62b15); similarly the Renaissance: 'the heroical . . . is not only a kind, but the best and most accomplished kind of poetry' (Sidney, *A Defense of Poesie*, 1583).

17 And a stylistic variety richer and more subtle than the 'chonicle' versus 'poetic' style distinction suggested by Leo 1913. See Goldberg, p. 31 below.

18 See, e.g., Edward Phillips, *Preface To Theatrum Poetarum* (1675): 'There is also a decorum to be observed in the style of the heroic poem: that is, that it be not inflate or jingling with an empty noise of words, nor creepingly low and insipid, but of a majesty suitable to the grandeur of the subject.'

19 For details here see Newman 1986: 249–50.

20 According to the elder Seneca (*Controversiae* 4, Preface 2) the tragedian and historian Asinius Pollio (76 BCE–4 CE) was the first Roman writer to recite his work to an invited audience. The practice quickly established itself as a dominant feature of Roman literary and social life. Juvenal's disdainful attitude to *recitatio* (especially of epic and tragedy) is apparent from *Satire* 1.1 onwards.

21 The reference is to Skutsch 1985.

22 Discussed by Conte 1986: 72ff.

23 Discussed by Conte 1986: 57ff., who (66ff.) draws attention to distinctions between 'integrative allusion' practised by Virgil, and 'reflective allusion' typical of Ovid, the latter signalling overtly its own artifice.

24 Conte 1986: 76, 'The opening is the place where all the signals point to the originality of the work or to its position within literary production.'

25 See Boyle in Boyle and Sullivan 1991: 272.
26 Actually erected by Quintus Lutatius Catulus, a supporter of Sulla and leader of the optimate party after Sulla's death.
27 See White 1982: 56ff., and Saller 1982: esp. 27–9.
28 See pp. 99–102 below.
29 For references see Goldberg 1989: 247 n. 1.
30 Boyle in Boyle and Sullivan 1991: 298. See also Ahl, Davis and Pomeroy 1986.
31 For details, see Bardon 1956: 229–30. Both Domitian and Statius' father wrote epics on the civil war of 69 CE.
32 See Baldwin 1982.
33 Apuleius, *Florida* 7; Nemesianus, *Cynegetica* 63–85. It is perhaps worth mentioning that the author of the life of Gordian I (acclaimed emperor in 238 CE) in *Historia Augusta* credits the emperor with the composition of a thirty-book epic, the *Antoniniad,* on the lives of Antoninus Pius and Marcus Aurelius, as well as an epic *Marius* and other poems, all of which the future emperor composed while a 'little boy' ('et haec quidem puerulus', *Gord.* 3). If there is any truth in this (which I doubt), these would almost certainly have been schoolboy exercises.
34 One might add possibly Albinus' hexametric *Res Romanae,* perhaps fourth-century.
35 On these five African epyllia see Bright 1987; on Dracontius see also Roberts 1989.
36 Roberts 1985; see also Roberts 1989 for comments on other late antique epic.
37 Roberts 1989: 12 and *passim*; and Nugent 1990b.
38 See Curtius 1953: 430.
39 See Roberts 1985: 224.
40 I allude to the judgment of Spencer 1968: 98, quoted by Sullivan below in chapter VIII, p. 157.

II

SATURNIAN EPIC: LIVIUS AND NAEVIUS

Sander M. Goldberg

In the early days of the Roman republic, Titus Aebutius Helva, Master of Horse to the Dictator Postumius, took a pounding at Lake Regillus. The historian Livy only records the fact. Lord Macaulay gives it life:

> And brave Aebutius Elva
>   Fell swooning to the ground:
> But a thick wall of bucklers
>   Encompassed him around.
> His clients from the battle
>   Bare him some little space,
> And filled a helm from the dark lake,
>   And bathed his brow and face;
> And when at last he opened
>   His swimming eyes to light,
> Men say, the earliest word he spake
>   Was, 'Friends, how goes the fight?'
>   (*The Battle of Lake Regillus*, XVI)

Such brave and patriotic moments fill the stanzas of these once-famous *Lays of Ancient Rome*, conjuring up the images of old Roman virtue and the sounds of old Roman minstrelsy. The images are in fact borrowed from Livy, but the sounds belong only to Sir Walter Scott. Macaulay's monument to Victorian sentiment could not draw directly on the bardic tradition it was seeking to evoke because no such bardic tradition survived from antiquity. The historian B. G. Niebuhr had certainly claimed one for the Romans: its existence helped him account for the poetic colouring of so much early Roman history. Macaulay, himself a keen admirer of folk poetry, naturally found this a congenial notion, and the introductory essay to his 'collection' of lays remains the best argument in English for Niebuhr's theory. Why should the Romans *not* have had a bardic tradition, and why would it *not* have vanished since they lacked a Scott or a Bishop Percy to collect and preserve its songs? The case has obvious appeal, but it is short on evidence to support it.

19

The Romans were certainly composing verse before they produced anything that we would call literature. The elder Cato had referred to a custom, long obsolete by his own day, of singing the praises of great men at dinner, and Cicero sought to connect this custom with the development of epic.[1] The *carmina* Cato describes, however, have nothing in common with Macaulay's lays. They were amateur efforts sung in turn by diners reclining at the table, and their subject was the praise (*laudes*), not the deeds (*res gestae*) of great men. These were apparently not narrative poems. The circumstances of their performance suggest the informality of those drinking songs that the Greeks called *skolia*, not the formalities of epic structure and the conditions of epic recitation. Nor was high polish in demand. Itinerant professionals who offered their services on such occasions were mocked as flatterers. Small wonder that the Romans, as Cato knew and Cicero would regret, were slow to respect the poets' art.[2] There was little in that earliest poetry to command respect. Cicero's effort in the *Brutus* to wrestle such spotty and intractable testimony into an evolutionary scheme is a bold but ultimately unconvincing experiment in literary history. Hymns and liturgies, dirges, epitaphs and encomia were certainly known – and have left their traces – from early times, but there is no hint of narrative verse among the Romans until the later third century, when a Greek freedman from Tarentum named Livius Andronicus sat down and composed the first Latin epic.[3]

It was not a completely original work. Andronicus' gift was for the interpretation, not the invention of literary forms. He is best known for launching the tradition of Roman theatre with productions at the *ludi Romani* of 240 BCE. These plays were Latin versions of Greek originals, and their adaptation of Greek plots and metres to Roman requirements established the norms of what soon became a flourishing genre. The first Roman epic was also an adaptation, a Latin version of the *Odyssey*, but Andronicus' changes in the epic form were more radical than his innovations in drama. He did not, for example, reproduce the Greek hexameter or turn any of the quantitative metres in his dramatist's arsenal to the task of narrative verse. He chose instead to use the Latin Saturnian, a decision that opens the history of Roman epic with a mystery.

Over two thousand years have passed since anyone has understood Saturnian verse. Debate over its pedigree (native Italic or Greek import?) and prosody (quantitative or accentual?) is at least that old. No solid conclusions have ever emerged. Only some 125 Latin Saturnians survive – a few Oscan ones have also been claimed – and this sample is too small and erratic to support any definitive explanation. We cannot even test proposed scansions against the norms of the Latin language, a crucial step in distinguishing deliberate metrical features from accidents of Latin phonology. Two formal features, however, are certain. The Saturnian line is divided by a caesura into two uneven cola, and the second colon is usually one to three syllables shorter than the first.[4] These comparatively rigid characteristics inevitably affect the arrangement of ideas in the line and the author's choice of stylistic ornament. The epitaph for Lucius Scipio Barbatus (consul 298 BCE) probably dates from the second half of the third century and illustrates some common devices of Saturnian composition.

> Cornelius Lucius   Scipio Barbatus
> Gnaivod patre prognatus   fortis vir sapiensque
> quoius forma virtutei   parisuma fuit
> consol censor aidilis   quei fuit apud vos
> Taurasia Cisauna   Samnio cepit
> subigit omne Loucanam   opsidesque abdoucit.
>
> (no. 309, Degrassi)

> Cornelius Lucius Scipio Barbatus
> Father Gnaeus' offspring, a brave and educated man,
> whose beauty matched his character.
> Consul, censor, aedile was he among you.
> Taurasia, Cisauna, Samnium he conquered.
> He subjugated all Lucania and brought back captives.

The cola here themselves form significant units of sense. Some are discrete phrases; others separate verbs from their complements. Only the last line puts a complete thought in each colon. Yet there is also a larger sense of organization in the arrangement of these lines: the epitaph falls into two equal parts, the first treating Scipio's character and the second his achievements.

The whole set of Scipionic epitaphs reflects similar principles of composition, but the Saturnian was not just the metre of epitaphs. Its functions were, if anything, too broad to create any particular generic associations. Honorific inscriptions could take Saturnian form, and so could witticisms. As late as the 140s, Lucius Mummius commemorated his destruction of Corinth with a Saturnian inscription, and the Metelli's famous jab at Naevius became the metricians' paradigm: 'malum dabunt Metelli Naevio poetae' ('The Metelli will make trouble for the poet Naevius'). Saturnian cola, or at least Saturnian tendencies, are even recognizable among the archaic gibberish of the Arval Hymn. The choice of metre that freed the Latin *Odyssey* from an important set of Greek associations also anchored it in the distinctly Roman experience of poetry. Andronicus' verse established a distinctly Roman form for a story with famous Italian associations. The choice also imposed some serious burdens. The Saturnian structure may seem ill suited to the demands of extended narrative, and its rhythmic possibilities are

21

certainly limited. Such apparent obstacles sometimes encourage the belief that the poem was crude, perhaps simply an exercise for school-boys. We know that Andronicus himself earned a living as a *grammaticus*, and the young Horace eventually studied his epic at a grammarian's knee. Horace's classroom torment, however, came over a century later, by which time the Latin *Odussia* had claimed its own, somewhat musty niche in the curriculum. It could never serve as a crib, for it was too free and too abridged – apparently but a single book – to substitute for the original.[5] Nor did Andronicus' poem lack art. He developed an epic style and an epic decorum quite distinct from his model, and in doing so launched Roman epic on its own unique course.

The opening line of the *Odussia* reveals his craft:

> Virum mihi, Camena,   insece versutum.
> Tell me, Camena, of the clever man.

Comparison with its famous model enables us to pry into the Latin poet's intentions as well as his techniques.

> Andra moi ennepe, Mousa, polutropon . . .
> Tell me, Muse, of the clever man . . .

Andronicus has immediately declared his capacity for close but clever translation. Thought and word-order are, given the shorter compass of the Saturnian, almost identical to the original, but with small changes suited to the new surroundings. One of the Camenae, nymphs identi-fied with a spring outside Rome's Porta Capena, has replaced Homer's Muse, an Italian equivalent with appropriate associations and a name sounding something like *carmen*. With *insece* he offers a rare Latin word of similar meaning, sound, and accent to Homer's own uncommon *ennepe; versutum*, built on *verto*, renders *polutropon* with a Latin version of the same metaphor. Metrical features are made to serve the needs of sense. Andronicus reverses the order of Homer's vocative and verb to accommodate the mandatory caesura and the naturally enclitic vocative. The alliteration of *virum . . . versutum* links the two cola by using sound and word-order to create a calculated relationship between them. This becomes a frequent device, creating relationships that may be parallel (e.g. 'argenteo polubro aureo eglutro', fr. 6) or chiastic (e.g. 'ibidem-que vir summus adprimus Patroclus', fr. 10).

A second device for bridging the caesura developed from the avoid-ance of patronymics, a Greek form that never found a comfortable Latin equivalent. Athena, for example, addresses Zeus in *Odyssey* 1 as 'pater hēmetere Kronidē' ('our father, the son of Kronos,' 45, 81), which Andronicus rendered with characteristically flexible fidelity as 'pater noster, Saturni filie' (fr. 2). This semantic bridge became a Saturnian mannerism:

> sancta puer Saturni   filia regina
>
>   (fr. 12)

> blessed child, Saturn's daughter, queen

> apud nympham Atlantis   filiam Calypsonem
>
>   (fr. 13)

> with the nymph, Atlas' daughter, Kalypso

> nam diva Monetas   filia docuit
>
>   (fr. 21)

> for the goddess, Mnemosyne's daughter, taught

or, varying the pattern,

> Mercurius cumque eo   filius Latonas
>
>   (fr. 19)

> and Mercury with him, Leto's son.

Significantly enough, these lines lack single, clearly identifiable Greek models. The Saturnian lines have transformed their originals beyond recognition.

Homeric metaphors presented a different kind of challenge. To make them into succinct but comprehensible Latin, Andronicus moved still further from his model. Zeus, for example, answers Athena's appeal in *Odyssey* 1 with a common Homeric expression:

> teknon emon, poion se epos fugen herkos odontōn?
>
>   (64)

> My child, what word escapes the barrier of your teeth?

Andronicus is again as faithful as possible in matters of vocabulary and word-order.

> mea puera, quid verbi ex tuo ore supra fugit?
>
>   (fr. 3)

> My child, what word escapes up out beyond your mouth?

Yet while *fugio* easily assumes the metaphoric sense of its Greek cognate, Latin cannot so readily describe a 'barrier of teeth'. *Supra* perhaps echoes the idea of an obstacle surmounted, but Andronicus must translate the meaning rather than the words. *Os* provides a far easier metaphor for 'lips'. So too with a common Homeric expression of fear:

kai tot' Odussēos luto gounata kai philon ētor.

and then Odysseus' knees loosened and his own heart.

Andronicus again keeps what he can.

> igitur demum Ulixi   cor frixit prae pavore.
>
> (fr. 30)

> only then did Ulysses' heart freeze for fear.

He, too, uses the narrative particles and keeps the name in the genitive at the caesura. He preserves the extended notion of 'heart' and avoids prosaic circumlocutions or explanations. Metaphor translates metaphor. The metaphor itself, however, must change to something Latin can more easily bear. *Frigesco* may be bold – it has only the metaphorical sense of waning enthusiasm in Roman comedy – and the effect is heightened by the alliteration of *prae pavore*.

One final example of the altered metaphor survives to tell us something else about Andronicus' taste. The original is in *Odyssey* 8. Alcinoos has commanded the young men Halios and Laodamas to entertain their guest with a solo performance.

> And then the pair danced (*orcheisthēn*) upon the all-nourishing earth, exchanging places often (*tarphe' ameibomenō*). The other young men standing about beat time, and a great sound arose.
>
> (*Od.* 8.378–80)

One Latin line from the passage is preserved.

> nexebant multa inter se   flexu nodum dubio.
>
> (fr. 20)

> They wove much between themselves with tangled bend of knots.

We may hear a Greek echo in the adverbial accusative *multa* and perhaps a hint of the dual in *inter se*. The complex dance itself, however, has become not a matter of exchanges back and forth, but of weaving in and out. The text does not render Homer directly. It offers a more familiar metaphor, so familiar that it also found its way into the minor Homeric scholia, which gloss the phrase *tarphe' ameibomenō* as 'weaving rapidly between themselves in their exchanges'.[6] Andronicus has applied his schoolmaster's mentality to the reading of Homer, employing a metaphor drawn not from the text, but from its margin.

A fourth sign of accommodation to a Roman readership involves the matter of epic decorum. The easy familiarity with which the gods and men of the *Odyssey* communicate across the barrier of mortality undergoes a curious change in this Latin version of their story. At *Odyssey* 3.102ff., for example, Nestor recounts for Telemachus the high cost of the Trojan campaign:

then perished there so many of the finest men. There Ajax lies, the man of Ares, and there Achilles, and there Patroclus, the gods' equal as counsellor, and there my own dear son, both strong and flawless, Antilochos.

(*Od.* 3.108–12)

Andronicus' tenth fragment seems to come from this passage.

> ibidemque vir summus   adprimus Patroclus.

> and then the best and very first of men, Patroclus.

Ibidemque strongly suggests that Andronicus has repeated Nestor's sequence, but the poet shies away from calling Patroclus 'the gods' equal as counsellor' (*theophin mēstōr atalantos*). He prefers an epithet still emphatically distinguished, but also decidedly human in its measure. He will not equate his mortal hero with the gods. A similar scruple seems to be operating in fragment 7, which also has a fairly certain model.

> tuque mihi narrato   omnia disertim.

> and you tell me   everything clearly.

> all' age moi tode eipe kai atrekeōs katalexon.

(*Od.* 1.169)

> but come, tell me this, explaining it clearly straight through.

Two Greek verbs of telling have become one, but Andronicus' omission is more significant than his compression. What has happened to Homer's *all' age*? Latin has the same expression. Characters in Plautus frequently say things like 'come now, first tell me your name' ('agedum nomen tuom primum memora mihi, *Tri.* 883). Why has Andronicus left it out? An answer lies in the context and in his new sense of epic decorum. Telemachus here is being gracious to the (disguised) Athena. It is a polite but colloquial moment, evidently too colloquial for the new epic audience. The Latin Telemachus is much more formal in his address to a god. A colloquialism disappears, and the rather solemn future imperative enters.

A related phenomenon occurs in fragment 18, based on Laodamas' comment in *Odyssey* 8 on the destructive power of the sea (138–9).

> ou gar egō ge ti phēmi kakōteron allo thalassēs
> andra ge sugkheuai, ei kai mala karteros eiē.

> I say for sure that nothing's more destructive than the sea:
> it overwhelms a man, however powerful he may be.

25

Andronicus renders these lines as follows (fr. 18):

        namque nullum peius   macerat humanum
        quamde mare saevom: vires cui sunt magnae,
        topper confringent   inportunae undae.

        for nothing wounds a mortal worse than
        a savage sea: he whose strength is great,
        the remorseless billows shatter at once.

The comparative structure parallels Homer fairly closely, and Andronicus has even preserved an appropriate nuance of vocabulary: *macerat*, like *sugkheuai*, takes its metaphorical sense from liquids. Yet tone and emphasis have shifted. The colloquial emphasis woven into Laodamas' 'ou gar egō ge ti phēmi' is, like Telemachus' casual grace, entirely gone. Andronicus' notion of epic decorum is once again not Homer's. Neither is his organization. This longest fragment of the *Odussia* also offers a rare glimpse into how the poet expresses a complex thought within the comparatively rigid Saturnian structure. Andronicus expands on *peius* with *saevom* and *inportunae*, and he doubles the verb (*macerat, confringent*). The expansion has a technical reason. Homer's concessive 'ei kai mala karteros eiē', coming almost as an afterthought, poses a challenge to the ordered sequence of Saturnian cola. Andronicus meets this challenge by reordering the thought. He expands on his model to give himself space, beginning with a more general statement than Homer's (*humanum* replacing *andra*) and then narrowing the thought with a specific example (*cui*). Word-order heightens the effect. Postponement of the relative, eventually a familiar mannerism in hexameter poetry, juxtaposes *vires* and *mare saevom* in unequal rivalry. The movement from general to specific restates and thus emphasizes the primary thought. It becomes the functional equivalent of Homer's concessive clause. A complex idea is expressed by short cola in asyndeton.

The asyndeton itself is of interest because the strong stop occurs at a caesura, not a line-end. Andronicus prefers to link thoughts between lines. Enjambment is rare, but lines frequently open with conjunctions. *Namque* and *quamde* here are typical. Enclitic *-que*, rarely attached to the first word of a hexameter verse, occurs in six of the thirty apparent line-openings of the *Odussia*. Others begin with *neque* and *atque*. Ten more begin with sequential adverbs like *nam, igitur,* and the archaic *topper*. A small group of single lines with clause-breaks at the caesura probably also indicates this tendency to prefer strong stops there rather than at line-end. These include:

        in Pylum deveniens,   aut ibi<dem> ommentans
                                             (fr. 9)

        coming to Pylos or remaining there

> quando dies adveniet,   quem profata Morta est
>   (fr. 23)

> when the day comes which Morta has foretold

> topper facit homines   ut prius fuerunt
>   (fr. 25)

> she at once made the men as they were.

Saturnian composition, however, does not necessitate parataxis. Fragment 15 preserves a different type of complex sequence.

> ibi manens sedeto   donicum videbis
> me carpento vehentem   domum venisse.

> Sit waiting there until you see
> I have come home, carried in my cart.

The context seems to be Nausicaa's instructions to Odysseus towards the end of *Odyssey* 6, and editors usually cite lines 295–6 as the model.

> Sit waiting there a time (*entha kathezomenos meinai*
>   *khronon*) until we have
> come to town and entered my father's house.

They may then puzzle over the logic (or perhaps topography) of the situation. How can Odysseus remain where he is and yet see Nausicaa return home? It helps to read on a little further.

> but when you think that we have reached the house
> (*autar epēn hēmeas elpēi poti dōmat' aphichthai*),
> then enter the Phaeacians' city and ask for
> the house of my father, greathearted Alcinoos.

Nausicaa, in rather leisurely fashion, is saying two things to Odysseus: wait here until I get home. When you think sufficient time has passed, follow after. Andronicus compresses these thoughts. He translates the first part of 295 closely, but *videbis* has the figurative sense 'think' and actually renders *elpēi* of line 297. The correspondences are really quite close:

> ibi manens sedeto ~ entha kathezomenos meinai khronon
> donicum videbis me . . . domum venisse ~ epēn hēmeas elpēi
>   . . . dōmat' aphichthai.

Where Homer has built his thought gradually, however, Andronicus condenses his. Each colon contains a discrete verbal idea (sitting, seeing, riding, arriving), but they are joined to develop a single complex

27

sequence: 'ibi . . . donicum' unites the first line around the caesura and 'me . . . venisse' bridges the second. The central idea ('donicum videbis') is surrounded by the injunction and the infinitive clause.

The cart, Andronicus' apparent addition to the passage, is itself of interest, for it reflects another aspect of the new epic decorum. Nausicaa's entourage in Homer carried a good deal of laundry piled into a four-wheeled wagon (*apēnē*, *Od.* 6.69, 252). We might expect the Latin *plaustrum*, the familiar wagon of everyday life. Instead we get *carpentum*, a lady's two-wheeled cart. It is the more suitable conveyance for a king's daughter, if not necessarily for a load of washing. In the choice of detail, as in the manner of dialogue, Andronicus seeks a uniformly elevated tone, altering or omitting those graphic and homely touches that anchor the Homeric *Odyssey* in the familiar realities of daily life. He develops a different kind of epic dignity that looks not back to Homer, but forward to Virgil.

Andronicus' poem opened the world of epic to Latin literature. Gnaeus Naevius, his successor, a Campanian of multiple talents and great originality, made that world Roman by elevating current events to epic proportions.[7] His *Bellum Punicum* treated a war he knew at first hand (fr. 44), but it did not lack debts to Andronicus' *Odussia*. Naevius also chose to employ the Saturnian metre and with it key features of Andronicus' style. He also cultivated echoes of the Greek heroic age. The poem told of Aeneas and Troy (frr. 5–7) and contained Odyssean allusions that Virgil would eventually borrow in his turn (fr. 15). There were divine debates and interventions of the epic type (frr. 9, 14). Naevius also mentioned Aeneas' visit to Carthage (frr. 21–3) and the founding of Rome (frr. 25–9). Yet his combination of mythic and historical narrative was not simply a history of Rome from the fall of Troy to the peace of 241 BCE. It was too compact and too intricately structured to ramble in annalistic fashion. Because the poem was divided into books some time after Naevius' death, our sources cite many of its fragments by book number, and a curious pattern emerges when we reconstruct the original sequence. The first book refers explicitly to the consul Valerius' expedition to Sicily in 263 BCE (fr. 3), but it also described Aeneas' flight from Troy. His visit to Carthage came in Book 2, and by Book 3 he was in Italy. The historic narrative had certainly resumed by Book 4, which mentions a Roman invasion of Malta dated to the early 250s (fr. 32). As unassigned fragments are fitted within this framework, it becomes clear that the legendary material was surrounded by the historical narrative.[8]

How Naevius moved to and from legendary time remains uncertain, but attention often centres on fragment 4, which comes from the first book:

inerant signa expressa, quo modo Titani,
bicorpores Gigantes magnique Atlantes
Runcus ac Purpureus, filii Terras.

Figures were modelled on it, how the Titans,
double-bodied Giants and great Atlases,
Runcus and Purpureus, sons of Earth.

The curious plural *Atlantes* put Hermann Fränkel in mind of the
'atlantes' that were a famous architectural feature of the Temple of
Zeus at Agrigentum.[9] These were a set of colossal male statues over
twenty feet tall that, like the Caryatids of the Athenian Erechtheum,
supported the architrave of the building. Fränkel suspected that the
architectural term has crept into a description of the Gigantomachy
that adorned the east pediment of this temple. He therefore associated
the fragment with the historical narrative. Readers have presumably
followed the consul Valerius to Sicily and now stand with him before
the temple at Agrigentum. Since the west pediment of the temple
showed the Homeric heroes at the fall of Troy, one of Naevius' Romans
may then have recognized Aeneas among them. One association would
bring on another, leading to the story of his flight and subsequent
voyage to Italy. The effect would be similar to *Aeneid* 1, where the
pictures of Troy on Dido's Temple of Juno prefigure Aeneas' narrative
in Book 2. This appealing reconstruction is unfortunately far from
certain. Other contexts are equally plausible, but the tentative quality
of Fränkel's suggestion must not obscure a basic fact: *some* such device
joined the historical and legendary narratives. The link was not purely
chronological. The *Bellum Punicum* had an interesting and intricate
structure.

It also had a style that reflected the technical innovations of Andronicus' *Odussia*. The invocation that opened the poem, for example,
contained a line – 'novem Iovis concordes filiae sorores' ('nine like-
minded sisters, Jupiter's daughters', fr. 1) – recalling Andronicus'
fondness for bridging the caesura with a patronymic phrase. A simple
description, 'ferunt pulcras creterras, aureas lepistas' ('they bear
beautiful bowls, golden goblets', fr. 54) echoes the content, structure
and stylistic ornament of Andronicus' 'argenteo polubro aureo eglutro'
('with silver basin, golden pitcher', fr. 6). Naevius may also arrange his
thoughts chiastically around the caesura, as in fragment 8: 'res divas
edicit, praedicit castus' ('he decrees the sacred rites, declares a state of
chastity'; cf. *Od.*, fr. 10). These are, if not signs of explicit modelling, at
least indications of a common approach to narrative composition that
marks the emergence of a distinct epic style. Because many fragments
of Naevius' poem are slightly longer than the remains of Andronicus'
Odussia, we can better gauge the effect of such features.

Epithets so easily fill the short cola that descriptive phrases sometimes pile up over several lines in Naevius, as in fragment 10:

> senex fretus pietatei   deum adlocutus
> summi deum regis   fratrem Neptunum
> regnatorem marum.

> The old man buoyed by piety called upon the god,
> brother of the gods' great king, Neptune
> ruler of the seas.

This layering of epithets avoids the predictable diminuendo so common
in sub-literary Saturnians. The layered style can also build power and a
certain tension into the lines:

> dein pollens sagittis   inclutus arquitenens
> sanctus Iove prognatus   Pythius Apollo.
>
> (fr. 20)

> Then mighty with arrows, the famous bow-holder,
> blessed son of Jupiter, Pythian Apollo.

Readers may well suspect at once that the god to be associated with bow
and arrow is Apollo, but that expectation only heightens the effect as
Naevius sets one epithet in each colon, culminating the sequence with
the proper name. The famous Giant-fragment (4) represents a more
elaborate form of the same technique. The sequence of three generic
titles ('Titani . . . Gigantes . . . Atlantes') sets each title in a two-word
phrase and again climaxes with proper names. Naevius then rounds off
the expression, which must have been the expanded subject of the
quomodo-clause, with the dignified archaism of 'filii Terras' ('sons of
Earth'). The crescendo of the lines thus suggests movement even
though the thought itself is standing still.

The static quality of such elaborately ornamented fragments is to
some extent an accident of their preservation. Layered expressions of
this kind are in any case a matter of choice. Other stylistic devices could
be employed to heighten the effect of actions. Fragment 5, for example, describes how the wives of Anchises and Aeneas fled the
destruction of Troy.

> amborum uxores
> noctu Troiad exibant   capitibus opertis
> flentes ambae, abeuntes,   lacrimis cum multis.

> Their two wives
> fled Troy by night, heads covered,
> weeping both, leaving with many tears.

Each colon, shaped as so often by alliteration and homoioteleuton, contains a discrete idea, while the nearly parallel ablative phrases link successive verses. A combination of participles and finite verbs creates the action, revealing the picture piece by piece to dramatic and poignant effect. Not all of Naevius' effects, however, depend on the juxtaposition of small pieces. In fragment 25, entire verses, not their constituent cola, are the primary units of meaning.

> postquam avem aspexit   in templo Anchisa,
> sacra in mensa penatium   ordine ponuntur;
> immolabat auream   victimam pulcram.

> After Anchises saw the bird in flight,
> offerings to the household gods were duly set out.
> He began sacrificing a fair, golden victim.

Here there are no significant breaks in phrasing at the caesurae. Each verse reports a discrete action: their structural integrity is emphasized by patterns of sound in the first and third lines and by a grammatical shift in the second, which introduces a new, plural verb.

This passage is narrative, and we might well expect a change in style when action demands a rapid pace. This undeniable difference between narrative and description has become a significant crux of Naevian criticism. The dignified directness of narrative passages in the *Bellum Punicum* led Friedrich Leo to distinguish 'an elevated chronicle style' from the more artful effects we find in a description like that of the women's flight from Troy (fr. 5) and in the numerous references to a divine apparatus. This stylistic distinction is now widely perceived as a defect or at best as an inevitable consequence of archaic crudity. As one noted Virgilian put it: 'We cannot expect at that era any special sensitivity to style, any strong sense of the incongruity between annalistic history and Homeric narrative.'[10] The problem is that, as we have seen, Saturnian epic never lacked a sensitivity to style. It was, if anything, quite highly stylized. It was never merely crude or naive. Would it then tolerate the kind of incongruity Leo's distinction implies? We need a clearer sense of the Latin *Chronikstil*. It is a legitimate herring, but need we paint it red and hang it on our wall?

An 'official style' was certainly recognizable at Rome by the late third century. Bold declarations of conquests that piled actions up in ablative phrases, detailed accounts of spoils taken, and the full name and titles of the conqueror are among its salient features. Plautus could always draw a laugh by aping it, and Livy preserves numerous examples – mostly later, but no matter – of the type. In 179 BCE, for example, the censor M. Aemilius Lepidus dedicated a temple to the Lares Permarini to fulfil the vow of L. Aemilius Regillus at the battle of Myonnessus

31

eleven years before. Livy's history preserves a somewhat garbled version of its dedicatory inscription (40.52.5–7):

> duello magno dirimendo, regibus subigendis, caput patrandae pacis haec pugna exeunti L. Aemilio M. Aemilii filio [. . .] auspicio imperio felicitate ductuque eius inter Ephesum Samum Chiumque inspectante eos ipso Antiocho, exercitu omni, equitatu elephantisque, classis regis Antiochi antehac invicta fusa contusa fugataque est, ibique eo die naves longae cum omnibus sociis captae quadraginta duae. ea pugna pugnata rex Antiochus regnumque [. . .] eius rei ergo aedem Laribus permarinis vovit.

> For ending a great war, for subduing kings, as a way to establish peace, this battle (was granted to) L. Aemilius, the son of M. Aemilius, when he took the field. Under his auspices, command, good fortune, and leadership near Ephesus, Samos, and Chios, while Antiochus himself watched them, the entire army, cavalry, and elephants, the fleet of King Antiochus though previously undefeated was routed, shattered, and put to flight, and on that same day forty-two warships with all their crews were captured. With this fight fought, King Antiochus and his kingdom (were conquered). For this victory he vowed a temple to the Lares of the Sea.

This formidable, 'annalistic' record of achievement does not lack stylistic embellishment. The ringing phrase 'auspicio imperio felicitate ductuque eius' was already formulaic (cf. *Amph.* 196), but Lepidus' inscription also contains stylistic features of its own. It is, for example, deliberately and conspicuously alliterative. The archaic form *duello* is doubtless chosen for effect, and so is the cognate accusative of *pugna pugnata*. The grouping 'Ephesum Samum Chiumque' may merely serve to place the battle geographically, but 'fusa contusa fugataque est' is certainly an artfully powerful tricolon that plays on the repetition of syllables and the increasing length of its components. This is writing for maximum effect. In fact, the 'chronicle style' here blends so easily into literary composition that the Neronian grammarian Caesius Bassus, plucking 'duello magno dirimendo, regibus subigendis' from its clearly unmetrical context, claimed it for a Saturnian along with an equally striking tricolon culled from a triumphal inscription of Acilius Glabrio: 'fundit fugat prosternit maximas legiones' ('He scattered, routed, smashed the greatest legions').[11] We need not share Bassus' conviction that these are Saturnians to agree that the official style has created such flamboyant effects by using the very ornaments characteristic of literary compositions. There is no great stylistic gap between official and literary narrative. Neither was necessarily plain, and Naevius found little difficulty in integrating historic narrative into his epic.

A trace of that integration remains in the alliteration across the caesura of even the prosaic fragment 3, referring to the Roman expedition to Sicily in 263 BCE:

> Manius Valerius
> consul partem exerciti in expeditionem
> ducit.

> Manius Valerius
> the consul led part of his army
> on a foray.

The unembarrassed pride of the Roman honorific inscriptions finds its best parallel, however, in one notoriously difficult fragment of the *Bellum Punicum*. The text should probably read like this:

> transit Melitam
> exercitus Romanus. insulam integram
> urit vastat populatur, rem hostium concinnat.
>
> (fr. 32)

> The Roman army
> crossed to Malta. It burned, pillaged, destroyed
> the entire island. It disrupted the enemy's affairs.

It employs not just the kind of tricolon and syllable play so common in military inscriptions, but a thought sequence characteristic of epic composition. We have already seen how a poet may present an incomplete idea in the first colon of a line and then resolve or explain that idea in the second colon. Thus the modifiers *novem Iovis concordes* are resolved by the nouns *filiae sorores*, and the *sanctus Iove prognatus* is then identified as *Pythius Apollo*. This mannerism is also found in historical contexts such as fragment 2, which apparently refers to the declaration of war with Carthage: 'scopas atque verbenas sagmina sumpserunt' ('they took up the *sagmina*, shoots and sacred boughs'). The *sagmina*, tufts of grass used by the Fetial priests in declaring war or making treaties, stand apart here in the second colon in apposition to 'scopas atque verbenas'. In fragment 33, the first colon ('simul atrocia proicerent') makes little sense without the object and subject nouns provided in the second ('exta ministratores'). So here. The last line describes the violence done to Malta with three verbs in the first colon and then summarizes the result of that violence with the declaration that the enemy has been discommoded. The parataxis of the fragment may recall the flatness of official prose, but Naevius' distribution of ideas in these lines reflects a familiar epic mannerism. Strong stops occur only at the caesurae, a pattern we have observed in Andronicus

33

(18) and which can be found in both mythological (8, 23) and historical (32, 34) fragments of the *Bellum Punicum*. The poet creates a tension between thought sequence and verse-structure by obscuring the line-ends with enjambment while slowing the pace at the caesurae.

Stylistically, fragment 32 is thus of a piece with Saturnian epic as a whole. Naevius may vary his art to fit his subject – good poets generally do – but he is never entirely without art. Taken as a group, the fragments of his poem show stylistic variety, not incongruity. Naevius' historical narrative wore a stylistic garb not so very different from his mythological passages. One final example may summarize the point. Fragment 34 is generally associated with events of 260 BCE, the only time we know the *praetor urbanus* to have held a military command.

> virum praetor adveneit,   auspicat auspicium
> prosperum.

> The men's praetor comes. He takes propitious
> auspices.

We find some familiar features here: strong break at caesura rather than verse-end, ubiquitous alliteration, a *figura etymologica*. The crowning flourish is the odd phrase *virum praetor*. Scevola Mariotti took *praetor* back to its root in *prae-itor* and explains the phrase as modelled on the Homeric 'lord of men' (*anax andrōn*). This clever suggestion has been dismissed as inappropriate to 'a terse, factual statement about a Roman magistrate', but only by putting the matter exactly backwards.[12] Factual statements among the surviving fragments are rarely without ornament. Naevius' decision to write a poem about the war with Carthage made this struggle quite literally an epic conflict, and the possibility of a Homeric echo here should not be so easily dismissed. We cannot press a distinction between 'chronicle' and 'poetic' styles. There is a stylistic unity to the *Bellum Punicum* that reflects Naevius' desire to extend the epic manner pioneered by Andronicus to include the narration of historical events. The Saturnian aesthetic expands its scope in this poem, though the impetus for that expansion would soon take Roman epic in a rather different direction.

The poets of a later day would have little praise and even less time for Saturnian epic. The metre itself became distasteful. Ennius dismissed it as the rhythm of fauns and fortune-tellers, and Horace would liken its demise to the draining of a marsh.

>   sic horridus ille
> defluxit numerus Saturnius, et grave virus
> munditiae pepulere.

>   (*Ep.* 2.1.157–9)

Then that harsh
Saturnian rhythm drained away, and elegance
drove off the brackish scent.

In the course of the second century, a Latinized form of dactylic hexameter became the recognized epic metre at Rome, and elegiac inscriptions began replacing Saturnians on tombs of the great. The greater appeal of this Greek import proved undeniable and unstoppable. Yet the stylistic changes that brought Latin verse from Saturnian thud to hexameter flow did not immediately or entirely eclipse the work of the earliest epic poets. Even while Horace was heaping his faint damns on Andronicus' *Odussia*, Romans were still reading Naevius' *Bellum Punicum*, and the *horridus numerus* was still recognized as poetry. That would soon change, of course, but the change in taste does not change a basic fact. Rome's perennial fascination with epic clearly begins, however oddly, with Livius Andronicus. He created the medium that supported Naevius' more ambitious and original *Bellum Punicum* and inspired in turn the still grander design of Ennius' *Annales*. The Saturnian created Rome's first epic aesthetic, and its more enduring sequel would certainly have been quite different without it. The road from Tarentum to Mantua was long and tortuous, but the journey proved fruitful and momentous.

NOTES

The present essay draws on material from my forthcoming book, *Ruined Choirs of Roman Epic Verse*. It cites Andronicus from the edition of Büchner (1982) and Naevius from that of Strzelecki (1964). The inscriptional evidence follows Degrassi (1957). Warmington (1957) provides the only widely available English translations of these early Roman poets, but his texts and notes are not always reliable. Translations provided here are my own.

1 Cic., *Brut.* 75; cf. *TD* 1.3 and 4.3, *Leg.* 2.62. Varro *ap.* Nonius 107L has a slightly different version. Less direct testimony in Val. Max. 2.1.10 and Quint. 1.10.20. I am summarizing what is usually presented as a long and complex argument. Momigliano 1957 and Zorzetti 1990 are the best guides to this controversial subject.

2 Cato *ap.* Gel. 11.2.5: 'Poeticae artis honos non erat. Si quis in ea re studebat aut sese ad convivia adplicabat, "crassator" vocabatur'. Cf. Cic., *TD* 1.3.

3 See Suerbaum 1968: 1–8 and 297–9 and now Gruen 1990: 80–92 for the biography and social context.

4 Cole 1969 provides the most accessible guide to the riddles of Saturnian verse, but see the critical survey of Waszink 1972: 875–85. The ancient testimony is conveniently gathered by Luiselli 1967: 105–14.

5 Suet., *Gram.* 1.1; Hor., *Ep.* 2.1.69–71. Formal instruction in grammar did not actually begin at Rome until the arrival of Crates of Mallos in the 160s. See Garbarino 1973: 356–62.

6 Σ V ad 379, first recognized by Fränkel 1932: 306–7. The V are pedestrian,

not learned scholia. There is no evidence here of the Alexandrian erudition claimed for Andronicus by Mariotti 1985.

7 Suerbaum 1968: 13–27; Gruen 1990: 92–106.
8 Thus Rowell 1947: 21–46, building on the landmark work of Strzelecki 1935.
9 Fränkel 1935: 59–61; cf. Fraenkel 1954 for alternatives.
10 Otis 1964: 21. The idea goes back to Leo 1913: 80–81 with development by Fraenkel 1935: 639.
11 GLK 6.265, citing simply 'in Acilii Glabrionis tabula'. The context is unknown. Mummius' dedication on the temple of Hercules Victor dates from 144 BCE and really was in Saturnians (no. 122, Degrassi).
12 Skutsch 1958: 47 on Mariotti 1955: 72.

III

FROM GREECE TO ROME: ENNIUS' *ANNALES*

William J. Dominik

Ennius ut noster cecinit, qui primus amoeno
detulit ex Helicone perenni fronde coronam,
per gentis Italas hominum quae clara clueret.

As our own Ennius sang, who first from pleasant Helicon
Carried off a perennial crown of laurel,
Destined to win renown among Italian peoples.[1]
(Lucretius, *DRN* 1.117–19)

hic canet illustri primus bella Itala versu
attolletque duces caelo; resonare docebit
hic Latiis Helicona modis nec cedet honore
Ascraeo famave seni.

He first will sing Italian wars in noble verse
And praise their leaders to the sky; in Latin metres
He will teach Helicon resonance, nor in fame or honour
Yield to the Ascraean sage.
(Silius, *Punica* 2.410–13)

Quintus Ennius – to Lucretius – was the immortal father of Roman poetry. 'ENNIus . . . perENNI' ('ENNIus perENNIal', *DRN* 1.117f.; cf. 121). To Silius Italicus he was a poetic icon of the past. Born in 239 BCE at Rudiae, a town in Calabria, Ennius observed that he had three hearts (or minds) because he spoke Greek and Latin as well as Oscan (Gel. 17.17.1). He had one foot firmly in the Greek tradition and one firmly in the Italian, a reflection of his cosmopolitan upbringing and perspective, but, although he reveals in his epic an understanding of both traditions, it was his Latin 'heart' that he was destined to develop to its full potential.

The epic of Ennius in its original version contained fifteen books covering the fall of Troy to 189 BCE. The material appears to have been organized into triads with a concentric, symmetrical structure. The first part of the *Annales* deals with events before his time (Books 1–7), while

37

the second part (Books 8–15) treats events of his own age. Books 1–3 cover the period from the sack of Troy through the death and deification of Romulus to the reign of Tarquinius Superbus. Books 4–6 deal with events of the early republic down to the war with Pyrrhus (281–271 BCE). The central, emphatic part of the epic (Books 7–9) deals briefly with the first Punic war, then covers events of the second down to Scipio's campaign in Africa and the peace in 201 BCE. The rest of the original work treats events in the East. Books 10–12 treat the second Macedonian war down to events of the Syrian war, possibly to the commencement of hostilities with Antiochus III (192–191 BCE); Books 13–15 cover the war with Antiochus down to events of the Aetolian war through 189 BCE. Later Ennius added three books which deal with events of the Istrian and third Macedonian wars from 189 to 171 BCE. Whether Ennius designed the original *Annales* with only fifteen books in mind, or designed it as an 'open' work on to which other books could be added if desired, is problematical. Since only about six hundred lines survive in fragments, it is difficult to determine what level of structural and thematic counterpoint is at work in the *Annales*. The later addition of three books does at least reveal some consciousness of structure on the part of the poet, since it keeps the total number of books divisible by three; but if the addition were to achieve little more than this, or if the structure of the original *Annales* comprised three pentads instead,[2] it would suggest a lack of structural sophistication.

ENNIUS: SELF-CONSCIOUS EPICIST

Self-consciousness is a principal feature of Ennian epic. This is apparent even before the first line of the *Annales*. Judging by an early reference to the epic in Lucilius (*Annales Enni*, 'the Annals of Ennius', 343 Marx), Ennius named his epic by this title, probably after the title of the pontifical records. By this obviously historical title, Ennius immediately metamorphoses the Homeric tradition of mythological epic and thereby departs from as well as challenges that tradition. The title asserts a consciousness of a time frame which is thoroughly un-Homeric; furthermore, it consciously asserts not only historical (or annalistic) epic but also the importance of Roman history.

The first fragment of the *Annales* further reveals the poet's self-conscious epic intention:[3]

> Musae, quae pedibus magnum pulsatis Olympum . . .[4]
>
> Muses, who beat your feet upon mighty Olympus . . .

Here Ennius uses the Muses of Hesiod (see *Th.* 22ff., 36ff.) rather than Homer's Muse (see *Od.* 1.1ff., *Il.* 1.1ff.) but has them dance not on Helicon but on Homer's Olympus (see *Il.* 2.484).[5] Ennius is the first poet in extant literature to portray himself as *ascending* the Muses' mountain, whereas Hesiod describes his meeting with the Muses *beneath* Helicon (*Th.* 22f.). Hesiod was often contrasted with Homer, and the use of Hesiod's Muses on Homer's Olympus in the Proem of the *Annales* not only recalls Homer and Hesiod but also distinguishes Ennius from them.

The use of *Musa* in the *Annales* distinguishes Ennius from his Roman predecessors. In the opening line of the *Odussia*, Livius Andronicus self-consciously commutes *Camena*, a Roman fountain goddess, for Homer's *Mousa*: 'Camena, insece' ('relate, Camena'). Naevius modifies Andronicus slightly in the opening of his *Bellum Punicum* by invoking 'novem Iovis concordes filiae sorores' ('nine blessed sisters, daughters of Jupiter'), and his epitaph suggests he knew them as *Camenae* ('flerent divae Camenae Naevium poetam', 'the divine Camenae would weep for the poet Naevius'). In another self-conscious change, Ennius rewrites Andronicus' 'Camena, insece' to read 'insece, Musa' ('relate, Muse', *Ann.* 10 fr. 1). Elsewhere he draws attention to his conscious use of *Musae* for *Camenae*:

> Musas quas memorant nosces nos esse Camenas.[6]
>
> > (*Ann.* sed. inc. fr. 487)
>
> You will know we are Camenae whom [the Greeks] call Muses.

Ca(s)menae may be a play on the word *carmina* ('songs'). Just as Ennius does not claim inspiration from the Camenae, he does not write *carmina*; he writes *poemata* ('poems'):

> latos <per> populos res atque poemata nostra
> <clara> cluebunt.
>
> > (*Ann.* 1, fr. 11)
>
> Among peoples far flung my subject and poem
> shall win renown.

This use of *poemata* for *carmina* seems a conscious attempt to distinguish his craft from the practices of his predecessors. No Greek or Roman poet prior to Ennius had (to our knowledge) made such a claim on behalf either of himself or any other poet.[7] Earlier poets such as Homer (*Il.* 2.484–93), Apollonius Rhodius (*Arg.* 4.982–97) and Naevius (see Gel. 17.21.45) do refer (infrequently) to themselves, but what distinguishes Ennius from them is his poem's proud claim to originality and fame, the assertive – almost aggressive – intrusion of his own personality in the poem, and the periodicity of his self-conscious references (judging from the fragments).

The dream of Ennius and his encounter with Homer dominate the Proem of the *Annales*. There are enough surviving fragments from the

Proem to allow a reconstruction of its contents.[8] In it Ennius relates how he falls asleep (and dreams) on Helicon[9] –

> somno leni placidoque revinctus
> *(Ann.* 1, fr. 2)

fettered in soft and gentle sleep

– or in a dream is transported to that mountain, a place renowned for the making of powerful poetry; and he may even have described a meeting with the Muses. The poet Homer subsequently appears to him:

> visus Homerus adesse poeta.
> *(Ann.* 1, fr. 3)

Homer the poet appeared by my side.

Homer then addresses Ennius:

> O pietas animi!
> *(Ann.* 1, fr. 5)

O piety of your heart!

The use of *pietas*, a term of familial bonding, is extraordinary, since Ennius uses it to establish the poetic relationship between him and Homer as one of poetic father to poetic son.

At some point in the dream Homer outlines some basic principles concerning *natura rerum*:

> desunt rivos camposque remanant
>   terra<que> corpus
> quae dedit ipsa capit neque dispendi facit hilum.
>   *(Ann.* 1, frr. 6f.)

[The waters] leave the streams and flow back into the fields
                         and earth who
Bestowed the body seizes it herself and wastes nothing.

As part of his general exposition of life's principles, Homer uses the egg analogy to explain the separate origins of the body and soul:

> ova parire solet genus pennis condecoratum,
> non animam. [et] post inde venit divinitus pullis
> ipsa anima
>
>   *(Ann.* 1, fr. 8)

The feather-adorned flock is accustomed to produce eggs,
Not life. And from that time forth life itself comes to the
  chicks
By divine influence.

And he reveals that his own soul had transmigrated from a peacock into the body of the Roman poet:

> memini me fiere pavom.
> *(Ann.* 1, fr. 9)

> I remember becoming a peacock.

Just before or after his dream vision, Ennius (probably) drinks from the Hippocrene, the fount of poetic inspiration (cf. Prop. 3.3.2, 5f.; Pers. prolog. 1).

Ennius is indebted to Hesiod and Callimachus for the conception of this passage in which he describes the source of his poetic inspiration and (specifically) epic aspirations in terms of a dream. Hesiod describes how he received rustic abuse and poetic instruction from the Muses on Helicon and was infused with their divine voice (*Th.* 22ff.). Hesiod, the founder of didactic poetry, looms large in the thoughts of Callimachus. The Alexandrian poet claims Hesiod, not Homer, as his inspiration (*Anth. Pal.* 7.42). Callimachus too is instructed by the Muses (*Anth. Pal.* 7.42.7f.; cf. *Th.* 22f.), but he catechizes them in a notable departure from the Hesiodic technique.

The dream encounter to Ennius is much more than a literary *topos*: a manifestation of his literary self-consciousness, the careful manipulation of the dream motif enables him to stress the magnitude of his poetic conception, inspiration, poetic mission, and place in Latin literature. Through his meeting with Homer and focus on Pythagorean metempsychosis in the prologue, Ennius suggests that the *Annales* represents the rebirth of Roman epic rather than an imitation of its Greek predecessor. As the pavomorphic Homer transforms into Ennius, so Greek epic transmutes into Roman. Hence Ennius' dream encounter acquires its real significance: he is not Homer, the creator of a tradition, but Homer reincarnate, the adaptor of that tradition to a new Roman context. Ennius brings much that is new to the content of epic, including aesthetic and philosophical eclecticism (apparent alone in the Pythagorean cast of the narrative, esp. *Ann.* 1, frr. 2–9), conscious didacticism (evident especially in the proemia, 1, frr. 1–11, 7, fr. 2), euhemeristic techniques of characterization (as in the deification of Romulus, 1, fr. 62; cf. 1, fr. 33), and Epicurean tendencies (witness the scene of Servilius Geminus' companion, 8, fr. 12). The dream denotes the effort and versatility of the powers required to achieve this:

> nec quisquam sophiam, sapientia quae perhibetur,
> in somnis vidit prius quam sam discere coepit.
> *(Ann.* 7, fr. 2)

Nor has any man seen wisdom (the word assigned to knowledge)
In his sleep before he has begun to learn her mysteries.

The poet owes his inspiration and *sophia* ('wisdom') to intellectual
exercise and constant devotion to the task. The burning self consciousness of his mission is evident in other poems such as the *Satires*:

> Enni poeta salve, qui mortalibus
> versus propinas flammeos medullitus!
>
> (*Sat.* 3, fr. 1)

> Hail, poet Ennius, who pledge to mortals
> Flaming verses from your inmost marrow!

The narrative of the first book features another dream passage in which
Ilia, daughter of Aeneas, relates how she is ravished by Mars (*Ann.* 1, fr.
29). In conception the passage reveals a significant debt to Homer, as it
is modelled closely on the scene in *Odyssey* 11.235ff. Mars rapes Ilia by a
river (*Ann.* 1, fr. 29 (36f.)), while in the *Odyssey* Poseidon does the same
to Turo by the river Enipeos (11.241–5); Aeneas attempts to comfort
Ilia by informing her that she will endure hardship before she sees her
fortunes reversed with the birth and rescue of her sons (Romulus and
Remus) from the river Tiber (*Ann.* 1, fr. 29 (42f.); cf. 1, frr. 37f.), while
Poseidon assures Turo by revealing his identity and the future greatness
of their sons (*Od.* 11.246–50; cf. 254–7); and Ilia marries Tiber (cf. *Ann.*
1, fr. 29 (34)), while Turo's lover is Enipeos (*Od.* 11.238–40), whose
form Poseidon takes before ravishing her (241f.). Ennius' adaptation of
the Homeric scene in the narrative of Book 1 is an extension of his
referential strategy, as the allusion to the text of Homer complements
his explicit reference to that poet in the Proem. As he does in his
encounter with Homer, Ennius conveys essential details in the form of
a dream, thus linking the two scenes and suggesting a particular
significance: Ilia's dream, through her rape by Mars and the offspring
she bears, creates Rome; Ennius' dream, through the transmigration of
Homer's soul into his body, creates Roman epic.

The Proem to Book 7 elaborates on the themes Ennius raises in the
first book. Not yet had anyone been inspired by the *Musae* ('Muses') to
compose epic in the Latin hexameter:

> scripsere alii rem
> vorsibus quos olim Faunei vatesque canebant.
> [cum] neque Musarum scopulos . . .
> nec dicti studiosus [quisquam erat] ante hunc.
> nos ausi reserare . . .
>
> (*Ann.* 7, frr. 1–1ª)

Others have written of the war
In verses which once the Fauns and bards used to sing.
[when] neither . . . the rocks of the Muses . . .
Nor [was anyone] before this man conscious of style.
It was I who dared to unbar . . .

The reference here is apparently only to Naevius, who Ennius says 'used to sing' ('canebant') in the manner of 'Fauns and bards' ('Faunei vatesque'); however, one cannot avoid thinking also of Andronicus, who composed the first Latin epic in the Saturnian metre, thereby awakening poets to the aesthetic possibilities of this distinctly Roman verse-form. Andronicus' epic manner contained a number of innovations or variations upon Homeric technique which influenced the epic of Ennius, including the omission of Homeric epithets or patronymics (e.g. *Od.*, frr. 2, 21;[10] cf. *Ann.* 1, fr. 32, 8, fr. 24), a fondness for alliteration (cf. *Od.*, frr. 20, 30; e.g. *Ann.* 1, fr. 60, sed. inc. fr. 451), the use of archaic forms to create an atmosphere of sublimity appropriate to epic (e.g. *Od.*, frr. 13, 29; cf. *Ann.* 1, fr. 26, 7, fr. 16), and the Romanization of Greek deities (e.g. *Od.*, frr. 11, 23; cf. *Ann.* 7, fr. 24).[11] A few years later Naevius reinvigorated the native Saturnian verse-form in his treatment of the first Punic war. Ennius was heavily indebted to Naevius (see Cic. *Brut.* 19.76), and declined to narrate in detail events which had been treated previously by Naevius in his epic (*Ann.* 7, fr. 1). Where Ennius follows Naevius is in approaching his subject chronologically (as the title *Annales* suggests), merging poetry and history into Roman historical epic, glorifying contemporary Roman figures, and composing narratives which do not revolve primarily around the adventures of a single hero. Despite this indebtedness, Ennius asserts that no one before *him* had been *dicti studiosus* ('conscious of style', *Ann.* 7, fr. 1a),[12] and he consigns Naevius to a group of poets he considers to be primitive because of their use of the Saturnian metre. To Ennius the rustic *versus* ('verses') of the *Faunei* ('Fauns') and *vates* ('bards') were inferior to the poems of a poet who had been infused with the creative spirit of the immortal Homer by the divine *Musae* ('Muses'), thereby enabling him to manipulate the Latin language to fit the quantitative requirements of the hexameter. Even though Ennius' hexameters appeared rough and crude by Augustan standards of technical versification (see Prop. 4.1.61f.; Ov., *Trist.* 2.259, 424, *Am.* 1.15.14, 19), this was no mean feat. The heavily spondaic rhythm (e.g. *Ann.* 1, fr. 47 (72, 81)), unusual word-order (e.g. 10, fr. 1), accidence (e.g. *agea*, sed. inc. fr. 61; *aethera*, sed. inc. fr. 88), diction (e.g. *induperator*, 1, fr. 47 (78), 10, frr. 1, 13; *induvolare*, sed. inc. fr. 41) and sound-effects (e.g. 1, fr. 40, sed. inc. fr. 9) were unique to Roman verse.

The Greeks, not the Romans, were the first to create historical epic. But Ennius appears to owe little to them. The poet makes a conscious decision to diverge from the path established by recent Greek (especially Alexandrian) and Roman epicists and to seek his poetic inspiration directly from the creator of the epic genre. Consequently, as might be expected, there is a distinctively Homeric touch to Ennius' narrative in

1 authorial voice: the conceit that the poet is the person through whom the Muse sings his lines (e.g. *Ann.* 10, fr. 1; cf. *Il.* 1.1ff.);
2 setting: oracular and prophetic scenes (e.g. *Ann.* 1, fr. 47; cf. *Il.* 15.63ff.), Olympian *concilia deorum* (e.g. *Ann.* 1, frr. 30–3; cf. *Il.* 1.533ff.);
3 epic and mythological apparatus: the catalogue of troops (e.g. *Ann.* 7, fr. 15; cf. *Il.* 2.494ff.), supernatural causation (e.g. *Ann.* 1, fr. 13; cf. *Il.* 22.208ff.), intervention in human affairs (e.g. *Ann.* 1, frr. 36f., 8, fr. 1; cf. *Il.* 17.319–32);
4 style: personification of natural phenomena (e.g. *Ann.* 1, fr. 28, 10, fr. 14, 16, fr. 19, sed. inc. fr. 109; cf. *Il.* 8.1f., 21.1ff.), extended similes based upon Homeric passages (e.g. *Ann.* 10, fr. 7; cf. *Il.* 10.183ff.), similes depicting social institutions and portraying scenes from daily life (e.g. *Ann.* 1, fr. 47 (79–81), 10, fr. 7; cf. *Il.* 2.474ff.), use of compound adjectives (e.g. *Ann.* 14, fr. 4, sed. inc. fr. 6; cf. *Il.* 14.222, 24.597), formulaic phrasing (e.g. *Ann.* 7, fr. 3, 8, fr. 7, 17, fr. 4; cf. *Il.* 1.121, 21.49).

But Ennius asserts his individuality as a poet and his differences from Homer in matters of

1 theme: the predominant national scope of the thematic design, the epicizing of *contemporary* events;
2 characterization: the realistic and approving descriptions of men from the middle classes (e.g. *Ann.* 8, fr. 12), the attention given in the narrative to the exploits of junior military officers (e.g. Caelius, 15, fr. 5) rather than just *imperatores* ('commanders'), the heroicizing of ordinary men and famous heroes, contemporary and ancient characters, actual and mythical figures;
3 style: the predominantly spondaic patterns of his verse (e.g. 6, fr. 9 (179), sed. inc. fr. 48), puns on proper names (e.g. *caerula* ('blue') with *Caeli* ('Caelius'), 2, fr. 12[13]), use of strictly onomatopoeic words (e.g. *taratantara* to imitate the sound of a trumpet, sed. inc. fr. 9).

That Ennius conceived of his *Annales* being completed at the end of the fifteenth book is apparent from a statement (possibly) at or towards the end of the original Epilogue, where he likens a distinguished *poeta* finishing a demanding literary task to a champion racing-steed in retirement:

sicuti fortis equos spatio qui saepe supremo
vicit Olympia nunc senio confectus quiescit.
(*Ann.* sed. inc. fr. 69)[14]

Just as the powerful steed, who often in the last lap
Has won at Olympia, now worn out in old age, takes rest.

This simile continues Ennius' pattern of self-conscious authorial comment. Later Ennius decided to resume his epic (Pliny, *NH* 7.101),[15] as the Prologue to the sixteenth book reveals:

post aetate pigret sufferre laborem.
quippe vetusta virum non est satis bella moveri?
reges per regnum statuasque sepulcraque quaerunt,
aedificant nomen, summa nituntur opum vi.
postremo longuinqua dies confecerit aetas.
(*Ann.* 16, frr. 1, 3–5)

He is averse to endure the toil so late in life.
Surely it is enough that the old wars of men were portrayed?
Kings seek statues and sepulchres during their reign;
They establish a name and strive with all their strength.
Finally the long age of the day has worn out.

His years and the arduous labour cause Ennius to question whether he should take up again a task he had thought finished; however, he decides that he must endure the labour involved in resuming the epic. Why does he draw attention to the appended section of the *Annales*? No rhetorical ploy, this Prologue represents a further statement of his intentions and accomplishments in the *Annales*. Just as kings strain to acquire a reputation for themselves that will endure after death, so Ennius will achieve no small measure of fame through his own laborious efforts in epic composition. And the epigrams preserved by Cicero demand:

aspicite o cives senis Enni imaginis formam.
hic vestrum panxit maxima facta patrum.
(*Epig.*, fr. 1)

Look, citizens, upon the portrait of the aged Ennius.
This man recorded the greatest deeds of your fathers.

And self-consciously assert:

nemo me lacrimis decoret nec funera fletu
faxit. cur? volito vivos per ora virum.
(*Epig.*, fr. 2)

Let none honour me with tears or prepare my funeral
With weeping. Why? Alive I fly between the mouths of
men.

Ennius is assured of immortality just as (and because) he has ensured
the fame of his countrymen's ancestors. Whether the first epigram was
part of Ennius' epitaph or instead accompanied a statue on the tomb of
the Scipios,[16] it bears testimony to the achievement of Rome and her
people, especially eminent citizens such as Scipio Africanus. Ennius has
him declare:

> si fas endo plagas caelestum ascendere cuiquam est,
>   mi soli caeli maxima porta patet.
>
> (*Epig.*, fr. 4 (23f.))

If it is right for anyone to ascend the regions of the gods,
For me alone the great gate of heaven stands open.

It is a sentiment that Ennius expresses equally well on his own behalf at
various points in the *Annales* (and elsewhere, e.g. *Sat.*, fr. 1). The
proemia to the first and seventh books of the *Annales* (1, fr. 11, 7, frr.
1–1ª) especially reflect a strong and decisive personality and assert the
rugged individualism and independent spirit of its author.

One of the longest fragments of the *Annales* also suggests these
qualities:

> haece locutus vocat quocum bene saepe libenter
> mensam sermonesque suos rerumque suarum
> comiter impertit,[17] magnam quom lassus diei   270
> partem fuisset de summis rebus regundis
> consilio indu foro lato sanctoque senatu;
> quoi res audacter magnas parvasque iocumque
> eloqueretur † et cuncta † malaque et bona dictu
> evomeret si qui vellet tutoque locaret;   275
> quocum multa volup
>   gaudia clamque palamque;
> ingenium quoi nulla malum sententia suadet
> ut faceret facinus levis aut mala: doctus, fidelis,
> suavis homo, facundus,[18] suo contentus, beatus,   280
> scitus, secunda loquens in tempore, commodus, verbum
> paucum, multa tenens antiqua, sepulta vetustas
> quae facit, et mores veteresque novosque tenentem
> multorum veterum leges divomque hominumque
> prudentem qui dicta loquive tacereve posset: 285
> hunc inter pugnas conpellat Servilius sic . . .
>
> (*Ann.*, 8, fr. 12 (268–86))

46

Having said this, he calls to one with with whom he right
  often shares
Willingly and amiably his table, conversations,
And matters of business, when he, exhausted, had spent   270
Much of the day in directing the most important affairs
By taking counsel in the broad forum and hallowed Senate;
One to whom he would speak out boldly on matters great
  and small,
And joke, and blurt out all manner of good and bad things
  to say
If he wished, and would place them in safe keeping;   275
One with whom [he could share] many pleasures
And many joys both secretly and openly;
Whose nature no trifling or ugly thought persuades
To commit a bad deed; a learned, loyal,
Pleasant man, eloquent, content with his lot, happy,   280
Shrewd, saying the right thing at the right time, obliging,
Of few words, preserving many ancient customs
Which a buried past age makes, and maintaining ways old and
  new
And the laws of our many ancestors, gods and men;
One who, being prudent, could express words or be
  silent.   285
Servilius addresses him between battles in this way . . .

Is the scholar L. Aelius Stilo correct in asserting that these personal
qualities attributed to a trusted non-military friend of the general Cn.
Servilius Geminus, consul of 217 BCE,[19] are really those of Ennius
himself (Gel. 12.4.4)? While in the *Annales* the self-conscious confidence
of the poet in his own abilities is revealed in the representation of
Homer's spirit being reborn in him and his self-portrayal as the
architect of a new poetic tradition, it is evident elsewhere when he
pokes fun at his own frailties:

> numquam poetor nisi si podager.
> > (*Sat.* lib. inc. fr. 5)

> I never poetize unless I am rheumatized.

Given the self-representation of the poet, it is scarcely surprising that
Stilo should ascribe to Ennius the philosophical qualities, profound
knowledge of antiquity and bonhomie attributed to Servilius' 'good
companion', for they are consonant with those attributes Stilo would
expect Ennius to claim for himself, especially being *doctus* ('learned', 8,
fr. 12 (279)), *suavis* ('pleasant', 280), *facundus* ('eloquent', 280), *suo
contentus* ('content with his lot', 280), *beatus* ('happy', 280), *commodus*

('obliging', 281), *scitus* ('shrewd', 281), as well as *multa tenens antiqua,
sepulta vetustas quae facit* ('preserving many ancient customs which a
buried past age makes', 282f.), and *mores veteresque novosque tenentem*
('maintaining ways old and new', 283) and *multorum veterum leges
divomque hominumque* ('the laws of our many ancestors, gods and men',
284). Just as Stilo does not find it difficult to imagine the portrait of
Servilius' friend to be that of Ennius, some modern scholars believe
that Ennius intends the description to apply (equally) to himself.[20]
However, Ennius is (almost) certainly not referring *directly* to himself in
this passage, since he did not arrive in Rome until 204 or 203 BCE (Nep.,
Ca. 1.4), twelve or thirteen years after Servilius died at Cannae in
216 BCE.[21]

ANNALES: THEME, CHARACTERIZATION AND STYLE

Even though the description of the 'good companion' is not of Ennius
specifically, it suggests personal qualities of social and political importance. The poet could be reacting mainly to the *novae res* of the age in
this description. But what survives of the *Annales* appears to reflect the
informing social and literary context of its age and images Roman
leaders and their companions as men of high character, profound
learning and even temperament. Ennius portrays these men willingly
sacrificing personal fame for the greater glory of the state. Elsewhere
he writes:

> moribus antiquis res stat Romana virisque.
>
> (*Ann.* 5, fr. 1)

> On ancient customs and men the Roman state stands firm.

Whatever the context of this fragment – it may belong to the story of
the consul T. Manlius, who condemned his own son to death for
disobeying his command[22] – it illustrates the important idea that the
national achievement is based upon respect for tradition, personal
discipline and individual sacrifices of its citizens.

As Roman successor to the Greek Homer, Ennius faced the problem
of adapting the mythological cyclorama of Homer to the historical
setting of his epic. For the *Annales* is not an epic of a distant heroic age:
though its cast is heroic, its focus is contemporary and real. Accordingly
its characters – although depicted in heroic terms – are contemporary
and real. Ennius (re)constructs historical and contemporary figures –
commanders, consuls and tribunes – and converts these into Homeric
heroes. He was fully conscious that the intrusion of the common
interest in his epic (e.g. *Ann.* 1, fr. 47, 15, fr. 5) ran contrary to
the tradition and spirit of heroic poetry. Indeed, the euhemerizing

tendencies of Ennius inclined him towards the belief that his accounts of real people and historic events were worthy of epic. Ennius translated or assembled into Latin the *Hiera Anagraphē* ('Sacred Scripture') of the rationalist Euhemerus, in which the gods were humans who had been apotheosized for their heroism (cf. Lactant., *Div. Inst.* 1.11.33; Cic., *ND* 1.42.119); this lack of a clear division between gods and great men of state also pervades the *Annales*. To Ennius Homeric divine and super-human figures had been great men of the distant past; hence distinguished Roman heroes of the recent past and of his own day, even a relatively minor historical figure such as the tribune Caelius (*Ann.* 15, fr. 5), were entitled to their superhuman status along Homeric lines (cf. *Il.* 16.102ff.). Ennius' treatment of Roman soldiers as Homeric heroes bears close comparison with Homer's moulding of Greek warriors into figures of heroic stature. Just as Agamemnon, Achilles and other Homeric warriors were representatives of a past Hellenic society, such disparate figures as Romulus, Numa, Hannibal, Scipio and the Greek kings in the *Annales* form the core of the Roman historical imagination. Even through the Homerization of recent Roman heroes, Ennius presents his audience with a Roman view of the world. The portrayal of the war between Rome and Carthage in Homeric terms suggests that to the poet the Roman struggle with Hannibal was equal to that of the Greeks at Troy and the heroes of the Punic wars equal in stature to the Homeric heroes. This could account in part for his attempt to bridge the gap between historical and legendary characterization in his portrayal of contemporary and historical figures. In the matter of characterization Ennius claims individuality from Homer and other Greek epicists in one quite important way: the narrative of the *Annales* sheds lustre upon individual figures (see 10, fr. 1), but there is no individual at the centre of Ennius' world, as Achilles and Odysseus loom over the Homeric epics and as Aristomenes dominates the *Messeniaca* of Rhianos. Instead of a personal hero Ennius seems to glorify a civilization and an ethos.

Epic was already the recognized medium for exalting the great men of the recent past (for Ennius was not the first Latin epicist to glorify contemporary figures: that honour goes to Naevius), and Horace observed that Ennius' praise of Scipio Africanus did more to glorify him than any public inscription (*Carm.* 4.8.13ff.) – alluding to such praise of Scipio in the *Annales* as we now find in the *Epigrams*:

> hic est ille situs, cui nemo civis neque hostis
> quibit pro factis reddere opis pretium.
> a sole exoriente supra Maeotis paludes
> nemo est qui factis aequiperare queat.
>
> (*Epig.*, frr. 3 (19f.), 4 (21f.))

Here lies that man to whom no one, citizen or foe,
   Can render a fair reward for his deeds.
From the rising sun above the marshes of Maeotis
   There is no one whose deeds can compare with his.

About such praise Cicero says:

> carus fuit Africano superiori noster Ennius . . . at iis laudibus certe non solum ipse qui laudatus, sed etiam populi Romani nomen ornatur. in caelum huius proavus Cato tollitur: magnus honos populi Romani rebus adiungitur. omnes denique illi Maximi, Marcelli, Fulvii non sine communi omnium nostrum laude decorantur.
>
> (Arch. 22)

> Our Ennius was dear to the elder Africanus . . . But to be sure not only did he exalt him by his praises, but adorned the name of the Roman people. He raised to heaven the great-grandfather of our Cato, and thereby brought great honour to the Roman people. In short, the works that celebrate the names of Maximus, Marcellus and Fulvius bring glory to all Romans.

And Ennius' deification of heroes such as Romulus has a similar purpose and effect:

> Romulus in caelo cum dis genitalibus aevom
> degit.
> (Ann. 1, fr. 62; cf. 1, fr. 33)

> In heaven with gods who gave him birth Romulus
> Lives for ever.

From a post-republican perspective, it is ironic that Ennius, in dramatizing the events and glorifying (or 'Homerizing') and deifying the heroes of the recent past, especially heads of state, may have contributed to the establishment of the aesthetic and ideological basis for the ruler cults of the empire. For his mythologizing of historical characters and events in order to celebrate the Roman national achievement later became a means of celebrating the divinity and heroic status of the imperial house.

In shaping momentous events and great men (and even men of ordinary stature) in the Homeric mould according to his own interpretation, Ennius helps to shape the historical tradition of epic. He seems to do this especially in Books 16–18 by concentrating upon the exploits of young military officers rather than the deeds of important men of state. Above all, the Annales serves as a vehicle of poetic-imaginative expression of the developing power of the Roman nation:

Ennius' depiction of the national achievement, the collective Roman hero, through portraying individual human action, is entirely consonant with his epic purpose of glorifying the Roman nation in a form appropriate to her evolving greatness. And Ennius takes poetic licence in creating characters and shaping events appropriate to his nationalist objectives.

One of the substantive methodological questions that arises in dealing with a fragmentary work is the extent to which valid assumptions can be made about the original text on the basis of its remains; since the literary critic is restricted to making observations about the incomplete text, he/she is left with a feeling of uncertainty about the whole text. This is the case with Ennius and the *Annales*. Although on one level he glorifies Rome, the possibility cannot be dismissed completely that elsewhere (in lost sections of the text) Ennius reveals an ambivalence towards his subject not apparent in the surviving fragments.[23] However, the remains of the *Annales* are too scattered to demonstrate with certainty whether or not Ennius undermines the superficial presentation of such Roman heroes as Romulus and Scipio as figures of great moral incorruptibility and profound knowledge. If the fragments are a true reflection of the *Annales*' spirit, Ennius appears to relate political and military heroes and events in a way that would have appealed to fervently nationalistic and public-spirited Romans; there is, for instance, no hint of ambiguity and contemporary allusion in the class struggles between the patricians and plebeians that would have reflected unfavourably upon the Roman achievement. Indeed, rather than challenging the Romans' public self-image, Ennius seems to have chosen deliberately to portray the relationships between historical and contemporary figures as ones of harmony and to ignore sensitive issues that could give the impression of social and political disunity in Rome.[24] He does warn, however, of the consequences of military solutions in the public arena:

> proelia promulgantur:
> pellitur e medio sapientia, vi geritur res;
> spernitur orator bonus, horridus miles amatur;
> haud doctis dictis certantes, nec maledictis
> miscent inter sese inimicitiam agitantes:
> non ex iure manu consertum, sed magis ferro –
> rem repetunt regnumque petunt – vadunt solida vi.
>
> (Ann., 8, fr. 1 (247–53))

> Battles are made known:
> Wisdom is thrust from our midst, an affair governed by
>   violence,
> The good orator is despised, the rough soldier loved;

51

Striving not with learned words, nor harassing one another
With abusive language, men arouse enmity:
They make joint seizure not by law, but rather with the sword;
They demand their rights, attack the realm, advance by pure
force.

These lines suggest the questioning of military strength, but Ennius does not (apparently) exploit the possibilities of the situation. Although there is no evidence that this fragment refers to distinctly Roman circumstances, it could apply to any situation, including that existing towards the end of the republic.

Or when Rome was founded. Ennius portrays the struggle for supremacy between Romulus and Remus in terms immediately recognizable to Romans of his day. The longest and most important fragment that survives from the *Annales* shows Romulus and Remus taking the auspices to establish which of the two brothers should be the ruler of the new city (cf. *Ann.* 1, frr. 33, 62):

> curantes magna cum cura tum cupientes
> regni dant operam simul auspicio augurioque.
> in † monte Remus auspicio sedet atque secundam
> solus avem servat. at Romulus pulcer in alto   75
> quaerit Aventino, servat genus altivolantum.
> certabant urbem Romam Remoramne vocarent.
> omnibus cura viris uter esset induperator.
> expectant veluti consul quom mittere signum
> volt, omnes avidi spectant ad carceris oras   80
> quam mox emittat pictis[25] e faucibus currus:
> sic expectabat populus atque ora timebat
> rebus utri magni victoria sit data regni.
> interea sol albus recessit in infera noctis.
> exin candida se radiis dedit icta foras lux   85
> et simul ex alto longe pulcerrima praepes
> laeva volavit avis. simul aureus exoritur sol
> cedunt de caelo ter quattuor corpora sancta
> avium, praepetibus sese pulcrisque locis dant.
> conspicit inde sibi data Romulus esse propritim 90
> auspicio regni stabilita scamna solumque.
>
> (*Ann.* 1, fr. 47 (72–91))

Taking great care and desirous of royal power,
They give themselves to auspice and to augury.
On a hill Remus waits for the auspices and alone
Looks for a propitious bird. But fair Romulus seeks
reply   75

On high Aventine and watches for the high-flying
   breed.
Their fight was whether they call the city Rome or
   Remora.
All men were anxious as to which of the two would
   be leader.
They wait, just as when the consul means to give
   the sign:
All look eagerly at the start of the racecourse as to   80
How soon he will send forth the cars from the
   painted jaws.
Thus the people waited and their faces showed
   fear as to which
Should be granted victory of great power by the
   affair.
Meanwhile the white sun retreated into darkest
   night.
Then a glittering light, illumined with rays, shot
   forth   85
Just as far to the left a bird, most fair and lucky,
Flew from on high. At the same time the golden
   sun bursts forth,
Four blessed shapes of birds move down three
   times from heaven
And perch upon places lucky and propitious.
From this Romulus sees that the throne and land
   of a kingdom   90
Have been given rightly to him, made firm by the
   flight of birds.

Romulus' duel with Remus foretold what was to become the archetypal Roman event of the games – the gladiatorial combat. Rome was founded as the result of an internecine struggle between two brothers, as 'certabant' ('their fight was', 1, fr. 47 (77); cf. 1, frr. 48–50 (92–95)) reminds us (cf. 'certantes', 'men strive', 8, fr. 1 (250)). To later Romans the founding of Rome upon Romulus' slaying of Remus seemed to foredoom her to eternal civil strife (see Hor., *Epod.* 7.17ff.).

There is a vivid and picturesque quality to this passage; the mental images are clear and striking. The setting is realistic, with close attention being paid to contemporary Roman ritual;[26] the atmosphere is one of solemnity, appropriate to the taking of the auspices; and the descriptions of the characters suggest a quiet nobility and intensity of feeling consistent with those qualities popularly believed by contemporary Romans to have been found in their ancestors. Contemporized in the comparison of the solicitude of the crowd in the Circus at the taking of the auspices with a crowd waiting for the presiding consul to start the chariot race, this proleptic auspicial scene is the Ennian version of Callimachus' *Aetia*, the origins of the Roman *res publica*. While the effect of the ritual and racing simile is to suggest to the contemporary Roman audience the long and uninterrupted history of Roman religious, political and social institutions, the passage as a whole defines the Roman imagination and reveals the distinctively national feeling of Ennian epic. Its style is sparse and simple, even rugged; the language is plain, concrete, imagistic; and the expression is what might be expected of a national epic – dignified, concise and direct. The careful structure of the passage – with its rapid shifts of viewpoint – reinforces the tension and impressiveness of the occasion. The passage commences with a general description of the brothers (72f.), focuses on the activities of Remus (73f.), then (with an abrupt change in mid-line) on those of Romulus (74f.), before shifting focus back to the pair, portraying them as rivals for political and eponymous power (77); the point of view next changes to the *viri* ('men') as spectators (78–83), who along with the brothers observe the celestial phenomena (84–9), then finally moves back to Romulus (90f.). After the brothers are mentioned as possible eponyms of the new city (77f.), dramatic suspense is created (for an audience willing to suspend its prescience) by the delay in naming the monarch-designate until late in the passage (90f.). These afore-mentioned descriptive, expressive and structural qualities help to shape the distinctive style, form and meaning of the *Annales*.

What specifically of Ennius' versification and phraseology as revealed in this fragment? The heavily spondaic rhythm (e.g. 1, fr. 47 (81, 88)), assonance of *u* (e.g. 72, 78), *au* (e.g. 73f.) and *i* (e.g. 84f.), and ubiquitous (external and internal) alliteration – mostly of *c* and *q* (e.g. 72, 81, 88), *r* (e.g. 77f.) and *s* (e.g. 90f.) – of many of the lines heighten the impression of the dignity and importance of the scene. The solemnity and impressiveness of the scene are suggested immediately in the heavily spondaic first line (72), and the striking alliteration of *c*, assonance of *u*, and ponderous etymological figure ('CURAntes cum CURA') add to the atmosphere. Ennius, ever sensitive to the possibilities of auditory suggestion, follows this initial play on sounds with word-play on *ave-*, 'bird' (cf. *AVEntino*, 75, *AVEm*, 76); this further heightens the effect of the scene to be played out on the *Aventinum* (rendered textually prominent by its placement between the asyndeton *quaerit servat*), as the name of the hill was said to have been derived from the birds who settled upon it (cf. Varro, *LL* 5.43). Both syllabic word-plays draw attention to the etymology of Rome's name (cf. *ROMulus*, 75, *ROMam*, 77), whose origin is the subject of the passage (cf. 77). Sometimes the rhythm and alliterative quality (and resultant onomatopoeic effect) of the lines reinforce the action. The dactylic and alliterative patterns of lines 84–7 and 90f. suggest a quickening of the pace, the rapid flight of birds, and the quick but certain conclusion to the auspice-taking, while the spondees and alliteration of lines 88f. seem to stress the authority and weight of the auspices. At the same time the predominant use by Ennius of the historical present – a narrative device adopted from the Saturnian poets – in the first eleven lines of the passage (72–83) conveys a vivid sense of the immediacy and urgency of the scene; there is a change to the historical (narrative) perfect (84–7), but then a change back to the historical present at the close (87–91).

The style of this fragment is characterized by other distinctive features: there is an absence of periodic sentence structure (e.g. the asyndeton *quaerit servat*, 1, fr. 47 (76)); some verses relate a single action or idea (76–8); syntactical pauses appear often at caesurae (e.g. 75, 82) and at the end of lines (e.g. 84, 89); enjambment is a common device (e.g. 74f., 85f.); there is frequent coincidence of foot and word (e.g. 85, 88); there are a number of first-foot spondaic words (e.g. *regni*, 73, *avium*, 89); elisions are few (e.g. 73, 82); and the caesurae are predominantly penthemimeral (75ff.). To modern ears the rhythms of some verses may seem over-ponderous (e.g. 72, 81) and uneven (e.g. 85, 87), lacking in balance (e.g. 80, 87), and composed of awkward monosyllabic endings (*lux*, 85, *sol*, 87, *dant*, 89) and weak endings in - *que* (73, 91); in places the diction may strike one as archaic (e.g. *induperator*, 78) and awkward (e.g. *altivolans*, 76), the language as redundant (e.g. *ex alto*, 87, 'from on high', *de caelo*, 88, 'from heaven'); and there may appear to be an overworking of simple verbs (e.g. forms of *dare*, 73, 83, 85, 89f.), compound verbs (*spectare* and its compounds, 79f., 82), nouns (*auspicium*, 73f., 91) and vapid adjectives (e.g. *pulcer* and variant forms, 75, 86, 89). In matters of style, versification and diction, Ennius is perhaps a casualty of Augustan (and modern) sensibilities: not only do the qualities of his verse complement each other and the content of the *Annales*, but also it must be remembered they did not violate contemporary standards. Although his verse represents the earliest stage in the development of the Latin hexameter, it possesses poetic merit, dignity and strength.

Ennius understood the creative possibilities of allusive epic. Unencumbered by the weight of his own tradition (though of course not devoid of its influence), he saw in Homeric epic a model worthy of imitation and recreation. His dream encounter with Homer is a symbolic (and self-conscious) acknowledgement of his indebtedness to Homer and his own place in the Graeco-Roman poetic tradition. A Roman metamorphosis of Homeric epic on a grand scale, the *Annales* in its conception and final form asserts consciously not merely the supremacy and grandeur of Rome but also the Latin literary genius. But Ennius too articulates in style, form and function not only the differences between his own creative achievement and that of his Roman and Greek contemporaries and predecessors, including Homer, but also (through the inspiration his model provides) the creations of his successors. Ennius created a new tradition that maintained itself as a vehicle of poetic-imaginative expression for centuries by providing a solid artistic base on which a subsequent Roman epicist such as Virgil could develop the genre further. The role of Ennius in the development of Latin epic is best seen in terms of the continuity from Greek to Roman, for Ennius borrows much above all from Homer.[27] But the influence of his own epic upon subsequent literature was immense, for he gave a new beginning and a new direction to the epic genre.[28]

NOTES

1 All translations in this essay are mine.

2 Cf. Cornell 1986: 249f.

3 Skutsch 1985: 143f. argues that this verse containing *Musae* ('Muses') was probably the *second* line of the *Annales*. Evidence for *Musae* appearing in the first line lies in the opening verse of Homer's *Odyssey*, of Andronicus' *Odussia*, and the line usually assumed to be the first in Naevius' *Bellum Punicum*, which refer to the Muses, but it is difficult to ascertain whether the Ennian line in which *Musae* appears came first or second.

4 The edition of the *Annales* used in this essay (with a few important emendations in text and numerous minor punctuative and orthographical alterations) is that of Skutsch 1985; references are to book and fragment numbers, sometimes with line-numbers indicated in parentheses (e.g. *Ann.* 1, fr. 47 (79–81)) except for *sedis incerta fragmenta*, which are cited as 'sed. inc. fr.'. (I do not necessarily give the whole fragment of text on each occasion a fragment is cited.) Text, fragment and line-numbers in Skutsch's edition of the *Annales* sometimes differ greatly from Vahlen 1928 and Warmington 1973. References to fragments in other works of Ennius are those of Vahlen 1928 (e.g. *Epig.*, fr. 4 (23f.)).

5 The *Annales*' Proem is obviously meant to bring to mind Hesiod *and* Homer. In Homer Olympus is said to be the home of the Muses (*Il.* 2.484); furthermore, Ennius' *magnum Olympum* specifically recalls Homer's *megan Olumpon* ('mighty Olympus', *Il.* 1.530 et al.). Although Varro, *LL* 7.20 observes that the Greeks understood *Olympum* to mean *caelum* (('sky'), and this is certainly the case, for instance, in Hom., *Od.* 20.103, where *Olumpos* means *ouranos* (= *caelum*)), that is not the sense in *Il.* 1.530, 2.484 and the first verse of the *Annales*. (How, for example, in Ennius, would the Muses '*beat* their feet *on* the mighty sky'?) The placing of Hesiod's Muses on

Homer's Olympus is a part of Ennius' allusive strategy in the Proem to the *Annales*. I cannot agree with Skutsch 1985: 147, who asserts that this was 'a subtlety not to be expected from the man who first introduced [the Muses] in Rome'.

6 Skutsch 1985: 649f. assigns this line to Book 15. If he is correct, then Ennius' celebration of the Muses in this book complements his praise of them in the proemia to Books 1 and 7.

7 Callimachus and Hesiod come close: the former in the observations he makes on the poetry of Heraclitus of Halicarnassus (*Epig.* 2); the latter in his suggestion that the Muses have accorded him a special poetic status (*Th.* 22–34).

8 There are numerous reconstructions of the Proem to the first book; recent studies include those of Marconi 1961: 224ff.; Waszink 1962: 113ff.; 1964: 327ff.; Grilli 1965: 43ff.; Kambylis 1965: 190ff.; Reggiani 1979: 13ff.

9 Or (less probably) Parnassus, as maintained first by Leo 1913: 164f. and later by many others. Propertius mentions Helicon as the place of Ennius' dream (3.3.1) and Lucretius describes it as 'amoeno Helicone' ('pleasant Helicon', *DRN* 1.117) whence Ennius brought down 'perenni fronde coronam' ('a perennial crown of laurel', 118). Helicon is the mountain of poetic inspiration in the second century BCE, while Parnassus does not appear in extant literature until the first century BCE (e.g. Virg., *G.* 3.291; cf. Latte 1960: 224 n. 3).

10 References to Andronicus are from the edition of Morel 1963.

11 For further discussion of Andronicus' style, see Goldberg in chapter II above, pp. 22ff.

12 Cicero makes clear that Ennius means *hunc* to refer to himself, not Naevius: 'ait ipse de se' ('this very man speaks of himself', *Brut.* 18.71); cf. Skutsch 1985: 374f.

13 Cf. Heraeus 1930: 271.

14 This fragment may have formed part of the original ending of the *Annales*; however, it may have belonged to Book 18 (if this final book had been completed at the time of Ennius' death) or even Book 16 (cf. 16, frr. 1–5). Cf. Skutsch 1985: 673.

15 This is well documented; see Skutsch 1985: 565ff.

16 The latter was the case, according to Suerbaum 1968: 208ff.

17 *comiter impertit* Gel.; *consilium partit* Sk.

18 *facundus*, Gel.; *iucundus*, Sk.

19 Servilius is certainly not the consul of 252 and 248 BCE, as Badian 1972: 180f. believes; cf. Skutsch 1985: 447ff.

20 Norden 1915: 133, Steuart 1925: 152f., Skutsch 1968: 94, 1985: 450, and Badian 1972: 180ff. think it probable that Ennius wrote the description as a self-portrait.

21 Cf. Suerbaum 1968: 142f. n. 455; Jocelyn 1972: 994; Goldberg 1989: 259f.

22 Skutsch 1985: 316ff.

23 Cf. Mommsen 1881: 916 (followed by Bilinski 1954: 9ff. and Friedrich 1968: xxviiif.), who conjectures that Ennius was an opponent of the patrician class on the basis of the extant dramatic fragments, his residence in the 'plebeian quarter' of the Aventine, his modest lifestyle and non-Roman background; however, this view rightly carries little authority among modern scholars because of the lack of textual and topographical evidence.

24 For qualifications to the picture of Ennius as panegyrist of individual Romans such as Fulvius Nobilior and M. Claudius Marcellus, see Goldberg 1989: 247ff.

25 *pictis*, Cic.; *pictos*, Sk.
26 Skutsch 1968: 62ff.
27 For another treatment of Ennius' role in the development of Latin epic, see Hainsworth 1991: 76ff.
28 I am indebted to Anthony Boyle (USC), Sander Goldberg (UCLA), Bronwyn Williams (Sydney) and Edward George (Texas Tech) for their many valuable suggestions on earlier versions of this essay. I am, of course, alone responsible for any perceived shortcomings.

IV

NEOTERIC EPIC: CATULLUS 64

David Konstan

The term 'epic' in modern usage connotes heroism on a large scale, and the notion of a short epic suggests a forced or unnatural compression, like a bonzai tree or miniature Shetland. The image is not altogether inappropriate for the compact poem composed in the epic manner by Catullus, which occupies the sixty-fourth place in the traditional ordering of his verses. Catullus 64 has a dense, abbreviated quality, as though it contained too much in too small a space; it is a bit nervous, like a diminutive breed of dog.

The form is today called an epyllion, or 'little epic'. Though there is no evidence that ancient critics recognized a separate genre of this description, I am inclined to agree with Hollis (1990: 25) that 'the category is a genuine one. Roman poets who composed such works as Catul. 64 or the pseudo-Virgilian *Ciris* – not to mention lost poems like Cinna's *Zmyrna* or Calvus' *Io* – must surely have believed that they were using a recognizable form inherited from the Greeks.'[1]

The Greeks in question were, in the first instance, the circle of craft-conscious poets centred at Alexandria in the third and second centuries BCE, where they were supported and encouraged by the court of the Ptolemies. Like their Roman disciples, the Alexandrians eschewed and despised voluminous effusions of hack verse, and cultivated instead a dense and learned style.[2] They composed terse didactic poems like Aratus' *Constellations* (*Phainomena*) or Nicander's treatise on snakebites, and stitched short narratives together in a series like Callimachus' *Origins* (*Aitia*), which indulged the passion for recondite aetiologies. Apollonius of Rhodes brought his epic on the voyage of the *Argo* to four books before abandoning the project, but it retains the crisp cleverness prized by his contemporaries.[3] Among the works produced by this coterie, one stands out as possible model for Catullus 64: Callimachus' *Hecale*, which, the fragments indicate, centered on an encounter between the hero Theseus and the old woman named in the title. Callimachus' poem seems to have been at least three times as long as Catullus'; nevertheless, as Hollis (1990: 32) suggests: 'For Roman poets

poems of a certain type

the *Hecale* may have had a special position as one of the earliest, finest, and most substantial specimens of the epyllion.'

Catullus belonged to the first generation of Roman lyric poets, who reproduced complex Greek verse-forms in the Latin language. Drama and epic had been domesticated for almost two hundred years; verse satire was more recent and something of an indigenous product. A few attempts at epigram around the turn of the first century heralded the new movement, but high technical virtuosity was the achievement of a group of poets whom Cicero dubbed with the Greek label *neōteroi*, 'neoterics' or, roughly, 'modernists'.[4] The term captures the Hellenic leanings of the group. Catullus himself translated a poem by Callimachus (66) and another by Sappho (51), in homage to whom he chose Lesbia, 'the woman of Lesbos', as the poetic name of his beloved. Several of Catullus' contemporaries, like Calvus and Cinna, also tried their hand at miniature epic, though their works are lost save for a few scraps.[5]

Like the Alexandrian experiments, Catullus' epyllion is a precious, artful composition, full of self-conscious tricks and learned allusions. While it has some of the immediate lyricism of Catullus' personal love poetry, it demands a sophisticated readership, and is unabashed about it. Beyond the Hellenistic precedents, however, the inspiration for Catullus' poem goes back, I believe, centuries earlier to an odd work associated with the archaic bard who was much admired and adapted by the polished Alexandrians – Hesiod, best known today for his didactic poems on agriculture (*Works and Days*) and the genealogy of the gods (*Theogony*), but regarded in antiquity also as the author of several other texts, including a short narrative poem conventionally entitled *The Shield of Heracles*. The *Shield* originally belonged or was attached to a verse catalogue of mythological women, but it circulated independently in antiquity and is preserved in the manuscripts of Hesiod as a separate composition.[6]

The poem begins with an account of Heracles' battle with Cycnus, the son of the war god Ares, but the poet then pauses to include a detailed description of the pictorial decorations on the hero's shield, along the lines of the more celebrated description of the shield of Achilles in the eighteenth book of Homer's *Iliad*. The Hesiodic *Shield* is remarkable, however, in that the ecphrasis (a literary transcription of a work of art) takes up almost half the entire work: 179 lines out of 480 (the vast scale of the *Iliad* can comfortably accommodate such an excursus). For another example of near equality in size between narrative frame and embedded description one must await the appearance precisely of Catullus' own epyllion towards the middle of the first century BCE, where the ecphrasis is indeed the dominant element (214 verses out of 408). Further analogies between the two poems will be indicated below.

Catullus chose for his theme the marriage between Thetis, a sea-Nymph and granddaughter of the god Ocean, and the mortal Peleus, and the poem is sometimes referred to as an epithalamium or wedding song, although the wedding song proper is an inset piece of some fifty-nine verses towards the end of the poem. Peleus was traditionally one of the heroes who participated in the expedition of the Argonauts, and Catullus ties his account of the marriage to that famous voyage, and thereby also to Apollonius' precedent in Hellenistic epic, by an elegant innovation. Apollonius had already indicated (4.928ff.) that the Nymphs of the sea, including Thetis, emerged to wonder at the extraordinary vessel, sometimes taken to be the first ship. Catullus shifts the timing of this baroque scene to the moment of the launching, and makes it the occasion on which the passion between Peleus and Thetis had its beginning (14–21). Although the rest of the poem is devoted to the wedding day itself, Catullus is thus able to connect it with the ancient saga of the *Argo*, and more specifically with the artful treatment of the theme by Apollonius, whom he acknowledges by direct quotation.[7]

But the *Argo* also carried associations with the story of Medea and her ill-starred affair with Jason, as dramatized in the enormously popular tragedy by Euripides. Catullus alerts the reader to this aspect of the voyage through echoes of the opening of Euripides' *Medea*, as well as of the Latin adaptation of Euripides' play by Ennius in the early second century BCE, and he continues to allude to this episode throughout the epyllion. From the beginning, then, Catullus establishes a pattern of references to at least two distinct genres and a complex of themes including marriage between a mortal and a divinity, the heroic quest of the Argonauts in pursuit of the golden fleece, and the abandonment and bitter revenge of Medea, whose love for Jason had enabled the success of his mission.

Opening with the *Argo* is a bold move in another way. The wedding itself will not take place until after the voyage is over, and thus there is a large gap in time between Peleus' and Thetis' initial encounter at sea, which occupies the first thirty verses of the poem, and the festivities themselves, which take up the balance of the narrative. Catullus negotiates the transition with an apparently casual formula: 'quae simul optatae finito tempore luces advenere' ('As soon as the time had lapsed and the desired day arrived', 31–2). But the abrupt switch of locale and date from the launching of the *Argo* to Peleus' palace in Thessaly long afterwards is not conventional in classical epic, which prefers a more gradual development of plot and the illusion, at least, of a continuous flow of time. The device in Catullus 64 is reminiscent of modern cinematic technique, where the spectators may be given an initial view of past events as a kind of prologue to the main action of the story.[8]

In ancient *epos*, the nearest parallel I know of is the first 56 verses of the Hesiodic *Shield of Heracles*, which narrate the birth of Heracles and Iphicles, his twin half-brother (since his father is not Zeus, but the mortal Amphitryon); the author then turns abruptly to his central theme, the battle between Heracles and Cycnus, which occupies the rest of the poem (the pivotal formula is simply, 'And he also slew Cycnus' ('hos kai Kuknon epephnen', 57)). The story of the hero's birth links the duel with Cycnus to the opening business concerning Heracles' mother Alcmene, who is the hinge by which the narrative as a whole is attached to the *Catalogue of Women*. For Catullus (or a Hellenistic intermediary), however, the passage on the birth of Heracles may well have provided the model for a proem that functions as a prologue, providing a synopsis of a past event that is part of the background to the main theme.[9]

By using the launching of the first ship as the occasion for the enamourment of Peleus and Thetis, Catullus also altered inherited versions of the myth, in which Thetis is represented as coerced and resentful at marrying a mortal, and (in some accounts) abandoning her husband's bed after their first night together.[10] Some sources mention a prophecy that the son of Thetis was destined to be greater than his father, in response to which Jupiter, to protect his power, decides that she must be given to a mortal. In Catullus' version, however, Jupiter (if it is he who is identified as 'father') merely sanctions the couple's spontaneous choice:

> tum Thetidis Peleus incensus fertur amore,
> tum Thetis humanos non despexit hymenaeos,
> tum Thetidi pater ipse iugandum Pelea sensit.
>
> (19–21)

> Then, they say, Peleus was fired with love for Thetis,
> Then Thetis ceased to despise a mortal marriage,
> Then the father himself saw that Peleus was to be
> joined to Thetis.

In the allusion to Jupiter's role, Catullus may be signalling the novelty of his own account. Such a mutual accord is remarkable in affairs between a human and a goddess, and places the two on the same level.[11] This is not without a purpose. When the scene shifts, a few lines later, to Peleus' mansion in Pharsalus, where the wedding takes place, Catullus models his description on a Roman villa, complete with atrium and marriage chamber.[12] The hero of antique saga and his immortal watery bride step easily into the roles of Roman notables, joined in wedlock with the pomp and panoply of great aristocratic families. They are not divided by a social barrier.

At the same time, there is a hint of condescension in Thetis' change of heart, and Catullus expresses his own surprise at Peleus' good fortune in marrying the granddaughter of the world-encircling Ocean, whom Jupiter himself had desired (25–30). The marriage has perhaps an allegorical dimension. As a Nymph Thetis may symbolize the sea (e.g. Virgil, *Eclogues* 4.32); a few lines earlier Catullus uses the name of Neptune's wife Amphitrite metonymically for the sea in connection with the launching of the *Argo* (11). Thetis' submission to a union with the mortal Peleus seems analogous to the conquest of the oceans by mankind, which has just been achieved by the invention of seafaring.

Given the negative attitude that conventionally attached to the origin of seafaring, which was associated with unnatural greed and ambition, one might have expected a note of transgression in the description of the voyage and the marriage, but Catullus apparently suppresses any such judgment.[13] Rather, he interrupts the narrative with a direct apostrophe to the heroes, and in particular to Peleus, in the manner of the invocation in a hymn.[14] It has been pointed out that Catullus' phrase, 'heroes salvete, deum genus' ('Hail heroes, offspring of the gods') resembles Apollonius of Rhodes 4.1773, 'hilat' aristēes makarōn genos' ('Thrive champions, offspring of the blessed'), but it is worth remarking also that immediately following the ecphrasis in the Hesiodic *Shield of Heracles*, Athena addresses Heracles and his charioteer, Iolaus, with the words: 'Greetings, offspring of far-famed Lynceus' ('khairete, Lugkēos geneē tēlekleitoio', 327).

In other poems, Catullus celebrates his beloved Lesbia as a 'brilliant goddess' ('candida diva', 68.70), compares the man who sits opposite her to a god (51.1, in the translation from Sappho), and reports (not without irony) her declaration that she would rather marry him than Jupiter himself (70.1–2; cf. 72.1–2); and it has been suggested that the love between Peleus and Thetis may capture an ideal moment in Catullus' own adoration of 'Lesbia', whom the ancient novelist and orator Apuleius identifies in real life as Clodia, wife (in all likelihood) of the senator Metellus and sister of Clodius, Caesar's notorious political henchman.[15] We need not suppose an autobiographical intention in such intertextual allusiveness within the Catullan corpus; the divinization of the beloved was one of the motifs available in the repertoire of classical erotic literature, and Catullus subtly appropriates it in his novel treatment of the myth.

With the shift of scene to Pharsalus and the wedding, Catullus turns his attention from the betrothed couple to the appointments of Peleus' palace, glittering with gold, silver and ivory: the splendour is enhanced by contrast with the countryside, which Catullus portrays as utterly deserted while everyone gathers at the capital (38–42).[16] Catullus then contracts the focus to the ivory wedding couch in the centre of the house, and the dark red embroidered coverlet that is the subject of the ecphrasis.[17] Thus, after forty-nine lines that are divided between the Proem on the Argonauts (1–30) and an intermezzo on the arrival of the wedding guests, the progress of the nuptials gives way to a new sequence of episodes involving Theseus' voyage to Crete and his desertion of Ariadne, as they are pictured on the divan tapestry.[18]

Once again, the structure of Catullus' epyllion resembles that of the Hesiodic *Shield*, where the prefatory account of the birth of the hero yields to a description of Heracles' and Cycnus' eagerness to do battle, followed by a scene in which Heracles dons his armour (57–138). The putting-on of arms (122–38: a stock scene-type in Homer), leading up to the shield that is the subject of the ecphrasis, corresponds to the description of the decorations in Peleus' palace, culminating in the embroidered coverlet.

The disjointedness and discontinuity of the presentation lend Catullus' epyllion a mannered quality, in which the individual scene or description stands out against the continuous narrative as an independent element or individual *tour de force*. This predominance of local rhetorical effect over the sense of global coherence has its roots in Hellenistic craftsmanship, both literary and plastic, with its penchant for miniature detail, and comes into its own in late antique poetry and art which is marked by what Michael Roberts (1989) has called the jewelled style.

The description of the coverlet is divided into five major tableaux (though these are susceptible to further subdivision).[19] The first, third, and fifth segments are given over to events on the island of Naxos (which Catullus calls by the archaic and more obscure name of Dia), where Ariadne awakens to find that Theseus' fleet has departed and left her behind. The second and fourth sections are, respectively, a flashback covering Theseus' expedition to Crete (76–85), Ariadne's infatuation with the newly arrived hero (86–102), and the battle with the Minotaur (103–15), and a flashforward describing Theseus' return to Athens, under the curse that Ariadne has called down upon him in the central panel: this passage begins (202–14) and ends (238–50) with the account of the hero's failure to remember his father's instructions, which are quoted in the central segment (215–37).

The first tableau (52–75) introduces Ariadne standing upon the shore and gazing out at the departing vessels as the waves lap about her feet (67). Catullus conjures up her anxiety with the still fresh metaphor of 'great waves of care' ('magnis curarum . . . undis', 62), suggesting a correspondence between her inner state and the tossing sea around her. Catullus models his description of Ariadne's pose upon a popular portrait type that represents her looking out to sea, and he compares the appearance of the stunned but tortured girl to a stone statue of a maenad possessed by Bacchus (61). The ecphrasis thus remains anchored in the plastic arts, and the embroidered figure carries a reference to sculpted images.[20]

The final panel, too, sticks close to the fiction of pictorial description, as the god Bacchus (here called by the cult name Iacchus) arrives on the scene inflamed with love for Ariadne, and accompanied by satyrs, sileni, and a troupe of bacchantes (255: the reference back to Ariadne's appearance is unmistakable) acting out the orgiastic rituals with dismembered limbs of cattle, live snakes, and a small orchestra of raucous instruments. Like the motion of the waves, the suggestion of strident noise is an easy inference from the embroidered images, and Catullus recalls the reader's attention to the coverlet in the formula that introduces the section: 'But from another part . . .' ('at parte ex alia . . .', 251), i.e. of the tapestry.

In the central sections of the ecphrasis, Catullus is less concerned with the pretence of a faithful transcription from one medium to another, and does not hesitate, for example, to introduce an epic simile comparing the fall of the Minotaur – half man, half bull – to the collapse of a tree buffeted in a storm (though as a kind of literary joke he situates the tree precisely on the peak of the Taurus, or 'Bull', mountains, 105); the inclusion of lengthy speeches by Ariadne and by Aegeus, Theseus' father, also undermines the illusion of copying a work of art. Indeed, Catullus begins the flashback to Theseus' departure from Athens with the phrase 'For they say that once . . .' ('nam perhibent olim . . .', 76), and Aegeus' words are introduced with a synonymous expression ('namque ferunt olim', 212), replacing the conventional ecphrastic tags with formulas of verbal report. The most notable example of this cross between media is the transition from the second panel to the central section dominated by the lyrical lament of Ariadne, where Catullus interrupts his own flashback to the events surrounding Theseus' arrival at Crete with the words: 'But why should I digress from my original song and mention further details' ('sed quid ego a primo digressus carmine plura commemorem', 116–17) – details which he proceeds to summarize before resuming his theme.

In the central tableau, Ariadne gives voice to charges of betrayal (132–63), a mood of despair (164–87), and finally the wish for revenge (188–201). Several motifs in her complaint, like the conceit that a lion, the sea, or some briny monster must be the parent of so cruel a man (154–7), or the complaint that she has no hope of refuge (177–87), look back to the reproaches that Euripides' Medea hurls against Jason (cf. 1342–3; 502ff.), and Catullus has manifestly drawn inspiration from denunciations in tragic drama, though he substitutes a soliloquy for the *agōn* or confrontation typical of Greek tragedy.[21]

At this point the reader may be wondering what possible bearing the story of Ariadne deserted by Theseus on an isolated shore might have on what is ostensibly the primary subject of the epyllion, the marriage of Peleus and Thetis. Variety itself was prized by the Alexandrian poets, and Catullus is at the very least offering a virtuoso display of what the Greeks called *poikilia*, the intricate and variegated patterning characteristic of fine needlework.[22] Commentators have remarked on the very general contrast between the unhappy episode inscribed on the ornamental bedspread and the felicitous tale of love at first sight consummated by marriage that is narrated in the frame (Klingner 1956: 45). Some have detected an analogy between Bacchus' love for Ariadne in the final panel of the ecphrasis and Thetis' assent to marriage with Peleus: two instances of passion joining a mortal and a divinity.[23]

We may recall, moreover, that Catullus deviates from traditional versions of Thetis' marriage to Peleus by associating the original enamourment with the launching of the *Argo*, and through this event with the story of Jason and Medea as it is recounted in tragedy and Hellenistic epic. Apollonius of Rhodes had already called attention to the close correspondence between the myth of Jason and Medea and that of Theseus and Ariadne (3.997ff.; see Dyck 1989: 460): in each, a hero sails to foreign shores, and accomplishes a dangerous task with the help of a royal maiden who follows him at the cost of a breach with her own family, only to be carelessly abandoned. Catullus embellishes the analogies by suggesting that Ariadne, like Medea, sacrificed her own brother for Theseus' sake (150–1): the reference is to the death of the Minotaur, strictly speaking Ariadne's half-brother, the offspring of her mother Pasiphae and the bull with which she fell in love – rather a grotesque conceit, when all is said and done.

In addition, Catullus ingeniously connects Theseus' treatment of Ariadne and her prayer for revenge with the death of his father Aegeus, thus bringing the denouement of the episode into line with the Medea story, in which the heroine destroys not the father but the children of her faithless partner. Catullus follows the tradition that Aegeus instructed his son to change the black sails on his ship to white if he proved successful in his mission to Crete (225–37). Theseus forgets to do so, and Aegeus, on watch for the returning vessel from a citadel or promontory, leaps to his death in the belief that his son has perished (241–5). Catullus emphasizes that this is condign punishment, since thanks to a lapse of memory Theseus has brought upon himself the same grief that his heedlessness had caused Ariadne (246–8, 200–1; see 135, 207–9 for Theseus' obliviousness of Ariadne and of his father's mandate, respectively). No one before Catullus seems to have connected the story of the sails with the abandonment of Ariadne in this way.[24]

It may thus be argued that the digression on Ariadne and Theseus is foreshadowed in an oblique way in the Proem to the epyllion.[25] By means of continued allusions to earlier treatments of the Medea theme in the ecphrasis, some of which we have noted above, Catullus keeps the reader alert to the sub-text of the poem, which he established by beginning his epithalamium for Peleus and Thetis in an unorthodox fashion with the adventure of the Argonauts. He also fills in the hiatus between the launching of the *Argo* and the wedding at Pharsalus with the parallel narrative of Theseus and Ariadne, which does duty for the omitted account of the fortunes of Jason and Medea.

Nevertheless, the thematic connection between the subject of the ecphrasis – that is, the desertion of Ariadne – and the marriage of Peleus and Thetis, which occupies the frame, remains elusive, not to say tenuous. What is the function of the set of associations generated by the reference to the *Argo* in the Proem, and kept alive by a sequence of subtle allusions? If Catullus wished, as critics have argued, to darken the bright picture he draws of the marriage of Peleus and Thetis with a tale of faithless passion, what was his purpose? Variety in tone and feeling may be a sufficient motive, and perhaps it is only the over-earnest critic who feels impelled to seek an ethical significance behind this scintillating composition. Richard Jenkyns, who makes an elegant case for an aesthetic approach to the poem, remarks: 'I have been struck by how frequent are the attempts to make Catullus into a moralist', and the first of his examples is Konstan 1977, who 'calls the poem a "penetrating critique of Roman values"'.[26]

It appears to me (still) that Catullus signals a critical relationship between the frame story and the embedded tale of Ariadne and Theseus in the verses that constitute the transition to the ecphrasis. In Latin, they read:

> pulvinar vero divae geniale locatur
> sedibus in mediis, Indo quod dente politum
> tincta tegit roseo conchyli purpura fuco.
> haec vestis priscis hominum variata figuris
> heroum mira virtutes indicat arte.
> namque fluentisono prospectans litore Diae . . .
>
> (47–52)

Here is how these lines are rendered in the recent and faithful translation by Guy Lee (1990:83):

> Indeed, there in the midst, the Goddess's bridal
> Divan is placed, inlaid with Indian tooth and spread
> With woven purple dipped in rosy murex dye.
> This coverlet, embroidered with old-time human figures,
> Reveals with wondrous art the virtues of heroes.
> There, staring out from Dia's surf-resounding shore . . .

Nothing in this version suggests that the ecphrasis is a commentary on the frame narrative, or that the designs on the coverlet convey a particularly gloomy story, reminiscent of Medea's tragedy and in counterpoint to the happy marriage of Peleus and Thetis. It would appear that the heroic adventures of Theseus are on a par with the exploits of the Argonauts, and that Peleus naturally has images of a comrade in myth like Theseus on his wedding couch.

On this reading, the relevance of Theseus and Ariadne to the primary narrative is independent of Theseus' treatment of Ariadne and his consequent omission to change his sails to white, resulting in the death of his father. Catullus is unconcerned with the issue of perfidy and punishment that he himself seems to have introduced into the narrative by making the abandonment of Ariadne the cause of Theseus' subsequent forgetfulness and loss.

There is surely something harsh, however, in taking the image of Ariadne abandoned in her sleep on the island of Naxos as the immediate example of heroic deeds: the word *namque*, 'for' or 'thus', in line 52 makes it certain that the following episode is illustrative of the previous statement (Lee translates 'there', which misses the force of the particle).[27] It may be that Catullus is letting the irony of the juxtaposition speak for itself. But there is, I believe, at least one term in the Latin text that unmistakably invites us to read the ecphrasis as a critical comment on traditional conceptions of heroism. The word is *indicat*, which can mean simply 'reveal' or 'portray', as Lee, along with most translators and editors, takes it. Just as often, however, it has the loaded significance 'expose', and is used, for example, of uncovering the truth behind the testimony of a witness or defendant in court.[28] The tapestry not only shows but unmasks the things that heroes do.

There is another feature in the description of the spread that may point up the immorality of Theseus' behaviour. Its dark red hue is expressed by a series of four more or less synonymous colour terms, the last of which is *fuco*. *Fucus*, literally a purplish dye derived from the Greek name for the archil, commonly denotes fraud. Indeed, it was barely a live metaphor in Catullus' time, and Cicero employs it regularly in the transferred sense without the compulsory 'as it were' that good Latin style requires with figurative expressions. If one listens to the overtones, it may sound as though the tapestry that exposes the deeds of heroes is 'dipped in rosy deception'.[29]

The irony in 'the virtues of heroes' is not so heavy-handed as the translation inevitably suggests. While the word *virtus* in Catullus' time connoted ethical goodness in addition to the older meaning of martial courage (*OLD*, def. 3), the plural form *virtutes* retained the primary sense of valiant deeds or accomplishments, with the emphasis on success rather than on the morality of the means. Thus the historian Sallust, who was more or less a contemporary of Catullus and much concerned with the moral decline of Rome, employs *virtus* ubiquitously in the singular, but systematically eschews the plural because it might suggest that he approves of success irrespective of how it is achieved.[30]

It appears, then, that Catullus does signal the surprising move by which a cruel and thoughtless action is cited in illustration of 'the virtues of heroes', and deliberately undercuts the ideal image of the heroic age evoked in the Proem with an episode revealing the effects of a hero's cold indifference.

A poem by Moschus on the rape of Europa contains a brief ecphrasis illustrating the parallel fate of Io, and this might have provided Catullus with the model for a unified story in the digression, as opposed to the diverse designs on the shields of Achilles and Heracles. Catullus avoids the self-evident connection between the parts of Moschus' poem, in which, as Perutelli (1978: 92) puts it, 'one can read the one myth through the other'. But he perhaps found a prototype for an implicit contrast between ecphrasis and frame in the Hesiodic *Shield* if, as Peter Toohey (1988: 20–5; cf. Janko 1986: 40) has recently argued, the role of Perseus, whose exploits grace the centre of the shield, is meant to comment contrastively upon the career of Heracles.

The motif of the seafaring hero who is assisted by the daughter of a local king goes back to the *Odyssey*. Odysseus, shipwrecked, is washed up upon the Phaeacian shore, where he meets the princess Nausicaa, who has come to clean the garments she is saving for her wedding. Their conversation has hints of courtship formulas, and it is possible that Homer is alluding to a traditional story type in which the erotic interest is more fully developed.[31] As it is, however, Nausicaa merely facilitates the introduction of Odysseus to her parents, and the amatory business remains latent. Apollonius of Rhodes develops the romantic plot implicit in the encounter between Odysseus and Nausicaa in the third and fourth books of his *Argonautica*, in which Medea falls in love with Jason and helps him to recover the golden fleece. Apollonius' narrative breaks off before the couple's arrival in Corinth, where, according to Euripides, Jason deserts Medea for the daughter of his royal host. But Apollonius alludes proleptically to Jason's perfidy in a scene in the fourth book, where Jason contemplates surrendering Medea to the Colchians (4.379–81).[32]

It was Catullus who, with an obvious debt to Euripides' tragedy, made the hero's exploitation and subsequent desertion of the heroine central to epic narrative. Virgil in turn took the episode of Theseus and Ariadne as a model for Aeneas' desertion of Dido, and in the process effected a transformation in the literary image of the Carthaginian queen, who in an alternative tradition was regarded as a paragon of chastity.[33] While Dido's accusations against the fleeing Aeneas at the end of Book 4 of the *Aeneid* echo the charges of Catullus' Ariadne, Virgil earlier allows his hero to defend his actions in Dido's presence, on the pattern of an exchange of speeches in tragedy. The reader is thus made aware of Aeneas' reluctance to desert his paramour, and of the claims of fate that drive him.

No such insight into Theseus' motives is vouchsafed us by Catullus. The perspective is entirely that of the abandoned heroine, and in this respect Ariadne's lament has more in common with the subjective lyricism of elegy than with the dialectical style of Virgilian epic. Thus Ovid, in his collection of verse epistles to absent lovers entitled the *Heroides* or 'Heroines', where he draws upon the conventions of elegiac poetry, largely eliminates in the letter of Dido (7) the epic dimension of Aeneas' historic destiny. In an anonymous epistle of Dido to Aeneas dated to the third century CE or later, the author, faithful to both classical models, reintroduces the theme of the hero's fate into the lyric complaint, and, in the words of a recent commentator, 'finds himself accordingly in a precarious balance between the Virgilian and Ovidian models'.[34] Catullus 64 is thus pivotal in the evolution of multiple and intersecting traditions in the representation of feminine passion and heroic callousness.

Pitilessness, ingratitude and perfidy – the failure to abide by his promises – are at the heart of Ariadne's indictment of Theseus. He is *perfidus* (132–3, 174), that is, wanting in *fides*, 'trustworthiness' or 'good faith'; his declarations, like those of all men, she says, are not *fideles* (144). Furthermore, he fails to recognize his debt to her for saving his life (149–53). Both these deficiencies are captured in the term *immemor*: Theseus is 'unmindful' of his obligations and of his perjured oaths (135; cf. 145–8), and it is this heedlessness, as we have seen, that forms the link between his treatment of Ariadne and the lapse of memory that brings about his father's death.[35]

Ariadne's charges contain echoes of complaints against faithlessness that Catullus utters in his own person in the lyrical poems and epigrams addressed to Lesbia and other members of his circle; one may compare, in particular, the bitter reproaches that he levels at Alfenus in poem 30 ('immemor', 1; 'perfide', 3; compare also 30.9–10 with 64.142). A number of critics have, consequently, seen Ariadne as a vehicle for Catullus' own feelings of betrayal. He 'identifies with Ariadne', according to one scholar, who adds: 'Her love is described in terms which had been used to describe Catullus' love for Lesbia' (Small 1983: 139, 140). Harkins 1959 interprets Ariadne's lament as a kind of 'autoallegory'.[36] If Peleus' love for the divine Thetis is taken as a reference to Catullus' adoration of Lesbia, then the contrasting tones of the frame and ecphrasis may be read as encapsulating two moments in Catullus' experience: initial enamourment and idealization of the beloved, followed by the disillusionment and resentment occasioned by betrayal (Small 1983: 138–9).

The parallels that have been adduced between Ariadne's lament and Catullus' lyrics are not entirely compelling, however, apart from the poem to Alfenus.[37] Nor are the two cases strictly analogous. Lesbia's inconstancy is libidinous: she seeks sexual pleasure rather than an abiding love (see especially lines 17–20; 58). Theseus is not accused of sexual infidelity, but rather of violating his oaths, the same charge that Medea hurls at Jason in Euripides' tragedy (and that Catullus levels against Alfenus). Theseus' neglect of Ariadne is cruel and unjust – he will pay the penalty for his thoughtlessness through the death of his father – but his mind is on other things than women. He is a hero, with a hero's virtues, and simultaneously an example of the callous indifference and ingratitude towards outsiders that accompanies a dedication to great deeds undertaken selflessly and at the risk of one's life for the sake of fellow citizens (81–3). Athens is dear to Theseus (81), not, it appears, a girl from Crete, whatever her feelings and acts of kindness. The paradigm of betrayal characteristic of tragedy and epic, which Catullus elaborates in his treatment of Ariadne's desertion, is distinct from the lyric formula of erotic waywardness.

Ariadne's lament is emotionally expressive, and Perutelli (1978: 97), without insisting on an autobiographical dimension, argues that resonances with Catullus' lyric poems intersect with allusions to Greek verse so as to form 'two systems of reference'.[38] He adds (98) that the lyrical elements 'definitively abolish the limits of the literary genre', since they constitute 'an open violation in the epic coherence of the composition'. The clash between a lyric voice and epic conventions may be seen as an instance of the mixture of genres favoured by Hellenistic poets, congruent with the incorporation of *amor* in a form given to the representation of heroic *virtus*.

Ariadne's infatuation with the handsome foreigner ('dulci . . . forma', 175; 'hospes', 176, cf. 98), which induces her to abandon her father and home (180–1), is answered by the arrival of the impassioned Bacchus and his frenzied band. Love is madness ('furores', 94), even in the bosom of a naive girl, and it corresponds to the frenzy ('lymphata mente furebant', 254) of the bacchic host, who seem less a rescue party than a symbol of Ariadne's own mad desire which overcame her sense of filial responsibility.[39]

Returning from the ecphrasis to the wedding scene in the palace, Catullus describes in an elaborate simile the departure of the mortal guests, as they make way for the arrival of the gods (267–77): they are like waves stirred by the west wind on the morning sea, flowing away from the purple light of the rising sun. The colour evokes the dark red tapestry on which the Thessalian youths had gazed, and the simile

71

seems to signal the resumption of epic grandeur, albeit applied, in the Alexandrian fashion, to a humble rather than a heroic subject (cf. Apollonius of Rhodes 4.215; Homer, *Iliad* 4.122).

First to arrive among the deities is the centaur Chiron, tutor of Peleus and later of Achilles, with floral wreaths as house gifts; next comes a local river god, Penios, bearing whole trees to shade the entrance way (like the flowers, the trees are very probably symbolic of fertility).[40] Prometheus follows, still carrying the marks of his bondage upon the cliffs. According to the tragedy *Prometheus Bound* attributed to Aeschylus, he knew that the son of Thetis would be greater than his father, and used the secret as a weapon against Jupiter, who was angry at him for giving fire and other skills to mankind. In a sense, then, he acted as matchmaker for the union with Peleus, though his role belongs to a different tradition from the tale of love at first sight that Catullus presents in the Proem. Perhaps too his patronage of technical arts associates him with the launching of the *Argo*. Last come Jupiter (now reconciled, one supposes, with Prometheus), Juno and their children, except for Apollo and Diana, who scorn to join in the celebration for Peleus and Thetis. Apollo is the enemy of Achilles in the *Iliad*, and Achilles' actions at Troy, revealed to him, it may be, by his oracular powers, perhaps induce him to boycott the wedding of Achilles' parents. Certainty is impossible: the learned wit of Alexandrian poetry is on display in the guest list.[41]

When the gods are seated at their tables, the ancient Fates or Parcae, dressed in white robes with a purple border and red ribbons in their snowy hair, begin their song, continuing the while to work at their spinning, which Catullus describes in the homely detail relished by Alexandrian sophistication, down to the bits of wool that stick to their dry old lips (316). The Parcae celebrate the mutuality of the love (*amor*, 330, 334–5, 372) between Peleus and Thetis, as well as the unique bond or compact (*foedus*, 335, 373) and harmony (*concordia*, 356, cf. 379) that join them, and they conclude with a good-humoured reference to the consummation of their desire, which, as they predict, will be fruitful.[42] Here are themes that recur in Catullus' most idealistic expressions of the sanctity of love and marriage, both in his personal lyrics and epigrams (see especially 109.6: 'aeternum hoc sanctae foedus amicitiae', 'this eternal compact of sacred affection') and in his formal epithalamia, above all the lovely marriage hymn for Manlius Torquatus and his bride Junia Aurunculeia (61).[43] In the union of Peleus and Thetis, Catullus paints, as Brian Arkins (1982: 330) says, 'an unequivocal portrait of happy marriage' – save for the disquieting pattern of allusions to the Medea and Jason story, which hint at a darker image of heroic virtue.

The song of the Parcae is stanzaic, with groups of two to five verses separated by a refrain. Three initial and three final stanzas surround a central set of seven devoted to the achievements of Peleus' and Thetis' great son, Achilles (338–70), in the war that will devastate Troy (346).[44] The hallmark of Achilles' success is carnage, fields flowing with blood (344), bodies cut down like wheat (353–5), heaps of corpses choking the river Scamander (359–60). Bereaved mothers will be witnesses to his glory:

> illius egregias virtutes claraque facta
> saepe fatebuntur gnatorum in funere matres,
> cum incultum cano solvent a vertice crinem,
> putridaque infirmis variabunt pectora palmis.
>
> (348–51)

In the elegant translation of Guy Lee again (1990: 101):

> His extraordinary virtues and famed deeds
> Shall mothers often own at their son's funeral,
> When they shall loose dishevelled hair from their white
>   crowns
> And with impotent palms shall bruise their withered
>   breasts.

The collocation here of *virtutes* with *clara facta* makes evident the specifically martial reference of the word 'virtues': they are achievements on the battlefield, irrespective of the pain they bring to aged women.

The final witness to Achilles' 'great virtues' (cf. 'magnis virtutibus', 357) or heroism will be Polyxena, the Trojan princess who will be slain at the tomb of Achilles as a sacrifice to his spirit (362–70). Tradition had it that Polyxena had been promised to Achilles as a bride (see Euripides, *Hecuba* 484ff.) as a condition for ending the war, and in her immolation to the dead hero some critics have seen a macabre travesty or perversion of a marriage union.[45] 'Come therefore', the Parcae continue, 'and consort in long-imagined love' (tr. Lee) – it takes a moment to realize that the Parcae have returned to Peleus and Thetis as their subject, and the juxtaposition of the brutal sacrifice with the bright joy of the wedding ceremony is jolting.[46]

The structure of the epithalamium sung by the Parcae thus replicates the pattern of the epyllion as a whole, in which the celebration of the perfect love between Peleus and Thetis surrounds the description of Theseus' heroic victory over the Minotaur (cf. Knopp 1976: 211); his *virtutes*, 'virtues' or 'deeds of valour', are, like those of Achilles, represented chiefly through their effect upon a foreign girl, whom he leaves to her death without a thought. While the heroic age offers an outstanding example of a great couple united in a loving marriage, military virtue is exhibited through the pain it casually inflicts on a would-be bride.

Catullus concludes his epyllion with a moralizing Epilogue, in which he contrasts the piety of bygone days, when the gods revealed themselves to mortals, with the perversity of present times, in which they have turned away and disdain to be seen in daylight. The viciousness of today is illustrated exclusively through offences within the family: brothers shedding fraternal blood, sons failing to mourn the death of fathers, a father eager for the funeral of his son so that he can freely enjoy his daughter-in-law, a mother deliberately seducing her son without fear of the household gods (399–404).[47] With this image of moral decline following a heroic age, Catullus exploits a popular diatribe tradition on the corruption of Rome, like that which Sallust, for example, embroiders in connection with Catiline's depravity (cf. Lucretius 3.72–3). At the same time, he alludes to a convention in didactic literature beginning with Hesiod's *Works and Days*, in which the golden age gives way in successive stages to modern vice. In Hesiod, Shame and Retribution abandon the earth after human beings have become hopelessly evil; Aratus, in the *Phainomena*, substitutes Justice for Hesiod's more archaic abstractions. Catullus varies the formula with the phrase, 'all drove Justice from their passionate minds' (398), linking his work implicitly with yet another genre favoured by the Alexandrians.[48]

Among the most virulent of Catullus' epigrams are those that accuse their addressee of incest and other violations of familial bonds, like Gellius, who is charged with seducing his aunt to keep his uncle in line (74, 88.3, 89.3) and sexual congress with his mother and sister (88.1–2, 89.1–2, 90, 91.5–6), or Gallus, who encourages a liaison between his sister-in-law and his nephew (78.1–4), or finally Lesbia herself, who, Catullus implies, enjoys her brother as a lover (79).[49] The moralizing finale to the epyllion, with its emphasis on perversion within the household, resonates with these poems, but, as with the topics of the divinity of the beloved or perfidy in love, the theme appears to be less an allusion to personal lyric than a reference to a literary tradition.

The idealization of the past, in contrast with present depravity, locates Theseus and Ariadne, as well as Peleus and Thetis, in a world of heroic virtue. Formerly, the gods visited 'the chaste homes of heroes' ('domos . . . castas heroum', 384–5). Catullus identifies three general situations in which divinities revealed themselves to human eyes: in temples during the performance of sacred rites, when Jupiter himself might be seen; on the summit of Mount Parnassus, where Bacchus led his band of bacchantes; and in war, when Mars or Athena 'encouraged in person the armed troops of men' (396). The bacchic celebration recalls the rescue of Ariadne, while Mars and Athena encourage the military virtues exemplified by Theseus and Achilles, and by Peleus himself ('virtutibus', 323). Catullus' image of the heroic past seems inclusive.

The Epilogue, however, does not cancel the critical representation of valour implicit in the casual cruelty of Theseus and Achilles.[50] Their victims are strangers and enemies; the suffering they cause is the consequence of a single-minded commitment to victory, not a sign of deliberate depravity within the family. In the modern age, fathers desire the death of their sons and sons have ceased to grieve (*lugere*, 400) for their fathers. While Theseus' conduct towards Ariadne indirectly causes his father's death, the point of her curse is that the loss will inflict upon Theseus a grief (*luctum*, 247) comparable to hers. Aegeus' suicide, in turn, illustrates the intensity of the paternal bond. The present, by contrast, is characterized by the open corruption of familial values and of the integrity of the household.[51]

Catullus 64 is a learned and technically spectacular poem; an example is the triple anaphora

> tum Thetidis . . .
> tum Thetis . . .
> tum Thetidi . . .
> (19–21)

in one of the passages quoted above, where Catullus gives a virtuoso display of the name Thetis in three grammatical cases. At the level of genre, the poem incorporates epic, tragic, lyric and didactic elements in a mixture that defies neat classification. The term 'epyllion' may, indeed, be misleading if it suggests that the work is to be read as an abbreviated version of traditional epic; as Ferguson (1985: 193) observes, it is 'a poem of its own type, moving according to laws of its own'.

Catullus exploits the intricate structure, density of texture, and generic variety of poem 64 to represent multiple themes and perspectives. A celebration of a happy marriage sits side by side with a lyrical expression of despair by a woman who has been carelessly abandoned; epic warfare, bacchic frenzy, homely realism, moralizing commentary jostle each other in startling succession. In its allusiveness and complexity, the poem seems to call attention to its status as a refined work of art. At the same time, it insists on an ethical reading, inviting judgment of Theseus' betrayal of Ariadne and the sacrifice of Polyxena, which coexist with the glamorous nuptials of Peleus and Thetis. Mortals have conquered the sea, but the celebration of the marriage to which the expedition gives rise is coloured by allusions to another affair in the wake of the *Argo*, that of Jason and Medea, and the callous indifference it represents to the suffering of foreigners and women. The Epilogue, with its image of decline drawn from the tradition of didactic verse, puts the reader in the position of a moralist and judge. 'One must acknowledge ... a sense of surprise in the movement taken by the poem, a sense of shifting direction which confuses our overall response, and leaves us uncertain if we should have one, or if we should simply accept what is being offered at the moment' (Hutchinson 1988: 309).

Catullus 64 has a dual quality, combining aesthetic self-consciousness with ethical critique. It announces itself as both a literary artefact and a commentary on human behaviour. Neither those scholars who defend an aesthetic reading nor the critics who interpret the poem as an indictment of Roman values are wrong: it demands both approaches, simultaneously foregrounding its technique as a literary construct by a display of artifice, and problematizing the morality of heroic action through its complex representation of *virtus*. Catullus does not conceal the junctures and sutures by which he shifts generic codes, nor does he soften or flatten out the conflicting perspectives on the action that accompany an epic or a lyric voice, hymnic praise or tragic complaint. He exploits the Alexandrian delight in novelty and the mixture of forms as a vehicle of Roman moral criticism, but the morality remains a function of the artistry, because the ideological content is mediated by the mixture of genres. Thus the Epilogue, for example, is not so much a direct expression of Catullus' view of Roman corruption as an appeal to a literary form that carries with it a conventional notion of moral decline. The poem speaks through its generic components.[52]

The combination is tense and unstable, like the epyllion form itself in the hands of Catullus. As Hutchinson (1988: 302) remarks: 'The organization of the poem shows a wilfulness quite without parallel in extant Hellenistic poetry', and no interpretation that makes the poem clear and easy is likely to be satisfactory. But the coexistence of aesthetic artifice and ethical interest as simultaneous values in the poem helped to open up the elite conventions of Hellenistic verse to an engagement with immediate social issues. The fruits of Catullus' experiment were to be realized by Virgil.

NOTES

1 Cf. Gutzwiller 1981: 3.
2 See Catullus 22, 36, 95; Callimachus, *Aitia*, fr. 1 Pfeiffer; Hutchinson 1988: 296; Watson 1990: 13–14.
3 Stories of a quarrel between Callimachus and Apollonius over the propriety of long epic poems are late, and must be treated with scepticism; see Hutchinson 1988: 85–7.
4 Cicero's *neōteroi* may simply mean the 'newer' or 'younger' poets; for the term 'neoteric', which is a later coinage applied only in modern times to Catullus' circle, see Schmidt 1975.

5 Some of the narratives in Ovid's *Metamorphoses* have affinities with \
 epyllion. Closest to Catullus 64 is the *Ciris*, attributed to Virgil; see Ly
 1978: 32–5.

6 See West 1985: 136.

7 For Catullus' Greek sources, see Braga 1950, esp. p. 160. In Apollonius'
 account, Peleus and Thetis are married and Achilles is born prior to the
 voyage.

8 The Proem thus has the function of the Prologue in Euripidean tragedy or
 New Comedy.

9 There is a curious cinematic parallel in the film *Twins*, starring Arnold
 Schwartzenegger and Danny di Vito: the opening shot shows the twins, who
 are the result of a genetic experiment, as infants, one large and contented,
 the other a cranky runt.

10 Cf. Harmon 1973: 325; for a possible hint in vv. 379–80 of a future
 separation between Thetis and Peleus, see Konstan 1977: 81–2.

11 Cf. Stehle 1990: 92–4.

12 Vv. 43–6, with Kroll 1960 and Fordyce 1961.

13 On seafaring, see Heydenreich 1970: 13–62. Cairns 1984 argues on the basis
 of a passage in Artemidorus' handbook on the interpretation of dreams
 (2.37–8) that the appearance of the Nereids is a good omen.

14 See Homeric Hymns to Hermes 579–80 and Delian Apollo 14; Callimachus,
 Hymns 1.91–2.

15 Small 1983: 137; cf. Wiseman 1985: 161–2. On the identification of Lesbia
 with Clodia, see Deroux 1973; Wiseman 1985: 15–26.

16 The picture of the countryside evokes a golden age when no one needed to
 toil at farming, but there is a falling note in v. 42 suggesting decay and
 desolation; see Konstan 1977: 31–3.

17 On the use of colour in the epyllion, see Harmon 1973; O'Connell 1977:
 751–4; Small 1983: 136–7.

18 On the apparent contradiction between the representation of Theseus'
 voyage on the coverlet and the *Argo* as the first ship, see Weber 1983.

19 Ferguson 1985: 194 analyses the structure of the ecphrasis into eleven
 sections, arranged in a ring structure; see also Bardon 1943: 38; Richardson
 1944.

20 See Klingner 1956: 32–46; O'Connell 1977; contra Tartaglini 1986.

21 See Klingner 1956: 55–7; Roman tragedy favoured the extended soliloquy;
 see Boyle 1988: 78ff. Lyne 1978: 270 suggests that a lament by the heroine
 'became more or less *de rigueur* in later epyllion'; see *Ciris* 404–58, and Ovid
 Metamorphoses 8.108 ff. (Scylla).

22 Cf. Klingner 1956: 78ff.

23 Klingner 1956: 70; Small 1983: 146.

24 See Lafaye 1894: 175; Klingner 1956: 60–2.

25 Cf. Ferguson 1985: 202.

26 Jenkyns 1982: 90; see also 93–4. Harmon 1973 and Bramble 1970 come in
 for similar criticism.

27 See Konstan 1977: 39; Ferguson 1985: 204.

28 See Konstan 1977: 40; *OLD* s.v., defs. 2, 3; Kinsey 1965: 916 takes *indicat*
 ironically.

29 Cf. Konstan 1977: 40; *OLD* s.v., def. 4.

30 See Earl 1961: 28; 1967: 83.

31 See Woodhouse 1930: 54–65; Hague 1983.

32 Dyck 1989: 455; cf. Pavlock 1990: 51–63.

33 Cf. Macrobius, *Sat.* 5.17.5–6; Solimano 1988: 10–11. Lucius Ateius Praetextatus (first century BCE) is said to have written a declamation entitled 'Whether Aeneas Loved Dido' ('An Didum amaverit Aeneas'), according to Pliny *serm. dub.* = *Grammaticorum romanorum fragmenta* 137, Funaioli.

34 Solimano 1988: 15; cf. *fatis* in *Epistula Didonis ad Aeneam* 13.

35 For the enlargement of this concept, *immemor*, into ideological and experiential obliviousness in the case of Virgil's epic hero Aeneas, see Boyle in chapter V below, pp. 85f.

36 See also Putnam 1961; Thomson 1961; Ferguson 1985: 199; Pavlock 1990: 118–29; more cautiously Wiseman 1985: 176–80.

37 See Kinsey 1965: 912; Perutelli 1978: 96; Jenkyns 1982: 88 n. 2.

38 A brief Catullan lyric (poem 60) echoed in Ariadne's lament (64.154–6) is itself based in part on Euripides' *Medea*, and thus unites the two systems of allusion.

39 See Wiseman 1985: 179–80; for a summary of interpretations of Bacchus' role see Konstan 1977: 60–1; Small 1983: 146.

40 See Arkins 1982: 135; Konstan 1977: 89–90 sees the flowers as feminine symbols, the trees (carried by Penios) as masculine.

41 The absence of Apollo and Diana has been taken by some critics as a note of gloom in the otherwise glorious representation of the wedding; so too, the song of the Parcae (see below) disrupts the idyllic picture.

42 On *foedus* and *concordia*, see Ross 1969: 80ff.

43 Cf. Arkins 1982: 137; Wiseman 1985: 116, 178.

44 Some editors bracket the refrain at v. 378 as an interpolation, thereby reducing to two the number of stanzas following the Achilles segment of the epithalamium, but there is no compelling reason to do so.

45 See Curran 1969: 190–1; Bramble 1970: 25–7.

46 On the harsh transition, see Hutchinson 1988: 308. Boës 1986 sees no irony in the collocation of festive joy and images of wartime brutality.

47 On the perversions described in the Epilogue, see Arkins 1982: 152; Jenkyns 1982: 96–7; Watson 1984; Forsyth 1987.

48 It is an editorial decision to capitalize *Iustitia* as a personification, but it is warranted, I believe, by the allusion to Aratus.

49 See also Cicero, *Pro Caelio* 13.32.

50 Forsyth 1975: 51 argues on the contrary that 'man has *not* changed his character over the ages'; the Epilogue 'asks the reader to "rethink" the entire epyllion' (50), and to realize that human beings were as corrupt in the heroic age as they are today.

51 Curiously, Ariadne, who out of *amor* for Theseus assists him in the murder of her brother, seems closer than any other figure of the heroic age to the kind of behaviour condemned in the Epilogue.

52 On genre as a signifying element, see Conte 1984: 62–82; Pavlock 1990: 2. I am pleased to express my gratitude to Yasmin Haskell, Frances Muecke and Bronwyn Williams for their encouragement and help.

V

THE CANONIC TEXT: VIRGIL'S *AENEID*

A. J. Boyle

me iuvet hesternis positum languere corollis,
  quem tetigit iactu certus ad ossa deus;
Actia Vergilium custodis litora Phoebi,
  Caesaris et fortis dicere posse ratis,
qui nunc Aeneae Troiani suscitat arma
  iactaque Lavinis moenia litoribus.
cedite Romani scriptores, cedite Grai!
  nescio quid maius nascitur Iliade.

  (Propertius 2.34.59–66)

My pleasure to languish with yesterday's garlands,
  Whom the sure-aiming god touched to the bone;
For Virgil the power to tell of Actium's shores
  In Phoebus' guard and Caesar's gallant ships,
Who now wakes to life the arms of Troy's Aeneas
  And walls cast down on Lavinian shores.
Surrender, writers of Rome, surrender, Greeks!
  Something greater than *Iliad* is born.[1]

The contemporary reception of Virgil's *Aeneid* was extraordinary.
Heralded by Propertius even before its publication (perhaps as early as
26 BCE) as surpassing the epics of Homer,[2] Virgil's ambitious, radical,
unfinished poem became an instant canonic text. At the precise
moment when the genre seemed to many outmoded and uncreative,
Roman epic produced its paradigm, one which all later practitioners of
the genre would acknowledge through allusion and response, as they
worked at generating new kinds of epic in the wake of Virgil's
achievement. Virgil of course had his critics. His poem was as poetically
and generically radical as it was morally complex and profound. He was
accused of *kakozelia* or 'affectation' by M. Vipsanius Agrippa, and of
Homeric *furta* or 'thefts' by many.[3] There was even a parody of the
Aeneid, entitled *Aeneidomastix* or 'Aeneid-Scourge', written by the

otherwise unknown Carvilius Pictor (see Servius, Gellius 9.9.12, Macrobius 6.5–6). But the great poets of the period – Propertius, Horace (*Ep.* 2.1.247), Ovid (*Am.* 1.15.25f.) – saluted Virgil's masterwork, as did the Roman people. It quickly took its place as a central text in the school curriculum. Knowledge of Virgil's narrative of Rome defined in part what it was to be Roman.

So quickly and successfully did the *Aeneid* take up its position at the apex of Roman epic that the revolutionary nature of Virgil's achievement is often overlooked. Chapter I of this volume demonstrated (pp. 2ff. above) how prior to Virgil the Roman epic tradition was essentially one of historical and (certainly after Ennius)[4] panegyrical epic. Mythological epic was written, but it was definitely secondary, indeed apparently rare (various translations of Homer's *Iliad*, a *Cypria Ilias*, Valerius Atacinus' *Argonautae* are attested), and almost certainly neither allegorical nor historico-symbolic. Mythology too was introduced into the historical narratives of the mainstream epics either as early history or as embellishment, sometimes – so Naevius – in digressions. But before Virgil there seems to have been no mythological historico-symbolic Roman – or Greek – epic. Faced with what they saw as a dead literary form, the neoterics had recoiled from epic, cultivating in its stead what modern critics refer to as the epyllion. Cinna's *Zmyrna*, Caecilius' *Magna Mater*, Valerius Cato's *Dictynna*, Cornificius' *Glaucus*, Calvus' *Io*, in addition to the more famous and extant *Peleus and Thetis* of Catullus (poem 64), constituted a poetic challenge to the established genre and one which might have succeeded if Virgil had followed their example. In fact Virgil took a great deal from the neoteric epyllion, which obviously attracted him greatly – he had shown his fascination with it in *Eclogue* 6 and his mastery of it in the Aristaeus–Orpheus section of *Georgic* 4. But his solution of the genre problem was not to develop this new form (the extreme Alexandrianism of which must have seemed destined to marginalize the genre) but to revivify the old one and to revivify it so successfully as to change the ground-rules permanently for Roman epic. This essay attempts to clarify some of the features of the *Aeneid* central to Virgil's transformation of the genre and to the *Aeneid*'s status as a canonic or (Eliot) 'classic' text.[5]

THE *AENEID* AS RECUPERABLE TEXT: MYTH AS SYMBOL

> mox tamen ardentis accingar dicere pugnas
> Caesaris et nomen fama tot ferre per annos,
> Tithoni prima quot abest ab origine Caesar.
> (*Georgic* 3.46–8)

Yet soon I'll arm myself to tell Caesar's burning battles
And bear his name in glory for as many years
As separate Tithonus' distant birth from Caesar.

In the Proem to Virgil's third Georgic the poet-narrator, using
metaphors of temple, triumph, chariot and games, voices his intention
(*G.* 3.8–22) to write a poem to honour Caesar Octavian (the later
Augustus), in which the focus of attention will be Caesar's military
prowess, victories, triumphs and glorious ancestry (*G.* 3.22–39; 46–8).
Conspicuous references to Ennius and Pindar early in the Proem[6]
confirm that the envisaged work was to be a Roman, historical,
panegyrical epic. There was considerable pressure upon the poets at
Rome to write precisely this kind of epic, as Propertius 2.1.25ff. and
other texts attest. But Virgil did not write it. To have done so would
have been a task incompatible with both moral sensibility and artistic
integrity. Such a poem would have been poetically dead, politically
restrictive and morally false. Nor could it have addressed the issues
dominating Virgil's mind. What had happened to the Roman world in
Virgil's lifetime raised questions about Rome and the Roman achievement which went far beyond the contemporary period. The first
mythological historico-symbolic epic was written to deal with them.

In some ways what happened was a development of Virgil's symbolic
use of myth in his first two works. The pastoral myth of his *Eclogues*
as well as the neoteric deployment of myth in *Eclogue* 6 and *Georgic* 4
demonstrated both his appreciation and mastery of myth's semiotic
possibilities. Catullus' *Peleus and Thetis* had paved the way here
(see chapter IV above), as had Alexandrian aetiology and the symbolic
use of myth in Greek literature (especially tragedy and lyric) and art.
But no one had written a historically recuperable mythic poem on this
scale before. As to how he would suggest and control the myth's
recuperability, Virgil could rely in part on the generic expectations
produced by the predominantly politico-historical character of pre-
Virgilian epic and made explicit in the Propertian passage quoted at
the head of this chapter. But he also found inspiration in the earliest
'Roman' epic, written in Saturnians, the late third-century *Bellum
Punicum* of Naevius, whose narrative priorities he inverted. Naevius'
historical epic seems to have relegated Rome's mythic history to
digressions. Virgil made myth the main narrative and history the
digression and subtext, insinuating references to specific historical
figures and events into divine speeches, prophecies, revelations, ecphrases and occasionally the narrative itself, and making it clear from
the opening lines of the epic onwards that the myth was not simply
narrative, but narrative recuperable at the level of history. Thus the
Aeneid's first verses:

arma virumque cano, Troiae qui primus ab oris
Italiam fato profugus Laviniaque venit
litora, multum ille et terris iactatus et alto
vi superum, saevae memorem Iunonis ob iram,
multa quoque et bello passus, dum conderet urbem
inferretque deos Latio; genus unde Latinum
Albanique patres atque altae moenia Romae.

(Aeneid 1.1–7)

Arms I sing and a man, who first from Troy's shores
Fate's exile came to Italy and Lavinian
Coast, hard driven indeed on both land and ocean
By Heaven's violence, for savage Juno's unforgetting
    wrath,
Hard suffering too in war, till he might found a city
And march gods into Latium; whence the Latin race,
The Alban fathers and the walls of soaring Rome.

'Whence', *unde* (line 6), is cardinal. The word ties the poem's mythic narrative aetiologically to Roman history and Roman institutions, and intimates the rules for reading Virgil's text. The rules are then re-inforced through an almost systematic interpenetration of myth and history, a sustained infusion of the narrative's mythic presentation with historical allusions and references which bind both the human and divine figures of the epic to Rome's history, values, ideals and practices. Juno, for example, from *Aeneid* 1.4 onwards is not simply the Greek goddess Hera or an outraged female Poseidon, or even a fusion of these with her status as Roman goddess of marriage and member of the Capitoline triad, but also the Carthaginian goddess Tanit, Carthage itself,[7] and the divine embodiment of *furor*, the moral and ideological antithesis of the central (historically proclaimed) Augustan value, *pietas* ('reverence', 'duty' towards family, nation and gods). Neptune's restoration of the natural order at the conclusion of the *Aeneid*'s opening storm scene is not allowed to pass without explicit revelation of the historical sub-text in a simile (*A.* 1.148–54) which indexes the divine action as in part a trope for the triumph of individual human *pietas* over mass civil *furor*. And when Venus enters the epic, she is defined by her care not simply for her son Aeneas, but for the promised *imperium* of Rome (*A.* 1.227ff.). From the start the *Aeneid*'s fictive gods are not simply imaginatively realized characters in the narrative fantasy of the poem but ones which, aligned with the human figures of the epic and the historical processes they lay bare, are designed to contribute substantially to the narrative's *historical* function.[8]

Especially effective in underscoring the poem's historical recuperability is the well-known quartet of ideologically related mytho-historical passages, placed strategically at the edges and centre of the work: Jupiter's historical prophecies of Book 1 (257–96) and Book 12 (830–40), and the revelation of Rome's future to Aeneas in Book 6 (756–899) and Book 8 (608–731). Appropriately it is at the centre of the *Aeneid* that the emblematic function of the mythic narrative's hero is made most explicit, as Anchises addresses his son as 'Romane':

> tu regere imperio populos, Romane, memento
> (hae tibi erunt artes), pacique imponere morem,
> parcere subiectis et debellare superbos.
>
> (*Aeneid* 6.851–3)

> You, Roman, remember to rule nations with your command –
> These will be your arts – to stamp peace with men's
>   practice,
> To spare the humbled and to crush the proud in war.

'You, Roman' – 'tu . . . Romane': singular. It is Aeneas, not 'Romans', *Romani*, whom Anchises exhorts. But it is Aeneas as emblem of Rome.[9] The point is important. Virgil directs the reader to construe his mythic narrative as historically symbolic, not as allegorical. Allegory, as commonly understood, crudely equates. The *Aeneid*'s intricate recuperability operates on several levels often simultaneously. Aeneas, for example, both is and is not Augustus. Certainly the representation of Augustus on the great shield of Book 8 is designed to promote an analogy between the *princeps* and Aeneas[10] (similar to that achieved a decade later by the sculptural reliefs of the Ara Pacis), and elsewhere in the epic there are episodes where Aeneas clearly prefigures Augustus (e.g. *A.* 3.278ff., 6.69ff.). But it is as emblem of *vir Romanus* that Aeneas primarily functions. There is much in him, for example, of Mark Antony, Julius Caesar, Marius, Scipio Africanus, Camillus, Romulus and other Roman heroes, with several of whom Virgil had already associated Augustus himself (*G.* 2.167–72, 3.27). The effect of Aeneas receiving and shouldering the great shield of Roman history at the end of Book 8 before he goes into battle is to ensure that Aeneas' wars in Latium are seen not simply as the wars of Augustus (although they are the wars of Augustus) but as the wars of Rome. Virgil's revolution in epic went beyond producing a historically recuperable mythic text; the recuperability he aimed for was complex and multi-layered in accordance with the complex and multi-layered political, historical and moral issues which his poem was written to explore. Later writers of mythic epic, such as Ovid, Statius and Valerius, could assume complex recuperability precisely because of Virgil's achievement.

THE *AENEID* AS MORAL TEXT: NARRATIVE AS CRITIQUE

But the *Aeneid* is not only a mythological historico-symbolic text. It is a moral text.[11] The political, panegyrical function of most previous Roman epic shaped contemporary expectations for Virgil's poem, which the *Aeneid* both encourages and attempts to subvert, organizing its text to confront the principal social and moral issue of Rome's world: the nature and value of empire. The narrative critically presents, rather than eulogizes, the world of political and military power (*imperium* and *arma*) and its idealizing self-image, examining the relationship of that image to Roman reality and the effect of the political world and its imperial achievement on human values and human history. The poem sets up an image–reality structure for its narrative by including at critical points in the epic – Books 1, 6, 8 and 12 (the relevant quartet of passages is cited above, p. 83) – overt statements of empire's claim to bring a civilizing, socio-moral order to the world, and then setting against those statements the narrative of Aeneas' emblematic exploits, which index the gap between imperial ideology and practice. Especially important here are the battle-books of 9–12, the culmination and climax of Aeneas' search for empire, in which the moral justification of empire's mission is placed seriously in doubt. Empire is presented as achieving its goal not through the operation of *pietas*, as Jupiter had prophesied (*A.* 1.257–96), or clemency, as Anchises had instructed (*A.* 6.851–3), but through violence, rage, vengeance and *furor*, and the mindless dissolution of bodies. Aeneas' appearance at the battlefield in Book 10 (260–75), his bloody vendetta after Pallas' death (*A.* 10.510–605), his slaying of Lausus and Mezentius (*A.* 10.762–908) and live sacrifice of prisoners to Pallas' shade (*A.* 11.81f.), his blood-letting in Book 12 (especially 494ff.), duel with Turnus and killing of him (*A.* 12.697–952) present the ancestor of the Julian family not as the imperial figure of the new Roman world but as a prime embodiment of the values and behaviour of the old heroic world of bloodlust, violence, 'honour' and the senseless pursuit of fame. Indeed into all the above depictions of Aeneas' behaviour Virgil insinuates a telling analogy with Achilles in order that the Trojan hero may be seen as the reincarnation of the very figure at whose cruelty and violence he had groaned in *Aeneid* 1 (453ff.).[12] Of course Aeneas, unlike Achilles, carries with him the imperial dream; Rome's history and *imago* are revealed to him in the ideological core of the epic – a fact to which attention is drawn at crucial moments in Books 10 (especially 521ff., 821ff.) and 12 (especially 175ff., 311ff., 829ff., 930ff.). The failure of this *imago* to be realized in the narrative makes of the narrative a refutation of the imperial *imago* itself. At the end of Book 8

Aeneas is described as 'ignorant of reality, rejoicing in the image' ('rerumque ignarus imagine gaudet', *A.* 8.730). The battle-books of the *Aeneid* show what that reality is. The epic ends on a note not of imperial triumph, but of individual suffering and loss, as Aeneas evidences the values for which empire in practice stands by sinking steel in human tissue:

> hoc dicens ferrum adverso sub pectore condit
> fervidus; ast illi solvuntur frigore membra
> vitaque cum gemitu fugit indignata sub umbras.
> <div align="right">(<i>Aeneid</i> 12.950–2)[13]</div>

> As he speaks he sinks steel in the facing breast
> Burning. The other's limbs go limp with cold.
> With a groan protesting life flees to the darkness.

Other moral issues are explored in Virgil's text: the worth of fame, central value of the Roman political and military ethos, against the human cost of its pursuit; the moral possibilities of man as against his psychological vulnerability and irresistible potentiality for violence; the nature of human action and motivation, the relationship between circumstance, psychology and behaviour; the paradox of human aspiration, the dehumanizing splendour of man's finest ideals; the human inability to learn from experience and the resulting inevitability and tragedy of history's repetitive cycle; the relationship between man and art, and the moral impotence of the latter; the human primacy of compassion and its failure as a force in history.

Central to these issues is the motif of Aeneas *immemor*, the hero who 'fails to remember'. In the first half of the epic Aeneas displays an enormous potentiality for commitment to the values of the private world, the values of compassion, understanding, friendship and love (e.g. *A.* 1.220ff., 459ff., 2.790ff., 3.709ff., 4.393–5, 5.869, 6.133, 332, 455, 476) – values which assert the primacy of the claims of the individual and the person rather than those of destiny or the state. There is no greater moral outcry in Latin literature against the injustice of history's treatment of the individual than Aeneas' response to his father's dynastic joy at *A.* 6.719–21 (discussed below, pp. 95f.). The hero's ensuing commitment, however, to Anchises' imperial vision and the passion for fame which it engenders ('famae venientis amor', *A.* 6.889) ensure that, like the souls destined for reincarnation (*A.* 6.750f.), he loses memory of all he has experienced before emerging into the imperial light. It is not merely that in Books 7–12 Aeneas never recalls the individual suffering which he has witnessed in his past, the tragic deaths, for example, of Creusa, Palinurus, Deiphobus or Dido; more importantly he forgets the inability of fame to compensate for the loss and the tears of history. One of the poem's most revealing moments is when Aeneas offers 'fame' to the young warrior Lausus as compensation for the dissolution of his life (*A.* 10.829f.). In Book 6 the epic's hero had seen the worthlessness of the *aeternum nomen*, the 'undying name' (*A.* 6.235, 381). It is not accidental that Trojan epithets continue to be applied to Aeneas, even after the 'Romanization' of Books 6 and 8; they are used to point up the hero's failure to learn from his past. Indeed Aeneas not only resurrects the Trojan war in Italy, repeating the violence he had criticized in his narrative of Book 2, but becomes himself the 'other Achilles', *alius Achilles*, prophesied by the Cumaean Sibyl (*A.* 6.89), a reincarnation in history of the paradigm of brutality ('saevum . . . Achillem') he had observed in Book 1 (459f.). Forgetting the past, Aeneas *immemor* resurrects it as the future. He is the most tragic of the poem's list of history's victims.

There were precedents for the use of myth for moral and political scrutiny, most recently Virgil's own *Eclogues* and *Georgics* and the seminal *Peleus and Thetis* of Catullus. Also Lucretius' *De Rerum Natura* had furnished an example of a sustained moral critique in non-narrative hexameter verse. But again there was nothing like this in Roman epic before Virgil. Even the Homeric epics, which are certainly moral texts, contain little to match the profound historical, political and moral critique of Virgil's narrative. Indeed Virgil's transformation of the genre here and the demands he made upon his readers were so radical that the critique was largely misread. But the *Aeneid* left to the epicists who followed a tradition of epic's function as critique of the political world. To Virgil's great successor Lucan this function was so central to the genre that he removed Virgil's veil of myth to make his critique unambiguous.

THE *AENEID* AS POETIC TEXT: STYLE AS POWER

The *Aeneid* classicized epic narrative style.[14] Virgil was indebted, of course, to Homer, whose formulaic descriptions, phrases and similes are often recalled in the Latin text, contributing an 'epic' flavour or atmosphere to the narrative. He was also indebted (substantially) to earlier Roman epic, especially to Ennius, who not only introduced the hexameter to Roman epic poetry but developed a weighty, non-strident epic manner and a rugged, compact narrative style which had a profound impact on Virgil. The *Aeneid*'s text is studded with Ennian tags and allusions, especially in Virgil's rendering of stock epic situations; but more important than these is the overall stylistic mode of the poem (which is that of Ennian 'high' epic) and the many passages of visually particularizing narrative, often at critical points in a book, reminiscent of Ennius' technique:

sic fatur lacrimans, classique immittit habenas
et tandem Euboicis Cumarum adlabitur oris.
obvertunt pelago proras; tum dente tenaci
ancora fundabat navis et litora curvae
praetexunt puppes. iuvenum manus emicat ardens
litus in Hesperium; quaerit pars semina flammae
abstrusa in venis silicis, pars densa ferarum
tecta rapit silvas inventaque flumina monstrat.

(Aeneid 6.1–8)

So speaks Aeneas weeping, and gives the fleet its head
And at long last glides to Cumae's Euboean shores.
They turn their prows seawards; anchors made fast the
    ships
With biting hooks and circling sterns embroider
The beach. A band of warriors bursts blazing
Onto Hesperia's shore; some look for seeds of fire
Hidden in veins of flint, some raid the tangled forest
Haunts of wild beasts and point to springs they have
    found.

Note the simplicity, economy, tightness of the writing, the powerful sparseness of the style. The visual effect is essentially impressionistic – specific, arresting details selected for immediacy and potency of impact, encapsulated in tough, aggressive, concrete, highly imagistic language with a dense concentration of epithets and verbs. Particularly Ennian (and indeed 'Homeric') is the way in which the absence of sub-ordination thrusts each detail momentarily into the position of fore-ground so that the detail itself, the percept, may be grasped and savoured. What is Ennian and non-Homeric is the use of the historic present to perceptualize the scene.[15] But though the stylized simplicity of this kind of narrative may be Ennian, the alliteration is more subtle and the poetic language more highly charged: observe the pictorial sharpness given to the normally lame *curvae* (here = 'circling', 4), and the development of metaphor into action evident in 'emicat ardens' (lit. 'flashes blazing', 5).[16]

Not all Virgilian narrative is of this kind. The *Aeneid* frequently adopts a more flowing, less staccato mode for much of its text, and employs a more complex, periodic structure for sentences dealing with an intricate situation or state of mind. The *Aeneid*'s narrative is, however, essentially pictorial and progresses substantially from carefully etched scene to carefully etched scene with a minimum of connecting detail. Every book ends with a pictorial tableau or vignette, climaxing what is in effect iconic narrative. For this iconic technique Virgil owes more to the neoterics, especially Catullus (*Peleus and Thetis* again), than to Ennius, and it is central to both his solution of the genre problem and the power of his style. Using tableaux and vignettes as the building-blocks of his epic ensured a sharply focused, rapidly changing narrative and a perceptually engaged reader, who was constantly challenged to build the selected details of the tableaux into coherent pictures and the juxtaposed pictures into coherent narrative.

From the neoterics too (and their Hellenistic predecessors, especially Callimachus and Apollonius) Virgil derived a love of the intellectual possibilities of language, the power of irony, paradox, ambiguity, polyvalence, thematic imagery, as well as a taut, crisp concision of utterance. Virgil was especially strong and radical (he was criticized for this by Agrippa) in what Horace later called *callida iunctura* (*AP* 47f.), the 'shrewd juxtaposition' of common words to generate fresh meaning. Examples abound: 'sunt lacrimae rerum' of Dido's frescoes ('there are tears for/in things', *A*. 1.462), 'animum pictura pascit inani' of Aeneas' response to the frescoes ('he feeds his soul on an empty picture', *A*. 1.464), 'discolor . . . auri . . . aura refulsit' of the golden bough ('the diverse-hued breath of gold reflected', *A*. 6.204), 'stant lumina flamma' of Charon ('his eyes stand with flame', *A*. 6.300). Like the neoterics too he was interested (perhaps most of all) in the use of poetic language to analyse human psychology and human relationships. Catullus and the *poetae novi* had treated their own emotions and psychology with a depth and seriousness hitherto unknown in the Roman tradition and they had started to extend this use of poetic language to fictive creations such as Attis in Catullus 63 and Ariadne in *Peleus and Thetis*. Virgil developed this further, using all the resources of neoteric personal poetry in his presentation of the thinking, feeling and the emotional interrelationships of the fictive characters of his epic. Indeed he developed a technique for psychologizing the narrative itself, so that events are frequently presented as they are experienced by a participant in the narrative. The foot-race of Book 5 (315ff.), for example, and the arrival of Aeneas in Carthage in Book 1 (418ff.) are presented from the point of view of a participant. When Aeneas views the frescoes at *A*. 1.450ff., the reader is not presented with an omniscient narrator's 'objective' description of them, but a description of the frescoes as experienced by Aeneas. The values embodied in the text's description of them are the values Aeneas reads into the scenes. This 'subjective' style of Virgil, as it has sometimes been called,[17] which the poet developed in the Orpheus narrative of *Georgic* 4 (453ff.), is a most important ingredient of the *Aeneid*'s stylistic power. It cuts through the distance between reader and text, embroiling the reader in the experience of the events and issues of the narrative.

Much of Virgil's interest in presenting the psychologies of his characters in some intricacy and depth seems to derive also from the Graeco-

Roman tragic tradition, in which he was deeply imbued. Indeed critics have drawn attention to the dramatic style of many of the *Aeneid*'s most moving episodes,[18] especially those which are dramatic in a technical sense, featuring a preponderance of dialogue, interleaved with narrative stage-directions, and the kind of psychological conflict likely to advance the action. The Dido–Aeneas quarrel scene of Book 4 (296–396) and the Italian council of war in Book 11 (225–444) are obvious examples here. But critics have also noted the use of tragic irony, insight and revelation elsewhere in the work of a kind and to a degree that it is clear that Virgil has gone some way towards conflating the genres of epic and tragedy into a new powerful tragico-epic style. Of course epic had always had affinities with drama (Aristotle, *Poetics* 1449b9ff.), but Virgil intensifies those affinities, achieving greater interiority for his epic story (the *Aeneid* in one sense is the story of the progress of the mind of Aeneas) and structuring episodes to move spectacularly and speedily towards a striking climax – as in the narrative of the death of Priam in Book 2 (506–58), for example, or the sequence of episodes in Book 2 ending with the Trojans dragging the wooden horse into the city (*A.* 2.13–249). Sometimes such episodes culminate in a speech of astonishing emotive power, preceded by acute, psychologically specific description – as at the turning-point of Book 12, when Saces rides out from the city of Latinus and begs Turnus to have mercy on his people ('miserere tuorum', *A.* 12.653):[19]

> obstipuit varia confusus imagine rerum
> Turnus et obtutu tacito stetit; aestuat ingens
> uno in corde pudor mixtoque insania luctu
> et furiis agitatus amor et conscia virtus.
> ut primum discussae umbrae et lux reddita menti,
> ardentis oculorum orbis ad moenia torsit
> turbidus eque rotis magnam respexit ad urbem.
> ecce autem flammis inter tabulata volutus
> ad caelum undabat vertex turrimque tenebat,
> turrim compactis trabibus quam eduxerat ipse
> subdideratque rotas pontisque instraverat altos.
> 'iam iam fata, soror, superant, absiste morari;
> quo deus et quo dura vocet fortuna sequamur.
> stat conferre manum Aeneae, stat, quidquid acerbi est,
> morte pati, neque me indecorem, germana, videbis
> amplius. hunc, oro, sine me furere ante furorem.'
>
> (*Aeneid* 12.665–80)

Stunned and confused by the world's shifting image,
Turnus stood silently staring; in one heart
Surges immense shame, and madness mingled with grief,

And love whipped up by rage, and conscious valour.
As soon as shadows parted and the mind's light returned,
He turned his eyes' blazing orbs to the ramparts
Frantic and looked back at the great city from his
    chariot.
Look! from floor to floor a rolling spire of flame
Was billowing upwards and clutching a tower,
A tower which he had raised himself from jointed beams
And set on rollers and laid with high gangways:
'Now, now, sister, the fates prevail; do not hold me
    back.
Let us follow where god and hard fortune call.
I am resolved to fight Aeneas, to suffer in death
All its bitterness; you'll see me, sister, shamed
No more. Let me, I beg, rage this final rage.'

The fusion of psychological focus and tragic revelation impresses. When the clouds of confusion dissipate, Turnus stands revealed as a man not only of honour, pride, compassion, love and courage but of self-awareness and tragic perception. As the tower which Turnus had built and emblem of much of his past life and purposes (*A.* 12.674–5) burns before his eyes, it generates in the Italian champion an insight into the inevitable imminence of his own destruction and a recognition that the engagement with Aeneas, which he must now face because of his own honour and grief for his people (*A.* 12.667, 679), will be but an exercise in futile heroics and self-dissolving *furor*. The sense of high tragedy is unmistakable; epic and drama combine to stir the reader's moral and emotional sensibilities.

THE *AENEID* AS WELL-WROUGHT TEXT: FORM AS MEANING

The *Aeneid* took a decade to write. It is one of the European tradition's most carefully wrought texts, a paradigm of poetic structure and intratextual relationships.[20] The neoterics appreciated the importance of poetic structure, as did Lucretius, who may have been the first poet of the Latin tradition to use the book (i.e. single papyrus roll) architecturally, as an integral unit of the poem's structure.[21] But Virgil went beyond his predecessors in the number and intricacy of the inter-related narrative structures he imposed on both the poem and its parts, creating in his verbal artefact the kinds of detailed correspondences, contrasts and relationships associated contemporarily with the visual arts, especially architecture and monumental sculpture. The *Aeneid* itself is designed both as bipartite and as tripartite – on the bipartite structure: Books 1–6, Virgil's '*Odyssey*' (Aeneas' wanderings in search of a kingdom), Books 7–12 (Aeneas' war to win the kingdom) Virgil's '*Iliad*';[22] on the tripartite structure: Books 1–4, Tragedy of Love (Dido), Books 5–8, Destiny of Rome, Books 9–12, Tragedy of War (Turnus). The various parts themselves embody several organizational principles. The two halves of the *Aeneid* can be seen both as parallel panels (Book 1 correlating thematically with 7, 2 with 8, 3 with 9, 4 with 10, 5 with 11, 6 with 12) and as halves of a single recessed panel (Book 2 correlating with 12, 3 with 11, 4 with 10, 5 with 9, 6 with 8 – 1 and 7 initiating the two halves); the tripartite structure reveals an arrangement of books within each tetrad on a thematic alternating system (e.g. Books 1 and 3, Aeneas' wanderings; Books 2 and 4, Tragic Departure). These correlations are reinforced by analogous episodes and intratextual motifs: thus Books 1 and 7 are linked by major interventions of Juno, 6 and 8 by the revelation of Rome's future, 5 and 9 by interventions of Juno via Iris, attempted ship-burnings, a Nisus–Euryalus episode, an Ascanius episode, etc. The individual books themselves are organized on similar principles, every book being clearly tripartite and disclosing in its various parts alternating, parallel and recessed panel schemes.

Thus the *Aeneid*'s narrative complexity is given disciplined form. But form is also meaning. Juxtaposition is often implicitly evaluative; intratextual correlation frequently judgmental. The framing of the ideological core of the epic (Books 5–8) by the tragedies of love (Books 1–4) and war (Books 9–12) not only focuses on the inextricable connection between Rome's glory and its cost but challenges the reader to evaluate the constituents of this conjunction. The many connections binding Book 12 (Future Secured/Birth of Rome) to Book 6 (Future Revealed) and 2 (Death of Troy) imply an analytic judgment: Rome's future revealed in Book 6 (756–853) is secured in Book 12 (especially 930–52), but in a manner which simply repeats the events and values of Book 2,[23] and thus undermines the ideology and promise of the revelation itself (*A.* 6.851–3). The organization of individual books and episodes similarly dictates focus and elicits judgment. The intricate recessed panel structure governing *Aeneid* 4 centres on Aeneas' defence of his behaviour to Dido at 333–61, the moral core of the book; and when Aeneas plucks the golden bough in *Aeneid* 6, that action too is at the centre of the concentrically structured account of his encounter with the Cumaean Sibyl, which opens the book (9–263). Sometimes the narrative is laid out in a parallel fashion to draw from the reader a comparative judgment. Book 10's account, for example, of the death of Pallas at the hands of Turnus and the reaction to it of Aeneas (*A.* 10.362–605) is followed almost immediately by a parallel account of the death of Lausus at the hands of Aeneas and the reaction to it of Lausus' father, Mezentius (*A.* 10.689–908), which makes any explicit comparison of the two events unnecessary.[24] Designed interplay between the endings of each book or major section of the *Aeneid* similarly generates meaning. Each book ends in a tableau focusing the reader's attention on major figures and (implicitly) their involvement in the movement towards Rome. The first tetrad ends with the focus on the death and suffering of Dido (*A.* 4.693–705), the final tetrad with the focus on the death of Turnus (*A.* 12.930–52); between these two are the tableaux that conclude Books 6 (893–9) and 8 (729–31), each of which focuses not only upon Aeneas' reception of the imperial dream but upon his deluded reception of it: at the end of Book 6 Anchises sends his son through the ivory gate, through which 'the dead send false dreams to the upper world' ('falsa ad caelum mittunt insomnia Manes', *A.* 6.896), and at the end of Book 8 Aeneas 'rejoices in the image' of Roman *imperium* on the shield, 'ignorant of reality' ('rerumque ignarus imagine gaudet', *A.* 8.730). Intratextual correlation again makes explicit comment otiose.

Much of this attention to intratextual connections Virgil had already displayed in his *Eclogues* and *Georgics*, which like the *Aeneid* reveal a fastidious concern with correlation and contrast between the various parts of each poem. The conspicuous dialectic between the finales of each Georgic is well known, as are the tripartite structure and recessed panel or mirror technique of *Eclogues* 1–9.[25] What is less well known is how Virgil in his early works uses motifs and images to bind poem to poem, episode to episode for comparative, as well as 'structural', purposes. *Eclogue* 10, for example, is virtually a composite of allusions to *Eclogues* 1–9, which serve to make the final eclogue an evaluative commentary on the issues of the *Eclogues* book. Virgil continues and expands this technique in the *Aeneid* using motifs and imagery to bind episode to episode and event to event to challenge the reader to ponder the interconnections and enlarge his/her perception of the action and the issues it realizes. The motif of 'failed resistance', for example, signalled by the sparse and discriminate use of *cunctari*, unites Dido (*A.* 4.133), Palinurus (*A.* 5.856), Turnus (*A.* 7.449, 12.919), Vulcan (*A.* 8.388) and Aeneas himself (*A.* 12.940), and is given the force of enigmatic symbolism by being associated with one of the epic's most important and emblematic events, the failed resistance of the golden bough (*A.* 6.211). The *geminus* motif unites Romulus and Remus (*A.* 1.274, 6.779, 8.631), the Tenedos serpents (*A.* 2.203f., 225), the Atridae (*A.* 2.415, 500, 8.130), the gates of sleep and of war (*A.* 6.893, 7.607), Allecto's, Hercules' and Cleopatra's serpents (*A.* 7.450, 8.289, 697), Aeneas (*A.* 7.280, 11.72), Augustus (*A.* 8.680), the *Dirae* or Furies used by Jupiter to render Turnus helpless (*A.* 12.845) – and again the golden bough (*A.* 6.190, 203). Many other pervasive motifs could be cited here: the use of *inanis*, *condere*, *fama*, *imago*, *res*, *lacrimae*, *furor*,

pietas, or *dolor*. Sometimes the mere repetition of poetically powerful lines serves to link major events, such as Aeneas' frustrated attempts
to embrace Creusa and Anchises (*A*. 2.792f., 6.700f.) or the departure of
Camilla's and Turnus' protesting life into darkness (*A*. 11.831, 12.952).

Perhaps the most important linking device in the *Aeneid* is its systemic
use of imagery. The fabric of the *Aeneid*'s narrative is permeated by such
symbolic images as serpent, fire, wound, storm, gold, brightness, bee,
deer, hunting, sacrifice, beast, dream, shadow and darkness,[26] which
occur at signal junctures of the epic and bring to the contexts in which
they appear associations derived from their appearance in other
contexts as part of an imagistic system. Thus the deer image links the
tragedies of Dido (*A*. 4.69–73) and Turnus (*A*. 12.749–55) with the
slaying of the pet stag of the family of Tyrrhus (the proximate cause of
the war in Latium: *A*. 7.483–502) as instances of history's annihilation of
the individual, whose vulnerability and value are suggested by the
image itself and whose destruction is ironically foreshadowed by
Aeneas' slaughter of deer for food when driven to the coast of Africa in
Book 1 (184ff.). But more important than the deer image is the
constellation of serpent, fire, wound and storm, signalled early in the
Aeneid as major imagistic representations of *furor* (e.g. *A*. 1.29, 36, 50,
81ff., 660ff., 2.199ff., 302ff., 416ff., 469ff., 529, 561, 575, 587), and
serving as indices of its manic, violent and destructive presence
throughout the epic. The constellation figures in association with
Dido's destructive passion for Aeneas, especially in Book 4, with the
start of the war in Latium in Book 7 (especially *A*. 7.323–571), with the
battle fury of Trojan and Italian warriors in Books 9–12 (*passim*) – and
most tellingly and most continuously with Aeneas' exploits from Troy
to Rome.[27]

The *Aeneid*'s final lines (*A*. 12.919–52) document the poem's status as
a well-wrought text in which intratextual correlations and intricacy of
form are ingredients of the epic's discourse. The constellation of *furor*
imagery explodes in this passage as Aeneas' behaviour is indexed by
storm (921ff.), flame (946), wound (948), sacrifice ('immolat', 949)[28]
and – sonally – serpent (949), and his actions not only invert the
ideology of Book 6 and recall the *furor* of Book 2 but provide ironic re-
enactment of the frescoes he had viewed in Book 1 and ironic fulfilment of the epic's opening lines.

> ille, oculis postquam saevi monimenta doloris
> exuviasque hausit, furiis accensus et ira
> terribilis: 'tune hinc spoliis indute meorum
> eripiare mihi? Pallas te hoc vulnere, Pallas
> immolat et poenam scelerato ex sanguine sumit.'
> hoc dicens ferrum adverso sub pectore condit

fervidus; ast illi solvuntur frigore membra
vitaque cum gemitu fugit indignata sub umbras.

(*Aeneid* 12.945–52)

Thus Aeneas, when his eyes drank in the plunder's
Reminders of savage grief, inflamed with rage,
Terrible with anger: 'Are you, decked with spoils of my
    men,
To be snatched from me? Pallas with this wound, Pallas
Sacrifices you and draws payment from guilty blood.'
As he speaks he sinks steel in the facing breast
Burning. The other's limbs go limp with cold.
With a groan protesting life flees to the darkness.

Turnus is Hector (and Priam), Aeneas is Achilles (see below, pp. 96f.);
the very conduct and figure the Trojan hero had deplored in Book 1
(453ff.) are here repeated, as the images on Dido's temple become the
reality of Roman history. The epic narrator began his text promising to
sing of 'arms and a man'; his text concludes with an emblematic tableau
of that man and his *arma* in full operation, as *Aeneid* 1's words and
images ironically return. The anger and fire of Juno and her eternal
wound, *aeternum vulnus*, introduced in the first book's opening lines (*A.*
1.4, 11, 25, 29, 36, 50), even the savagery of her grief ('saevi dolores', *A.*
1.25), are recalled in the fire of Aeneas' anger (*A.* 12. 946), the savage
grief ('saevi . . . doloris', *A.* 12.945) and the final wound itself ('hoc
vulnere', *A.* 12. 948), as Aeneas sinks the steel full in Turnus' breast. And
the word which Virgil uses of this, Aeneas' final act – English 'sinks',
Latin *condit* – he had used twice in the opening thirty-three lines of
Book 1 of the founding of Rome itself: 'conderet urbem', 'found a city',
A. 1.5, 'condere gentem', 'found a race', *A.* 1.33. The sinking of Aeneas'
sword in Turnus' breast – *condit* – aetiologizes the founding of Rome
and realizes one of the epic's cardinal themes: history's unimpedable
cycle. The cyclic structure of Virgil's well-wrought text is not simply a
property of poetic form, but a function of the poet's vision of reality:
time future as repetition of time past. In the beginning is the end, in
the end the beginning – in both poetic *imago* and in *res*. Virgil's well-
wrought text images the Virgilian world.

THE *AENEID* AS PALIMPSESTIC TEXT: INTERTEXTUALITY AS CODE

Internal structure is not everything. What generates much of the
Aeneid's meaning and canonic force is the epic's relationship to and
rewriting of other texts, especially its allusions to and rewriting of
Homer. Livius Andronicus began his adaptation of Homer's *Odyssey*

with the word *virum*, translating Homer's opening word *andra*. Virgil's opening phrase, *arma virumque* (which became the title of his epic) rewrites both Homer and Livius to reveal an ambition to unite the *Iliad* and the *Odyssey* in a larger, all-encompassing work. But of course the *Aeneid* reverses the order of the Homeric epics. The *Odyssey* dealt with the more civilized, humane, moral world of Odysseus, whose values of intelligence, survival, home, family and justice replace the one-dimensional heroic ethos of the warriors of the *Iliad*. Virgil begins with his *Odyssey*, *Aeneid* 1–6, and not only narrates an individual's wanderings in search of a homeland, city and kingdom, but examines the humanity of that individual, his growth in perception, compassion and understanding as a result of his own experience. Aeneas enters the epic at *A.* 1.92ff. quoting Odysseus' words from *Odyssey* 5 (306f.) and reveals himself throughout Books 1–6 to be no archetypal empire-man but a more Odyssean than Iliadic figure: vulnerable, sensitive, reflective, uncertain of the future (e.g. *A.* 5.700ff.), possessing an immense potentiality for deep, personal involvement (Creusa, Dido, Anchises), responsive to individual suffering and loss (e.g. *A.* 1.220ff., 459ff., 3.709ff., 4.393ff., 5.869), and able to progress from Troy to Italy because at each crucial stage there are motives of a personal kind to drive him onwards.[29] The result of Aeneas' experiences is a growth in perception and a realization of the cost in human dissolution and suffering of fame's pursuit. The culmination of this intellectual and moral growth occurs in the underworld scene of Book 6, the most 'Odyssean' episode in the poem, where the poet not only alludes constantly to Homer's *Nekuia* of *Odyssey* 11 but follows Homer's example in using a *Nekuia* to achieve a confrontation between the hero and his past and to reveal the hero's values, especially that of compassion. But there the similarity ends. For Aeneas' response to the scenes of human misery, hopelessness and dissolution for which he and others have been responsible is not simply a display of compassion but a recognition of the hollowness of *fama*, 'fame', as a value, the inadequacy of the 'eternal name', *aeternum nomen* (*A.* 6.235, 381), as compensation for the human cost of its pursuit.[30] This perception of Aeneas is encapsulated in a brilliant rewriting of Homer. When Anchises asks his son to rejoice with him in the glorious roll-call of their descendants, souls due to be reincarnated as future Roman heroes, Aeneas inverts Achilles' retort to Odysseus in *Odyssey* 11 to express a profound sense of the pointlessness of human endeavour, the futility of human life:

> o pater, anne aliquas ad caelum hinc ire putandum est
> sublimis animas iterumque ad tarda reverti
> corpora? quae lucis miseris tam dira cupido?
> > (*Aeneid* 6.719–21)

O father, must it be thought some souls ascend from here
To the sky's vault and return once more to clogging
Bodies? What perverse lust for light grips the wretches?

In the *Odyssey* passage to which Aeneas' words allude, Achilles had proclaimed to Odysseus the supreme value of life and the incomprehensibility of anyone choosing to descend to the underworld: 'How could you endure to descend to Hades, where senseless corpses dwell, images of perished mortals?' (*Od.* 11.475f.). Aeneas' experiences have taught him differently. His view of earthly existence is one of unremitting anguish. Odysseus' sense of the value of the individual and humane pity have been developed in Aeneas into a rejection of the values of empire and a kind of existential despair. If this state of mind were to remain, the imperial mission would stop. Anchises then reveals the future to Aeneas and the socio-moral ideology of his mission. The stirring apocalypse of *Aeneid* 6.847ff. proves irresistible to Aeneas because it not only offers Aeneas a way of compensating for the human loss he has witnessed but translates to the public world the cardinal value of Aeneas' private world, compassion – in Anchises' apocalypse, 'mercy' ('parcere subiectis', 'to spare the humbled', *A.* 6.853). Anchises then inflames Aeneas with love of the value which more than anything the mission requires: *fama* (*A.* 6.889), the central value of Homer's *Iliad*. To remind the reader of what is being lost in terms of Aeneas' Odyssean consciousness and sensibility Virgil takes the reader again to Homer's *Odyssey* and has his hero depart from the underworld through that epic's gate of false dreams (*A.* 6.893ff.; cf. *Od.* 19.562ff.). The *Odyssey* was a poem about moral and emotional growth and the re-establishment of identity; the *Aeneid* is about to become a poem about moral and emotional degeneration and identity's loss. The poet now proclaims the commencement of his *Iliad* (*A.* 7.37ff.). The heroic ethos of Book 2, which Aeneas himself criticized and had grown beyond, is to return.

There is thus more than narrative point in Virgil's reversal of the order of Homer's poems. Virgil invites the reader to construe this reversal as part of his epic's discourse. The movement of Aeneas from 'private' to 'public' man, from personal motivation and responsibility to emblem of Roman history, ironically inverts the Homeric movement from an amoral, heroic ethos to a moral, civilized world. Intertextuality here functions as code. And part of this code is the epic's numerous allusions to the *Iliad*'s hero, Achilles. The shadow of Achilles dogs Aeneas throughout the journey to Italy. The Venus–Jupiter colloquy at *Aeneid* 1.223ff. (recalling Thetis' visit to Zeus on behalf of Achilles at *Iliad* 1.493ff.), the association with Achilles' son Pyrrhus in *Aeneid* 2 (379ff. and 471ff.) and 3 (469), the funeral games of *Aeneid* 5 (modelled on those held for Patroclus by Achilles in *Iliad* 23), the enigmatic prophecy of the birth of 'another Achilles', *alius Achilles*, by the Sibyl in *Aeneid* 6 (89f.), prepare the reader for Aeneas' *re*presentation of Achilles in Virgil's *Iliad*. Ironically Aeneas groans at the savagery of Achilles and the tragic suffering he had caused, depicted on the walls of Dido's temple at Carthage (*A.* 1.453ff.). But this does not prevent him from becoming *alius Achilles*. And when Virgil concludes Aeneas' 'Romanization' with the presentation of armour made by Vulcan, alluding to Achilles' armour in *Iliad* 18, Virgil initiates a whole series of signal analogies between the Greek and the Trojan warrior,[31] which reach their culmination in the duel of Book 12 and the final scene itself, in which Virgil rewrites Priam's comment on Achilles in *Iliad* 22 ('He too had such a father in Peleus', *Il.* 22.420f.) and insinuates it into Turnus' request for mercy ('fuit et tibi talis / Anchises genitor', 'You too had such a father in Anchises', *A.* 12.933f.). Constant allusions to Homer in the preceding duel had reinforced the analogy between Aeneas and Achilles and between Turnus and Hector.[32] Virgil here uses Homer to enrich the texture of his final scene, in which the conflation of Turnus with both Hector and Priam underscores not only Aeneas as the new Achilles but the very Achilles pictured on Dido's temple in Book 1 (*A.* 1.483ff.). The epic's final line recalls many things. But by echoing the line which Homer used to describe the death of Hector in *Iliad* 22 (22.952) it signals the return to the *Iliad*'s flesh-dissolving ethos without the reparation of *Iliad* 24. Virgil's *Iliad* ends at the nadir of Homer's epic.

The Homeric code is extensive. The above observations are illustrative only. And there are many other significant intertextual codes than the Homeric one. There are many allusions to Greek tragedy (either directly or in the Latin versions of Ennius, Pacuvius and Accius – Accius' plays especially were popular in the late republic), to Pisander (in *Aeneid* 2, according to Macrobius 5.2.4), to Apollonius Rhodius (from whom according to Servius 'the whole of Book 4 (*totus hic liber*) was translated'!),[33] to Naevius and Ennius (the focus on Carthage at the opening of the poem, *A.* 1.12ff., establishes the *Bellum Punicum* and the *Annales* as sub-texts, models and narrative sequels),[34] to Lucretius, to Catullus – to mention the more important – to the great prose-writers too, especially the historians Polybius, Diodorus Siculus, Livy,[35] making Virgil's own poetic text a palimpsest with many texts beneath it. There are also numerous allusions to Virgil's own texts, the *Eclogues* and the *Georgics*, which serve both to clarify the *Aeneid*'s own discourse and to map Virgil's intellectual movement. Dido's Carthage in *Aeneid* 1, for example, recalls the civic paradigm of *Georgic* 4 (cf. especially *A.* 1.421ff. and *G.* 4.162ff.), her court bard Iopas sings lines from *Georgic* 2 (475ff., cf. *A.* 1.742ff.) with reminiscences of *Eclogue* 6 (especially *E.* 6.64), while Dido herself evokes the Daphnis ideal of *Eclogue* 5 (*A.* 1.609 quotes

E. 5.78). Evander's Arcadia in *Aeneid* 8 (102ff.) recalls the pastoral vision of *Eclogue* 4; Saturnian Juno recalls and undermines throughout the whole epic the *Georgics'* Saturnian dream. The apparent eulogies of Augustus in the speeches of Jupiter in *Aeneid* 1 (286ff.) and Anchises in *Aeneid* 6 (789ff.) echo Virgil's own apparent eulogies of the same political figure in the politico-historical frame of his preceding work. Even the focus on Rome as *urbs* or 'city' in the Proem to the *Aeneid* (*A.* 1.5ff.) recalls a similar opening focus in Virgil's earliest text (*E.* 1.19ff.; cf. *E.* 9.1ff.). In each case either the ideals of earlier texts are recalled to be criticized and undermined, or the surface value-assumptions of the final text are juxtaposed with earlier criticism. Imagery too gains semantic force from intertextual allusion. The image of gold, for example, associated in the *Eclogues* and the *Georgics* with the ideal visions of those works, the golden age of *Eclogue* 4 ('gens aurea', *E.* 4.9) and the rural life of *Georgic* 2 ('aureus . . . Saturnus', *G.* 2.538), is associated right from the start of the *Aeneid* not with socio-moral visions but with death, suffering, failure and *furor* (see especially *A.* 1.349, 3.57, 6.32, 6.136ff.). Gold is first associated with political and social idealism in the *Aeneid* in the revelation scene itself, when Anchises jubilantly declares to his son:

> hic vir, hic est, tibi quem promitti saepius audis,
> Augustus Caesar, divi genus, aurea condet
> saecula qui rursus Latio regnata per arva
> Saturno quondam, super et Garamantas et Indos
> proferet imperium.
>
> (*Aeneid* 6.791–5)

> Here is the man, here, whom you hear often promised,
> Augustus Caesar, son of god, who will found again
> The golden ages in fields of Latium where Saturn
> Once ruled, and beyond Garamantian and Indian
> Extend his empire.

'Aurea condet / saecula': 'will found the golden ages'. *Condere* again: the ultimate *vir*'s reflection in history of Aeneas' final act in the text. Aeneas at this point seems unimpressed.[36] As the reader should be. Unlike the *Eclogues* and the *Georgics*, the *Aeneid* delays the association of gold with political and social idealism until its connections with the darker side of man's condition have been firmly established – connections that reflect upon and undermine both Anchises' exultation and the claims of Augustan ideology. This marked divergence from Virgil's earlier texts exposes the mendacious splendour of empire's promise and the naivety of the poet's earlier idealism. The intertextual code functions here as self-criticism and an index of intellectual change. The palimpsestic text becomes self-reflexive.

THE *AENEID* AS SELF-REFLEXIVE TEXT: ART AS THEME

Virgil's inter/intratextual strategies shaped epic writing to come. So too – and importantly, especially in the cases of Ovid and Lucan – did his structuring of the poetic text to reflect upon itself. A central device, which he took from Catullus' *Peleus and Thetis*, from Hellenistic poetry and from Homer,[37] is the use of ecphrasis, the extended description of a work of art. Virgil had employed this device in both the *Eclogues* (especially 3.35ff.) and *Georgics* (especially 3.26ff.), where he had begun to transform it into an instrument of poetic self-reflexion. The *Aeneid* contains three major ecphrases: the description of the frescoes on Dido's temple in *Aeneid* 1 (453ff.); the account of the temple doors engraved by Daedalus in *Aeneid* 6 (20ff.); and the description of the great shield made by Vulcan in *Aeneid* 8 (626ff.).

In Book 1 on arriving at Carthage Aeneas encounters a temple built by Dido on the walls of which he views a series of frescoes depicting the Trojan war. The frescoes are emphasized at the outset as the product of artistic skill and toil:

> namque sub ingenti lustrat dum singula templo
> reginam opperiens, dum quae fortuna sit urbi
> artificumque manus inter se operumque laborem
> miratur, videt Iliacas ex ordine pugnas
> bellaque iam fama totum vulgata per orbem,
> Atridas Priamumque et saevum ambobus Achillem.
> constitit et lacrimans 'quis iam locus', inquit, 'Achate,
> quae regio in terris nostri non plena laboris?
> en Priamus. sunt hic etiam sua praemia laudi,
> sunt lacrimae rerum et mentem mortalia tangunt.
> solve metus; feret haec aliquam tibi fama salutem.'
> sic ait atque animum pictura pascit inani
> multa gemens, largoque umectat flumine vultum.
>
> (*Aeneid* 1.453–65)

> As Aeneas views each detail beneath the vast temple
> Waiting for the queen, as he marvels at the city's
> Fortune, the rival craftsmen's work and the product
> Of their toil, he sees Ilium's battles set out in order
> And wars whose fame had spread now through all the world,
> The Atridae and Priam, and Achilles savage to both.
> He stopped and, weeping, said: 'What place now, Achates,
> What district on earth is not filled with our suffering?
> Look! Priam! Even here are due rewards for worth;
> There are tears for things and mortality touches the
>   heart.

Away with fear; this fame will bring you some safety.'
So he speaks and feeds his soul on an empty picture
Heavily sighing, his face wet with a river's flood.

Aeneas sees in the frescoes both *fama*, 'fame', and 'tears', *lacrimae rerum*, 'tears of/in/for things'.[38] But in the ensuing description of the frescoes at *Aeneid* 1.466ff., which we see through Aeneas' eyes ('namque videbat uti . . .', 'for he saw how . . .', *A.* 1.466), the emphasis is on tears, futility, loss, on the 'reality', *res*, of the suffering of the individual in history. There is no reference to *fama*. The fresco scene in fact raises the issue of the relationship between fame and its cost, between fame, reality and tears, and then presents the reader with the reality and the tears, *lacrimae rerum*. What the poetic text suggests is the hollowness of fame as a value.

Aeneas himself responds to the frescoes with tears (*A.* 1.459, 465, 470, 485), and his immediate behaviour accords with the values they embody. From here in Book 1 to the mid-point of Book 4 Aeneas effectively gives up the mission, forsakes the pursuit of fame,[39] and opts for Dido and love (*AMOR*, the literal inversion of *ROMA*). But the frescoes are to return. And when Aeneas resumes the mission, moves in Book 6 from the *lacrimae* of the opening lines ('sic fatur lacrimans', 'So speaks Aeneas weeping', *A.* 6.1) to the *fama*-directed passion of its close (*A.* 6.889), and resurrects the Trojan war in Italy, the *imago* of the frescoes becomes the *res* of Roman history. The scenes which Aeneas laments in Dido's temple in *Aeneid* 1 are re-enacted in the battle-books of *Aeneid* 9–12, where Aeneas becomes the very Achilles whose savagery he had condemned. When the text describes Aeneas' response to the frescoes at *Aeneid* 1.464 as 'feeding his soul on an empty picture' ('pictura pascit inani'), i.e. on a picture that fails to nourish, it foreshadows both the ending of the *Aeneid* and the failure of the Carthaginians' creative toil. The artefact on Dido's temple – in the end – changes nothing.

Related points may be made about the artefacts of Books 6 and 8.[40] In Book 6, when confronting the doors carved by Daedalus with their record of death, suffering and sacrifice, especially the sacrifice of the young (*A.* 6.20ff.), Aeneas responds forcefully to their statement of pain and loss, as his immediate behaviour in the underworld shows, but does so only eventually to forget that statement and reproduce in his own imperial quest a further sacrifice of the young. The mendacious gleam of empire's promise triumphs over Aeneas' perception of the suffering of the individual in history. Indeed in Book 8, faced with the shield's ideological picturing of Roman history – with which his experiences neither in the underworld nor at Troy and Carthage accorded – Aeneas ignores the gap between imperial image and Roman, historical reality and 'ignorant of things rejoices in the image' ('rerumque ignarus imagine gaudet', *A.* 8.730). Underscoring the movement of Book 6 from *lacrimae* to *fama* as a movement from knowledge to delusion, Aeneas now embraces the 'fame and fate/death',[41] *fama* and *fata* of his descendants (*A.* 8.731).

From the *Aeneid*'s three great works of art Aeneas learns nothing – at least nothing that lasts. Neither the imbalance between fame and its cost in the Dido frescoes nor the record of human suffering and sacrifice in the Daedalus reliefs, to both of which he responds most fully, in the end affect his behaviour in history. Even the transparent gap between imperial image and historical *res*, which he could have seen in respect of the great shield and to which the shield itself seems subtly to point, passes unseen; as with Anchises' apocalypse, only a false *imago* impresses (in both cases Aeneas 'marvels': 'miratur', *A.* 8.730, 'mirantibus', *A.* 6.854). As a group these three entexted artefacts, products of *ars* and *labor*, seem designed to reflect on the artefact which entexts them, the *Aeneid*, constituting a poetic self-critique, in which the epicist locates his scepticism, if not pessimism, about the power of his own artefact to affect the Roman world. They signal Virgil's awareness of his didactic impotence.

They signal too the kind of *imago* the *Aeneid* is. It is not accidental that both Dido's frescoes and the great shield are emphasized as commissioned works – and antithetical ones: Dido's frescoes focus on *lacrimae* as against *fama*; the shield, commissioned by the imperial ancestress Venus, on *fama* as against *lacrimae*. By setting up two antithetical models of the commissioned work, the text invites a comparison between them and its own so-called 'commissioned' status. The comparison intrigues. For while in a sense commissioned like the Vulcan shield for transparently partisan purposes, the *Aeneid*'s rendering of human history, *res gestae*, makes it closer to the frescoes of Book 1. For the compassion shown in the frescoes' treatment of the Trojan war and their displayed criticism of heroism and heroic values are evidenced in the *Aeneid*'s own account of the fall of Troy in Book 2 and (most tellingly) in the battle-books of 9–12, when the Trojan war is resurrected as Aeneas' war in Italy and the Trojan hero becomes Achilles reborn. On the other hand, the shield's ideological rhetoric seems undermined by the events of the narrative and in a way which draws attention to the gap between the *Aeneid* and the shield as instances of the commissioned work. The ending of Book 8 is again important here. When Aeneas rejoices in the false image of the shield and shoulders his descendants' fame-and-death-bringing future, not only does he accept the values which the frescoes, his own experiences and the *Aeneid*'s narrative have shown to be hollow, but he accepts them in a way designed to recall the dehumanized Achilles of *Iliad* 18, just prior to his brutal and murderous re-entry into battle. Homeric allusion here ironically confirms not Aeneas as renascent man, but the hero's increasing proximity – as against the rhetoric of the shield – to the very paradigm of brutality which in Dido's temple he had deplored. The end of *Aeneid* 8 reminds the reader not only that the frescoes have been forgotten, but that the tragedy there depicted is about to be repeated. The battle-books of the *Aeneid* are Dido's frescoes writ large.

Daedalus' artefact, however, was not commissioned. It was the product of the artist's grief, and like the *Aeneid* was unfinished.

> tu quoque magnam
> partem opere in tanto, sineret dolor, Icare, haberes.
> bis conatus erat casus effingere in auro,
> bis patriae cecidere manus.
>
> (*Aeneid* 6.30–3)

> You too would have a large
> Place in the great work, if grief allowed, Icarus.
> Twice he had tried to fashion the fall in gold;
> Twice a father's hands failed.

Daedalus was the paradigm maker and artist.[42] Several things seem suggested about the *Aeneid* by this central ecphrasis. Particularly striking is its focus on the artist's failure to represent fully – and thereby compensate for – the pain of human loss. Also important is the emphasis given in this ecphrasis to the artist's own experience, his suffering, grief, *dolor*, and their relationship to the created work. For the Daedalus reliefs are a kind of autobiography, a record of the loss and suffering which Daedalus had witnessed and attempted to alleviate, and of the pain, *dolor*, of the artist himself. The text seems to be denying that it is itself simply a public, 'commissioned' work, but one profoundly personal, product of the poet's experience and *dolor* – and one which can never fully represent, far less compensate for, the suffering of the individual in history. Artistic representation, as Aeneas saw in Book 1, is itself a form of *fama*; and *fama* atones for nothing.

Ecphrasis is not the only instrument of self-reflexion employed in the *Aeneid*. As adumbrated above, thematic and verbal allusion to Virgil's earlier works often functions as self-critique. The issue of poetry's or art's ability to affect the political and historical worlds was one that preoccupied Virgil in the *Eclogues* and the *Georgics* too, and the marked development of Virgil's position from scepticism (*Eclogues*) through ambivalence (*Georgics*) into certainty and pessimism (*Aeneid*)[43] renders the *Aeneid*'s treatment of this issue in part criticism of earlier naivety. At issue here is a view of human reality, *res*, exemplified most clearly in the *Aeneid* by its final scene, where Aeneas, overwhelmed with *dolor* on Pallas' behalf, rejects the appeal to compassion and *pietas* which Turnus makes and ends the poem in a crazed and bloody act of self-deceived *furor*. Readers cognisant of the endings of both previous Virgilian texts would appreciate fully the significance of the *Aeneid*'s final scene as critical self-reference. For though both the *Eclogues* and the *Georgics* focus in their concluding lines on the subservience to *furor* and its vitiation of human aspiration and toil (*E.* 10.64ff., *G.* 4.485ff.), they follow and qualify those lines with complex, ambivalent epilogues in which there seems, even in the *Eclogues*, the fragment of a hope. No such qualifying passage follows Aeneas' slaying of Turnus, which stops Virgil's epic in its narrative tracks. Self-reference functions as index of intellectual change, even as it underscores the universality of the thesis embodied in the text. Functions too as self-conscious index of poetic impotence.

> hoc dicens ferrum adverso sub pectore condit
> fervidus; ast illi solvuntur frigore membra
> vitaque cum gemitu fugit indignata sub umbras.
>
> (*Aeneid* 12.950–2)

> As he speaks he sinks steel in the facing breast
> Burning. The other's limbs go limp with cold.
> With a groan protesting life flees to the shadows.

Umbras, 'darkness' or 'shadows', is the final word of Virgil's final text; its occurrence echoes not only the identical description of the death of Camilla at *Aeneid* 11.831, but more significantly its triple use to mark the closure of Virgil's first text, the *Eclogues*:

> surgamus: solet esse gravis cantantibus *umbra*,
> iuniperi gravis *umbra*; nocent et frugibus *umbrae*.
> ite domum saturae, venit Hesperus, ite capellae.
>
> (*Eclogues* 10.75–7)

> Let us rise: *shade* is oppressive to singers;
> Juniper's *shade* oppresses; crops too are stunted by *shadows*.
> Homeward, little goats, full-fed – Hesperus comes – homeward.

The forces of darkness, *umbrae*, that almost triumph in the *Eclogues*, triumph in the *Aeneid*; so too what the earlier text presents as the echoic Muse, poetry which simply reflects itself, didactically impotent, only an internal echo of the poet's fictive world.[44] The *Aeneid*'s climactic echoes of both the beginning of itself (see p. 94 above) and the ending of Virgil's earliest text confirm the epic's and the *oeuvre*'s status as echoic Muse, signalling the closed internal system of Virgil's poetic world, the impenetrable walls separating the world of text and the world of history. Self-reflexion becomes established not only as a prime epic mode, but as potential index of the gap between word and world.

Such are six central aspects of the Virgilian transformation of Roman epic. The poet died in 19 BCE leaving his epic 'unfinished'. Had the instructions contained in his will been carried out, Roman epic, indeed Roman literature both prose and verse, would have evolved quite differently. Ovid's experimentations, Lucan's dismemberment of the genre and its Flavian reconstitution only make sense as creative responses to Virgil, whose profound reformulation of the ground-rules for epic verse influenced everything that followed.[45] The self-reflexive *Metamorphoses* and *Bellum Civile* (or *Pharsalia*), the palimpsestic, morally incisive *Thebaid*, the mytho-symbolic *Argonautica*, the intertextually fertile *Punica*, the iconic *De Raptu Proserpinae* – all well-wrought texts – acknowledge the canonic nature of Virgil's epic of Rome.

NOTES

For more detailed argument in respect of the main interpretative theses of this essay, see Boyle 1986: 85–176. Three recent studies (Hardie 1986, Cairns 1989, Feeney 1991) have adopted a neo-traditionalist approach, resurrecting with modifications and development the pro-Augustan interpretation of Otis 1964 and others. There is much to learn from each of these books, but their general position – exemplified in the claim (Feeney 1991:137) that 'an ideal synthesis of the natural order and of Rome's historical order is something which the poem strives to establish as attainable' – seems to me incapable of being sustained. Only a fraction of the many excellent critical books and essays that have appeared in the last thirty years can be cited in these notes. Several of those cited contain useful bibliographies, particularly of more recent work.

1 The translations in this essay are my own.
2 Not without irony; see Sullivan in chapter VIII below, pp. 147ff.
3 The ancient life of Virgil (*Vita Vergilii Donati* 45) even mentions a collection of eight volumes of these made by Quintus Octavius Avitus.
4 That Rome's early epicists – Livius, Naevius and Ennius – were politically more independent than traditionally thought is well argued by Goldberg 1989. On the Graeco-Roman epic tradition and the problems it posed for Virgil see Otis 1964: 5–40.
5 It should be observed at the outset that the aspects of the *Aeneid* examined here as contributing to its canonic or 'classic' status differ markedly from those advanced by Eliot in his 1944 address to the English Virgilian Society. Eliot's concluding affirmation, however, that 'Our classic, the classic of all Europe, is Virgil' (Eliot 1944: 70), is of course one with which this chapter concurs.
6 *G.* 3.9, 'victorque virum volitare per ora' ('fly victorious across the lips of men') echoes Ennius' famous self-epitaph, 'volito vivus per ora virum' ('alive I fly across the lips of men', quoted in Cic., *Tusc.* 1.34). The Georgic poet's chariot is indebted to Pindar's chariot of song (*O.* 6.22ff., 9.81; *P.* 10.65; *N.* 1.7; *I.* 2.1f., 5.38, 8.61) and his poetic temple to Pindar's visualization of poetry in terms of architecture and sculpture: *O.* 6.1ff.; *P.* 6.5ff., 3.113, 4.81; *N.* 1.8. See Wilkinson 1970.
7 For the complexity of this presentation of Juno see Feeney 1991: 116–17,

130–4, who, however, misses the programmatic association of Juno with *furor*, essential to the poem's ideological system.

8 This contribution is particularly forceful in the final book of the epic, in which the presentation of deities associated with the losing Italians (Juturna and Faunus) contrasts sharply with that of the triumphing Olympians (Venus, Jupiter and – finally and paradoxically – Juno) aligned with history and with Rome. See Boyle 1986: 103–6.

9 *Romane*, 'Roman', figures emblematically in various formal contexts, especially in oracles as at Livy 5.16.9, Ovid, *Met.* 15.637 and *Fasti* 4.259 cited by Austin 1977 *ad loc.* The context of the father–son address and the personalized *tu* make the *A.* 6.851 use both personal and emblematic.

10 Cf. especially *A.* 8.680f. with *A.* 8.620, 10.261 and 10.270f.

11 In Newman's terminology a 'vatic' text. See Newman 1986: 158, 'We do not understand the *Aeneid* unless we see that it is in the first instance a *vatic* epic.'

12 On this analogy between Aeneas and Achilles, which is not restricted to the battle-books of the *Aeneid* (9–12), see pp. 96f. below and Boyle 1986: 154–6.

13 The final scene of the *Aeneid* has been much discussed. For excellent analysis see Putnam 1966: 200f., Quinn 1968: 271–6 and Anderson 1969: 101–9. Anderson's view, however, that Aeneas' conduct is a momentary aberration seems to ignore Aeneas' similar conduct earlier, especially in the Pallas vendetta of Book 10. On this scene see further below, pp. 93f., 102f.

14 On Virgil's narrative style see the excellent comments in Quinn 1968: 72ff., 355ff., to which this section is indebted.

15 The historic present, used by Livius, Naevius and Ennius, is not used by Greek epic writers. It is, however, not a little absurd to claim that it 'may stand as the Latin contribution to poetic narrative style' (Hainsworth 1991: 82).

16 See Quinn 1968: 161.

17 The term belongs to Otis 1964: 41ff., where the footrace of Book 5 and other passages are analysed with perception and precision.

18 E.g. Quinn 1968: 74–6, whose comments instruct my own.

19 For illuminating comments on this scene see Quinn 1968: 330–2, Johnson 1976: 148f.

20 On structural schemes in the *Aeneid* see especially Otis 1964: 217ff.; Quinn 1968: 64ff., 98ff. Duckworth 1962 *passim*, though not always persuasive, may also be consulted with profit.

21 Possibly Ennius preceded Lucretius in this, but the evidence is too fragmentary for conclusions to be drawn.

22 This division is promoted by Virgil, whose 'second Preface' (*A.* 7.37ff.) announces the commencement of his *Iliad*, his *maius opus* ('greater work'). The division is reflected in the titles of Otis' (1964) two main chapters on the *Aeneid*: 'The Odyssean *Aeneid*' and 'The Iliadic *Aeneid*'.

23 Especially important here is the way Book 12 brings to final realization the text's presentation of Aeneas' war in Italy as a repetition of the Trojan war itself – only this time Aeneas is Achilles. In addition to the detailed modelling of the duel between Aeneas and Turnus on that between Achilles and Hector in Homer's *Iliad* (cf. *A.* 12.725–7, 749–55, 760–2, 764f., 786f., 908–12, 952 and *Iliad* 22.208–13, 188–93, 205–7, 159–61, 276f., 199–201, 362f. respectively), notice the analogy between Aeneas' assault upon Latinus' city at *A.* 12.554ff. and Pyrrhus' attack upon Priam's palace at *A.* 2.469ff. (reinforced by verbal echoes: cf. *A.* 2.479, 494, and *A.* 12.579, 577).

24 See Quinn 1968: 342f. Book 10 in fact anticipates its own narrative structure by emphasizing the parallel destinies awaiting Pallas and Lausus, when they meet at *A* 10.433–6.

25 On the structure of Virgil's *Eclogues* see Rudd 1976: 119ff.; Boyle 1976: 10ff.

26 Excellent works on the *Aeneid*'s imagery include: Pöschl 1950, Knox 1950, Brooks 1953, Putnam 1966, Segal 1965–6, Hornsby 1970 and Northrup 1978. For further discussion of the issues raised here see Boyle 1986: 124–32.

27 For association with Dido's passion: *A.* 4.1f., 23, 54, 63–73, 101, 160–8, etc.; with Aeneas' exploits: *A.* 2.302–17, 379–81, 575ff., 679ff., 10.260–75, 565–70, 602–4, 12.451ff., 521ff., 573ff., 720, etc.

28 The word has significant intratextual resonance: Creusa, Dido, Palinurus, Misenus, Nisus, Euryalus, Pallas, Lausus, Camilla, Amata and Turnus are all in a clear sense 'sacrifices'. In particular *immolat* recalls Aeneas' Pallas-vendetta of Book 10, the only other context in the *Aeneid* where the word appears (*A.* 10.519, 541).

29 Aeneas leaves Troy in order to save his family (see especially *A.* 2.559–63, 596–8, 635–6); he leaves Carthage primarily to fulfil his personal obligations to Anchises and Ascanius (*A.* 4.272–6, 351–5); he leaves Sicily again in order to fulfil his personal obligation to Anchises, but also that he may meet him once more (*A.* 5.722ff.).

30 On the *aeternum nomen* and its value as compensation for individual dissolution see especially the twin articles of Segal 1965–6.

31 For details see Boyle 1986: especially 155f.

32 Cf. *A.* 12.725–7, 749–55, 760–2, 764f., 786f., 899f., 908–12, and *Il.* 22.208–13, 188–93, 205–7, 159–61, 276f., 12.445–50, 22.199–201.

33 Servius on *A.* 4.1. Macrobius is less sweeping: 'Almost the whole (*totum paene*) of *Aeneid* 4' (5.17.4) was taken from Apollonius.

34 Indeed it should be noted that the important colloquy between Venus and Jupiter at *A.*1.223–96 is a rewriting not only of Homer as noted above, but also of Naevius (frr. 14–16; see Macrobius, *Sat.* 6.2.31), who may have been the first to extend epic prophecy to include events in the poet's own world. See Feeney 1991: 109–13.

35 One important allusion deserves mention. Part of the irony of Aeneas' account of the fall of Troy to the Carthaginians in Book 2 lies in the use – by historians from Polybius onwards (Polybius 38.22, Diodorus Siculus 32.23ff.; cf. later Appian, *Pun.* 132) – of the Greek destruction of Troy as a historical (and rhetorical) analogue for Rome's razing of the city of Carthage in 146 BCE.

36 Notice his silence when Anchises tries to elicit a response at the end of the Augustus segment (*A.* 6.806f.).

37 See especially Theocritus 1.29ff., Apollonius Rhodius 1.721ff. and *Iliad* 18.478ff.

38 *Lacrimae rerum* is a typical example of Virgilian polyvalence achieved through syntactic ambiguity. *Rerum* may be taken as both objective genitive 'for things' or subjective, possessive genitive 'of, i.e. belonging to, things': there are tears for the world and the world has tears built within its structure.

39 As Mercury observes in his (successful) attempt to return Aeneas to the mission in Book 4 (272): 'If you are not stirred by the glory of these great things (*gloria rerum*) . . .'.

40 For more detailed discussion of these artefacts see Boyle 1986: 136ff., 172ff.

41 *Fatum* may mean either 'fate' or 'death'. Poets like Virgil (and Lucan and Valerius after him) knew how and when to exploit this potential ambivalence.

42 'The most celebrated genius of the creative arts', to translate Ovid, *Met.* 8.159: 'Daedalus ingenio fabrae celeberrimus artis'.

43 This development is the central thesis of Boyle 1986.

44 On this see Boyle 1977.

45 See now Hardie 1993.

VI

FORM CHANGED: OVID'S *METAMORPHOSES*

William S. Anderson

The title of Ovid's great poem, which we conventionally give in its Greek form, was not impossible, but quite difficult for the poet to fit into the hexameter, and he always referred to it in Latin, which allowed him to break up the long word into two shorter words that he could separate and fit conveniently to the metrical rhythm or even to identify the poem by a short epitome of its contents. At the opening of the *Metamorphoses*, then, Ovid announces his Latin title and provokes his audience into some curious questions about the kind of poem he has chosen to create:

> in nova fert animus mutatas dicere formas
> corpora: di, coeptis (nam vos mutastis et illa)
> adspirate meis primaque ab origine mundi
> ad mea perpetuum deducite tempora carmen.
> (M. 1.1–4)

My spirit impels me to speak of forms changed into new bodies. Gods, breathe favourably on these beginnings of mine (for you have changed them also) and from the first creation of the universe draw out a continuous poem down to my times.

The Latin title, like the Greek, uses the plural: the poet intends to deal with many occasions of form changed. And he goes on to amplify his purpose, referring to the new bodies into which the original forms are altered. It remains to be seen how Ovid will actually engage this topic, to what extent he will focus on the forms incurring change and to what extent on the new bodies that result, and that is a first question for the audience's curiosity. A second question arises from the teasing provocation of the second word *nova* (which seems to announce poetic innovation) and from the parenthetical remark to the gods in line 2: what are the changes to the poetic form that Ovid wishes us to notice and think about, and how fundamental and continuous are they in this 'continuous poem'?

Let me explain more fully how Ovid teases us in the opening two lines. When we first read or hear *nova* ('new'), we do not realize that it goes as an adjective with *corpora* ('bodies') in line 2, and so we start by translating the first four words as a sense-unit: 'My spirit takes me into new things.' Hardly have we finished correcting ourselves, than Ovid plunges us and himself into the parenthesis which for perhaps fifteen hundred years has been misunderstood. All our manuscripts, which go back to sources no later than the fifth or sixth century, give the reading *illas* for the final word of 2, which means that the scribes understood the pronoun 'them' to refer to the forms of line 1, not the beginnings. So for centuries it was assumed that the parenthesis rather ineptly gave the gods credit for causing metamorphoses. However, Kenney (1976) and Kovacs (1987) show that the correct reading is neuter plural *illa*, to refer by the pronoun to *coeptis* ('beginnings'). That explains why Ovid placed his qualifying remark where he did: he asks the gods' favour on his poem as it starts, because the gods have often exerted their power to change a poem at the outset, and it might even be felt that they have altered this very poem. When Ovid embarks on this parenthesis, he has written in line 1 a normal hexameter (constructed in two sections with a caesura after *animus*), and in line 2 he has brought us to the middle, where he again places his caesura. The parenthesis completes the hexameter. For a first-time audience of the poem, however, this would be a unique moment. Never before had they experienced a poem by Ovid which consisted of continuous hexameters: he was the greatest master of the elegiac metre alive in Rome, and he had been unchallenged for fifteen or twenty years, since Propertius stopped writing verse. What Ovid in fact made a caesura would normally, in his elegiac couplets, have functioned as the break between the halves of the *pentameter*. Thus, as the admiring audience start to sit back to another elegant Ovidian performance in elegiacs, they suddenly hear a metrical conclusion to the line, emphasized by the many long syllables of the spondees, which transforms their expectations and the poetic form from elegiacs into hexameters. And that meant that, incredibly or at least paradoxically, the world's most successful elegiac poet was suddenly an epic poet. Could he, with the help of the gods, really carry through this transformation, no matter what it demanded of him? Or might his approving audience have put the question in a more benevolent fashion, such as: Could Ovid's innovative genius work as creatively and delightfully with the conventions of epic as it had worked in mastering the elegiac form? What kind of epic has he achieved?

This essay deals with the two related questions or problems that Ovid raises by his enterprise, implies by his introductory lines, and has forced on my ambivalent title: (1) What does this poem on the subject of changed forms discover that is new, significant, entertaining, and capable of challenging Virgil's *Aeneid?* (2) How far does Ovid the elegiac poet change, as he composes this poem, and how far does he change the epic form in which he has chosen to work? Because I believe that the poem is more important than the form in which it is composed, I shall start with issues of generic form and thus gradually approach the principal problems and marvellous successes of the *Metamorphoses* itself.

TENSION BETWEEN ELEGY AND EPIC

When one pauses to think how slight the difference is between a pair of hexameter lines and an elegiac couplet, especially when both sets have been created by Ovid, it might seem astounding how much scholars have argued over the essential nature of the *Metamorphoses* and how the poem, if it is epic, differs from previous and contemporary elegiac verse of Ovid and from the previous and contemporary epic, particularly that of Virgil. Clearly, to generations of scholars, this change of form has been far more than a matter of versification. To scholars, but not so much to poets, generic form is a decisive critical tool; we might even describe it as a critical 'crutch'. It enables us non-poets to put poets and their verse in the proper pigeon hole, trap them in the test tube and under the microscope, where we can have our scientific way with them.

The most influential of such scientific investigations of the distinction between the two Ovids and their generic styles was that of Richard Heinze some seventy years ago. He ingeniously chose several pairs of Ovidian accounts, in elegiacs and hexameters, on the same subject and argued that there were consistent differences in each pair that must be attributed to the essential generic conventions of elegy and epic.[1] Heinze was really more interested in clarifying the nature of elegiac narrative than in promoting the interpretation of the *Metamorphoses*, but the methodology that he had devised was quickly exploited by the students of Ovidian hexameter to investigate more fully the special nature of Ovid's epic narrative. As if choosing to write in continuous hexameters meant a radical change of generic form, scholars hammered out and on to the *Metamorphoses* a series of definitive features that made it 'epic' (serious, moral, expansive, grand, etc.), decisively distinct from the frivolous and jerky qualities of elegy. That has proved to be a great disservice to Ovid's hexameter masterpiece. The methodology was faulty from the beginning in trying to impose a generic label on the observable differences between the two narrative styles of Ovid (which in fact Heinze much exaggerated while minimizing and ignoring the obvious similarities). More than a decade earlier, Benedetto Croce had defined that error in his discussion of what he named the Generic Fallacy (1902).

Moreover, any serious reflection on the practice of other Latin poets during the late first century would have indicated that all the poets were mingling the genres and consciously creating rich mixtures by rejecting the hard, fixed distinctions which nineteenth- and twentieth-century scholars then insisted on requiring long after the event. The invention of the genre called the 'epyllion' does almost nothing to improve our understanding of Catullus 64, but it comforts critics who need a category. Catullus was mixing modes, in anticipation of Ovid. Horace constantly mixed his modes and effects: did he create the genre of Roman satire or rather so change the Lucilian form that his product became unique? Are his *Odes* recognizable in terms of traditional lyric poetry, or are they a unique and inimitable generic mix, a rich complex of Aeolic or Lesbian lyric, Anacreon and Pindar and Simonides, Hellenistic epigram, and Roman moralism? Did not Ovid's admired 'teacher' Propertius radically stretch the range of elegy in his Book 4 (and pave the way for Ovid's own elegiac experimentation in the *Heroides*, the *Art of Love* and the *Fasti*)? And finally, what about Virgil and his 'canonic text'? Did he not succumb to innumerable non-epic Hellenistic features and, by his masterful employment of them, make his *Aeneid* that ambivalent poem and canonic problem that it remains even today?

In 1966, almost a half-century after Heinze, Brooks Otis published his study of the *Metamorphoses* and proclaimed his intention to deal with the generic problem once again by his title, *Ovid as an Epic Poet*. Although his instincts kept telling him that the best parts of Ovid's poem turn out to be what he considered 'non-epic' or epic parody, nevertheless Otis could not break free from Heinze's barren methodology and the Generic Fallacy. He had to see that Ovid was trying to write an Augustan epic, after the model of Virgil's *Aeneid*, and thus that Ovid failed disastrously in his goal. 'It seems clear that there was in fact a conflict between his heart and his head, between the epic he really wanted to write and the epic he felt he ought to write. And this conflict was obviously a quite fundamental one.'[2] The book and its thesis have had a special history in Ovidian studies. The book aroused so much controversy and sold out so fast that Cambridge University Press encouraged Otis to bring out a second edition and answer his critics in some detail. This new edition offers a second Preface and a completely changed Conclusion, but leaves totally unchanged the original eight chapters constituting the heart of the study. Warned by the new Preface, the reader can deal with the obvious inconsistencies that result and then let Otis explain them in his new Conclusion. But in a way Otis' study turns out to be a document of the conflict between his own head and heart rather than of Ovidian inconsistency. 'I posited two "Ovids" – an Augustan and a comic-amatory Ovid so to speak – who continually got into each other's way. In fact I even stated (preface to the first edition, see p. xiii) that the Augustan Ovid prevented the comic-erotic Ovid from realizing his full purpose and in fact condemned him to a good deal of inferior poetry, to "fustian and bathos". This is a view that I now completely repudiate.'[3] Even in this repudiation, Otis clamped down on the generic labels that earlier he had too freely employed; earlier, he would confidently have claimed that the purposes of Augustan epic had crippled further development of the anti-epic and elegiac successes of the first eleven books of the poem.

Although Otis bravely recanted some main points of his analysis of Ovid, particularly on the postulation of two 'Ovids' at odds with each other in the same way that elegy and epic are opposed, he could not entirely overhaul his interpretation or abandon the methodology of Heinze. But others have dealt more directly with this generic fallacy in the years since. Little has mounted a severe attack on Heinze (1970). Two studies of the mid-1980s have taken us further. Hinds has attempted to rescue some of Heinze's ideas and then put the distinction between elegy and epic not to classify the whole Ovidian enterprise, but to suggest the way Ovid plays with programmatic announcements in particular passages (1987). Knox, on the other hand, has reversed the bias of Otis and argued forcefully that Ovid remains committed to Hellenistic poetic interests and to his own elegiac experience in his hexameter poem: 'Ovid's distinctive achievement in the *Metamorphoses* is that he draws on the entire range of Roman poetry composed in the Alexandrian tradition, including also, of course, the epyllion.'[4]

What I have said so far suggests that it is more damaging than helpful to approach Ovid's poem with the expectation of finding an epic. Expecting and insisting on epic, critics have missed or protested against the many elegiac (and other generic) elements that Ovid has consciously and flagrantly employed to enrich his poem. We might obviate the difficulty by calling it a work that embraces the entire poetic tradition at work in Rome, regardless of genre; or we might avoid the generic label and merely describe it as a hexameter poem – remembering that Roman poets wrote didactic and satire as well as epic in that metrical medium. However, I propose to leave the general category unspecified and, looking at particular passages, to turn rather to consideration of the way Ovid used the 'canonic text' of Virgil's special epic in his *Metamorphoses.* By that devious method, I shall eventually make my transition to discussion of the poem itself in my second section.

Ovid was in Rome in the early 20s and presumably shared the interest of the literate public in the promised *Aeneid*, which was published after Virgil's death around the time Augustus was celebrating the Secular Games in 17 BCE. If *Amores* 1.15 belongs with the original poems of the

first edition, then it shows Ovid openly recognizing the total achievement of Virgil and aiming to vie with its immortality:

> Tityrus et fruges Aeneiaque arma legentur,
>   Roma triumphati dum caput orbis erit.
>
> (*Am.* 1.15.25–6)

> Tityrus and crops and the arms of Aeneas will be read,
>   as long as Rome is the head of the conquered world.

In 'the arms of Aeneas', Ovid refers unmistakably to the opening of the
Aeneid, arma virumque (just as Tityrus refers to the opening of the first
Eclogue). Ovid's first sustained challenge of Virgil's epic was in *Heroides*
7, where he viewed Dido as a disappointed and suicidal lover in the
elegiac mode, in contrast to the grand style, a combination of epic and
tragic techniques, with which Virgil had presented her disaster. Virgil
allows her a tragic soliloquy before she stabs herself with Aeneas' sword;
Ovid has her write a letter to Aeneas, in which she consciously and
unconsciously deploys histrionic methods in order to persuade him
(and us) of her pathetic condition.[5] He brings down Virgil's proud
queen and makes her appealingly human. Humanization of epic
seriousness and rigidity is but one of the purposes the poet has for the
Aeneid in the vast scope of the *Metamorphoses*.

The obvious place to consider the relationship between the two Latin
poets and their poems is the section of *M.* 13 and 14, where Ovid uses
the experiences of Aeneas from the fall of Troy until his defeat of
Turnus to structure his own narrative. It is evident to all readers that
Ovid refers to the *Aeneid* and expects his audience to use this connection in its interpretation. Galinsky devotes a chapter to this subject
(1975: 217ff.). In his more recent study, Solodow examines Books 13
and 14, but he also compares in detail episodes of the two poems for
style and narratological techniques, and he does not limit himself to
those two books which are often summarized as 'Ovid's *Aeneid*'.[6]
Arguing that Ovid turns away from heroic and grand characters and
sets out to humanize the heroes he inherits from previous literature,
Solodow rejects the view that Ovid criticizes or parodies Virgil's epic
directly. 'Instead Ovid's poem is the representation of an alternate
view' (154). He goes on: 'Truths are multiple, not single. Ovid objects
to literature which assumes an exclusive point of view. More narrowly,
the *Metamorphoses* challenges the possibility of epic' (155). Despite this
provocative last sentence, however, Solodow does not try to prove that
epic was *impossible*: since the *Aeneid* did exist and was obviously the most
impressive Latin poem ever written, there could be no question about
its *possibility*. What he means and what he believes Ovid targets is the
validity of the epic vision, of the concept of heroic patriotism that Virgil

presents. An alternative view may raise questions about a rival view-point; it does not need to deny the very *possibility* of the other.

I wish to start with a passage that obviously relies on an intertextual connection with the *Aeneid*, whose 'alternate view', however, can hardly be shared by Ovid or his audience. In *M.* 3 and 4, Ovid narrates the founding of Thebes by Cadmus and the promising, but ill-starred, careers of his grandsons, Actaeon and Pentheus; he goes on to the destruction of Ino's family, more grandsons; and finally, bereft of all successors, Cadmus departs into self-imposed exile and chooses to be de-humanized as a snake. It has long been recognized that as he proceeded Ovid kept reminding his audience of the *Aeneid*. Recently, Hardie has taken that observation to its extreme and tried to prove that this Theban section was possibly the first of many 'anti-*Aeneids*' composed after Virgil's death.[7] Hardie contents himself pretty much with showing that the foundation-legend that Ovid follows for Thebes reverses that of Rome, but he ignores the deeper ramifications of the topic. We have to look much closer at the Theban characters that Ovid presents and what features of the Virgilian themes he makes them represent.

In using Virgil's epic, Ovid from the start alludes to situations and characters of the *Aeneid* while making clear some critical differences between Thebes and Rome, between Cadmus and Aeneas. We hear that Cadmus has wandered the world and is *profugus* ('an exile', *M.* 3.6–7), but he has no purpose matching Aeneas': he is looking for his sister. Only when he fails to locate her does he seek an oracle about where he should settle down (since his father has forbidden him to return home without the girl). Thebes, then, is a purely personal home for Cadmus and his family; that a people should collect at the spot is sheerly accidental. Before he can settle in the fated location, Cadmus has to kill the serpent that guards the spring. Ovid reminds us verbally at this point of the occasion when Hercules killed the monster Cacus and made the site of Rome safe for Evander (and for Aeneas, who will follow). Again, though, the poet marks the differences: Cacus (whose name is merely the Greek word for Bad transliterated into Latin) is the incarnation of the thematic force of Evil and Madness which Aeneas and Rome are dedicated to bringing under control. On the other hand, the Theban dragon seems little more than an ill-tempered guardian-monster from fairy-tale; and after Cadmus kills him, Ovid introduces another story motif that connects with his basic interest in meta-morphosis (not with the symbolic foundation of a city and nation). A mysterious voice predicts to Cadmus that, just as he now looks at this serpent, so one day people will look at him and see a serpent (*M.* 3.98). Ovid has decisively avoided the heroic, nationalistic themes of Virgil.

When Cadmus grows old, he hands over the rule to his grandson

Pentheus. As Ovid and his audience knew, Pentheus had been the subject of several Greek tragedies (of which Euripides' *Bacchae* today alone survives), which had been adapted by Roman playwrights. Ovid saw an opportunity, too, to allude to Virgil's epic as he began his account. He introduces Pentheus, then, as *contemptor superum* ('despiser of the gods above', *M.* 3.514). The Latin phrase immediately reminds the audience of the great blasphemer of the *Aeneid*, Mezentius, whom Virgil presented as *contemptor divum* ('despiser of the gods', *A.* 7.648). Again, though, we quickly recognize the differences between these two impious men. Mezentius is a mature warrior and king, who has been a vicious tyrant; in the course of Virgil's narrative, he becomes humanized for us when his son Lausus dies trying to protect him, and Mezentius willingly accepts death to join the boy. Pentheus is but a young man himself, the age of Lausus, and he will die at the hands of his mother and aunts, violent maenads, but not at all humanized or sympathetic to Ovid's audience and certainly not heroic. In a long speech, however, Pentheus is made to echo, in an unattractive manner, several stirring and heroic motifs of the Virgilian poem. Let us look at part of that speech:

> 'quis furor, anguigenae, proles Mavortia, vestras
> attonuit mentes?' Pentheus ait; 'aerane tantum
> aere repulsa valent et adunco tibia cornu
> et magicae fraudes, ut, quos non bellicus ensis,
> non tuba terruerit, non strictis agmina telis,
> femineae voces et mota insania vino
> obscenique greges et inania tympana vincant?
> vosne, senes, mirer, qui longa per aequora vecti
> hac Tyron, hac profugos posuistis sede Penates,
> nunc sinitis sine Marte capi? vosne, acrior aetas,
> o iuvenes, propiorque meae, quos arma tenere,
> non thyrsos, galeaque tegi, non fronde decebat?
> este, precor, memores, qua sitis stirpe creati,
> illiusque animos, qui multos perdidit unus,
> sumite serpentis! pro fontibus ille lacuque
> interiit: at vos pro fama vincite vestra!
> ille dedit leto fortes, vos pellite molles
> et patrium retinete decus!'
>
> (*M.* 3.531–48)

'What madness has stunned your minds, you snake-born offspring of Mars?' said Pentheus. 'Do cymbals beaten against cymbals have such power, as well as the flute of curved horn and deceptive feats of magic, that men whom no sword in battle, no trumpet has frightened, no battleline bristling with spears, are conquered by

115

the shrieks of women and drunken madness and crowds of perverts and hollow drums? Should I be surprised by you older men, who, after being carried over the long seas, established on this site Tyre and its fugitive Penates, but now allow it to be captured without a fight? Or should I rather be amazed at you young men of more vigorous age, closer to my own, who should be holding weapons, not thyrsi, whose heads should be covered by a helmet, not leaves? Be mindful, I beg you, of the stock from which you spring, and assume the spirit of the one that alone slew so many, of that famous dragon! He perished in defence of springs and a pool: you should conquer on behalf of your glory! He slew brave men; you should repulse cowardly perverts and preserve the honour of your fathers!'

Pentheus addresses his people as 'offspring of Mars' (like the Romans) and also 'snake-born' (unlike the Romans, 531). He protests their behaviour and brands it madness, much as young Ascanius had assailed the women's actions in burning the Trojan ships on the shore in Sicily: 'quis furor iste novus' ('What is this new madness of yours?', A. 5.670). But Ascanius was acting properly and trying to put a stop to what we recognize as serious damage; whereas Pentheus the blasphemer is trying to stop the legitimate piety of his people towards the god Bacchus, a benevolent deity when not wildly opposed. In opposing the god, though, Pentheus introduces military imagery ('vincant', 'conquer', 537) and the emotional contrast between religious trappings and army gear. This represents Ovid's Romanization of the traditional tragic themes (which focused on the antithesis between god and human being, female and male): Ovid modernizes the controversy, making it a matter of militant virility. In this and in his assimilation of Bacchic worship to that of Cybele, he aligns himself with Catullus and with Virgil. In A. 9.598ff., a hot-headed young relative of Turnus arrogantly taunts the Trojans with sneers about their effeminacy and ridicule of the flute and drum (see 'tibia' here in 533, 'tympana' at 537), un-Roman music for a deity. The epic quickly comments on the speaker's folly, when Aeneas' son Ascanius, with full approval of Apollo, kills the Italian with an arrow through the temples. So far, then, Ovid has used his Virgilian allusions to cast Pentheus as a major blasphemer-tyrant and as a chauvinistic young fool.

At 538, Pentheus divides his audience into older and younger men. The older seem to be viewed as survivors of the band that came with Cadmus from Tyre; the younger emerge as Theban-born descendants of the dragon's teeth. Thus, the ruler appeals to the seniors with language that reminds us of positive themes of the *Aeneid*, of the troubled voyage over the sea ('per aequora vecti', 538, direct repetition of a familiar phrase in *A*. 1.375, 3.325 and 6.355), and of the bringing of the ancestral Trojan gods, the Penates, to the new home (539). However, Pentheus' rhetoric comes out in such a tawdry way that he seems only a bad parody. Cadmus had no Penates when he set out in search of his sister; his goal was never the patriotic-religious foundation that Aeneas' is. Furthermore, Virgil would never have used the pathetic adjective 'fugitives' (*profugos*) of gods or fallen into the silly triple alliteration that goes with Pentheus' popping anger. Aeneas was a refugee (*profugus*, *A*. 1.2), but his gods are not so humanly feeble. Our awareness of Virgil's effective representation of Aeneas makes us view Pentheus' efforts at super-patriotism without sympathy: Ovid sees to it that this man is perceived not only for his likeness to negative Virgilian characters but also for his inept pose as another Aeneas, Virgil's hero. In the appeal to his own contemporaries, Pentheus uses his super-patriotism in an even sillier manner, as he argues shrilly that the dragon of the fairy-tale should be regarded as a 'heroic model', of fighting nobly against large odds and perishing in defence of one's land. That is to suggest that the basic allegory of the *Aeneid*, the conquest of monstrous disorder (such as Cacus or personified *Furor*, 'Madness'), should be inverted and disorder viewed as patriotic fervour!

Ovid does not, I think, produce an 'anti-*Aeneid*' here in this speech or in his mythical account of Thebes. The values that Virgil establishes in his epic remain valid, and Ovid uses them skilfully to interpret Pentheus as a wretched chauvinist and impious fool. The king fails to imitate closely either Aeneas or Ascanius, but does somewhat hysterically come off as a version of Mezentius and Numanus. Using Virgilian standards and situations to assess his mythical material is but one type of effective contextuality in Ovid. Because Pentheus lacks the epic nobility which he claims, we reject him. In other parts of his poem, Ovid himself seems to turn away from epic values and themes and to validate an alternative human, non-heroic viewpoint. What some critics label Ovid's 'Little *Aeneid*', therefore, emerges as very little concerned with the *Aeneid* at all, but with un-epic stories that Ovid loosely attaches to the narrative skeleton of Virgil's poem, concerning anything but Aeneas and his great mission. Here and there, Ovid even rationalizes and humanizes some of Virgil's own grand themes, notably in his reductionist epitome of the issues of the war between Aeneas and Turnus:

> habetque deos pars utraque, quodque deorum est
> instar, habent animos; nec iam dotalia regna
> nec sceptrum soceri nec te, Lavinia virgo,
> sed vicisse petunt deponendique pudore
> bella gerunt.

> (*M*. 14.568–72)

117

Each side has its own gods and what is as good as gods: human spirit. No longer do they fight for a kingdom that comes as dowry nor for the sceptre of a father-in-law nor for you, maiden Lavinia; they merely want to conquer, and they wage war from shame of giving it up.

The human spirit not only reduces the significance of Virgil's gods but also undermines the noble ideals of the war in Italy. Now, the war seems like any war when stripped of its rhetorical mask. We might not think very much of this 'human spirit' as it sabotages the *Aeneid* or animates Pentheus, but in the poem as a whole it constitutes the major concern in a most attractive way, and it gradually looms as a very real alternative to self-denying (but often self-deceiving and assertive) epic heroism. To that positive preoccupation of Ovid with humanity I now turn.

HUMANE EPIC

In the early books of the *Metamorphoses*, Ovid presents stories that focus on the relation of human beings and gods. For the most part, the human beings appear – unlike the arrogant Pentheus – as innocent victims of selfish, violent gods. Nymphs, raped by Jupiter (whose epic epithet, *pater omnipotens*, 'father omnipotent', exposes his ignoble lust), suffer trauma that Ovid renders symbolically as he describes their metamorphosis and effort to adjust to an ugly brute form. Io turned into a cow (1.610ff.) implies the brutalization that rape is. Jupiter transforms her only to escape the anger of his suspicious wife, but Io, losing her external form, retains her essential human awareness and feelings, so she feels the cruelty she has experienced, agonizes over her loss of communication with her family, and mourns over the selfish exploitation by Jupiter and the unjust anger of Juno to which she falls innocent victim. Juno even attacks and transforms another rape-victim of her husband, Callisto, and turns her into a gross bear (2.466ff.), which, because its *mens antiqua* ('original human rationality', 2.485) survives, is plagued by human misery. I would like to spend a little time with Pentheus' cousin Actaeon, a male victim of divine savagery who, though studied in the same book as Pentheus, for Ovid clearly has interest not as a representative of an 'anti-epic' theme but rather as an embodiment of what I call epic humaneness.

As Schlam (1984) has recently shown, the myth of Actaeon acquired several important variants before Ovid. Actaeon had been represented as a hunting-rival of Diana, a blasphemous challenger of her power, and even as a would-be sexual assailant of her virginity. However, once Ovid's version existed, it dominated subsequent narrations. His Actaeon is an innocent, whose only crime is the simple mistake of wandering into a grove where Diana was bathing.

118

at bene si quaeras, fortunae crimen in illo,
non scelus invenies; quod enim scelus error habebat?

(*M.* 3.141–2)

If you investigate correctly, you will discover his crime to have
been one of fortune, not guilt; what guilt is there in a mistake?

Ovid's Actaeon hunts all morning, and at high noon, hot, tired, and
content with his kill, he decides to call it a day, a day which he, with
unwitting irony, declares had enough fortune (149). Almost simultaneously, in another part of the woods, Diana also decides to rest from
the hunt. For transition from mortal to deity, Ovid simply gives a
description of an idyllic spot, which offers a shady recess and a spring
that pours out crystal-clear water into a grass-lined pool (155–62). It is
a place that automatically answers a tired hunter's or huntress's desires,
for it offers shade and water for drinking and bathing. Placed where it
is without explicit connection, it could be the perfect rest-spot for
either Actaeon or Diana. In the recently told story of Callisto, that
huntress grew tired and chose a grassy shaded spot at high noon
(*M.* 2.417–21); and there Jupiter raped her. Parry has nicely described
the basic elements of this forest landscape where violence rather than
peace overtakes the tired hunter.[8] Ovid can and does insert the
description of the place either before or after introducing the hunting
activity. But, once he has focused on a particular hunter, the idyllic
description that follows regularly applies to him or her. Thus, in this
story of Actaeon, the poet creates a certain expectation that violence of
an erotic kind will victimize this hunter. In fact, though, he connects
the idyllic spring and pool first with Diana, who starts bathing there
with her companion nymphs. Now *she* becomes an obvious candidate
for rape, not only falling into the Ovidian narrative pattern but also
fitting one of the earlier versions of the myth. Again, however, he
defeats expectations. Although Actaeon does indeed arrive at this scene
of tempting female nudity, he has not planned to do so and he has no
time to react before angry Diana, presuming the worst of him, acts first
to destroy him. Ovid brings him back into the story as though
completing a narrative pattern: Actaeon is simply looking for his idyllic
spot for relaxation, and he blunders into the same spot as Diana.

ecce nepos Cadmi dilata parte laborum
per nemus ignotum non certis passibus errans
pervenit in lucum: sic illum fata ferebant.
qui simul intravit rorantia fontibus antra . . .

(*M.* 3.174–7)

Enter Cadmus' grandson, who has postponed half his toil and,
wandering uncertainly through the unfamiliar woods, arrived in

119

the grove. Chance carried him that way. As soon as he entered the recess that dripped with water . . .

Note how emphatically Ovid insists on the planless, accidental aspect of Actaeon's behaviour, reiterating what he said earlier at 141. I have not cited the remainder of the long sentence that begins at 177, because I wanted the reader to feel the false drift of the narrative. Having dramatically brought Actaeon on stage with the significant adverb *ecce* ('look' or 'enter'), Ovid creates the expectation, by the way he starts 177 (with a relative pronoun that maintains our focus on the intruding hunter), that he will have much more to say about this lucky male among all these nude females. What red-blooded man would not have had some interesting thoughts, voiced words, and indicated some reactions by at least a few gestures? But Diana seizes the stage and the position of grammatical subject from Actaeon and, presuming him guilty (not of intending to rape her, but of planning to boast of having seen her nude, 193–4), she robs him of his ability to speak and act as a man. She transforms him into a deer.

Whereas, we saw, Pentheus alienated our sympathy by his arrogant and chauvinistic rhetoric (which was exposed by comparison with Virgil's *Aeneid*), Actaeon has been consistently delineated as an innocent, and from this point functions as a sympathetic victim, a human being who suffers from merciless divine violence. Ovid devised a special way to engage us with his metamorphosed mortals, a way that has continued to be productive ever since (as in Kafka's famous story, 'Metamorphosis'): he changed their forms only in so far as to give them all external features and *some* of the natural qualities of the beings they respectively assumed, but he insisted that animals retained one particular feature of the former human beings, the *mens* ('human consciousness'). Thus, having here described the way Actaeon grew horns, had his neck lengthened and ears tipped, fell down on all fours, and displayed a dappled hide, because of Diana's cruel action, the poet goes on with the psychological damage that afflicts an Actaeon who still has human awareness of what he is suffering and how much he has been disabled.

> additus et pavor est. fugit Autonoeius heros
> et se tam celerem cursu miratur in ipso.
> ut vero vultus et cornua vidit in unda,
> 'me miserum!' dicturus erat: vox nulla secuta est;
> ingemuit: vox illa fuit, lacrimaeque per ora
> non sua fluxerunt; mens tantum pristina mansit.
> quid faciat? repetatne domum et regalia tecta
> an lateat silvis? timor hoc, pudor impedit illud.
> dum dubitat, videre canes.
>
> (*M.* 3.198–206)

Fear was also added. The heroic son of Autonoe fled, and he
was amazed at his own speed as he ran along. But when he saw
his face and horns reflected in water, he tried to say, 'Woe is
me!'; no human voice or words followed. He groaned, and that
was his voice, and tears flowed down his changed face. Only his
former consciousness remained the same. What was he to do? Go
back to his home and royal palace or hide in the forest? Fear
prevented the one, shame the other. While he hesitated, the dogs
sighted him.

Ovid has created this incompletely changed Actaeon precisely so that
he could be represented as realizing what has happened to him and
struggling to assert his humanity over the animal nature with which he
has been afflicted. The deer-form is bad enough, but the deer-traits of
fear and swift flight un-man the heroic self-consciousness of the young
prince. He cannot speak his thoughts, but he feels all that a human
being would feel who fears against his will and is ashamed about what
this animal form does to him.

Worse is to follow. Although Diana's full intentions in this metamorphosis have not been revealed at first, they now work themselves
inexorably out with the sudden introduction of the dogs. She has not
merely robbed him of the power of speech so that he cannot inform
against her; she has robbed him of the ability to assert his mastery over
his own hounds and instead turned him into their prey, a deer with
human awareness of what he has lost, of his inability to communicate
with his hunting companions and dogs, and finally of the excruciating
agonies which he must endure, with only animal groans to utter, before
he is literally torn to pieces. As Ovid concludes, then, it was not until
she saw the innumerable fatal wounds in this deer (once Actaeon) that
Diana's savagery was finally appeased (251–2).

Actaeon, struggling to make his humanity work, in spite of the deer-
form and nature that has been cruelly imposed on him, unable to
communicate with other human beings and finally dying, killed as an
animal by his closest friends, epitomizes some of the striking themes
that Ovid developed in this poem. We could say that these Ovidian
themes vary some that are fundamental to epic and any serious literature which regularly explores the limits of human nature. When
Achilles talks with Priam and returns the corpse of Hector to the father
whom, though an enemy, he can pity, the wild Greek warrior recovers
some of the finest aspects of humanity. And when Aeneas savagely kills
the helpless, pleading Turnus, regardless of the many provocations to
such violence, Virgil expects us to ponder the inhumanity of Rome's
greatest hero at the moment of victory and to meditate sombrely on
imperial Rome (see chapter V above, pp. 85, 93f.). But in both epic

instances, the poets decisively imply that basic humanity can and should prevail, that human beings can master their lower emotional instincts. Ovid, on the other hand, has described a human victim, who cannot possibly act as the human being he wants to be, who dies helplessly and in excruciating pain to satisfy a cruel deity.

In the first five books of the *Metamorphoses*, Ovid portrays the connections between gods and mortals. We would expect the gods to have superior power, but we might not expect them to be so self-centred and devoid of benevolence as Ovid depicts them. Male or female, the deities pursue their passions ruthlessly at the expense of human beings, as Diana does with Actaeon, and as Jupiter does with his numerous rape-victims. A helpless sense of unmerited pain afflicts men and women, and their changed form regularly symbolizes the immoral operation of divine powers, who are content to bestialize human beings in order to gratify their corrupt desires. After the fifth book, however, Ovid tends to narrate stories where human beings become involved with other human beings. But the results are no better, indeed worse in their emotional effect on us in the audience. Human beings prove unable to manage their passions also, and they pursue illicit or impossible loves and frightful vengeance like the gods, but without the power to gratify themselves with impunity, without the amoral egotism to ignore their consciousness of doing what is wrong. Ovid's interest then focuses on the ways in which the human *mens* (reason and conscience) operates under the impetus of passion, struggling with genuine moral issues (as the gods never have to do) and eventually succumbing, to get no secure pleasure from passion, but lasting misery. The failure of human conscience to guide people to honourable behaviour and happiness leads eventually to metamorphosis, a changed form that now frequently has nothing to do with action of the gods – how could those amoral gods of the early books gain ethical authority here? – but seems rather to symbolize the failure of human moral effort and a permanent atmosphere of regret, occasionally modified by some partial compensation in the non-human existence of the changed forms.

The first purely human story in Book 6 is symptomatic. It features the violent triangular relationships of Tereus, barbaric ruler of Thrace, Procne, his wife from Athens and mother of his son Itys, and thirdly his sister-in-law, the lovely young Philomela. Tereus lusts after Philomela, lures her into accompanying him back to Thrace to visit her sister, and savagely rapes her. To accomplish this, Tereus lets his diseased imagination dwell on his sexual goal, day and night, and Ovid shows him cloaking his desires under the mask of *pietas* ('honourable family feeling', *M.* 6.474, 482, 503). His pose as a devoted husband and brother-in-law deceives the others, and thus morality becomes a central issue of the story, the misuse of moral values for human evil. When Tereus perpetrates his rape, Philomela has the *mens* (6.531) to exclaim over the way he has viciously confounded family relations. Frightened and angry, he only abuses her more savagely, first cutting her tongue out, then raping her again. He has bestialized her, robbing her of her human voice, in a manner that is far more horrifying than what gods do to human beings. However, she still retains her human intelligence, which is mightily stimulated by her passionate sense of indignation: she does communicate with Procne by means of a tapestry, in which she works her story. Unlike helpless Callisto, rape-victim of Jupiter, or helpless Actaeon, victim of Diana's unreasonable fury, Procne and Philomela can act on their feelings. Their minds have been twisted by what they have suffered gratuitously from Tereus, and they now dedicate themselves inhumanely to their vengeance on him. They decide to kill the boy Itys, cut him up, and serve him to Tereus as banquet meat! For Procne, that means destruction of her maternal feeling in the train of her savage hatred of her husband. Ovid shows her hesitating, then deciding that her *mens* is becoming too soft because of *pietas* (629), which she now totally condemns. As she declares, 'scelus est pietas in coniuge Tereo' ('family loyalty is a crime towards a husband like Tereus', 635). So the two women do kill Itys, and they watch with demonic glee while Tereus eats that meat, then reveal the truth to him. Lust and vengeance have wrecked a family and every member; they have done inhuman deeds, and lost their essential humanity and the power to direct their behaviour by a conscience focused on *pietas*. Most of the narrative has dealt with the psychological disintegration of these three people. Eight lines conclude the story (667–74), in which Ovid briefly records their transformation into three birds, who memorialize their human misery, Tereus especially. The changed forms provide an ending, but the meaning of the story lies in the careful delineation of the dismal failure of human *mens* and *pietas*, overwhelmed by wilful passion. These people have changed internally, partly as victims of each other, but partly, too, as their own victims, before the external change asserted itself.

Otis once called Ovid's great poem 'the only epic of love'.[9] There is much merit in that claim, once one spends some effort to define its parameters. Ovid does convey a positive valuation of the mutuality and responsibility of human love, but he does so by narrating stories where love fails and passion regularly destroys one or all the people affected (as the four people in Tereus' family). However, Ovid does not restrict himself to love, and so, while supporting the emphasis on the non-heroic character of Ovid's poem, I would prefer to emphasize the larger concern with human nature, its desperate and thwarted efforts to find happiness with other human beings. As he shows in the greater part of the *Metamorphoses*, we are responsible for the changes that develop in us, spreading from *mens* to body and external form. What the poet announced as an epic (or simply a poem) about changed forms has proved to be a much more searching study of changed humanity.

NOTES

1 Heinze 1919.
2 Otis 1966: 314–15.
3 Otis 1970: vii–viii.
4 Knox 1986: 2.
5 Anderson 1973.
6 Solodow 1988: 110ff.
7 Hardie 1990b.
8 Parry 1964.
9 Otis 1966: 345.

VII

FORM EMPOWERED: LUCAN'S *PHARSALIA*

Frederick Ahl

Most Roman poetry from Virgil onwards has a political soul, and none more so than Lucan's *Pharsalia*.[1] It is a political act as well as a political poem. When Lucan declares it the achievement he shares with Julius Caesar, he does not simply mean that Pharsalia is a battle (or war) Caesar waged and he, the poet, wrote about.[2] He is matching himself against Caesar on two counts: one literary, one historical. His *Pharsalia* opposes Caesar's *Civil Wars* as an interpretation of what the civil wars meant, and his assassination of the last of Caesar's house would, he hoped, undo the consequences of Caesar's victory. Lucan, then, is neither playing Homer to Caesar's Achilles nor claiming, with Statian false modesty, to be following in the wake of Virgil. He is poised to enter as the central figure as well as the writer of his own epic.

The *Pharsalia* is the epic of a youth whose life and poetry were shaped by an obsession with the giants of a century before. They inscribed his world, life, and thought even as he inscribed theirs. Lucan is as much a creation of the *Pharsalia* as the *Pharsalia* is of him. His rhetorical persona, didactic, satirical, ubiquitous, resembles Lucretius' rather than Virgil's; it is highly conscious of, and seeks to persuade, to change the reader.

Lucan is something of a Byronic figure, and his popularity as a poet in the similarly youthful poetic (and politically conscious) circles of Byron and Shelley should reassure readers that scholarly doubts about his poetry have not always been shared by his fellow poets. Shelley judged Lucan 'a poet of great genius and transcending Virgil'.[3] Even when Quintilian, writing a generation after Lucan's death, describes Lucan as a writer 'magis oratoribus quam poetis imitandus' ('someone orators [i.e. men in public life], rather than poets, should imitate'), he both praises and chastises (*Inst. Orat.* 10.1.90). His innuendo is that Romans in political life could take their cue from Lucan even if poets should not.[4]

Critics ancient and modern agree that Lucan adapted epic to his own needs. The *Pharsalia* describes a world dismembered, as do the *Iliad*, the *Odyssey,* and the *Aeneid.* What is new is Lucan's overt disapproval of the dismemberment of his world, his invective against those he feels responsible for it, his hope that his readers will not simply acquiesce. His aim is to provoke, not just to report, action. As a result he radically reshapes, some would say dismembers, the epic genre.[5]

Many objections to his changes pertain to matters of style, language and metre and are secondary attacks used to reinforce conclusions already drawn. They are not the real core of the matter. Lucan's frequent preference for prosy language to the conventional vocabulary of Latin poetry draws censure; but so does Apollonius' and Nonnus' use of poetically conventional, pseudo-Homeric Greek. And Dante is praised for jettisoning Latin altogether in favour of Italian. The issue is what Lucan says rather than how he says it. Although other surviving writers in the century after Octavian's death share Lucan's view of the Roman world, none proclaims (or wholly sympathizes with) the remedies he advocates. Tacitus, suspicious of Roman ideologues, follows Sallust in the *Jugurtha* and uses the voices of Rome's adversaries to convey (at a prudent distance) some memorable criticisms of Rome and Romans: they make a desert and call it peace (*Agricola* 30.3). The degree to which the sentiment reflects Tacitus' personal opinion is not always clear. Yet regardless of the degree of criticism voiced, writers of the first century CE rarely act as propagandists for an idealized Rome. There was no Octavian looking over their shoulders to bully, cajole or bribe them into giving lip-service to state propaganda of a 'golden age'. Roman literature of the first century CE strikes us as the product of a decadent age, a 'silver age', because no one forced writers to describe it otherwise. The dissident Augustan, in contrast, faced the task of incorporating criticism into sustained panegyric. Octavian read what they wrote and, as Suetonius indicates in his *Life of Horace,* noticed what was left out as well as what was included. 'Why am I not in your *Sermones*?' he asks Horace.[6] Most subsequent Caesars, notably Domitian, were (as Martial complains) less attentive to poets and less concerned with soliciting 'golden age' propaganda. A few moments of careful panegyric kept Domitian at bay.

Midway through his *Punica,* and directly after his account of Rome's most traumatic defeat by Hannibal at Cannae, Silius Italicus concludes that it would be better if Carthage were still standing than that Rome should be what it is in his own day.[7] No 'golden age' here. But no rallying cry either. Rather a cynical sense of despair. Valerius Flaccus strikes a similar note at the end of his first book: Elysium offers enticements for which nowadays there is no desire (*Arg.* 1.843–7). Statius shows more anger, but avows he is unable to tell of Flavian victories. The struggle between two mythical brothers for a penniless kingdom extends his vocabulary of horror and atrocity to its limits. He

126

has not yet the capacity to describe wars which brought all the lands and wealth of the Mediterranean under the rule of one man (*Theb.* 1.17–40).[8]

The only surviving Augustan poet who overtly satirizes the 'golden age', Ovid, spent his last years in exile on the Black Sea. To declare as he did in *Ars Amatoria* 2.273–8 that this was a 'golden age' because gold could buy you anything was not exactly what Octavian had in mind. Virgil is never so open, but keeps praise of the 'golden age' and censure of man's passion for gold judiciously apart. Like Statius, he is a commentator on the politics and aftermath of civil war, not a revolutionary, or even a member of the ruling class with a political agenda of his own. He is no challenger in the contest for power, as Lucan is. Criticism of Caesar and Caesarism is usually, and understandably, covert in the *Aeneid* – so covert that many read the epic as a paean of praise for Octavian's regime, a validation of the 'golden age'. For interpretation of the *Aeneid* remains enmeshed in a kind of Augustan apologetic. We invest in Octavian's imperial ideology despite the disquieting means he used to attain and institutionalize his power. We make Virgil's uneasy hero the symbol par excellence of that ideology and its morality for several reasons.

One is our propensity for what Danuta Shanzer calls 'flat' reading of ancient texts.[9]

MINIMALIST CRITICISM

Criticism of Latin literature is less influenced than that of Greek by consideration of what Michel Foucault calls the poet's struggles as 'he strains his ears to catch that "other language", the language without words or discourse, of resemblance', which lurks 'beneath the language of signs and beneath the interplay of their precisely delineated distinctions'.[10] We favour explicit, 'simpler' readings. 'The modern era', R. Palmer argues of classical scholarship, 'is something like the "golden age of literalism".' Maija Väisänen notes in her brilliant study of Catullus that minimalist interpretation, the intentionality of what is taken as explicit, still remains, for some, an article of faith.[11] That it should be so is odd at the end of a century when D. H. Kahnweiler sponsored such Cubist artists as Picasso because, Pierre Assouline observes, 'he wanted the painting to be more faithful, more precise, more exact than a photographic reproduction'.[12]

Minimalist or 'flat' readings of most Latin epics result in a division of interpretation between its apostles and those who see more elaborate rhetorical and artistic structures at work. The minimalist's *Aeneid* is an encomium of Augustus and the *Pax Romana*, the ultimate justification of historical inevitability and the imperial moral paradigm. A rhetorical reading yields a more polyphonic epic inviting reflection and self-scrutiny, prompting questions rather than answers, and challenging the very nature of Romanness.

Virgil lurks within a labyrinth of allusion, the product of his lifetime of study and eleven years of meticulous craftsmanship. His imagery is baroque rather than classical, and seems, at first glance, intent on making everything seem artificial and contrived. That is the nature of his illusion: at times a stage-set, at times a bas-relief in verse, with montages of anthropomorphic gods, mountains and winds where the underlying reality is not human but divine (as it never is in Lucan). Neptune scuds across waves and prises ships off rocks with his trident, or tears down Troy's walls. Yet Virgil's stylized art regularly and abruptly intersects with varying degrees of 'reality', as when Aeneas' eyes move from the sculpted Penthesilea on Juno's temple in Carthage to the living Dido, or when, in the epic's first simile, the baroque Neptune, calming warring winds, is compared to a pious human quelling civil strife (*A.* 1.490–7; 142–56).

This last instance illustrates Virgil's power of focusing myth on contemporary realities. The storm Neptune quells is caused by the *breakdown* of a cosmic system of checks and balances, much as Octavian's intervention in Roman affairs is precipitated by the civil collapse of Rome. Aeolus, empowered by almighty Jupiter to release or check the winds in accordance with fixed terms (*foedere certo*), has been bribed by Juno to ignore his mandate (*A.* 1.52–83). Yet Jupiter never notices, much less acts to prevent or punish, Aeolus' disobedience. There is sly irony when, shortly after Neptune calms the storm that should never have arisen, Jupiter smiles at Venus with that smile with which 'he calms sky and storms' ('caelum tempestatesque serenat'), then promises Rome empire without end (*A.* 1.254–6; 279). Is Jupiter sufficiently in control to guarantee his promise? Virgil leaves us to formulate the answer.

Virgil presupposes a learned contemporary audience and demands knowledge of everything from Homeric and Alexandrian epic to Roman and other Italian history and traditions. The need to simplify, codify, catechize Virgil's complex web of allusion arose long before medieval times, when the *Aeneid*'s historical and cultural context lay beyond the ken of commentator and reader alike.[13] In contrast, Lucan's historical and ideological focus, his compression of events and characters, produces a remarkably self-contained work. Lucan could (and still can) be read *in toto* and essentially understood by someone other than an expert. He offers a cast of Roman characters familiar to even his less learned contemporaries and presents them in a manner that makes no great, overt demands on their knowledge of history.

A measure of the enduring intelligibility of the *Pharsalia* as opposed to the *Aeneid* emerges in the contrast between what the first vernacular translations of the epics conserve for their less learned readers. The Gaelic *Aeneid* is greatly whittled down and modified for its audience. Only rarely do we have a powerful sense of the original. The *Pharsalia* is much closer to a verbatim translation – even though Caesar does have Scandinavia added to his conquests to impress the Irish, beleaguered by Viking onslaughts.[14]

The *Pharsalia*'s apparent directness, its classicism, as opposed to the *Aeneid*'s Alexandrian baroque, is Lucan's artistic *trompe l'œil*. Poets, like painters and architects, strive to deceive or counteract the eye's perceptions. Outer simplicity or explicitness is often built, as was the Parthenon, on complex mathematical and engineering calculations and on a grasp of the various vantage points from which the beholder is likely to be viewing the creation.[15] Similarly, ancient scholars warn repeatedly that being 'formidable in argument' involves creating a false illusion of explicitness.[16] As Horace observes of the dancer, even playful movements belie the agony of their creation (*Ep.* 2.2.124–5).

It is easy to be deluded by the crafted surface. Douglas Little admires the *Pharsalia* because it is populated by characters who are 'the solid actors of history' who 'seldom set foot on Ovid's airy stage', because it is engaged with the writer's contemporary world, in contrast to Virgil's work, in which 'the present appears only through the veil of visions and prophecies'.[17] Surely, however, we get a more *specific* sense of the poet's contemporary world from Virgil or Ovid than from Lucan, despite (or perhaps because of) their predominantly mythic discourse. Lucan's *Pharsalia*, though centred in history, is sparse in specific, datable, allusions to his own day. It focuses tightly on the civil wars a century before Lucan wrote. True, Lucan alludes to the succession of Caesars. Yet no other Caesar looms individually and ominously out of the text. Even Nero is mentioned only once, in the first book. But the contemporary Octavian is omnipresent in Ovid and Virgil. The baroque, myth-historical *Aeneid*, like Ovid's works, engages Roman history and politics from its opening and never disengages.

A comparison of the necromancies in *Aeneid* 6 and *Pharsalia* 6 clarifies my point. Lucan could have designed a parade of Caesars past, as in Seneca's *Apocolocyntosis* or in Julian's *Banquet of the Caesars*. Instead, he introduces no persons or events subsequent to Sextus Pompey's death in 36 BCE. In *Aeneid* 6, Virgil introduces the still living Augustus and the doomed, young Marcellus who died thirteen years *after* Sextus, and only four years before Virgil.

Although Lucan's choice of a historical subject is shared by Ennius, Naevius, and his older contemporary, Silius Italicus, and is thus very Roman and conventionally epic, Lucan uses history differently.[18] History works against, not for, his rhetorical vision, since it tends to validate the victor, if only as the force of historical necessity. The republic whose symbols and final moments he endows with historical life is, as Lucan writes, a long disembodied soul. By compressing time, Lucan brings us to the body as it dies, hoping, perhaps, that the power of proximity will give the soul another incarnation. His triumph is making history, his greatest potential enemy, the vehicle of a narrative whose purpose is to subvert history: to make the events which toppled the republic and gave Rome to the Caesars less morally and politically definitive.

He does not, therefore, begin 'at the beginning' or extend his narrative too close to his own day. Rather, he concentrates events into symbolic shapes. Into his 'Pharsalian' wars he subsumes those between Marius and Sulla, the Philippi campaign and the 'slave wars' of Sextus Pompey. He selects and develops a limited number of motifs, characters and events to convey his vision. By removing temporal markers of the hundred years since the civil wars, he brings the fallen republic *into and within reach of the present* and maintains that illusion of immediacy by positioning his narrative persona close to the events and personalities of those wars, as if he were an eyewitness to, or on the scene shortly after, the action. He shapes history into an ideological sword ready to plunge into the tyrant-dominated present or future at a moment Lucan fears will never come. Hence the continuing threat of the *Pharsalia*. Because the sword never struck its original target, since Lucan's plot against Nero failed, it remains for ever poised and threatening.

Lucan has been hurt less than other epic poets by minimalist interpretation not because he is less complex, but because he *appears* less complex: because he normally deploys his rhetoric, his figured usages, to underscore, not undermine, the explicit level of his narrative. His authorial voice assumes a fairly consistent persona, dominating the *Pharsalia* as Cicero's dominates his *Second Philippic*. He thus differs from Virgil, Ovid, Statius and Valerius Flaccus, who create a more complex counterpoint between their authorial voices and those of their other personae, between what they declare their narratives are doing and what they actually do.

Virgil's deconstructive rhetoric, what ancient rhetoricians called *emphasis*, invites (but does not compel) the reader to question the apparent import of his work. What is Dido about when she asks Aeneas what Diomedes' horses were like and how great Achilles was? Diomedes' horses were Aeneas' before Diomedes took them from him in *Iliad* 5, and Aeneas had to be rescued from both Achilles and Diomedes by Aphrodite.[19] Lucan inverts Virgil's procedure. He deploys rhetoric as Cicero does, to reinforce rather than to subvert the picture he sets forth. Virgil alerts us obliquely to the shortcomings in Octavian's vision; Lucan, like Cicero, usually wants to conceal the flaws in his own. Hence

Quintilian's comment that Lucan is a model for orators rather than for poets. Lucan's rhetoric is more typical of the orator than of the poet, and thus more open to adverse assessment than Virgil's.

Manipulation of myth is, in scholarly terms, permissible; manipulation of known historical data unforgivable. When Virgil has Dido (rather than Anna, as in Varro) die for love of Aeneas, we treat his change more lightly than Virgil's contemporaries, familiar with Varro and the Roman tradition of Anna, would have done.[20] We do not even think of Virgil as blending Anna with Dido, but assume Virgil is 'following' one tradition and 'rejecting' another.[21] When Lucan, however, merges Lentulus Crus and Lentulus Spinther into one composite Lentulus, or talks of Pharsalia and Philippi as if they were the same battle, we notice what he has done but often assume, incorrectly, that he did not know they were different.[22] The impulse is to validate Virgil's picture and invalidate Lucan's, to step over Virgil's carefully spaced gaps and hack at Lucan's careful sutures.

IDEOLOGICAL CONFLICT

Classicists admire, with good reason, many accomplishments of the Augustan age and focus on its positive achievements, especially its professional management system. The Caesars earn praise for bringing stability, prosperity and efficient government.[23] Literary scholars in particular tend to leave uncontested the less savoury aspects of a triumphant autocracy that accompanied the chameleon-like Octavian's metamorphosis from bloodied victor of civil war into the nobly adjectival 'Augustus'.[24] And Virgil's *Aeneid* is the supreme textual prop for the view that Augustan Rome was, as Octavian maintained, 'golden'.

Revisionist interpretations of the *Aeneid* questioning Virgil's enthusiasm for the imperial ideal were virtually unknown before Francesco Sforza's now largely forgotten (and poorly argued) article in the *Classical Review* for 1935 and still fall, largely, on deaf ears.[25] But Lucan was a challenge to scholarly Augustanism which came to view critics of the new regime, rather than the regime itself, as decadent. We can accommodate Virgil more easily than Lucan to the imperial paradigm but generally try to dispose of, rather than understand, Lucan's objections to Caesarism.

It is easy enough to enumerate the limitations of the republic the Caesars replaced and to deprive it of, or diminish its claims to, 'the moral high ground'. Construing the Roman republic in terms of liberty is inaccurate. The republic was a corrupt, inefficient oligarchy promising nothing but internal chaos and bloodletting. What its champions called freedom was merely aristocratic privilege. Yet Lucan would not dispute these statements with us: his condemnation of the *publica belli semina* in *Pharsalia* 1.158–82 makes precisely the same contention. He differs in that he contends that the republic's failure does not invalidate the ideal of *libertas*. For many of us it does.

Not only was the loss of 'liberty' meaningless; it was inevitable. Romans should have reconciled themselves to the Julio-Claudians, who, despite occasional weaknesses of character, did much good public building and made the grain ships run on time. Thus writers who support the Caesars (however anxiously) act sensibly. Those who resent and resist are sentimentalists, opponents of progress and common sense, who want 'to turn the clock backwards', to reject, that is, historical inevitability.[26] Thus Virgil acted sensibly; Lucan did not.

Attacks on republican *libertas* recall those on inefficient democracy in the political debates of the 1920s and 1930s. Mussolini described democracy as 'merely a verbal illusion for simple-minded folk', and Winston Churchill, for a while an admirer of Mussolini, declared that democracy had 'invaded the Council Chamber' and 'liquidated the prestige of the House of Commons'.[27] Churchill felt happier with the oligarchic nineteenth-century Parliament, and commented: 'The vote given to every one has been regarded as a trifle by many, and as a nuisance by many more'.[28] Rostovtzeff felt much the same disquiet. 'Is not every civilization bound to decay as soon as it begins to penetrate the masses?' he asked.[29] Such writers did not argue, as does Lucan's Caesar, in, of all places, a speech addressed to his mutinous troops, that the human race lives for the benefit of a few: 'humanum paucis vivit genus' (*Phar.* 5.343) – one of Caesar's many raw statements of distasteful reality. Rather they contended, as Plato's Thrasymachus does, that the ruler, however much he appears to act in his own interests, even unjustly, makes life better for the ruled as a kind of collateral benefit.

Lucan's *Pharsalia* was perceived as one of the most important ideological challenges to their view. Otto Forst de Battaglia observes that 'dictatorship resembles high treason – a crime from which at first it is barely distinguishable – in that if it fails it constitutes a felony which is severely punished, while its success is hailed as a highly patriotic and praiseworthy achievement'. The statement is little more than an elaboration of Lucan's *ius datum sceleri* and the notion expressed by his Caesar that victory and defeat are the measures of innocence and guilt.[30] Hence Lucan's famous declaration of the opposition between freedom and the absolutist state: 'par quod semper habemus/, libertas et Caesar, erit' ('we shall have the matched conflict we always have between liberty and Caesar', *Phar.* 7.695–6). De Battaglia echoes this contention too:

> To sum up: if we come to the conclusion that dictatorships have meant a positive gain for the countries in which they have been

established, it must be borne in mind that we have hitherto considered the matter only from the standpoint of the interests of the State, the primary need of which is to be governed and to secure internal unity without overmuch regard for the individual. But if we turn to the citizen of the State for his opinion, we find that the trial of dictatorship is merely an episode in the everlasting dispute *individuum versus societatem*.[31]

Lucan had glimpsed, if not explored, the idea that the apparent good of the body politic may conflict with that of the individual regardless of the system of government. But his voice of resistance to autocracy is readily identified with that of the individual in its battle with the state.

The glamour of success and power, de Battaglia argues, 'makes the triumphant ideology accepted as their own by the vast majority. A victorious cause is pleasing not only to the gods, but also to the masses, and a difficulty overcome is approved by the Catos.'[32] The Lucanian sub-text is now explicit: 'victrix causa deis placuit sed victa Catoni' ('the victorious cause pleased the gods, but the conquered cause pleased Cato', *Phar.* 1.128). Lucan's Cato, however, is not reconciled to the idea that success is the measure of virtue.

Scholars, such as Ronald Syme, who condemn the principate as usurpation and tyranny and find a resemblance between Octavian and Hitler agree with Lucan that the *Pax Augusta* was purchased at the cost of tyranny: 'cum domino pax ista venit' (*Phar.* 1. 670). Yet Syme concludes that, after a century of anarchy, twenty years of civil war and military tyranny 'if despotism was the price, it was not too high'.[33] 'To a patriotic Roman of Republican sentiments', Syme continues, para-phrasing Favonius' comment to Cato in Plutarch (*Brutus* 12), 'even submission to absolute rule was a lesser evil than war between citizens'. De Battaglia would concur. But not Lucan.

Ralph Johnson faults Lucan for being so obsessed with the 'momentary monsters' of his world, and for failing to grasp that human power and decadence are essentially cloudlike and unenduring.[34] In terms of cosmic time or even the experience of the twentieth century, he is right. Our monsters have been short-lived and thus, from a deterministic perspective, 'doomed' from the outset. In more general historical terms, and certainly those of Rome, Lucan had every reason to think (or fear) that liberty was gone for ever and to find the cloud monsters less momentary, less easily dispersed by winds of change. 'We are cast down', Lucan laments, 'until the end of time': 'in totum mundi prosternimur aevum' (*Phar.* 7.640).

In our recent experience, dictatorial causes perceived, at least in hindsight, as morally worse, tend to lose rather than win. We shy, of course, from outright Thrasymacheanism. When a case can be made that the winning side is also morally superior, the link between success and morality is rarely stated more strongly than: 'they lost because they were guilty'. Right is might. Not only are we ourselves vindicated, but so is our god who has not ignored our prayers. But when the morality of all parties to a conflict is less clear, or when a better moral case can be made for the losing side, the rhetoric becomes more complicated.

THE RHETORIC OF THE DIVINE

Of the structural changes Lucan makes in epic none is more striking (and necessary) than his radical modification of epic's traditional gods. Since Lucan wished to revive the 'losing' side, the cause (in his judgment) of liberty, traditional deities of epic were more an obstacle than a help. If gods offer any moral justification for events, they validate the winner rather than the loser if only as the agent of their wrath. They further offer those who acquiesce in the 'verdict of history' a pretext for doing so: what happened must be part of the divine plan. When Venus tells Aeneas that Troy fell because of 'heaven's lack of clemency' ('divom inclementia, divom', *A*. 2. 602), she excuses all human agents (including Aeneas) from responsibility.

Lucan could hardly use gods in the Virgilian manner since he was disputing the morality of history's 'verdict'. By his time, moreover, the Caesars' power prompted their claims to parity with the gods of state and of poetry. Their cults carried the Roman tradition which interwove offices of state with those of religion a decisive step further, affirming the oneness of absolute power both secular and religious, institutionalizing the doctrine that might is right. Since the gods of literature and cult were already barely credible symbols of justice and morality, such deification was not so obviously outrageous as it would be if presidents or prime ministers were canonized nowadays. But for Lucan, as for Seneca in the *Apocolocyntosis*, the new Caesarian Olympians ruined whatever credibility still remained in the pantheon: they were gods 'by whose name one is ashamed to swear' (*Phar.* 9.601–4). Although epic's Olympians are often mentioned in the *Pharsalia*, they are as mute and unresponsive as the avenging gods invoked in Seneca's *Thyestes*. The universe occasionally shudders at human behaviour in the *Pharsalia*, as in a Senecan chorus, but does not move against or for mankind.

With the cynicism of their age, Lucan and Seneca not only follow, but go beyond Socrates, who rejects the idea that 'might is right'. Seneca (*Ep.* 14.13) states categorically: 'potest melior vincere, non potest non peior esse qui vicerit' ('the better man has the capacity to win, but the man who actually wins does not have the capacity not to be the worse'). Lucan, perhaps allowing for the success of his own enterprise, restricts his inversion of Thrasymacheanism to one specific instance. Of the battle of Pharsalia he observes: 'vincere peius erat' ('it was worse to win', *Phar.* 7.706). Its consequences were *ius datum sceleri*, criminal behaviour given legal recognition (*Phar.* 1.2). Tacitus, in the context of the impending struggle between Vitellius and Vespasian – a context charged with reminiscences of the civil wars from Pharsalia to Mutina and strongly evocative of Lucan – finds similar cynicism in public opinion: 'the only thing you can know in a war between two opposing parties is that the winner will be worse' ('deteriorem fore qui vicisset', *Hist.* 1.50). He himself adds, prudently, that Vespasian turned out better than expected.

The doctrine of 'might is right' does, of course have a voice in the *Pharsalia*. Caesar tells his troops that if they win, they are innocent; if they lose, they are guilty (*Phar.* 7.259–60). But as Plato's Socrates challenges Thrasymachus, so Lucan's Cato challenges Caesar and becomes voice and symbol of values not based on military might. The immorality of the traditional pantheon, particularly as represented in poetry, troubled Plato as it did Lucan. Yet Socrates, if we accept Vlastos' argument, rather than denying the state's gods (though his accusers certainly claimed he did), rationalizes them 'by making them moral', and even suggests that god needs the services of the good man (such as Socrates) to do for Athenians what god would do if he could.[35] The gods, in short, need qualified human interpreters to demonstrate their goodness, not the whimsical wielders of power that the poets suggest. And Plato's Socrates claims to act as an agent of the gods.

Lucan drives a wedge between the good man and god: Cato's approval, not divine approval, makes a cause valid. Lucan does not deny that gods exist, but openly claims what Socrates only implies: that they exercise no real control over events – 'we lie when we say Jupiter rules' ('mentimur regnare Iovem', *Phar.* 7.447). Where Plato dismisses poets, Lucan dismisses gods. They have failed to act in a corrective moral capacity.

Paradoxically, the traditional forces dismissed loom large in both writers. Although Lucan's agenda is political rather than philosophical or religious, his displacement of epic gods moves epic towards rather than away from theological issues, preparing the ground for Prudentius, Dante and Milton. Dante, who bases most references to Cato on Lucan's *Pharsalia*, takes the political allegory of Cato's remarriage to Marcia in *Pharsalia* 2 as a religious allegory of God and the noble soul reunited and, in *Convivio* 4.28, declares Cato the most appropriate human to symbolize God himself.[36] I doubt that this was Lucan's intent. Yet, when Lucan expresses the hope that Cato will one day be deified, he comes close to making his good man not only god, but the only real god (*Phar.* 9. 601–4). In his rhetorical response to secular absolutism, he takes a decisive step in the direction of ethical absolutism, that is to say of monotheism. He moves epic to a threshold not crossed until the Christian era, when the notion of '"the good" become man' yields to the notion of 'god becoming (the good) man'.

We sometimes miss the significance of Lucan's rhetorical achievement here not only because we see, rightly, that Lucan's immediate goals are political rather than theological, but because we read back on to the pantheon of Virgil and Statius, and particularly on to Jupiter, a Judaeo-Christian notion of deity. Critics of Virgil and Statius still dally with an assumption alien to pagan poetry: that Jupiter and (or) fate represent a morally positive divine force. Rather, Lucan's immediate successors, particularly Statius, move back from Lucan's theologized politics and find the traditional, amoral gods of epic a more satisfactory means of expressing the human dilemma. Statius maps the causal web in all its details. Lucan, trying to resolve, not describe, the dilemma, marks threads one should follow.

John Sullivan correctly points out that the *Pharsalia* 'is too complex a work of art' to allow it to be a matter of Cato the 'moral hero' and Caesar a kind of anti-hero.[37] Lucan's Cato is more a symbol than a hero in our sense, urging men to fight for themselves, not for someone, or even something, else. In Lucan's terms, a physically or morally coercive central figure of power is the world's problem, not the world's ideal. Through Cato, Lucan extends *libertas* beyond its significance as the political slogan of the opponents of Caesarism to the individual's struggle against the enslaving power not only of tyranny and state, but of the yearning for life itself.

There is, of course, rhetorical sleight of hand here: the exhortation to live free or die, however extended and idealized, remains a political slogan to encourage rather than to quell civil war. Recognizing this, Lucan follows Marcus Brutus in making *libertas* precisely such a slogan in his editorial voice even though that voice condemns Brutus for becoming excessively enamoured of civil war as a result of hearing Cato speak. Yet Lucan is as careful to keep his symbol, Cato, as free from conscious responsibility for the behaviour of his admirers as Plato is to distance Socrates from Alcibiades and Critias.

In separating the essence of *libertas* from its ruins in the republic's last days, Lucan generates a rhetorical ideal whose inexorable logic reaches, as de Battaglia saw, beyond the limited political goals he probably had in mind. When an aristocrat assumes the persona of a slave struggling for political and intellectual freedom, he positions himself, rhetorically, beside the more genuinely oppressed: his own slaves, for instance. Common enemies create common causes.

The Julio-Claudian principate, through Lucan and St Paul, yields our first canonical definitions of Cato and Christ and confirms the divinity of those prepared to make a ritual offering of themselves, a *devotio*, for the community at large. Lucan's moral symbol, Cato, shares rhetorical ground with the shrewdly apolitical Christ who, like Cato, wishes his blood could redeem the peoples from suffering: 'hic redimat sanguis populos' (*Phar.* 2.312). And Christian rhetoricians targeted groups they sought to convert by talking in their terms, as Paul points out (1 Corinthians 9.19–23). As hopes of political *libertas* vanished, those who, like Lucan, idealized Cato gradually shifted allegiance to Christ and regenerated Rome as the *civitas dei*.

Lucan illustrates the importance of Neronian Rome as one of the great (if neglected) crossroads of western intellectual history. Recent studies of Nero's reign emphasize its Latin dimensions and do little to explore the parallel movements in Hellenized Jewish and Christian thought. Lucan's uncle Gallio crossed paths with the greatest rhetorician of antiquity, St Paul. The fire of Rome in 64 CE and its aftermath of upheaval claimed Paul's life and, *ut fama est*, St Peter's, as well as the lives of Lucan, Gallio and Seneca. Moreover the Christian tradition made the last of the Julio-Claudians its arch enemy, its anti-Christ, much as Lucan made the first of the dynasty his. The Christians, in time, claimed Seneca for their own, and even forged a collection of letters between Seneca and Paul.[38] But Lucan remained problematical. True, his Cato came to serve Dante as an allegory of God. Yet his rhetoric of opposition threatens all absolutist systems, ideological as well as secular.

THE HYPOCRISY OF IDEOLOGY

Lucan, like Seneca, knows it is easier to argue that the man of principle, the Stoic wise man, should stay outside the struggles for temporal power whose outcome lies beyond his control: involvement inevitably makes him as guilty as other participants.[39] Yet Seneca, whose own life was inextricably interwoven with politics, offers few more miserable pictures than that of the withdrawn, envied and affluent Vatia whose life, he declares, is a living death (*Ep.* 55). Similarly Lucan so phrases the argument for disinvolvement (put in Brutus' mouth) that it suggests Epicurean rather than Stoic philosophical principles and an abdication of responsibility.

There was, of course, a middle ground: the maintenance of what Lucan's Cotta calls 'the ghost of liberty' by being *willing* to do what one is told: 'si quidquid iubeare velis' (*Phar.* 3.143–9). Cotta's argument, one of discreet compromise, is as old as Zeno, the founder of Stoicism. Zeno declared a man is not a slave if he comes to terms with a tyrant, provided he acts of his own free will (Plutarch, *How the Young Man Should Listen to Poets* 33D). Although Lucan, like Cato, decides that he cannot justify himself morally by standing outside the conflict, he does not censure Cotta for this view, though it is a far remove from Cato's definition of Rome as liberty, whose empty ghost he will follow to the bitter end (*Phar.* 2.297–303).

His caution is too little and too late on this matter. His epic constantly implies the hypocrisy of such compromise and must have stung those who, though they disliked tyranny, rationalized their collaboration and suffered pangs of conscience for doing do. The historian Tacitus, for instance, secured his own career by careful compromise with the very emperor whose tyranny he so roundly condemns. Thus the failure of the conspiracy to kill Nero in 65 CE, in which Lucan was deeply involved, may have been a relief as well as a disappointment to contemporary Cottas. It also afforded a chance to counter-attack by subverting not only the idealist's ideals but the sincerity of his commitment to them.

Tacitus suggests (*Ann.* 15.49) that vehement personal hatred (*vivida odia*) for Nero, not ideological passion for liberty, drove Lucan into the Pisonian conspiracy. When the plot was discovered, Lucan, he adds, cracked under interrogation and even incriminated his own mother in a vain effort to save his life. Suetonius (*Life of Lucan*) is even more damning: Lucan implicated his mother in the hope of winning Nero's favour by emulating Nero's own matricide. Vacca, who alone among ancient writers shows much sympathy for Lucan, depicts Lucan as an apolitical poet who undeservedly became the victim of Nero's wrath.

We face an unresolvable, and in many ways irrelevant, conflict between such testimony and the evidence of the poem. If Lucan hated Nero, he was scrupulous to leave no trace of such personal animosity to Nero in his epic, even in books probably composed while he was plotting to kill the emperor. The *Pharsalia*, as a text, is deeply committed to *libertas* even if Lucan himself could not live up to it. Although I incline to agree with Ralph Johnson that Lucan depicts his monsters 'so wittily, so fiercely, so bravely', there is really no way of knowing whether his courage failed him at the end.[40] Readers usually make the decision for themselves on the basis of their attitudes towards his ideals.

The rhetorical advantage of siding with Tacitus is that it displaces the suspicion of moral relativism from critic to poet. Hence Bernard Henderson's brutal summation that Lucan betrayed his ruler and died 'young, but hardly prematurely . . . tangled on the briars of treachery and cold dishonour'.[41] The 'loyalty' argument, however, cuts both ways. Neronian and Flavian poets usually lose in modern value judgments regardless of how they inclined politically in Nero's reign. Silius Italicus, consul in the year Nero died, is often criticized for not *opposing* Nero.[42]

Admirers of Lucan, finding Tacitus' charges hard to refute, and worried about the possible 'irrelevance' of republican ideals in Neronian Rome, often defend him by denying the very basis of his work, arguing that the conspiracy against Nero did not have the restoration of the republic as its aim. Taking their brief from Vacca, with his politically innocent Lucan, they argue that Lucan was not really opposed to monarchy or Nero (though this does leave problems explaining his involvement in the plot to kill Nero). Rather, Lucan shares Tacitus' view in *Agricola* 3.1.2: under a new regime, principate and liberty, 'res olim dissociabiles' ('things once irreconcilable'), are ultimately brought together. Nero, by this reckoning, was in Lucan's eyes a realization of the Senecan notion of a 'Just King'.

The textual basis of the 'Just King' interpretation of Lucan is a curious invocation of Nero which leaves scholars divided (*Pharsalia* 1.32–67). Some (including myself) think it humorously mocking. It certainly lacks any vicious political undertow, such as is present in Statius' aside to Domitian in *Thebaid* 1.17–40.[43] Some, Douglas Little, for example, contend that it is purely 'conventional' flattery – though what ancient convention of flattery fails to be ambiguous, unless one thinks of Julian's flattery of Constantius, which is simply insincere, I do not know.[44] Cicero treats flattery as a form of aggression against which important people should always be on their guard.[45] Others, notably scholars writing in French, treat Lucan's flattery as sincere, which is itself something of an oxymoron.[46]

Now Seneca, writing in 55 CE as Nero was assuming power, possibly hoped to mould Nero into a 'Just King' with his *De Clementia*. At least he dangled such an ideal before the young emperor, as Dio Chrysostom in his *Kingship Orations* later tried to educate Trajan. What John Moles says about Dio and Trajan could be said with equal justice about Seneca's approach to Nero: he tried to teach his emperor 'true philosophy and thereby make him a better emperor. He failed, but the failure was not his but Trajan's: in the last analysis there was something irremediably wrong with Trajan's *physis*'.[47] Lucan probably began his epic after 60 CE when Nero's actions would have made his candidacy for such philosophical monarchy incredible, and when even Seneca began to be pushed aside or withdraw from the corridors of power. Seneca and Lucan, though both deeply influenced by Stoic thought, were following very different paths in the 60s.[48] As Seneca withdrew from, Lucan entered upon the political scene. But if Lucan had made public any suggestion that Nero was a candidate for some kind of philosophical kingship, he would hardly have been taken into, much less become standard-bearer for, a conspiracy whose intent was not only to kill Nero, but, in the opinion of at least some of its participants, such as Plautius Lateranus, to restore the republic.

This 'Just King' interpretation of the *Pharsalia* has, of course, the advantage of removing Lucan's challenge to our imperial moral paradigm altogether by showing that Lucan's proclaimed republican ideology need not be taken seriously. The problem is that Lucan contends from the first book of his epic onwards that the result of the civil wars was eternal slavery. If he thought such slavery worth while because it brought Nero to rule the world as a Stoic 'Just King', he buries that notion beneath a rhetorical and satirical avalanche of invective against monarchy in any form. There is not the most oblique suggestion, even among his characters who are themselves courtiers, of a paradox along Stoic and certain Christian lines that slavery to a 'Just King' or to God is its own kind of freedom. The *Pharsalia* bears the stamp of *libertas* as surely as do Brutus' coins after Caesar's assassination.

That is why the suggestion of personal animosity is, in rhetorical terms, precisely what Lucan, like Brutus, would have wanted to *avoid*. It would weaken, rather than reinforce, the ideological structure he so carefully builds. His opposition to the Caesars and Caesarism clearly includes Nero, but does not single him out for special attention. Absolutism is objectionable no matter who holds absolute power, not because a specific person holds power at a given moment in history.

Regardless of which view of the invocation to Nero one takes, the passage supports neither Tacitus' contention that Lucan was motivated by intense personal animosity towards Nero, rather than by ideological considerations, nor that of modern scholars such as Jacqueline Brisset and Eugen Cizek, that Lucan saw Nero as a 'Just King'. If we must generate a hypothesis about Lucan's relationship with Nero, we would do better to construe it in terms of the character from the *Pharsalia* who shared something of the poet's dilemma: Marcus Brutus. Lucan's obsession with *libertas* made it logically necessary for him to maintain the persona of a Brutus striking down a friend because that friend was the symbol of the absolutism he opposed.[49]

CONCLUSION

Lucan, more than any other ancient writer, codified the political rhetoric of liberty which bore important political fruit in the era of the French and American revolutions. He created in his *Pharsalia* something more far-reaching than he himself grasped, as did those who drafted the American Declaration of Independence and Bill of Rights. Lucan's satirical assault on the multi-national populace of his contemporary Rome shows that his view of *libertas* was narrower than Paul's and more socially restricted than that of most Caesars. Ironically too, his own family, of Spanish origins, probably owed its Roman citizenship, as Paul did, to the very Caesars he condemns. Much the same criticism may be voiced of America's founding fathers. Their goals too were limited and politically specific. They too owned slaves and probably never realized that their document, given the authority of law, would force their descendants to accept an equality they neither imagined nor desired. Indeed, slavery was abolished in the Britain from which they rebelled more than half a century before it was abolished in the United States. None the less, their rhetoric, like Lucan's, embodies the illusion (masked, with consummate rhetorical bravado, not only as truth, but as self-evident truth) that the human race does not, as Lucan's Caesar claims, live for the benefit of a few. The facts are still on Caesar's side. But the dissociation of truth from fact, of ideals from history, is a grand illusion capable of changing fact. That is why, as John Henderson urges, 'You must read Lucan.'[50]

NOTES

1　Unfortunately, political poetry is not widely approved in the English-speaking world, as Bowra 1966: 1 notes.
2　*Phar.* 9.980–6; see Ahl 1976: 326–32, and the sources cited there.
3　Jones 1964 (vol. 1): 432; cf. 429–30; cf. Ackermann 1896.
4　For Quintilian's figured uses, see Ahl 1984a: 174–208.
5　Boyle in Boyle and Sullivan 1991: 154–61.
6　See Ahl 1984b: 40–110 (especially 57).
7　*Punica* 10. 657–8; cf. Ahl, Davis and Pomeroy 1986; cf. Boyle in Boyle and Sullivan 1991: 297–304.
8　Cf. Ahl 1986: 2803–912.
9　Shanzer 1990: 239.
10　Foucault 1970: 49–50.
11　Palmer 1980: 346; Väisänen 1988: 9–28.
12　Assouline 1990: 99.
13　See, for example, Jones and Jones 1977.
14　Ahl 1989a: 173–98.
15　See, for example, Pollitt 1972: 71–9.
16　Ahl 1984a: 174–208.
17　Little 1990: 6.
18　Ahl, Davis and Pomeroy 1986: 2501–11.
19　For Aeneas, Achilles and Diomedes, see *Aeneid* 1.752 and 10.581; *Iliad* 5.311–454; 20.283–92; 23.377–513; also Ahl 1989b: 1–31, especially 26–9, and the sources cited.
20　Austin 1963, for example, does not even mention the other traditions of Anna.
21　For Varro, see Servius on *Aeneid* 4. 682; cf. Ahl 1989b: 21–3.
22　Ahl 1976: 71.
23　For an unusual and remarkably concise overview, see Thornton 1989.
24　For Octavian as chameleon, see Julian, *Banquet of the Caesars* 309A-B.
25　Sforza 1935: 97–108; for a fuller treatment of this issue, see Boyle 1986.
26　MacMullen 1966: 33.
27　De Battaglia 1930: 9–10. Churchill's scathing assessment of the United States (in his view a 'Limited Liability Dictatorship') rivals Lucan's description of republican political decadence.

28 Ibid.
29 Rostovtzeff 1957.
30 De Battaglia 1930: 287–8.
31 Ibid., 372.
32 Ibid., 374.
33 Syme 1939: 2.
34 Johnson 1987: vi (citing Alexander Pope).
35 Vlastos 1991: 162.
36 *Convivio* 4.28 is a line-by-line allegorical interpretation of *Phar.* 2.338–45 –
    the only major alteration Dante makes is in his reading of 344–5; elsewhere,
    Convivio 4.5 draws on *Phar.* 2.285 (see also *Aeneid* 6.841); *Convivio* 4.27 on
    Phar. 2.383; *Purgatorio* 1.31–6 and 71–5 on *Phar.* 2.372–8; also, possibly,
    Purgatorio 2.119–24 and *Vita Nuova* 19 on *Phar.* 9.256ff. Lucan's remarriage
    scene between Cato and Marcia (*Phar.* 2.326–91) probably interested Dante
    since it was suggestive of his own relationship with Beatrice (see
    Purgatorio 1.78–9).
37 Sullivan 1985: 151.
38 Barlow 1938.
39 See, for example, *Phar.* 2.247–76; cf. Seneca, *Ep.* 14.13 and 14.
40 Johnson 1987: 134.
41 Henderson 1903: 264–5.
42 Pliny, *Epistles* 3.7; Sullivan 1985: 88.
43 Ahl 1986: 2817–21.
44 Little 1990: 77–8.
45 Cicero, *De Amicitia* 99; cf. Seneca, *NQ* 4a, Preface 9 and Ahl 1984a: 197–208.
46 Cizek 1982: 244; cf. Brisset 1964: 171–94, 221. For details of the opposing
    view see my Ahl 1976: 25–61 and sources cited on p. 35 n. 33; also Narducci
    1979, especially 16, and Grant 1970: 176–7.
47 Moles 1990: 364.
48 Cizek 1982: 243, states that Lucan always approved the politics, philosophy
    and poetics of his uncle. I am not at all clear what his basis for that
    contention is.
49 If we want to reconcile Tacitus' *vivida odia* with this picture, yet sense that
    there is more than petty literary jealousy between Lucan and Nero involved,
    our best answer probably lies in Lucan's publication of a work, no longer
    extant, entitled 'On the Burning of Rome', which Statius includes among
    Lucan's notable works in a poem (*Silvae* 2.7) celebrating what would have
    been Lucan's fiftieth birthday in 89 CE. Statius' synopsis seems to indicate
    that Lucan blamed Nero for the fire of Rome in 64 CE. Nero could hardly
    have let such an overt (and arguably incorrect) political charge go
    unpunished. The personal breach between Nero and Lucan probably
    occurred then. See Ahl 1976: 333–53.
50 Henderson 1988: 123.

VIII
FORM OPPOSED:
ELEGY, EPIGRAM, SATIRE

J. P. Sullivan

The historical and social origins of oral or 'primary' epic (to use the convenient term) are well enough agreed on, whether Mesopotamian, Homeric, Anglo-Saxon, Icelandic, Turkic, Khergiz or Slavic;[1] less so the historical and social circumstances, or literary traditions, that give rise to different kinds of secondary or 'literary' epic, which in turn must influence the critical reactions a particular work or epic tradition provokes.[2]

Whatever their origins in oral tradition, the *Iliad* and the *Odyssey* established epic in Greek and, later, in Roman perceptions as *the* pre-eminent and most prestigious literary form in the evolving hierarchy of ancient genres, with tragedy a close second.[3] (The distinction nowadays made between historical and mythological epic would not be a distinction worth making for the Greeks.) Attempts to dethrone or subvert this dominant form were perhaps inevitable. As towering literary figures in the Greek or Roman tradition, first Homer and later Virgil became obvious targets of literary and critical assassins. The anxiety of influence prompts patricidal impulses, masquerading under various guises. Sometimes these impulses are prompted by literary awe or despair: what does one say of, how does one criticize, the two Homeric epics revered as the Bible of the Greeks? Crude parody, deriding heroic values and elevated language, was the first blasphemous answer, and so *Batrachomyomachia* ('The Battle of the Frogs and the Mice') and the Roman parody, *Culex* ('The Gnat') were still lively sellers for schoolboys in Martial's time (*Epig.* 14.183; 185). This all-purpose weapon never lost its edge, and only rarely was the humour unaccompanied by some degree of hostility.[4]

More forces are at work than artistic emulation or frustration. Primary epic is the product of monarchical or aristocratic milieux, in their prime or even in their decline; it flourishes in feudal periods: witness the *Chanson de Roland*. In resolutely autocratic societies, even before an absolutist state is established, both heroic and semi-historical epic make a political statement, consciously or not. For the driving force of epic, its essential subject, is the struggle for power, even when manifested as devotion to king and country, military prowess or chivalric honour. These overriding themes cannot entirely suppress the dialogic element implicit in ambitious narrative, but it can muffle it, just as Odysseus could scotch the protests of a Thersites.

Most mythological cycles, if they transcend local ritual and choral celebration, become embodied and preserved in epic narratives as one possible condition of their survival, but their ultimately tribal (or national) origins determine that the hidden text, if not the explicit charter text, is one of empowerment, rebellion against, or defence of, established religious or social structures and hierarchies.

Drama, in the hands of Euripides, might question the certitudes of heroic epic or capitalize on any subversion latent in the genre itself, but obvious counter-genres such as personal lyric and polemical iambic were the first formal expressions of deep doubts about heroic ideals, invoking easily understood symbols of abandoned shields and private passions. So Alcaeus, Sappho and Hipponax: Callimachus would be another story.

Inspired by Greek traditions and spurred on by the example of Livius Andronicus' version of the *Odyssey* (around 250 BCE), with the deities Latinized and the metre native Saturnians, Roman epic buds with Naevius' *Bellum Punicum* and flowers in Quintus Ennius' *Annales*, another endeavour to fashion a Roman *Iliad* around the heroes of the Punic wars. Both of these brave productions were undisguised attempts to justify the *novus ordo saeclorum*, while praising prominent contemporary Romans as embodiments of that new order.[5] Both epics were proclamations of a new heroic mission, skilfully utilizing the historical and mythical traditions refurbished, or specially concocted, for the Romans by ingenious Greeks. This epic strain of nationalistic and individual propaganda would have a long life, continuing well into the empire and beyond, although the heroes would change. Achilles and Hector would be replaced by a Fabius or a Scipio, by a Pompey or a Caesar, and later by emperors and their generals. The heroic events would be the battles of Cannae, Trasimene, Pharsalia and Actium, or even lesser encounters on German and African frontiers, rather than the Battles of the Titans and Giants or Diomedean *aristeiai*.[6]

How far Callimachean poetics denied the viability of literary epic in *any* form, as opposed to bloated inartistic poems such as Antimachus' *Lyde*, is a more complicated problem than it used to be, now that scholars discount a critical quarrel between the sharp-tongued arbiter of style and Apollonius Rhodius, the exponent of a sophisticated literary epic. Nevertheless, the Alexandrian critic's *obiter dicta* and his actual poetic practice were easily interpreted as blanket discouragement and a general warning. Indeed, how can we know whether

Apollonius Rhodius' modernistic *Argonautica* would have escaped Callimachus' strictures? Certainly to the Roman poets of the Catullan circle,
who welcomed, or were swept along by, the Callimachean revolution as
propagated by Meleager, Parthenius, and other didactic practitioners,
conventional epic was a highly suspect mode of poetic expression.
Catullus' attack on Volusius' *cacata charta* (*Carm.* 36) surely reflected
his critical stance. Reflected also in Catullus' *œuvre* is a change of
ideology (in the broad sense), not just a refinement of poetic technique. The poet's barely disguised contempt for political worthies such
as Pompey, Julius Caesar and (one suspects) Cicero becomes, with the
succeeding generation of elegists, a rejection of the political ideals of
Roman imperialism and military glory, and even a rejection of war itself
in favour of the quiet life in the country or the splendours and miseries
of romantic love. The choice was presented as valid for literature as well
as private life: *otium* vs *virtus.*

Elegy, as it developed in Rome in the first century BCE, provides a
cogent, if unsystematic, criticism of the epic genre in a manner not
unlike that of Sappho and her contemporaries. The complexity of the
reaction is best illustrated by Propertius. It is not just a question (in
epic terms) of choosing Lotus Land over the trials by combat or of the
voyage home to Ithaca, but rather of embracing the more rigorous and
testing alternatives represented by Calypso and Circe.

Since Homer remained the paradigm and symbol of all epic,
Propertius could grapple with him as the representative of the whole
epic tradition. He could serve as a convenient surrogate, even
scapegoat, for contemporary Roman writers of epic, not least Virgil.
There are consequently a number of significant references to Homer
and the Trojan war in Propertius' elegies, and, although the *Iliad* is
mentioned specifically in only three passages (2.1.50; 2.34.66; 2.1.14),
each of these references has a freight of symbolic connotation, and
each, on close inspection, exposes Propertius' attitude to the epic
itself, to its conventional reputation and to the poetic traditions it now
embodies.

A prime representative function of the *Iliad* for Propertius, and so
also for his audience, is that it is a classical narrative poem which has
immortalized its subjects. Without its existence, the poet argues, Troy
town and its citadel, the Greek and Trojan heroes who perished before
its walls, all would be unknown, buried in the oblivion of time:

> exiguo sermone fores nunc, Ilion, et tu
> Troia, bis Oetaei numine capta dei.
> nec non ille tui casus memorator Homerus
> posteritate suum crescere sensit opus.
>
> (3.1.31–4)

As Ezra Pound concisely puts it:

> Small talk O Ilion and O Troad
>   twice taken by Oetian god,
> If Homer had not stated your case.

To vindicate the claims that elegiac poetry (specifically love poetry) as a poetic discourse is at least equal, if not superior, to epic poetry, is the main task of the opening elegy of Book 3, when Homer's poetic powers are, somewhat minimally, acknowledged. In this long and complex poem Propertius first presents himself as an innovator in the Callimachean tradition, and then, almost immediately, he launches into a brusque dismissal of heroic and historical epic in general:

> a valeat, Phoebum quicumque moratur in armis!
>
> (3.1.7)

> Goodbye to whoever ties down Apollo in warfare![7]

Implicit here is the dismissal of any writer who would waste his time and inspiration on outdated epic productions that might begin with the words: *Arma virumque cano.* It is not the writing of such long-winded and ambitious epics, but rather the writing of *love poetry* that will bring a modern poet fame and tempt a triumphant Muse. Propertius admits that there will continue to be chroniclers of Rome's expanding empire, but he himself will concentrate on poems that can be read and admired in times of peace. Any temporary hostility that he may provoke in his audience will be compensated by his later reputation, posthumous if necessary: death, after all, ennobles all artistic achievement. And so, while it may be true that Troy and the heroes of its siege would have been forgotten without the songs of Homer, nevertheless love poetry can bring the writer similar glory:

> meque inter seros laudabit Roma nepotes:
>   illum post cineres auguror ipse diem.
> ne mea contempto lapis indicet ossa sepulchro
>   provisum est Lycio vota probante deo.
>
> (3.1.35–8)

And Rome will praise me among her later posterity: I myself predict that day will come when I am ashes. It has been settled, through Lycian Apollo's approval of my prayers, that a stone over no mean grave will mark my bones.

The case had been put just as strongly earlier (in 2.14), when Propertius had compared his emotions about a lovers' quarrel with Cynthia to the passions of certain epic and tragic heroes, notably Agamemnon in his hour of victory over Troy. This reinforces what Propertius has already

146

proclaimed, that out of the battles in the bedroom, from love-making with his mistress, he has found poetic material for an 'epic' narrative in every respect comparable to the *Iliad*:

> seu nuda erepto mecum luctatur amictu,
> tunc vero longas condimus Iliadas.
>
> (2.1.13f.)

Or if she struggles with me with her dress off, then we construct many *Iliads*.

This protestation that love poetry, particularly in modernistic elegy of the Alexandrian variety, is just as valuable, in an important sense, as hexametric narratives of war and its horrendous consequences is very radical and would hardly be acceptable to a conventional Roman audience. Propertius has therefore to keep hammering at the theme. The corollary that peace is preferable to war, that lovers venerate *peace* ('pacem veneramur amantes'), like the literary claim that refined Callimachean artistry, the miniature and the vignette, should be preferred to lengthy epic poems and the broad Homeric canvas, would be equally difficult to accept.

Another tack for the love poet to try, if in an ironic vein, is to undermine the traditional high status of the *Iliad* itself. Propertius argues that the mainspring of Homer's narrative is the immoral abduction of an all too willing Helen by the seducer Paris. This is a sordid tale, and so Cynthia, portrayed for the nonce as a faithful and devoted mistress, is ready to condemn the whole epic on the basis of this disreputable theme:

> si memini, solet illa leves culpare puellas
> et totam ex Helena non probat Iliada.
>
> (2.1.49f.)

If I remember, she often castigates unfaithful mistresses, and disapproves of the whole *Iliad* because of Helen.

In any case, Homer's achievement, as Propertius goes on to argue, is not something beyond a modern poet's reach. Virgil's still unpublished *Aeneid* may well wrest the crown from the ancient Greek, at least if the reports of its material are to be believed. Propertius briefly speculates about Virgil's work in progress, his epic on the foundation of Rome, which will also contain apparently complimentary allusions to Caesar's victory at Actium. He proclaims, not without a touch of irony:

> cedite Romani scriptores, cedite Grai:
> nescioquid maius nascitur Iliade. (2.34.65f.)

The neat paraphrase by Ezra Pound somewhat heightens the tone:

147

Make way, ye Roman authors,
   clear the street, o ye Greeks,
For a much larger Iliad is in course of construction
   (And to Imperial order)
Clear the streets, o ye Greeks!

By bringing the *Iliad* down to a level below the contemporary *Aeneid*, the elegist can now launch a critical attack at the whole concept of epic poetry without giving obvious offence.[8] Virgil, he argues, has taken, or been forced to take, the wrong track. For all his epic endeavours, the senior Roman author is fundamentally a love poet, with Alexandrian roots. As witness Propertius adduces the *Eclogues*, from which he cites appropriate erotic motifs at some length:

non tamen haec ulli venient ingrata legenti,
   sive in amore rudis sive peritus erit.

(2.34.81f.)

But these themes will come not unwelcome to any reader, whether
he is naive or experienced in love.

Propertius insists that *this* is the aspect of Virgil, Virgil the love poet, that the Roman audience should be applauding. From this it follows that love poetry, at least in the present historical circumstances, is as valid a genre as the traditional epic narrative with its glorification of power, honour and bloodshed.

The general argument now becomes clear. It is true enough that Homer's *Iliad* conferred immortality on Troy and the warriors and heroines involved in its story, but the glory conferred is tainted by the immorality of the central character, Helen, as well as by the bloodiness of its action. Virgil's themes, being Roman, are perhaps superior, and so his achievement may surpass Homer's in this style of writing, yet Virgil is also, more importantly, a love poet – like Propertius – and his love poetry is surely as good as, and as popular as, his still unpublished ventures into epic. If this is the case, then Propertius' love poetry too has as great a claim to contemporary recognition in itself, and as a medium for bestowing fame, as Homer's *Iliad*. He too can immortalize his subjects.

Propertius tendentiously chooses the *Iliad* as the most obvious and most famous example of the epic genre he is attempting to undermine. The choice of the older and more revered Greek epic would be acceptable and also safer, from a literary and perhaps even a political point of view, than attacking Virgil directly. Yet it is 'literary' epic in general that he is attacking, and what could be more effective than enlisting Virgil himself in the subversion of epic through the elevation of elegiac and pastoral love poetry?

It will be noticed that Propertius himself is deterred from epic by the warning of Apollo, here the symbol of poetic inspiration (3.3.15ff.). Ovid, on the other hand, claims that he was tricked by Cupid into writing love poetry instead of epic (*Am.* 1.1.1–4). The purport of the allegories, however, is the same. Tibullus does not refer to writing at all, but makes his critical position clear by attacking the main subject of epic, war itself (see 1.10). In deploying these critical symbols, the *Iliad* and the *Aeneid*, which represent epic narrative, 'Cynthia', 'Delia' and 'Corinna', who stand for personal passion and private concerns, and invoking Calliope, Cupid and even Apollo to validate these new poetic directions, the elegists are trying to effect a poetic revolution – and one utterly different from that effected by Virgil himself.[9] They are attempting to subvert or radically alter the 'canon' by turning the whole hierarchy of genres upside down.

The task is not easy and the argumentation must be subtle to be persuasive. Propertius has chosen to start by dethroning Homer in favour of a more up-to-date epic, but one which deals with matters closer to home, or to Rome. Then, by a logical progression, he proceeds to undermine this new candidate for the poetic crown by arguing that the genre itself leaves so much to be desired that the very attempt is *a priori* doomed to failure. For what is needed now is a Callimachean poetic and the more compelling themes of private life, love and Cynthia. And yet, as the later elegies make clear, even those specific themes are not vital; even Cynthia and the poet's passion for her can be abandoned. But the *poetic* discourse, the whole manner of writing, can survive the change of subject, as Book 4 will prove. Propertius, even with Cynthia almost abandoned as a topic, can still conclude his debate with the seer Horus over his poetic future (4.1B) with the inspired conclusion that elegy, in some form or other, is still to be his poetic *métier* and his claim to immortality.

The last of the Roman elegists, however, while subscribing to his forerunners' objections to old-fashioned nationalist epic, discovered, again looking to Alexandrian sources for help, an imaginative way out of the impasse facing a more ambitious poet. Ovid's solution was the highly imaginative *Metamorphoses*, whose structure could embody many moods and many styles: irony, pathos, tragedy, comedy, emotion, reflection and even eulogy. To interpret the work as some sort of 'epic' venture is therefore to miss its critical purpose and distort its achievement.[10] It was, supremely, a 'counter-epic', a creative critique of the most honoured ancient genre. Its misfortune was that it seemed inimitable – or, in the light of its author's fate, potentially dangerous.

Ultimately, of course, it would be the successors of elegy, the poets of the personal lyric or of meditative verse on love, death and nature, drawing on accessible experience and emotions, or, more self-consciously, examining the nature of art and the artist, who would, in the European tradition at least, take over many of epic's *poetic* aspirations, while jettisoning its style and its ideological and heroic values.

The elegists, including the last of their number, Ovid, launched their attacks on epic from comparatively high literary ground. But even humbler literary forms found champions who were willing on their behalf to challenge the traditional canon.

An interesting case is Phaedrus, the Macedonian-born freedman of Augustus, who finding perhaps that the superior kinds of poetry were pre-empted by such distinguished contemporaries as Horace, Virgil and Ovid, set himself up as a fabulist. In his keen desire to shine, he has no hesitation about making strong claims for this lowly kind of popular (and populist) composition, the fable, whose master was the semi-legendary slave Aesop,[11] and challenges epic and tragedy in various asides. Naturally, as with the elegists, satirists and epigrammatists, a pose of modesty is coupled with the claims of artistic merit or ethical utility:

> ioculare tibi videmur: et sane levi
> dum nil habemus maius, calamo ludimus.
> sed diligenter intuere has nenias;
> quantam in pusillis utilitatem reperies!
> non semper ea sunt quae videntur: decipit
> frons prima multos, rara mens intellegit
> quod interiore condidit cura angulo.
>
> (4.2.1–7)

> We seem to you to jest and it is true
> While we have nothing greater, we must play
> With lightest pen. But closely scrutinize
> These trifles, and what great benefits
> You'll find writ small! Appearance may deceive;
> First glance misleads the multitude. Rare minds
> Detect what care has hidden in a nook inside.

A little later, speaking *in propria persona*, Phaedrus attacks potential critics by claiming that even tragedy cannot live up to their literal-minded and puritanical demands:

> quid ergo possum facere tibi, lector Cato,
> si nec fabellae te iuvant nec fabulae?
>
> (4.7.21f.)

> What then can I do for you, Cato my reader, if neither folk-tales
> nor stage plays please you?

And in the Epilogue to Book 4, he promises Particulo, his patron and the rich freedman of Claudius, that his name will live in Phaedrus' writing as long as Latin literature is valued:

> Particulo, chartis nomen victurum meis
> Latinis dum manebit pretium litteris.
>
> (vv. 5f.)

Particulo, a name that will live in my lines as long as the value of Latin letters abides.

Making a virtue of his brevity, he finally attacks the larger literary modes:

> si non ingenium, certe brevitatem adproba;
> quae commendari tanto debet iustius
> quanto cantores sunt molesti validius.
>
> (vv.7–9)

If not its genius, surely its brevity you must approve, which should be the more justly commended, the more powerfully high-flying singers bore you.

Phaedrus' claims for fable, however, are modest enough:

> duplex libelli dos est: quod risum movet,
> et quod prudenti vitam consilio monet.
>
> (1 *Prolog.* 3f.)

The book brings a double dowry: it raises a laugh and is a stern and prudent guide to living.

Phaedrus at least honours the Horatian slogan that the most acceptable poetry combines usefulness with pleasure: 'omne tulit punctum qui miscuit utile dulci' (*AP* 343).

So much for the mock-modesty and the pleas for the reader's ear or his/her indulgence. But then what is the ideological content that Phaedrus, Babrius and the other fabulists propose to substitute for the heroic ideals of epic and tragedy? Phaedrus dwells more than Babrius on the injustices that spring from the tyranny of the strong over the weak (e.g. in such remarks as 'humiles laborant ubi potentes dissident' – 'the poor suffer, when great men fall out', 1.30.1). This is partly because he wishes to stress the injustice of his own treatment by Sejanus and by hostile fellow scribes, but his main theme is that sometimes the weak and the patient (or even passive) may assert power over the strong. The implicit aims of the fable are to undercut authority, predict an end to oppression, and mete out justice. Babrius puts it most succinctly in his story of the bull and the mouse, who finally squeaks: 'It's not always the big guy (*ho megas*) who has the power; there are

times when to be small (*mikron*) and humble (*kapeinon*) is a strength!'
(112.9–10), but Phaedrus conveys the same message in his story of the
fox and the eagle:

> quamvis sublimes debent humiles metuere,
> vindicta docili quia patet sollertiae.
>
> (1.28.1f.)

Personages, however lofty, should fear the humble people, for
shrewdness may learn and find a way open to revenge.

The fabulist's anti-heroic posture is particularly evident in stories that
satirize presumptuous aspirations or describe the punishments attendant on *hubris* of any sort. In the fable of the Battle of the Mice and
Weasels Phaedrus notes with grim satisfaction:

> quemcumque populum tristis eventus premit,
> periclitatur magnitudo principum,
> minuta plebes facili praesidio latet.
>
> (4.6.11–13)

Whenever a people is hard pressed by some dire crisis, it is their
rulers' high status that is jeopardized; the ordinary people find
easy refuge in obscurity.

A more articulate rejection of heroic epic and drama makes itself felt
when both satire and epigram press their claims to be *the* truly realistic
– and moralistic – modes of writing and representation. Love or the life
of passion is no longer central in literary discourse, partly because of
radical social changes. Instead writers turned, more pessimistically, to
the hard realities of life in a corrupt society. Accordingly Persius,
Martial and Juvenal all present roughly similar criticisms of epic. Epic
themes are unreal, not by contrast with the idealized and passionate life
of the lover, but by contrast with the everyday life of poverty, patronage
and power – and the virtuous or contented life in which alone lie
spiritual defence and protection. Elegy, after Ovid, was dead, but the
attack on mythological epic, its dethronement from the critical and
literary centre of artistic endeavour, could be taken up by satire and
epigram, which would include those realistic or personal short poems
that went for a time under the conventional title of epigram.[12]

Horace, it will be recalled, had gracefully and politely rejected the
siren call of epic composition: his talents were too slight and his literary
friends had pre-empted the genre. The less ambitious genres of personal lyric, satire and verse epistle were his poetic choices. Was this
modesty, friendship or literary instinct? Who can say?

Succeeding satirists make no bones about their choice and pick a
lively quarrel with epic, branding it as a form no longer viable or even
desirable. Their prime objection is to its unreality and remoteness from

the real world and the proper concerns of the writer, which must be mankind on the human level, and, ultimately, the structure of power in *contemporary* society, not in the mythical or even historical past.

Persius, for instance, in his *Prologue* attributes mercenary motives to epic poets: the loftier the genre, the deeper the pockets it picks. In *Satire* 1 he points the scornful, ostensibly complicit finger:

> ecce modo heroas sensus afferre docemus
> nugari solitos Graece . . .
>
> > > (*Sat.* 1.69f.)

> Look, here we go
> > teaching people to report (now, today!)
> the feelings of Heroes, when what they are used to
> > is playing Greek word-games.
>
> > > (Tr. Richard E. Braun)

Against such decadent writing he opposes as models the satires of Lucilius and Horace (*Sat.* 1.114–18), and later he passionately advocates the morality of that down-to-earth genre as against the bombast of historical epic and mythical tragedy (*Sat.* 5.1–18), which he has already connected with spiritual and sexual corruption (*Sat.* 1.15ff.).

Juvenal's objections are similarly high-minded, although he adds boredom and staleness as additional objections to epic, tragedy and the lesser literary forms that draw on myth for their subject matter (*Sat.* 1.1–14). Since his motivation for writing satire is the indignation aroused in him by the utter corruption of the present age, it follows that epic and similar well-established and conventionally prestigious forms are utterly inadequate to the tasks that face the civic-minded author in this worst of times. Since all art had for ancient authors and critics (apart from a few Epicurean demurrers) an implicit or explicit moral basis and justification, the satirist's overt objection to epic, rightly or wrongly, is a moral one, although it is easy enough to discern beneath this a more aesthetic and literary impulse in practice.[13]

Martial perhaps presents the case most cogently, since he speaks of *literary* choices rather than of uncontrollable moral disgust or Stoic zeal. He could have chosen to practise in any genre (*Epig.* 12.94); he chooses instead to attack the extravagant claims that epic, lyric and tragedy make on the critic's attention and the audience's admiration. In his classic defence of epigram and satire Martial rejects the worn-out mythological themes of epic, tragedy and elegy: his writings deal with mankind:

> qui legis Oedipoden caligantemque Thyesten,
> > Colchidas et Scyllas, quid nisi monstra legis?
> quid tibi raptus Hylas, quid Parthenopaeus et Attis,

153

quid tibi dormitor proderit Endymion?
exutusve puer pinnis labentibus? aut qui
   odit amatrices Hermaphroditus aquas?
quid te vana iuvant miserae ludibria chartae?
   hoc lege, quod possit dicere vita, 'Meum est.'
non hic Centauros, non Gorgonas Harpyiasque
   invenies: hominem pagina nostra sapit.
sed non vis, Mamurra, tuos cognoscere mores
   nec te scire: legas *Aetia* Callimachi.

                 (*Epig.* 10.4. 1–12)

Read of *Thyestes, Oedipus*, dark suns
   of *Scyllas, Medeas* – you read of freaks.
Hylas' rape . . . ? *Attis* . . . ? *Parthenopaeus* . . . ?
   Endymion's dreams changed your life? The *Cretan*
Glider moulting feathers . . . ? *Hermaphroditus?* –
   averse to advances of *Salmacian* fount . . .
Why waste time on fantasy annals? Rather
   read my books, where Life cries: 'This is me!'
No *Centaurs* here; you'll meet no *Gorgons, Harpies.*
   My page tastes of man. Yet you're incurious
To view your morals, view yourself. Best stick
   to *Callimachus* – the mythic *Origins.*

                 (Tr. Peter Whigham)

This call for a relation of literature to life, already foreshadowed even by Virgil (*Georgic* 3.3), will, of course, become the standard claim for various later authors working in different literary forms. Nor should the mock-modesty of the lesser genres of epigram and satire, an attitude inherited primarily from Horace, blind us to their covert pretensions. Persius, for instance, seemingly the poet with the lowest expectations of all (an audience of one or two), as he proceeds to analyse the Neronian literary situation, begins with sneers at epic writing, as was noted earlier, and only then goes on to savage the etiolated neo-Callimacheanism of other court poetry. Elsewhere in his satires, like Juvenal, he parodies epic conventions and language (see, e.g., the opening of *Satire* 5).

Admittedly both Martial and Juvenal are somewhat unfair, or at least literal-minded, in their refusal to acknowledge the allegorical and symbolic potentialities of epic and dramatic poetry. Seneca and Statius *were* debating, in however disguised a form, the recognizable problems of power and its attendant corruption, the nature of tyranny and ambition, the cruelty of war and arbitrary execution, and the bitterness of internecine struggle. Indeed they could reasonably counter that often the targets of the satirist and epigrammatist were trivial or modish, their performances more often intended to provoke amuse-ment rather than reflection. Modern defenders of Seneca the tragedian and of Statius the epicist can make persuasive enough cases for the 'seriousness' of each of them.[14] Yet the satirists had a point: whatever the merits of Valerius Flaccus, for example, his way of speaking to the human heart or the human condition was, at least superficially, over-elaborate, indirect and too dependent on stale traditions to compete with such a vigorous and comparatively new genre as satire.

Satire and epigram professed to reform as well as record; epic only to record. Epic easily fell into the pitfalls of rhetoric and rhodomontade; satire, like personal elegy, proclaimed its relevance and close con-nection to real life. Unlike elegy, however, it claimed to offer a more altruistic and universal message. Its exaggerations were justified by the lamentable state of society or the human condition, not by stylistic conventions. It therefore appealed to a more serious audience, to public-minded fellow citizens, disgusted with the decadence of the times, the corruption of public life and the pretensions of the powerful.

Satire, however, might be too limited and negative a form to satisfy all poetic aspirations. In the last decade of the fourth century Claudian, for instance, presents himself as both satirist and epicist. But here, surely, even in his sometimes powerful work, the reader is witnessing the playing out of the pagan classical tradition in derivative and opportunistic imitations.

Despite all this radical criticism from elegists and satirists, the writing of epic, now fully naturalized in Rome, and capable of achieving varying degrees of Alexandrian sophistication, continued as though such challenges had never been uttered.

Most contemporary criticism of Virgil's *Aeneid* was limited to niggling objections to his structure, his language, his style and his specific borrowings from Homer. Messala and Maecenas carped at his prolixity; lesser figures such as Herennius, Perellius Faustus and Q. Octavius Avitus provided lists of his faults and his literary thefts. Carvilius Pictor wrote a book with the title *Aeneidomastix* ('Scourge of the *Aeneid*'), filled with pedantic condemnations of Virgil's history and language.[15] Even emperors, such as Caligula and Commodus, might indulge in *épatant* sneers, parading their preference for the lighter works of Ovid and the epigrams of Martial. Perhaps only Vipsanius Agrippa was looking at larger issues when he described the author of the *Aeneid* as the inventor of a new and pernicious type of affectation ('repertorem novae cacozeliae'). Despite all of this the Mantovan remained the Roman Homer, and so the object of rivals' envy and emulation.

An important critical debate about the nature of epic in general and of Virgil's achievement in particular emerged in the frenzy of literary activity that centred on Nero's court. There one epicist stands out: the young Lucan. The patient Silius Italicus, a contemporary, would later continue Virgil's story of the founding of Rome through the time of its greatest external crisis, the Punic wars, meanwhile celebrating the poet's birthday each year. Silius was less allegorical than Virgil: his heroes were historical personages, standing for nothing but themselves; at most they were exemplars of Roman virtue. Yet he preserved the divine machinery of the epic tradition, however much it creaked, although he deployed it to a far lesser extent than Virgil.[16] Lucan, however, seems to have regarded the interaction of the human and the divine later to be seen in the *Punica* as supererogatory, if not downright factitious. Silius' own literary piety, on the other hand, might find congenial any contemporary objections to Lucan's deviation from Virgilian norms. Certainly the *Punica* conforms more closely than the *Pharsalia* to Eumolpus' recommendations for the writing of historical epic.[17]

Lucan's implicit criticism of the *Aeneid* is radical, and it was fuelled by partisan as well as artistic rivalry. He took issue with aspects of the *Aeneid*'s presentation of Rome and the empire, and although he paid his homage to his predecessor in linguistic allusions and stylistic echoes, he jettisoned the epic structural devices, notably the divine machinery, which Virgil had used in imitation of Homer and to provide a divine backdrop to Rome's history and the growing prestige of the Julian house. Lucan substituted a vaguer, more Stoic, supernatural dimension – fate and fortune – to narrate Rome's moral downfall and the tragedy of the republic in the civil wars. This repudiation of what many saw as Virgil's imperial optimism did not go unnoticed by hostile critics and by the keepers of the 'Virgilian' faith.

Somewhat unexpectedly, in the *Satyricon*, which was, among other things, a mock-*Odyssey* in a mixture of prose and verse, Petronius covertly criticizes Lucan's epic, without mentioning the poet's name. He targets Lucan's work for its inadequate learning, its reliance on historical facts and its abandonment of the operations of the divine in human affairs, not to mention the subversive depiction of Julio-Claudian legitimacy and current imperial authority. If epic is to be written, then it should follow the now traditional patterns of mysterious divine interventions ('per ambages deorumque ministeria', *Satyr.* 118.6). Yet despite this brave programme, the *Bellum Civile*, the 295-line sketch of a Virgilian treatment of the civil war, with greater emphasis placed on Caesar rather than Pompey and Cato, and with celestial and infernal deities playing a prominent part, is a disappointing effort that leaves the reader with uneasy feelings about its aims and its success. For all its obvious relationship to the *Pharsalia*, it is not what could be called a good parody. But if not a parody, it is certainly a 'para-poem'.[18]

The best available theory is that Petronius, for polemical purposes and in the context of Neronian literary politics, is using the disreputable poet Eumolpus to argue that if one sets out to write epic, then one must follow established, i.e. Virgilian, precedents in terms of *doctrina*, epic machinery, heightened imagination and smooth consistent style. Clever *sententiae* are no substitute for learning. But, and it is a significant but, such advice is subverted (as often in the *Satyricon*) by its source, a lecherous poetaster who is rejected by popular taste and by his sophisticated friends. His proferred counter-example, the sketchy fragment of an epic on the civil war, would hardly inspire a reader's confidence in the programme.

It is to the new dialogic, if not polyphonic, paradigm offered by the *Satyricon* itself, the loose sprawling Menippean novel, epic in length and scope with ludic (and ludicrous) allusions to the *Odyssey* in the Poseidon–Priapus theme, that the judicious reader must look for exemplary originality. The *Satyricon* as a whole should be considered Petronius' critique of epic. It has a legitimate claim to be regarded as the first extant picaresque novel, although it had its Greek antecedents. Its survival suggests that the artistic future lay with the apparently amorphous forms that would develop into the erotic or comic novel, the historical romance, the fictional biography of prince and philosopher, and even, with the advent of Christianity and its advocacy of a more passive but equally heroic virtue, the hagiography. There was clearly emerging a discernible literary (conservatives would say *subliterary*) genre in both languages.[19]

English literature offers a convenient analogy in the history of *Paradise Lost*, the last serious English epic, which itself incorporates Milton's own criticism of classical epic.[20] It has been said of this remarkable poem:

> Never was the death of an art form celebrated with such a magnificent ceremony, splendid in ashes and pompous in the grave. The death of tragedy was a mere decline into a whine and a whisper. But the death of epic was, in Milton's hands, a glorious and perfectly staged suicide.[21]

Much the same might be said, perhaps, of the explosion of epic in the Flavian period. Milton's epic was supplanted by, first, the religious allegory, notably John Bunyan's *Pilgrim's Progress* and *The Holy City*, and then by the realistic, sometimes comic, 'novels' of Aphra Behn, Daniel Defoe, Sterne, Fielding, Richardson and Smollett.[22] Other analogies may be found in French literature in the case of Rabelais, and in Spanish literature in the shape of *Don Quixote*, which rendered ridiculous the epic tales of chivalric *gestes*. It is of course dangerous to invoke so simple an example as Milton, for here we are dealing with what one might call 'tertiary' epic, since Milton does not go back for his models to the Old English or British heroic sagas for his primary epic models, and Homer he absorbs through the muffling medium of Virgil.

Indeed, anyone who looks for analogies in modern literatures runs up against the fact that, after the Renaissance and the revival of the classics, we are *always* dealing with 'tertiary' epic. The oral epics of the Anglo-Saxon and Germanic traditions had generated only vestigial secondary formations in the growth of their respective national literatures, since Renaissance, and in particular Italian, Humanism had weighted down the burgeoning vernacular tradition with the sometimes burdensome wealth of the classical heritage. This stifled any natural development of a literary or 'secondary' epic based on national oral epics such as the Old English *Beowulf* or the Merovingian *Nibelungenlied*. Instead would-be epic writers chose the alien classical models, not least Virgil, as the foundations of their literary efforts. So Milton professes to improve on pagan epic in his Christian epic, but it is not against *Beowulf* or even against the *Iliad* that his strictures are directed, but against Virgil, Statius and other adherents of the *Roman* epic tradition. It is significant that Milton's revolutionary endeavour is not a new beginning, as the author had hoped, but the end of the European epic tradition.

The assaults on Roman epic (not to mention tragedy) in the classical period by elegists, satirists, fabulists, and epigrammatists are symptomatic, then, of some literary or critical unease with the genre and the canon that enshrined its most famous exponents, even though the genre had a longer lease on life than either Latin elegy or Roman satire, and produced perhaps more remarkable artistic achievements than the more marginal literary forms. It is tempting to explain these various attacks as due to literary envy or self-promotion on the part of the 'modernists'. It is even more tempting to take refuge in generalizations about the inevitability of the rise, peaking and decline of all literary forms that cannot adapt to changing circumstances – and the relative inflexibility of epic theory is indicated by the tendentious criticisms of Virgil by Carvilius Pictor on the one hand and of Lucan by Petronius on the other.

Of course epic did adapt, as the essays in the present volume show, but not sufficiently, or with sufficient pertinency, for some of the empire's finest talents. For them the gloomy realities of the imperial present, the corruption of power and the ambiguities of loyalty, passion and courage that it engendered called for a satirist's eye rather than the epic voice.

NOTES

1 For a sketch of the variety of the many oral epic traditions from Ainu through Mongol to Serbo-Croat, see Hatto 1980: vol. I.

2 There is of course an overlap, and it would be interesting to know how many of the poems of the Greek epic cycle produced between 650 and 525 BCE would strike us as 'primary' and how many as 'secondary' epic. Inside the Trojan framework were such epics as *Cypria*, *Aethiopis*, *Little Iliad*, *The Sack of Troy*, *The Returns Home* and the *Telegony*; outside that frame, but impinging on it, were the poems of other epic cycles: *The Taking of Oechalia*, *Titanomachy*, *Oedipodeia*, *Thebais* and *Alcmaeonis*. See Davies 1989. The *Heraclia*s of Peisander and Panyassis and Antimachus' *Thebais* have the best claim to be the earliest 'secondary' epics.

3 Here the fifth-century Athenian tragic playwrights provide the paradigm and even deviant models. Tragedy's historical, social and ritual roots, hardly to be found elsewhere, at least in western art, suggest that the distinction between 'primary' and 'secondary' literary forms, as applied to epic, might be equally useful in the discussion of tragedy. Drama and epic were held in much the same esteem for partly historical reasons; hence Homer and the Attic dramatists are the main subjects of the first book of Aristotle's *Poetics*. For Milton, the story of the Fall was equally appropriate for dramatic or epic treatment, if his remarks in *The Reason of Church Government* are evidence. To Aristotle Yvor Winter's canonization of the short lyric poem would have been incomprehensible.

4 Contemporary parodies of Virgil attributed to Numitorius, Bavius and Maevius are largely lost. Significantly, when Dryden's translation of Virgil brought back the *Aeneid* to public attention, mock-epic and burlesque parodies of the *Aeneid* came back into vogue also, one example being Cambridge's *Scribleriad*. It will not be forgotten that the greatest translator of the *Iliad* was also the author of *The Rape of the Lock* and *The Dunciad*.

5 For some qualifications in respect of Ennius, see Goldberg 1989: 256–61.

6 Fragments or records survive of epics devoted to Pompey and other commanders. Obvious examples are Volusius' *Annales*, the *Bellum Actiacum*, the account of Germanicus' expedition to northern Germany by Albinovanus Pedo, Statius' proposed epics on Domitian's German wars, and so on. The craft of the professional epic writer is praised in Cicero's *Pro Archia* and by the younger Pliny (*Ep.* 3.21). Some typical examples are to be found in Morel 1963: s.v. Varro Atacinus; Varius Rufus; Albinovanus Pedo; and Cornelius Severus.

7 Unless otherwise indicated, the translations are mine and are meant to be interpretative rather than elegant.

8 Ezra Pound has not been the only one to find in Propertius' 'praise' of Virgil an underlying irony. Apart from myself, Stahl 1985: 180f. also believes that Propertius is not committed to Virgil's own estimate of what he is attempting. In Stahl's words (p. 181), 'the exuberant tribute to a New Homer and an epic even greater than the *Iliad* is a very dubious, because ambiguous, compliment'.

9 For which see chapter V above.

10 This is argued at length by, for example, Otis 1966. For criticism of Otis see Anderson in chapter VI above, pp. 111ff., who, however, takes a different view of the *Metamorphoses* from that suggested here.

11 Cf. 2.9.8–14; 3. *Prolog.* 61: 'iam mihi sollemnis dabitur gloria'; 4. *Prolog.*

17–20; 2.1–7; *Epilog.* 5–6. Interestingly enough, the Greek fabulist Babrius, who sees his iambics as a gentler successor to the blunt satiric iambics of Archilochus and Hipponax, may be dated no more than a half-century after Phaedrus. His achievement in the Greek tradition was similarly minimal and isolated.

12 The short poem as represented by Martial and a number of similar writers of the time, like the embryonic novel, ran into difficulties of nomenclature. Short pieces of verse of varying length and metre, when they were clearly not lyrical odes, were variously called *epigrammata, poematia, paegnia, lusus, nugae,*and so on.

13 See the still salutary warnings of Mason 1963: 94.

14 See, for example, Boyle 1983 and Ahl 1986.

15 The *Vita Donati* lists the critics and remarks wryly: 'obtrectatores Vergilio numquam defuerunt, nec mirum: nam nec Homero quidem' (Hardie 1966: 43). Many of the detailed objections surface in the scholia and the commentaries, not least in Servius, but they are apparent also in the discussions of Aulus Gellius and Macrobius. Georgii 1891 lists them, dividing them into three types: criticism of style and structure; criticism of historical accuracy; and criticism of borrowings from other poets.

16 To be precise, Silius' use of the divine dimension (excluding oracles) is confined to the following episodes: Book 2, the episodes of Hercules, Juno and Tisiphone (fewer than 300 out of 1,400 lines); Book 3, the discussion between Venus and Jupiter of Rome's prospects in the war; Book 4, Juno's spurring on of Hannibal; Book 6, Jupiter's diversion of Hannibal from his advance on Rome; Book 7, an aetiological episode concerning Bacchus and the introduction of wine; and an equally digressive encounter between Proteus and the Nymphs; Book 8, the aetiological encounter between Juno and Anna, Dido's sister; Book 10, Juno deterring Hannibal from a march on Rome; Book 11, Venus' participation in softening the Carthaginian troops billeted in Capua; Book 12, the rescue of Ennius by Apollo, and a further foiling by Juno and Jupiter of Hannibal's aggressive action against Rome; Book 15, the rescue by the goddess Italia of Claudius Nero; Book 17, Cybele's introduction to Rome; Neptune's storm, and the debate between Juno and Jupiter over Hannibal's fate. These constitute the sum total of parts played by heaven in human affairs in the *Punica* and are a mere fraction of the narrative by contrast with the close interaction between the two in the *Aeneid*.

17 Lucan also had his detractors, who criticized his oratorical style or his overly historical content; see Sanford 1931: 233. On Silius' mythological perspective on the causes and events of the Punic war, see Wilson in chapter XI below, pp. 219ff.

18 To use D. J. Enright's convenient term. The close relationship between the *Bellum Civile* and the *Pharsalia* has been denied by some, but the detailed evidence laid out by Rose 1971 is difficult to discredit. A recent implausible suggestion that the *Pharsalia* is inspired by the *Bellum Civile* goes too far in the opposite direction. What has troubled doubters perhaps is the fact that it is *not* a 'parody' in any ancient or modern sense of the term, and our literary theories are not sophisticated enough to distinguish intertextual relations other than (complimentary) 'imitation' and 'pastiche' or (hostile or derisive) 'parody'.

19 One has to qualify this by saying that the genre is 'discernible' in hindsight. Just as our own terms for certain forms of literature such as 'the novel' or

'romance' are diachronically and even synchronically problematic, and just as the Roman 'short poem' ran into definitional problems (*epigramma*, *poemation*, *lusus*, etc.), so these Greek prose fictions were variously described as *plasmata*, *dramata*, *mythi erotici*, *historiae* or *fabulae*, or were referred to by their subject matter or by the names of the characters, e.g. *Ethiopica*, *Satyrica* or *Chaereas and Callirhoe*.

20 See Pavlock 1990: 187.

21 Spencer 1968: 98.

22 On the death of epic and the rise of the religious and then the secular novel in England, see Hill 1989.

IX

FORM REMADE/
STATIUS' *THEBAID*

John Henderson

GATEWAYS TO THEBES[1]

We must want to get to the end as much as Aeneas did.[2]

As the story of Latin epic reaches the *Thebaid* of Statius, we confront for the first time the problem of a 'classic' which is commonly and even generally found disappointing by the scholarly consensus of our time.[3] While there have been voices outspoken in condemnation and, more rarely, in acclaim, this poem from the heart of the Flavian dynasty's court has most typically been coolly assessed as a disappointingly conformist product returning the epic genre to its ancient ways and means – with all the excitation and challenge that this description promises us (not) to expect! Vespasian in his humdrum dourness could be said[4] to have restored something of 'Augustan' dignity to the Imperial Order after the megalomania and self-destruction of Julio-Claudian excess, but ultimately failed to blind posterity to the obvious truth that he was the first emperor who was no 'Caesar' (made, not born). We could in similar fashion see his bard's laid-back aestheticism as a modest restoration of Virgilian classicism to epic's destiny after relegated Ovid's follies and Lucan's performance as 'human-bomb', but a restoration which must come across as a counter-reformatory venture doomed by its very logic to present its author as, ultimately, no true Poet (Purpose, yes, but inspiration? Hardly!'). Self-aware Sabine ruler and Neapolitan writer: just the team for an honest-to-goodness plod along roads, and *reads*, that would lead back to a gilt-edged Rome worthy of the name. Expect miles of post-Homeric machinery: Olympian inserts, Twin Catalogues and Teichoscopy, Necromancy and Underworld scenography, Funeral Games and *Aristeiai*, Prayer-sequences and Prophecy, Tragical Included Narrative and Aetiological Hymn, Developed Formal Similes, Battle-*Sturm und Drang*, Mountain Vastnesses tipping out twelve post-Virgilian volumes of torrentially surging verse – *in extenso*, the whole works! Such a view is outlined by the poem itself, both in its dedicatory Prologue and in the extraordinary Epilogue that

162

rounds off the text, in marked defiance of our generic expectations. It is also supported by Statius' own self-portraiture in his other extant poetry, his collections of occasional poems, the *Silvae*.

In the Prologue (1.1–45), Statius offers a *recusatio*, his remake of the poet's traditional 'apology' for his substitution of the work he can manage for the aspiration he can glimpse but not rise to realize. He makes it clear that we should recognize the decorum of an imperial subject's loyalty to Rome and its royals as the poet proffers *arma . . . / Aonia* (33f., 'the epic of poesy's Thebes') in place of what he marks as the goal deferred to the hope of his maturity, the real subject for epic, *Itala . . . / signa* (17f., 'Roman standards: a patriot's Latinity'). The *Thebaid*, then, *says* it is but an earnest of what may one day be written of the exploits of Rome's promised future, the dash of Domitianic campaigning towards a grand imperial victory and its inscription in triumphant verse . . . (Vespasian joined the gods while Statius worked on his epic.) The *Thebaid*'s promise is to trim its aspirations, then, in a responsible fit of callow producer to product. *Pierius . . . calor* (3, 'Inspirational heat from Pieria, near-enough to Thebes') will orchestrate this score for a *chelys* (33, 'The Greek word for tortoise, Greek noises to denote the lyre of art-writing and to connote an aesthete's devotion to learning the Graeco-Roman tradition'). As yet this poet's verses will *not* pretend to sing *Rome* with its Latinity. As yet he but brings the traditionally worthy but culturally irrelevant saga of Thebes for a new lease of life within classical art: *horrore canendus*, ends the Prologue, promising to 'sing a horror-show' (45), and at once the poet's hand plunges his stylus into the guilty eyes of cursed Oedipus, to write *impia . . . dextra* (46, 'with godless . . . hand') of the horror of the King of Thebes' self-blinding . . . The poet knows that this is, for now, *satis* (33, 'Enough'). The artist's 'Not Yet!'[5]

The Epilogue redoubles Statius' 'apology'. He breaks off his final scene, of post-*bellum* carnage, with 'vidui ducunt ad corpora luctus' (12.796, 'The women home on the men, as ever: widowed wives cleave unto the *dead* bodies of their males; in processional grief, voice after voice oblating laments'). This poet moderates his transports by fixing the widows' pain as beyond his powers to narrate. *This* calls for epic's traditional *recusatio*-formula: the poet would need more than 'a hundred hearts' to do justice to this theme, more than a fresh shot of 'the Apolline' within his chemistry (797–808). As it is, he speaks plainly and conclusively for himself, 'mea iam longo meruit ratis aequore portum' (809, 'My craft has now run the long course of its ocean-text and earned its haven').[6] At this moment of apparently final release, reminiscent of the ending of Apollonius of Rhodes' *Argonautica* where the Argonauts disembark back at Pagasae, Statius makes a further turn, towards his own heroine, '*Thebais*'. He tells his poem she is *multum vigilata* (811, 'night after night of lucubration: a finished product'). Initial reception at court and in Italy promises her a future once the usual envy of the writer gives way to deserved recognition (812–19): 'meriti post me referentur honores' (819, 'After I am gone all you have earned will be paid: honour after honour after honour' – the poem's last line). With one modest proviso, however: 'nec tu divinam Aeneida tempta, / sed longe sequere et vestigia semper adora' (816f., 'Don't take on the immortal heroine *Aeneis*! / No! Follow at the appropriate distance behind and for ever and ever worship the ground she has trodden!'). Statius knows all along, and inscribes, his 'post-Virgilian, propter-Virgilian' status.

These are privileged, authorized, self-positionings of the *Thebaid*. An 'ode' such as *Silvae* 4.7 can lend its voice in support.[7] This poem dramatizes Statius' writing-career within his social ambience, picturing the friendship, that 'Horatian' nexus of companionship and literary advice, of Vibius Maximus as the essential spine of his productivity. 'Maximus' figures a challenge for the poet whose work stretches from the understated renunciation of grandeur that befits a 'Callimachean' lyricist up to the sonorous greatnesses of epic tales of heroic expenditure. Vibius must return from his imperial labours in Dalmatia to rejoice in the recognition of a baby son and heir, *Maximus alter* (32, 'Maximus jr'): he is foil for Statius' writing, as the poet tells us Vibius helped 'nostra / Thebais multa cruciata lima' (25f., 'Our Thebaid, all that plastic surgery, the torture of criticism') take on 'the daring challenge of Virgilian-style glory', and is now needed for further poetic midwifery as Statius is 'stuck getting past his second epic's first bend into *Achilleid* book 2' (23f. Stuck there – he already knew? – for ever). The charm – ingenuousness, camaraderie, *urbanity* – of this fetching piece (one of *my* favourite Latin poems, as I imagine you can tell) adds the last touches to the self-portrait of a bachelor-scholar in his verse-workshop, turning out neatly crafted and self-critical works in tune with the canons of tradition and the best taste of the day . . . Would this poetaster *not* be satisfied if we found his epic progeny *competent*, declamatory entertainment for the Rome of the Younger Pliny – a sell-out fit to stir Juvenal's wrath?[8]

READING THEBES

The *Thebaid* cannot be said to be *about* anything.[9]

But the poem *knows* this 'humility' of its 'apologies'; it knows that their rhetoric is deflection and *meiosis*, the characteristic décor of urbane discourse under the empire.[10] From two points of view, at least, we can find that the poem's self-framing within its 'editorials' even points directly to its undisguisably explosive potential to mean, within the Flavian cosmos. When Statius promises his princeling the delectation of literary pirouetting in mythical Thebes from a *Pierio . . . oestro* (1.32, 'As Greek a gad-fly as the Muses can buzz into poetic frenzy'), he does more and less than direct attention away from Roman reality: he as good as pins the label to his tale, 'Read this text in and through its address to Domitian: look here and see "what His Divine Majesty deigns to give his time to" (12.814). *Think of the Flavians when you read this*' . . . This is not to say what readers are to find, only to frame *them* into finding *something*, a point in reading as searching to find 'it'. Since the Augustans, Roman readers of poetry had become used to the notion that a reading 'as if from, within, over against, the position of' a Caesar could produce a legion of tonal divagations, a proliferating release of meanings (e.g. Horace, *Epistles* 2, a meditation on its own, and any, such performance). Statius' readers would need no explicit mandate to explore ways in which his poem was declaring to them at one and the same moment both that the *Thebaid* was not 'about' their world and that it was not *not* about their world, too. In the second place, the story of 'Thebes' did not arrive on Statius' desk without its own set of meanings. A writer could insist, till he was blue in the face, that *his* treatment of this material was cleansed of any socio-political dimension, that he had only and precisely picked this legend because it allowed him to cut his teeth as a novice epic-versifier without taking a 'position' on *anything*, that . . . only to find that epic form denies any such facile abdication from vatic authority. 'Thebes' remains a live, civic paradigm, in no matter whose hands, under whatever waiver, in a declamation-hall, in a school textbook, in *this* book and in *your* life – but, especially, within any *imperial* order. (And *are* there any others?) I shall next explore both these points just a little.

ROMAN THEBES

The *Thebaid* is not a Roman epic; it has no national or patriotic motive.[11]

The *Thebaid*'s 'Prologue' moves in the shadow of Lucan's. Trumps 'cognatas . . . acies' (*BC* 1.4, 'battlelines of kin against kin') with 'fraternas . . . acies' (*Theb.* 1.1, 'battlelines of brother against brother'). But loses the *edge* of Lucan's *Bellum Civile*, its ambition to represent the ultimate epic amplification, 'Bella . . . plus quam civilia' (*BC* 1.1, 'Civil War – The Civil War, That Civil War, All Civil Wars – and then some'), as it disjoins its readers from its subject: in Lucan, the key textual moment is the appellation of readers into their positions as citizens of Rome, 'quis furor, o cives, quae licentia ferri?' (*BC* 1.8,

'*Citizens* – all you who participate in and are comprehended by Latin culture and Roman civilization – feel this madness, the anarchy, the killing, your *greatness*!'). If Statius himself as good as poses the problem for Flavian epic as : 'What has Rome to say after Lucan's holocaust?', we could find that he has only the wet answer that his text displaces civic with kin war – and the promise of his pre-text that he will (try to) turn up the horror-controls.

Flavian subjects, however, could scarcely resist reading into their 'Thebes' the post-Lucanian tragedy of the Caesars of 69 CE, 'The Year of the Four Emperors', when civil war in waves of invasion found what could conceivably be told as supervenient settlement by a new 'Theseus' of suicidal internecine stasis à la *Thebaid*, as Vespasian finally arrived to conclude the carnage left after Nero's fall by the struggles between Galba, Otho and Vitellius. This is *not* what Statius says. Nor does he claim to write of Father Vespasian's ('Pisistratean') legacy of the Roman World-State, the City of Man, to *his* two sons for their rule. But in his articulation of (the 'Zedekiahan') 'Oedipodae confusa domus' (1.17, 'That chaos, the Oedipal ménage'), which the Prologue presents as its designated 'limes . . . carminis' (1.16, 'the line/limit/path/ domain of the poem'), Statius' readers cannot avoid contemplating up close the collapse of a royal house, the end of such dynasties as the Julio-Claudian and . . . of *whatever* lineage will succeed it, the mass-destruction that absolutist monarchy must eventually spell for its cultural order, according to the age-old mytho-logic of epic Thebes. This was one 'secret' of power at Rome that could never be concealed. Had some kind of Labdacidal 'Tragedy' *not* befallen *their* Rome?[12]

Thebes was a classic terrain for epic, as 'Homeric' as Troy. The Cyclic *Thebaid* has now all but vanished, though the opening verse survives – to set us to think hard and long: 'Argos sing, goddess, a-thirst from where chiefs'.[13] Ever after, the Theban story must consider its Argos, Argos embroiled in the Theban nightmare: *innocent* Argos?[14] Athenian tragedy, to which we must return, attests in full the aptitude of the cities of Oedipus and Tantalus for the release of the Repressed. Among Hellenistic classics, Antimachus' *Thebaid* offered what we may guess to have been a massively recherché text of prevarication, starting from a grand 'Speak on, Muse-daughters of mighty Zeus, son of Cronus' and obstructing *his* Seven Warrior-Heroes from reaching Thebes with twenty-four books of preliminaries.[15] We just know the existence of a string of other Hellenistic efforts – by Antagoras, by a certain Demosthenes, and by Menelaus of Aegae[16] – before Rome's first dynastic inauguration called forth *its Thebaid*, in the very early 20s BCE. Again we have nothing left to go on, – so many textual *Thebaids* as utterly destroyed as the house of Laius, more thoroughly than Alexander could raze physical Thebes! – but it is worth taking a moment to wonder what Propertius' sparring-partner Ponticus can have been signalling by penning his epic of 'Cadmeae . . . Thebae / armaque fraternae tristia militiae' (1.7.1f., 'Cadmus' Thebes, where war turned sour on brothers-in-arms'). Was this but the recycling of recycled Greek melodramatics, a welcome reinvestment in the aestheticized sublimity of 'Classical Culture'? Or does Propertius find himself finding in Ponticus an explosive return to insistent relevance of those dinosaur alien city-scapes of early mythology, a theme for post-Actian Italy?[17]

LE ROMAN DE THEBES

L'anti-cité, la cité de la violence pure et de la stasis.[18]

'Thebes', then, was known throughout classical antiquity as a central theme for epic narration, for Homeric representation of *cacotopia*. To an extent, it is but a trick of time that makes Statius' the first extant narrative. On the other hand, there are powerful reasons why this tale suited best the Attic and then the post-Attic (Accian, Senecan, Racinian . . .) dramatic medium, why Theban narratives have died so many deaths and mainly survive to haunt theatre-scripts. It is in any case true that it is within the criticism of fifth-century Greek tragedy that the horror-show of Thebes has been most sympathetically registered. (May I merely remark, however, in passing that there has been a tremendous input of energy through the millennia to bound the reception and interpretation of the tragedy of the Athenian democracy this side of making any impact upon the political thought of our civilization? As if 'we' have ever been safely cordoned off from 'Thebes'! As if it simply is as we would wish it to be: our Other, the exteriority of our feared selves!) I shall next briskly summarize the 'story' so that we may then turn briefly to the Thebes of drama. Later I shall return to the difference that *narration*, epic narration, of the *Thebais* may make to its sense.

Here, then, is a paraphrase of the story that Statius remakes into his poem:[19] Oedipus carried within his nature *was* the curse of the Family (of King Laius). Parricide, Incest, Horror. After his own self-recognition and self-blinding he damned his two sons to rule Thebes in his place. Their agreement, to alternate power on an annual basis, broke down at the first try. Dispossessed by brother Eteocles, Polynices finds a band of guest-friends, new affinal relatives and warrior-comrades in Adrastus' kingdom of Argos, the 'Seven against Thebes', who will restore him to his throne. Considerable delay and obstruction held up the assault half-way, around Nemea, before bloody battle broke out, in which the 'Seven' and many of their opponents virtually wiped each other out. The climax was the brothers' hand-to-hand duel, which closed in reciprocal fratricide. The new king, Creon, denied burial to the invaders, but the women of Thebes and of Argos called in the dashing King Theseus of Athens to face him down. Thebes' royal house was as good as terminated in this tussle. With lamentation from the bereaved ends the tale.

THE TRAGEDY OF THEBES

C'est la Thébaïde, c'est-à-dire le sujet le plus tragique de l'Antiquité.[20]

If we are to feel Statius' poetry, we will need to grant it *something* of that 'form of attention' which we habitually lavish upon the genre of fifth-century Athenian tragedy, the presumption, that is to say, that in its struggles to tell us its world and in its own insistence that this is necessarily and importantly an incomplete, suspect, partial representation, 'Thebes' resounds with political intelligence. In a magisterial essay which you *must* read, Zeitlin (1990)[21] explores what 'Thebes' meant for the *dēmos* of Athens. She finds the boundaries of personal identity and the boundaries of alterity annulled, the relational structure of the family imploded, and the city a system entropically closed, folded up from articulation and locked into self-absorption:

> Thebes is the place . . . that makes problematic every inclusion and exclusion, every conjunction and disjunction, every relation between near and far, high and low, inside and outside, stranger and kin . . . When he . . . alternates between a condition of self-referential autonomy and involvement in too dense a network of relations, Oidipous personifies in himself the characteristics that Thebes manifests in all its dramatic variants, through all its other myths, and through the extant work of all the tragic poets of Athens . . . Thebes, the other, provides Athens, the self, with a place where it can play with and discharge both terror of and attraction to the irreconcilable, the inexpiable, and the unredeemable, where it can experiment with the dangerous heights of self-assertion that transgression of fixed boundaries inevitably entails, where the city's political claims to primacy may be exposed and held up to question.[22]

In Thebes, where Father is Brother, Mother is Wife, Mother-in-Law is Sister-in-Law, nothing can add up and make sense. Internecine hatred completes the undoing of the clan and its state. Barthes sees the confusion thus:

> Hatred does not divide the two brothers . . . (i)t brings them closer together; they need each other in order to live and in order

to die, their hatred is the expression of a complementarity and derives its force from this very unity: they hate each other for being unable to tell each other apart . . . What the brothers seek in order to vent their hatred is not battle, the abstract, strategic annihilation of the enemy: it is the individual clinch, the physical conflict and embrace; and this is how they die, in the lists. Whether it is womb, throne, or arena, they can never escape the same space that confines them, a unique protocol has ordained their birth, their life, and their death. And the effort they make to tear themselves away from each other is merely the final triumph of their identity.[23]

We begin to understand how powerful a scenario tragic 'Thebes' can be, through the eyes of the Athenian citizen we imagine ourselves to play: the very dimensions within which we can find any relations thinkable, the possibility for any story-pattern to be imagined – temporality, space, generational linearity – spin at Thebes into recycled repetition, glomerate in fusion. This is Statius' point of departure, the *guilt* of Thebes – locked into circles of revenge in which everything can only happen again:

> fraternas acies alternaque regna profanis
> decertata odiis sontesque evolvere Thebas
> Pierius menti calor incidit.
>
> (*Theb.* 1.1ff.)

Battlelines of brothers, the kingdom of alternation, cursed hatred's final solution, the guilty: Thebes . . . On heat with Poesy – Greece! – My Mind. *Falling.*

If the order here seems to be chronologically up-ended, so that the poem's first item must name its *telos*, the duel of Eteocles and Polynices, then the point will soon be clarified when the text has the voice of Thebes name as *fraternas . . . acies* those *Spartoi*, the 'Sown Men' of Cadmus with whose sowing and internecine strife the city came into being, total disaster from/as the start. An anonymous citizen reads Thebes for us as the abomination that lay at the end of founder Cadmus' 'search' (*quaerere*), the 'battlelines of brothers' his dynastic legacy, the omen of dissemination ('augurium seros dimisit ad usque nepotes', 1.184f., 'He handed on the omen to reach right through to all his late-comer grandsons'). It could still be the apogee of this senselessness that we come – perhaps with, perhaps in spite of, Theseus – to ponder on Statius' Killing Fields.

169

WAR AT THEBES

War is, first of all, at war with the rationality of its own participants
. . . Hatred assimilates each side to the other, the *Wechselwirkung*
becomes an oscillation as well as a mutuality, each side becoming
the other as the sides work each other up to a resemblance in
extremism. There is even an altruism of hatred, in which the other
becomes more important than the self. One is willing to give one's
life in order to take the foe's. This is the selflessness that gives war
its weird and inverted nobility. It is, in Clausewitz's view, a
necessary mark of fighting men. But it is hardly rational . . .
(w)hen we are most exalted by hostility and have the greatest
sense of wielding war to serve our purposes, war is wielding us,
carrying us away from ourselves in the nobility of self-sacrifice
inspired by hate. Shoulder shoving, on the largest scale, has
become an end in itself . . .[24]

At Thebes we look at Warfare afresh. A *Thebaid* is not cleanly the other
of civic/patriotic/national/imperialist fighting. It does not simply stage
a hyped-up mythic remake of the *Bellum Civile*. Rather, it makes itself a
messy collage from a cursed centrepiece of suicidal *Bruderkrieg* against
the background of a (hysterically primitivesque) blood-brotherhood-in-
arms. 'Thebes' has that unsettling status of not *not* confounding War,
Revolution, Civil War and Stasis. (Especially once Statius has removed
its shape by un-featuring the Walls, the Gates, the Seven Paired
Champions standing ready in the old story to structure a scene of
Attack/Defence.)

War is fought to decide a dispute, to impose a 'sense'. Thus the
fighters fight to impose their reading on anyone left alive to dispute
'Thebes'. We can set out some of the rival perspectives. For Adrastan
Argos, this is a Just War. An obligation to a guest-friend, with God on
our Side. And International Law. This blurs into: the Restoration of its
own Crown Prince to his full inheritance: (cloaked) military Annex-
ation. Not to mention: Adventure for 'Heroes'. And: Alliance in
operation. // Whereas, for Eteocles, this is a *Coup d'état*; it must be
stopped. So: patriotic Defence of the Realm. This is an elder son
reclaiming his own rights; and he maintains Internal Security and
restores Stability. An outlawed Enemy of the State leads an Invasion,
backed by the might of a Super-Power arsenal and economy; the
Intervention is but papered-over Self-Interest. // For Tydeus, next, the
attack is merited Revenge. The Cause is that foundation of International Law, Diplomatic Immunity. Theban Aggression assaults the
Argive Nation when it assaults the person of its (second) Crown Prince-
and-Envoy. // Polynices? Polynices is out to direct his own script: of
Restoration. He vindicates a Solemn Treaty, reclaims his Right to Rule,

170

grants Thebes *Anschluss* with Argos, and uses Minimum Force to punish the Usurper. // For Creon, this is the story of his son's Sacrifice to Save the Walls; for him the Enemy is one alien undifference, set below Human Rights. // Loser Jocasta must replay 'Veturia' failing to avert her 'Coriolanus': the mother whose son turns on his origins, his country, his people. // For Theseus, this is one more request to remake Man for Clement Civilization. There is, to be sure, some (Regrettable) Loss of Life – from Hostile Extremists, naturally, condemned by World Opinion. // For the Cities, for their Women, this is War – why discriminate further? This is that old refrain, 'And it's 1–2–3–What are we fightin' for?'. 'Thebes' is what takes the men away. It is why mothers bear sons: Victory, in that Body-Bag . . .

In war Humanity orders and imposes a distribution of meanings around a dominant 'reading'. A final solution, a rereading that 'remakes', it says, a (stab at) Truth. (As if there could ever be a dominant hierarchy that did not depend on the continuing resistance of the views and values it constitutively seeks to oppress! The defeated memorialize *their* stories even as they become cannon-fodder, notches on the belts of their conquerors.)

We have perhaps thought we know why a Wild West's *Magnificent Seven*, a World War's *Dirty Dozen*, must fight it out before us, why the champions of a *Thebaid*'s army of Argives must live their face-to-face code of 'heroism' for us. This western discourse of warfare has forever played its part in anchoring political sense between and within our human social structures. These are scenes of consecration for the Human Being conceived as civic pugnacity: 'at the bottom-line of national ideology, you'll find that the subject who "*is*" is man as male, and is a male male, a manly man. *And that's what he should be*'.[25] The 'Iliadic' myth of the Warrior's *aristeia* as the proving-ground of real existence pulls us (men?) back still into the regressive fantasy that we live in some individual-scale, directly cooperative, self-bounded tribal culture, where the localism essential to the heroic champion can pass as a plausible reading of our lives, our only text-to-be. Of course we 'know', like those imperial Romans, like those democratic Athenians, like even those social configurations which produced their 'Homeric' recitations in the first place, that this bears no *real* relation to any world we inhabit. It is the flame of ideological atavism that draws us, moths in the glare of its beacon. We, all of us, know our selves, the order of our being, in and through (the denial of) our very distance – our 'lapse'? – from this the nostalgia of Europe's origins: the positioning of the 'Man-at-Arms' as his City's Shield and Spear. Nothing could be so simple. No condensation, no image-repertoire so massively reinforced by centuries of inculcation with charismatic text and educational scene of training in militarist machismo, with or without the balm of pathos/the chauvinism of conquest. Yet, the ordeal of 'Thebes' may show, nothing is so reliant on carefully elaborated articulation and on insistently patrolled shepherding of the psyches it would condition.

The *Iliad*'s modelling round a transcendental design – the 'Plan of Zeus' – contributes to its narration a drive towards totalization that fetishizes 'The Duel' as the orgasmic finale, the Warrior binding the corselet of Power and Knowledge tight round his Self as he drives home the metal in his hand through the body of his partner. The narration constrains this paradigmatic primal scene to converge with the story that bears it in a teleology where we can know that Everything is all along directed towards the ending that is the fight 'to the end'. The point of the story-telling is to arrive at the conviction that human agency crystallizes when the Warrior decisively and conclusively drives home the point of his blade. Yet the scene depends on choreography for a Due*t*, for the victor needs his victim's cooperation for their *pas de de*ath. The absolute difference between life and death which is the stake and productivity of Combat is founded on an initial parity, the opponents must interlock in a blur of proximate interchangeability, and we and they must find each other's values from a mutuality in the 'fairness' of fight. The hero 'knows himself' through the foe he merits. There is even necessarily a bond between the participants that tends toward the homoerotic, for the show-*down* functions as show-*case*, for 'manliness'. They and we must find what we admire, or – Why not say it? – *love*, in the reflected ideal gleaming and dinning from the flashing weapons and thundering armour of that best of beetles, the hard-case *HuMan*. This way the thorax will fill with the spirit of prowess and . . . we'll – join the marines.

The *Aeneid* forces such a reading upon the *Iliad*, mightily establishes this as the epic tradition, classical tradition, Tradition *tout court*, how Fathers-who-were-Sons remake Sons-who-will-be-Fathers in their own form. Homer's text runs on from its dénouement dance of Achilles with Hector to shape its meaning through reception in and of the poem by way of memorializing scenes that feature and constitute 'commentary' and so risks side-tracking readers from its 'finality', or thereby courts a discursive, dialogical, suspended reaction from readers on out of the text and into their lives.[26] The immeasurably abrup— terminat— of the *Aen*—, in the very departure of Turnus' life from the body at Aeneas' fee—, insists, to the contrary, on running us through (with) the charismatic moment of slaughter, without compunction or softening. We are obliged, with the suggestive shadow of the *Iliad* in our minds and the promptings of the myriad variations, and discourses, on the paradigm of *arma virumque* that have been pressed into making up the entire duration of the Roman national epic before us, to 'remake' our own final reckoning up of the sense. The poignancy, the poin—

After Lucan's dejection of the *aristeia* from his own, open-ended, epic – dislodged from the text, perhaps, to await some patriot's revenge on the Caesars, some more conclusive Cassius Chaerea, a final conspiracy of Roman warrior-heroism, possibly a remake starring Annaeus Lucanus? – Statius returns the majesty of Roman story-telling to the sanctified ways of Western War. *His* pantheon of Warriors stakes out a mighty terrain for *virtus*, to be focused, perfected and topped by the duel between the rival commandants, the sons of Oedipus. Then the *Thebaid* continues its travail, with a full exploration of its signification through a panoply of aftermath scenes: struggles to memorialize the slain, fresh slaughter to that end, suffering on suffering, and the regime of mourning . . . Statius takes the space to fix the dynamics of 'Cadmean Victory' into his own, 'Theban', portrait of humanity; and the bard survives to carry through to completion and completeness the 'intent' of Virgil's narration. Statius shores up the sense of The Duel from the lability which its unpoliced termination risks at the hands of its readers – if he does not rather bring out the *necessarily* delicate poise of heroism above an abyss of our suspicion and mutiny, if he does not indeed even tarnish and topple the whole shooting-match. The 'remake' –

COMBAT AT THEBES

The Western Way of War, conceived by the Greeks as trial by ordeal, leads <us> their descendants into the pit of the holocaust.[27]

At its simplest, martial epic was purpose-built to hammer home cumulative thrusts with the hand-held sword. The 'wrong' scene would be the killing of the wrong – unfairly matched – victim, as when Aeneas' sword pierces the body of the female commandant Dido. (Destinedly, Aeneas had his alibi – we witness his absence, away with his fleet. And there were no finger-prints!) The Italian *vir* Turnus is contrastively defined by contrast as the 'right' object of 'the right war in the right place'. 'Bad' slaughter, however, was elaborated in terms of its positioning – even its 'morality', as the belligerent interpreter will always insist on lying to us. Thus Aeneas will become the *vir* fit to receive and bear his *arma* only when he has soldiered on through his ordeals to reach the site of the homeland he is readied to kill or die for. He journeys from Dido to occupy the *domus*, the *ara*, the *moenia* of the *Urbs*, the supreme, overriding, object of his desire. (Home. Stability. Spatial Selfhood. Identity. All he lost with Troy.) Consecrated by his *adventus* here, he can be embraced by Love, mother-love generating love of the fatherland his progeny; he can be wrapped henceforth in the divine *arma* that he has been forged to fit: *AMOR > ROMA*. You see, *Virtus* is

173

the use of *arma* in 'Defence', as we euphemize all warfare waged *pro patria*, after the archetype Hector. Aeneas wields 'the sword of Deathstiny' (*Aen.* 8.621, 'fatiferum ... ensem') once he has been positioned – joyful, rapt in wonder (617ff.) – as his society's 'Human Shield': as the Shield he both wears and, in both senses of the word, 'becomes' ('clipei non enarrabile textum', 625, 'the unsayable fabric of epic discourse, all that the sign "shield" shields from summation: the Shield-ensign that signifies the Warrior's worth, the mettle of his *Virtus*'). And just as we are to recognize in the 'bad' emblem of the trophy Aeneas makes of the 'bad' victim, who seizes the initiative, spoils the Duel, 'attacks Aeneas' sword-blade with his throat' (10.907f.), that the arms *are* the man – 'Mezentius hic est', taunts Aeneas over the emptied rig of armour (11.16, 'Introducing the great Mezentius, large as life!') – so we will see that the 'good' sword-thrust is powered by comradeship, the agent's adrenalin fired by soldierly *pietas*, when Aeneas slays Turnus at the sight of the despoiled sword-belt of Pallas round the 'wrong' frame: the arms signify and make present the whole force of the soldier's *virtus*, as good as driving the warrior by remote control. Such 'fraternal' solidarity valorizes the Warrior's valour: set alongside his like to make the paradigm of the patriot State, forbidden to 'fraternize' with the other side's brothers-in-arms ... – the alibi inside-out, as values must be, on the battlefield, where –

'Our' armies must forever massage themselves into making real for themselves the myth of Homeric epic and its remakes, where family-units – phalanxes of brothers – regularly stand shoulder to shoulder in action, naturalizing 'national service' as a system of 'blood-ties'. (Classic scenes at Hom., *Il.* 11.426ff., *Aen.*10.338ff., cf. e.g. 390ff., 575ff., especially 'morere et fratrem ne desere frater', 600, 'Be brothers in brotherly death!')[28] In this respect the *Thebaid* more than runs true to form. (Cf. *Theb.* 8.448ff., where twin brothers regret killing twin brothers; 9.272ff., where a true brother dies sooner than desert his brother; 292, one twin is spared, one is speared; 10.654, brothers metaphorically as well as literally fight side by side; 12.744, triplet brothers are slain by Theseus ...) For 'Thebes' tilts the whole epic apparatus towards negating this fundamental feature of its design precisely by working up to its climax of protagonist brothers 'fighting together'. The story fixates on the desecration of War and its categories as its Theban 'theme', unveiled from the first by Statius' disgustingly unforgettable catachresis *fraternas acies*.[29] Thus the curse on Thebes from (the dejected Cronian brother) Pluto, rewriting father Oedipus' mandate, takes the form: 'fratres ... fratres alterna in vulnera ruant' (8.70, 'Brother after brother, brother upon brother, taking turns to deal out the wounds, to dive on to the wounds, let Theban alternation commence!'); Tisiphone, Oedipus' hellish double, orders: 'non solitas acies ... sed fratrum' (11.97f., 'War gone strange – lines of brothers'); Polynices' bloodlust craves: 'scelus et caedem et perfossi in sanguine fratris / exspirare' (11.153f., 'wicked-ness/slaughter/a chunnel dug through my brother before I breathe my last in the lake of his blood'); Piety must make her vain appeal to: 'quis nati fratresque domi' (11.478, 'Calling all parents and brothers!') . . .

The *Thebaid* does present its readers with hallowed epic scenes of brothers-in-death, where the warriors love their death; it brings them closer than men can ever be, and locks them together in what Statian jaundice, however, pictures as a sickeningly eternal 'hug', 'The Kiss' of the sons of Ide (3.151, 'complexus . . . oscula'):

> procubuere pares fatis, miserabile votum
> mortis, et alterna clauserunt lumina dextra.
> (*Theb.* 2.642–3)

Undivided they fall. Deathstiny deals them a shared end. – Pray to die this way. You'll find, like them, a place in everyone who has a heart. – Their hands closed each other's eyes, they watched over each other's death, a twosome alternation of soldierly righteous-ness. The *right hand*, the sword hand, the Man's pledge, the hand of righteousness, *droit, son dieu*.

But this Man's Talk – Drool as Brother watches Brother die, closes the other's '*eyes* swimming still in *light*' (638f., 'oculos etiamnum in luce natantes') – is, as we shall see, stained by Statian lamentation and in any case figures as but foil to the guilty '*alternation*' of Theban brotherhood, along with all the other cues to 'think siblings' massed through the poem:[30] 'fratri concurro, quid ultra est?' (11.185, 'I invade my brother: the absolute limit'). The potential for Thebes to breed cameos of *virtus* is squandered, off the Killing Fields, in *Freitod*, defiant suicide – from Maeon, the bearer of bad news to a tyrant (3.91), then Menoeceus' devotion for the city, his *mortis amor* (10.804); in the deathstined 'fall' of Amphiaraus into hell's abyss (8.1, 'incidit umbris'), that 'one small step for Epic Originality' (8.101, 'nova fata'); in the last-minute reprieve of Hippomedon from drowning, for ('Palinuran') overwhelming – still 'no chance for him to die a hero, not with Statius' limited poetic resources' (9.491, 'nec magnae copia mortis'); in whatever Statius and we make of Capaneus' verbal theomachy, that thunder-struck display of 'infernal madness, was it? Or *virtus egressa modum*? Headlong glory? Mega-Deathstiny? Pride before Fall, Supernal Wrath smiling Death?' (10.831–6). Unless we find *virtus*, rather than its snuffing, displayed in that *tour de force* of romantic/tragic sentimentality, the exploits of mother Diana's ('Camilla'-esque) Arcadian-archer, *miserande puer* Par-thenopaeus (9.716, 'Virgilian pathos of immature death': cf. *Aen.* 6.882 of Marcellus). Unless it is to be found worked into that parody of

Patroclean comradeship, the blood-brotherhood-in-arms of Polynices and Tydeus, that grows into the chiefest martial sub-theme of the epic? In Tydeus we may find the *Thebaid*'s own favourite foil of *Warrior* idealism/fetishism, set to frame the ultimate scene of mutual fratricide with the contempt of perversion. In Tydean *virtus* shall we find, even, 'Das Hauptwerk des Statius'?[31]

EPIC AT THEBES

We are much less Greek than we believe.[32]

This boarish Calydonian (2.469ff.) one-man plague and brother-killer (1.397, 402, 'fraterni sanguinis', 2.113, 'fraterno sanguine') first enters the text outcast and in need, to remake 'beggar Irus vs beggar Odysseus' upon Argos' threshold. From 'alternation' of verbal abuse (1.410, 'alternis'), he proceeds to a 'duel' of feral *clawing* for brute needs, namely 'Shelter from the Storm', before he is taken up to play his opponent Polynices' 'Pylades' (1.473ff.), the perfect brother-in-law, 'that brother you never had': 'alius misero ac melior mihi frater ademptus' (9.53, 'the other and better brother it will hurt to lose'). Polynices' partner for a double royal wedding to the princess sisters becomes his diplomatic representative, his fly-weight champion and pocket-general. He joins, teams up with, represents, stands for and stands in for, his 'mate': they are a couple good as – married: their two hearts beat as one! (Eteocles treated Tydeus as if he *were* Polynices, see 7.540, 'nec frater eram', 'I wasn't even his brother!' And Tydeus' battle-cry calls *just* like an Oedipodionian for 'Anyone with menfolk I've slain – a father, perhaps? A brother or so, your other halves, your sem-blances?' for slaying next (8.668f., 'nulline patres, nulline iacentum / unanimi fratres').

Tydeus is to be Statius' answer to The Epic Tradition of the sturdy ('defensive') Warrior. This one-man army (2.491, 8.701f.) figures the mobile Wall and Human Shield, trusty stalwart of stability, the team-man's resistance 'For the Good of the Cause' – remade decoction of the *Iliad*'s Ajax, Ennius' Aelius, the *Aeneid*'s Turnus, Lucan's Scaeva . . .[33] But already in the introductory scrap with Polynices (à la Lawrence's *Women in Love*!), the *Thebaid*'s 'fighting' was pre-cultural, Oedipally regressive – homing in on the *eye-sockets*:

scrutatur et intima vultus
unca manus penitusque oculis cedentibus intrat.
(*Theb.* 1.426–7)

Digging right inside the *face*/some pre-human *claw* passes inside and the *eyes* give ground.

You will find that this is typologically prefigured by and textually prefiguring the mythological song-within-the-song of Statius' 'Alcinous'/'Dido'/'Evander'/'Latinus'-precipitate, the King of Argos Adrastus' aetiological hymn to 'Poetry', to *Phoebe parens*, which shuts this book that (as we remarked) was opened by Oedipus' gouged eyes, where the 'pre-human *claw* . . . and iron-clad *rippers*' ('unca manus . . . ferratique ungues') of Apollo's post-'Cacus' monster suffers when *his* 'Hercules', Coroebus, comes to '*rummage* in the dark' (*scrutatus latebras*) before the folk come to 'ogle the *eyes* bruising in death' (1.610ff., 'visere . . . liventes in morte oculos'). In this myth (fixing *Aen.* 8 with the end of *Aen.* 1) we will find, displaced and condensed, anticipated lineaments of the *Thebaid*, seeded *Hauptmotiven* of its paradigm: Python's 'hug' (1.564, *amplexum*), the rabid pack's, and the monster's, 'blood-baby-*munch*' (1.589, 'morsu depasta cruento'; 1.603f., 'morsu cruento / devesci') . . .[34]

Supposing this 'Man' Tydeus' charisma has survived his entrée's ferocious savagery, you'll have to be a Polynices if you don't find his last martial feat of *virtus* emetic. Recall first that Achilles was verbally smeared, by Hector's mother, uniquely smeared, as a bestial outsider with '*ōmēstēs*' (*Il.* 24.207, 'Eater of the Raw'). This was, then, once the worst that could be said on how people ought not to (tr)eat.[35] Well, you just watch the *Thebaid*'s dying 'Patroclus'/'Pallas'-deposit, Tydeus, as he has the head of his killer fetched and, as his admiring patron Athena comes to award him Herculean divinity, she and we must see him expire thus:

> illum effracti perfusum tabe cerebri
> aspicit et vivo scelerantem sanguine fauces
> – nec comites auferre valent.
>
> (*Theb.* 8.760–2)

Her *eyes* met Tydeus drowned in brain-pulp smithereens, pervert *jaws* wicked with lifeblood still alive – the comrades can't get it away from him.

This is 'ultimate' social deconstruction to set alongside incest and fratricide, approaching the Platonic Tyrant's endocannibalistic filicide.[36] This *Yukkh*, Tydeus' last memory and memorial, is the way 'Thebes' must see its feast of *virtus*: eating into the brain. As it does in reading – ingestion through the eyes . . . does the *Thebaid* not vomit, revile, its own story-patterns here? Manic vision had linked Tydeus to his killer in a gaze that has no ending: (Tydeus) 'vultu occurrit, vidit / ora trahique oculos, spectat atrox . . . gliscitque tepentis / lumina torva videns et adhuc dubitantia figi' (8.751–6, 'met him *face-on*, saw his *face*, *eyes* a-trailing, grimly *watched the sight* . . . grew expansive, *seeing the eye-*

lights grim, not yet decided to get fixed'). The guardian angel, soldier Athena of the flashing eyes, had managed her fighter Tydeus' martial career so far. But finally, even she must '*turn away in aversion*' and 'purge those luminous *eyes*, with mystic fire, with an epic river-flow of ablution': 'fugit aversata iacentem, / nec prius astra subit quam mystica lampas et insons / Elisos multa purgavit lumina lympha' (8.764–6: this the book-end, two-thirds through the post-Virgilian twelve-book plan, instructs you readers just what to do once you leave your study, turn for respite from the text!). We Oedipuses must burn out the sight – unless we blot Tydeus out with tears of derision. Statius!

Athena's *aversion* from Tydeus points forward to the most authoritative moment in all readings of the *Thebaid*, her (our) Almighty Father's 'imperative *aversion*' from the brothers' showdown, *auferte oculos*!' (11.126): 'ut . . . vidit pater . . . / "vidimus . . . licitas . . . acies . . . lateant . . . Iouem: sat . . . sontes . . . vidisse . . . turbanda dies . . . Ledaei videant neu talia fratres." / Sic pater omnipotens visusque nocentibus arvis / abstulit . . . ' (119–35, 'When the Father *saw* . . . he said, "We have *seen* lines of regular war . . . Let the brothers hide from Jupiter's *sight*; enough to have *seen* the guilty . . . I must smog the day . . . And *they* mustn't *see*, those twin boys of Leda, those *brothers*!" Thus the Almighty One. And he tore his *gaze* from the fields ploughed with guilt'). Tydeus' and Polynices' brawl already pre-patterned the brothers' Duel:

> coeunt sine more, sine arte,
> tantum animisque iraque, atque ignescentia cernunt
> per galeas odia et vultus rimantur acerbo
> lumine . . .
>
>   veluti . . .
>
>   sues . . .
> igne tremunt oculi, lunataque dentibus uncis
> ora sonant.
>
>   (*Theb.* 11.524–33)

Come together, right now: bare of skill, bare of style,/ pure mental drive plus hate; ablaze, they *eye* / loathing through helm, through helm loathing; and *faces rifle faces* with acid / *sight* . . . like . . . boars . . . quivering *optic fire*, and crescent, *claw-toothed*, / *mouth-faces* din.

The 'scopic drive' – all-consuming desire to watch the mirror-self (the brother) watch itself smashed to pieces – guides the Duel to/as its fetishized end: our readers' stand-in within the simile of the 'boars', the blenched hunter, turns spectator and stills his hounds to listen, while the sibling Furies play admiring arena-crowd (11.533–8); prematurely exultant Polynices tells dying Eteocles, 'You *see*, you've let yourself get out of shape!' (548, 'vides' . . .); he proclaims his victory, '*I see* the heavy *eyes* (of a Dido), a *face* swimming in death (558, 'cerno graves oculos atque ora natantia leto', cf. *Aen.* 4.688). Let someone go fetch sceptre and crown, fast, *while he can see!*' (559f., 'dum videt!'). The bard prays that 'But one *day* shall ever *see* this abomination, anywhere, any age' (577f., 'viderit una dies'). Aggression as the hot *light* of brotherly hatred will outlast their lives past the ignition of their bodies' shared pyre: 'ecce iterum fratres . . . exundant diviso vertice flammae / alternosque apices abrupta luce coruscant' (12.429–32, 'Brothers. Endlessly . . . Flames stream up with halved head and flash one crest, then flash the other crest, torn-off chunks of *light*, that Theban *alternation*'). In all this scopic horror, we shall recognize the curse of Oedipus' Thebes. Remade: its law of the eternal return, the 'Remake' –

The '*hooked teeth*' in the similitude here further relays us through the horrors of Tydeus' last mouthful (9.13, 'morsibus uncis') and when Polynices '*fell and crushed* brother with his panoply' (11.573, 'concidit et totis fratrem gravis obruit armis'), we are bound to recall that earlier he 'disarmed naked, *fell on* the now void corpse of his best of friends' to lament Tydeus (9.48, 'abiectis . . . armis / nudus in . . . corpus amici / procidit'), à la Nisus, transfixed upon the body of dear Euryalus (*Aen.* 9.444, 'super exanimum sese proiecit amicum'). The fratricidal Duel acts out the curse that caused it, and in turn the grief it evokes remakes the fighting:

> ut quaesita diu monstravit corpora clamor
> virginis, insternit totos frigentibus artus.
> (*Theb.* 11.599f.)

When daughter's cry *located* the bodies Oedipus *groped for*, he *spread his every limb over* their every cold limb.

The 'trick death-blow' of Eteocles (565, 'erigit occulte ferrum') is remade when father's suicidal grief has him '*hunt* the dagger(s)' in the corpses, only to find quick-thinking daughter has already spoiled his trick (628f., 'occulte telum . . . quaerebat'). The gouging of Oedipus' sockets is both what his sons must try to 'emulate', to outdo upon the body that faces them, and what their Father must wish vainly to repeat as his mimetic tribute to those bodies that the Curse of Thebes will not allow to separate off from their Origin but insists on reclaiming to its parental clutches.

Enter, then, Father Oedipus to feel (for) what he has done to his sons, 'that *face* far-away inside, / its cheeks/*sockets*, slag-heap of filth tracing lights out' ('ora genaeque / intus et effossae squalent vestigia lucis', 11.584f.).[37] The avatar of Theban Madness, Tisiphone-style

(1.104–12, 'Enthroned in *eyes* sunk deep in the skull: iron *light*', 'sedet intus abactis / ferrea lux oculis', 'venom-swollen skin', 'doubled gesticulation of Wrath', 'geminas quatit ira manus'), Oedipus 'feels his way round those helmets, *searches out* the hiding *faces*' (603, 'tractat galeas atque ora latentia quaerit'), wishes his '*sight* would return for a second dig, so he could do his thing, blitz his *face*' (614f., 'o si fodienda redirent / lumina et in vultus saevire . . . potestas'). He swears himself blind: 'That curse. It wasn't my fault, it wasn't, it wasn't' –

> furor illa et movit Erinys
> et pater et genetrix et regna oculique cadentes;
> nil ego . . .

(Theb. 11.619–21)

Put it down to: Madness / The Fury / Pa / Ma / Power Mania / My *eyes, falling*, / EVERYTHING / EVERYTHING – NOT ME.

Look! The gaze of Oedipus' Guilt detaches itself, with inexorable logic, from the retina of his ('Agamemnon' / 'Turnus') Ego! As 'Allecto'-remake Oedipus doubles up to play the bereft parent he cursed himself to be – 'Evander-parent-of-Pallas'-*revenant* – the 'Duel'-focused and 'Duel'-predicated epic narrative turns, it may feel, from the agency of Warrior deeds toward their reception, their aftermath of grief. Does the scene shift altogether – towards Woman?

WOMEN OF THEBES

> She was out in the darkness, out in some black waste strewn with corpses, and she was going from one to another, looking, peering, yet dreading to see; she was looking for Eliot. There were bodies lying on their faces . . . bodies on their backs with faces ghastly upturned, bodies twisted terribly. They were everywhere. She had to go to them all, with the other ghosts that wandered like herself in that black waste. Killed . . . blown to pieces, a voice was saying in her head, but still she had to go on looking and searching and wandering.[38]

Father Oedipus' newly fatherly wish is to join his sons, his brothers, the remakes of his Self, in what may amount to utterly implosive perversion, the *formula* of woman's grief cumulated and patterned through the length of the *Thebaid*'s lamentable lines:

> ei mihi, quos nexus fratrum, quae vulnera tracto!
> solvite quaeso manus infestaque vincula tandem
> dividite, et medium nunc saltem admittite patrem.

(Theb. 11.624–6)

A A A A A   A   A   A   G   H!
Brothers wound *tight together* round their wounds. My fingers feel
all. Unfasten, all I ask, hand from hand, these bonds of hate at last
/ undo, and let me in, between you, finally: Dad.

Statius earlier had his mother (Ide) emerge from among the herd of
matres who:

> scrutantur galeas frigentum inventaque monstrant
> corpora, prociduae . . .
> . . . lumina signant
>   . . . cervicibus ora reponunt.
>
> (Theb. 3.126–32)

They *ferret through* helmets of the cold ones, they identify the
bodies, they label corpses, they *fall on* the dead . . . they close the
eyes . . . they stick the *faces* back on their necks.

Double-death bound, Ide *rummages for* those sons (whose Last Kiss we
met already) through the cannon-fodder casualties ('quaerit. . . natos'),
clawing her face ('ora / ungue premens') as she mourns the lot of them
(3.134–9). She is come to bless Her Thespiad Boys with the pain of her
lamentation:

> quin ego non dextras miseris complexibus ausim
> dividere et tanti consortia rumpere leti:
> ite diu fratres indiscretique supremis
> ignibus et caros urna confundite manes.
>
> (Theb. 3.165–8, cf. 2.629–43)

I, only I can speak this Truth: listen! This mother would interfere
if she undid from their piteous embrace these right-arms, the true
Man's pledge to be true, to fight for right. (To '*stand and fight and
see your slain, / And take the bullet in your brain*') This epic death
celebrates a sacred togetherness that must not be broken. Claim
the Future, brother-to-brother, and merge once for all in joint
cremation. Fuse in the love you bear your spirits after death: one
urn, one pair.[39]

Statius will return to remake this set-piece of set-pieces – in 'para-
potamian', underwater transmogrification! His 'Thetis'-figure, Ismenis,
'redoubles' Crenaeus', Crenaeus', name (9.356, 'ingeminat'). *His* last
gulp had been: 'Mother!' (340). 'In grief she *seeks* her dead "Water-
Baby" in the murky depths' of River daddy's bed (363f., 'penitus . . .
occulta . . . funera nati / vestigat plangitque tamen'). 'She *rummages
through* the helmets and rolls back the bodies *face-down*' (369f., 'scrutatur
. . . manu galeas et prona reclinat / corpora'), *hugs* him to the bank

(373, *amplexa*) and mourns 'his *face* that reflects back her own, the *eyes* that looked back with papa's grim *look*' (381, 'hine mei vultus? haec torvi lumina patris?') – variant on Thebes' archetype: Ino with drowned infant Palaemon (401ff.) . . . 'Thebes', this is to say, even threatens to *become* a 'Mother's Lament': Ino – last but not least in the poem's augural opening catalogue of preterite topics, 'socio casura Palaemone mater' (1.14, 'child Palaemon with her for keeps, she is ready to take the plunge to death: Mother's *Mutterliebe*', cf. 1.122, 2.381, 4.59, 562, 6.10, 7.421, 9.331, 402); Jocasta – with 'grim *eyes*, bloodless cheeks/*sockets*' (7.474f., 'truces oculos . . . exsangues Iocasta genas'), she has Polynices chant 'Mother, Mother' (494f.), bids him 'overcome his *aversion* from brother' (508, 'fratremque – quid aufers lumina? – fratrem'); later she must try to halt the 'Coriolanus' within, Eteocles: she is compared with 'Mother Agave, son's head-in-hand!' (11.318ff.); Ide and Ismenis (see *above*); Eurydice (5.632, 6.35, 136, see *below*); Atalanta – her Parthenopaeus, the super-'Camilla/Pallas/Lausus'-in-one-bundle of gorgeousness, sexy gold tunic from mum's needle (9.691f.), lengthily talks his book out to curtains with his 'Poor Mama' refrain (9.885–907); and Atalanta's mortal equivalent, the *clawed* cheeks/*sockets* of Menoeceus' mother (10.818, 'ungue genas') – her lament the remake of *Aen.* 9's Euryalus' Mother's (792–814)[40] . . .

With the Women, pick up the pieces. Can *your* reader-*sockets*, your 'I', feel this Man's Curse, War, unmake persons into the Warrior Male's crustacean *virtus*, 'helmet'-hide the '*face*', '*hug*' those sons tight in these *Suppliant Women*'s 'mother's arms'? Does the *Thebaid* remake Epic – into Euripidean tragedy: 'With this . . . shift from the rhetoric of eulogy to the ugly facts of blood, wounds, and bodily decay, the pathos of loss resurges unabated, and remains unassuaged by the physical contact for which the mothers have longed (cf. 69–70, 815–18)'?[41] The case can be made that the poem *shows* this meaning. Short of *saying* so, it makes this its (bid for) 'truth' –

NARRATION OF THEBES

Masculinity and individuality will only be reassembled and spoken if *epos* becomes epic through narrative closure and through the delivery of the story.[42]

Much of any epic must consist in delay, obstruction, deferral: anachronic time for hermeneutic thickening, for atmospheric amplification. Much of the *Thebaid* spatially constricts itself to little Nemea, as against the worldwide dashes of Lucan's Caesar, the Odyssean charts of Virgil: cool Nemea's 'Herculean . . . thickets' (4.646f.), 'too small to deploy/catalogue (*evolvere*) an epic host' (5.43ff.)! Its poetic wood, a (Callimachean) place for poetics, for juggling perspectives on epic 'greatness', on heroic might. Here, the Horatian poet of the *Silvae* could scarcely forget, the Pharaoh's master-poet had once played off Hercules with Adrastus, Molorchus with Archemorus/Opheltes, to make a Victory-*Elegy* fit for his sophisticated Queen-'Muse': Callimachus' ludibund *Aitia* originated the Nemean Games, courtesy of Euripidean Romance, from the incineration of an infant and the invention of mouse-trap technology in a hovel, via the lesson of humble theoxeny, to put Theban Hercules' immortalizing Labour of *andreia*, his strong-arm strangling of the Nemean Lion, truly in the shade.[43] The passage was basic to Roman poesy, its sense well understood.[44] The turn away from the grand ('Pindaric'/'Homeric') Victor, towards the 'domesticity' of the Woman's World, will mark this epic's midway stage, as Berenice's va(r)nished Epinician in the *Aitia* heralded a midpoint turn in the form of their narration.

At Nemea, Statius offers, 'aside', a remarkable knot of 'combinatorial imitation':[45] a pathetic horror-show tale is told by its victim; thereby an innocent perishes senselessly; elaborate burial demands the 'heroic mockery' of funeral games . . . We recognize tableaux from the Epic Tradition – and an insistence on and in their remaking, their reconceptualization. With the Argive Warriors-to-be, we meet the persecuted former princess, now enslaved child-nurse, Hypsipyle, and we return *her* two sons, Euneos and Thoas, found among our company. Model brothers, these: 'Identical twins. Totally' (6.343, 'geminis eadem omnia', cf. 345, 434f., 477). Retrieved, they 'tear mother in half with greedy *hugs* taken turn by turn. No Theban *alternation*, this!' (5.722, 'complexibus . . . alterna . . . pectora mutant'). We are treated to, and created as readers by, the *Thebaid*'s demolition of the happiness of this family reintegration, for the positioning and framing of the moment serves, like Odysseus' performance before Arete and Aeneas' before Dido, as the epic's reflexivity upon the dynamics of its own voicing and reception.[46] In *this* epic, it is the post-Phaeacian 'Nausicaa'-figure Hypsipyle who will take the chance of hospitality-niceties to operate, know and bespeak narrative, taking over the post-war scarred Warrior's privilege and charisma. This promotion of the Woman's Voice to tell the underside of *virtus* displaces the site of epic from within: it is as if Virgil's Andromache were to step out of her narrated inclusion within Aeneas' perspective and take over the telling of *Aeneid* 2 and 3 for a *Troades*-style *narrative*.

We watch to see what narration does to the narrator and to the other 'readers in the text', what relations may obtain between the narrated and the narration, and what currents of textual electricity are generated from this laboratory of story-telling – how it may power the text that hosts the emblematic 'digression', what it might suggest to be the stake of the enfolding performance of narrative.

This – recognize its patterning from the remakes we have encountered – is what becomes of Hypsipyle as and because she plays narrator: Nurse Hypsipyle puts down her droopy child, (ominously) 'heavy-*eyed* and tired-*faced*' (5.502, 'graves oculos languentiaque ora'). Along crept Snake, 'bruise-torched *glare*, swollen venom, *claw*-teeth and all' (508f., 'livida fax oculis, tumidi . . . veneni, adunci / dentis'). And then? The boy's '*eyes* opened only for death' (540, 'in solam patuerunt lumina mortem'). Nurse comes 'a-*hunting*, runs through his little vocabulary, then runs through it again, in *duplicate*' (546f., 'ingeminans . . . visu . . . quaerens'). She '*leans down*' (*incumbens*), '*doubles*' her kisses (*ingeminat*), '*searches*' limbs for warm life (*quaerit*), to find 'sinew-*bindings*' awash with blood (562ff., *nexus*): 'No body. All. All is wound!' (594–8, 'totum . . . in vulnere corpus'). She grieves – 'for his lovely *face*' (613, 'heu ubi siderei vultus?'). Mother – Eurydice – burns 'to *throw herself on* the remains' (6.35f., 'super prorumpere nati / reliquias'), her women '*redouble*' their keening (*congeminant*), mother screams she is ready to die, to share a pyre with Hypsipyle – so long as she can first '*feast her eyes*' ('exsaturata oculos') on the revenge (175f.). At the epic funeral ceremonies, the soldiers stage their military-style rite of '*aversion* from the polluting *sight* of evil' (204f. 'prospectu visus interclusere nefasto') . . .

What Hypsipyle tells us, while she and we dump 'her' infant in the way of the passing Snake's fatally clumsy tail-swish so that Nanny can serve us Argives, is her 'Iliupersis'-with-a-difference, the tale of internecine massacre on Lemnos. This is Myth's show-place of anti-*virtus*, where gender turns turtle: the island was stocked of old with *armisque virisque* (5.305); but the men left their women/home/re-productivity/plough-ing's furrow-line, *non arva viri* (309), until the women dared to take up *arma . . . virum* (353). Eventually these un-Women are remade: 'arma aliena cadunt, rediit in pectora sexus' (309), when Venus and *Amor* insinuate into their minds the Argonauts' *arma habitusque virum* (447), and the isle is soon full of baby noises (462). But before that, Lemnian upset in gender-/power-relations has seen the poem's first conden-sation of the patterns of 'Killing' with those of 'Mourning': one Lemniad '*probes* where to wound her man' (210, 'vulnera rimatur'); one 'keeps *eyes* wide, gets her foe first with a quick *hug* – as he becomes aroused for his knifing, he *feels for* her' (216f., 'oculis vigilantibus hostem / occupat amplexu, . . . oculis . . . tremens . . . murmure Gorgen / quaerit'); a mother forces a sister 'to *see* herself in the *face* of *fratricide*: she *falls on* sibling's corpse' (226ff., 'heu similes . . . vultus / aspiciens . . . iacenti / incidit'); the scene is '*floodlit*' by Bacchus (285f.), and Sun '*averts light*' from Lemnos (297). Most markedly 'Theban' of all

Lemnian pre-echoes, Polyxo, 'cheeks/*sockets* erect and eyesight suffused with pulsating blood' (5.95f., 'erecta genas aciemque offusa trementi sanguine'), sets her stakes at '4 sons; + Pops': 'vulnera fratrum / miscebo patremque simul spirantibus addam' (5.125f., 'My recipe calls for brothers – with a dash of Dad; add before all the ingredients go flat'). She models for all the *Thebaid*'s Oedipal con-fusions of 'Brother + Brother – Add: Father' to follow, Tisiphone, for one, 'fratrem huic, fratrem ingerit illi, / aut utrique patrem' (7.467f., 'She piles Brother on *x*, Brother on *y*, or Daddy *z* on *x* + *y*').

Put 'Warrior Wives hugging their "men" on to their blades in bed' together with 'Epic Funeral Games for a "Patriarch-Anchises" Remake-as-Cot-Death' and feel the shift within narration *through* Hypsipyle. Infanticide, 'the killing of children', always spells, or threatens to spell, the suicide of narration, 'the killing of story-telling'.[47]

LAMENTATION AT THEBES

> The narrative concerning Niobe, with its story of slain children buried finally only after a delay, reflects something of the situation within the *Iliad*. But the telling of the tale does not end in burial . . . The story passes into an indefinite structure of openness beyond burial . . . in which it closes by suspending its statement of any final determinate meaning . . . The text does not stage a final, full revelation of meaning but rather achieves a certain suspended position of 'meaningfulness': that indefinitely open indication of a certainty of sense in the absence of any single, specific deter-minate meaning.[48]

With the Funeral extravagance for Hypsipyle's/ Eurydice's Dead Baby, the special service as previously used, a dozen times, by Niobe (6.517: the 'Theban mother', 1.711; cf. 3.193, 4.576, 9.682), we glamorize all the *Thebaid*'s Innocents, those Babes-in-Arms, Argia's 'Astyanax'-remake Thessander (3.683), Ino/Leucothea's Palaemon/Melicertes (cued in at 6.10f.), and Linus – featuring at Opheltes'/Archemorus' funeral as . . . embroidery (6.66: his mother 'abominated it to *aversion*', 'oculos flectebat ab omine'). And we may be primed to find Statius' Epic Militarism collapsing around its 'weakness' for the memorializing voice of the Warriors' bereaved womenfolk:

> unius ingens
> bellum uteri, coeuntque pares sub casside vultus.
> (*Theb.* 11.407f.)

One huge War. One huge Womb. Come together, *Face*, in your helmet, and *Face*, in yours. You are The Same.

The annihilation that is the Father's Curse – that Father who is also his children's Brother – can cry for the Mother/Sister's womb: the *Thebaid*'s 'primal scene' may *supplement* – more than comment upon and amplify; rather, substitute and displace – its staged paradigms of 'martial' *virtus*. The climax it could deliver as the 'marital' narrative of *sisterhood* forged in defence of Human Rights between Bride and Sister, the (Callimachean) alliance between Argia and Antigone, an 'altern-at(iv)e' 'battleline' to defy Creon, 'fraternize' with the Enemy, bury Polynices. (Cf. the simile of the *sisters* who bury Phaethon, 12.413ff.; anticipated at 3.173.) A comradely sorority: 'they *drop* together (*lapsae*) for an embrace *à trois* (*amplexu*), split the limbs fifty/fifty, and with a groan from her, then a groan from her, go back to his *face* (*ad vultum*), *take turns for* (*alterna*) possession of their favourite neck' (12.385ff.). These Sisters of Mercy will compete manically/manfully for Creon's punishment – in a 'Me, choose me!' verbal 'duel', a mock-'Thebaid' ('alternis ... verbis', 461), where 'you'd have thought it was the familiar Theban wrath and hatred!' (461f.) Is *this* what Thebes is fightin' for?

Woman – this time, the Bride – wades through Statius' Killing Fields:

> dum funus putat omne suum, visuque sagaci
> rimatur positos et corpora prona supinat
> incumbens, queriturque parum lucentibus astris.
> (*Theb.* 12.288–90)

She comes upon the dead – each one she assumes is hers. Eagle-*eyed* she *rummages through* the fallen, rolls over corpses *face-down*, *leans down*, wails: 'The stars won't *shine*'.

Argos' Wife of Wives, Juno, floods those Fields with *light* (312, 'infuso lumine'), until Argia:

> videt ipsum in pulvere paene
> calcatum. fugere animus visusque sonusque,
> inclusitque dolor lacrimas; tum corpore toto
> sternitur in vultus animamque per oscula quaerit
> absentem.
> (*Theb.* 12.316–20)

... She *sees* her man. In the dust. About flattened. Mind, *sight*, sound. All left her. Pain imprisoned epic tears. Every fibre of her body. She *spreads her Self on his face*. She *hunts* his life. His breath. Kiss upon Kiss. It is gone.

She, Aarghia, wails:

huc adtolle genas defectaque lumina . . .
sed bene habet, superi, gratum est, Fortuna . . .
   . . . totos invenimus artus.
ei mihi . . .
       . . . hoc frater?
       (*Theb.* 12.325–41)

'Here. Lift your *cheeks*. Those *sockets*. Dead, dead *eyes* . . .' Still.
Praise be to Heaven! Thank you, Fortune! . . . I have found him.
All of him. His body checks out.
A A A A A   A   G   H!
. . . This. This thing. This — ? A BROTHER – . . .

Next, Wife will be joined by Sister, out combing the corpses too, for the age-old unison of antiphonal lament (366, 375, their twin *search* for dead menfolk, 'quaeris . . . quaesitura'), 'Andromache'-and-'Juturna' remakes, joined in Humanity's Sisterhood. The text may have told us all along that it must give us but a semblance of the grief it must ultimately gesture to defer, the pain of the Women of Thebes – and Argos! – whose lamentations must lie in the next, impossible, epic narration, way beyond Statius' powers to realize. We must eternally imagine for ourselves widow Evadne's '*search*' ('quaesierit') for a bolt in her breast, too (12.801f.), and widow Deipyle's '*lying on* her corpse's kisses' (802f., 'iacens super oscula saevi / corporis'): all this for Capaneus, and for Tydeus! Then conjure up 'the bloodless *face*' of the *genetrix Erymanthia* Atalanta's Parthenopaeus, Every Mother's Son, 'lovely in death' ('consumpto servantem sanguine vultus'). The *text* can only treble the double mourning from its '*double* armies' ('geminae . . . pariter . . . cohortes') on both sides: 'Arcada . . . / Arcada . . . / Arcada . . . ' (805ff.).

POEM OF THEBES *THE BEST*HEBES

The *Thebaid* ends with lamentation for the dead, not with paeans for Theseus' victory.[49]

But the *Thebaid* has not *not* mourned the death of *virtus*. This has filled its plangent lines all along? It can only imagine what commemoration of Manhood could be like, can only lament that it can not lament:

quis mortis, Thebane, locus, nisi dura negasset
Tisiphone, quantum poteras dimittere bellum!
te Thebe fraterque palam, te plangeret Argos,
te Nemee, tibi Lerna comas Larissaque supplex
poneret, Archemori maior colerere sepulcro.
       (*Theb.* 6.513–17)

Man of Thebes, what an occasion for your death – how the poet could exploit the *topos* – if the iron law of Theban madness had not forbidden it, always already! Your city-nymph Thebe could show up for the funeral right next to your Brother, for all to see, and your other city Argos could join the mourning, with the neighbours (heroic-victor-proclaiming) Nemea (venomously seven-mouthed) Lerna, and (*non*-Achillean) Larissa, humbly offering ritual locks for your grave. You could be being memorialized right now: bigger than infant Archemorus, a greater epic send-off!

The *Thebaid* 'ends', as we saw, by explicitly representing itself as a successor to Virgil's *Aeneid*. In this very gesture of filiation and affiliation to the Augustan epic, the Flavian poem marks out a challenging difference from Virgilian epic's *decorum*. If we 'conclude' that Statius stages his work as an emulation, a challenge, a remaking of the classical tradition, we may find that the reverential disciple has *undone* the master-text by taking over the original, redirected it towards quite other ends. Statius' text was doomed from the start to fall punily short of its quintessentially strong predecessor – with its pious self-deprecation to mark its assent to this verdict: it knows the great days of Rome when the great books in Latin could be written were long since past! – but in the process the *Thebaid* infiltrates the structures of Virgilian epic with what reads as an intently revisionary, even 'subversive', replaying of the traditional values. The very subject of the Theban saga may have always connoted – perhaps, even, *stood for* – a contestation of the 'Iliadic' values of the Homeric civilization(s) of classical antiquity. Such a meaning may be lodged indelibly and unmistakably in the theme from the beginning, from the beginning, that is, of European literature.[50] But the particular interpretation by Statius may display a lability always already latent in the old vision of Warrior reality. The *Thebaid* can expose an uncomfortable instability at the heart of those old city-state paradigms for civic existence which ordered antiquity into a single temporality. The *Thebaid*'s fealty to Virgil can be veiling for attentive readers to read, through the very signal of its figuration, a 'strong' rereading of the *Aeneid* as itself a text *about to turn*, for ever, towards a plaintive critique of the militarism of its narrative of action. The suggestion then would be that Statius' 'rereading' strengthens and emphasizes an incipient tendency in Virgilian narrative so that it may reappear, amplified and strengthened, in full view. Not the Warrior display of *arma virumque*, but its disfiguration and displacement before the pain of Woman's Bereavement.

Theban Sphinx always already condenses, does she not? – the epic's Oedipal question for its readers – *she is, all along*, in her *Oedipodioniae domus*, the *Thebais*: 'cheeks/ sockets erect and *eyes* suffused with old blood' ('erecta genas suffusaque tabo / lumina'), she '*hugs*' (*amplexa*) human remains, '*gnawed* bones' ('semesa . . . ossa premens') clutched to her naked breast in hideous parody of Woman's grief carrying out the dead. She dominates the *visual-*/battlefield ('visus . . . frementi / conlustrat campos'), ready for allcomers with her 'cursed tongue, *claws* a-sharpening, *bite* drawn' ('dirae . . . linguae . . . acuens . . . ungues / . . . strictos . . . dentes', 2.505–15).

Not the paradigm of *virtus* hung on its age-old narrative peg, but the poetic affirmation of GUILT. If Theseus models all-too-distant a reader, sorting out Theban disaster all too firmly and cleanly, all too violently and vitiated a wind-up, then use those Oedipal sockets of yours, feel what you cannot see. With Statius? Perhaps – But *he* could not possibly confirm this!

NOTES

1 For this essay annotation is kept to a minimum. Readers desiring bibliographical effulgence may wish to consult my premake: Henderson 1991.
2 Gransden 1984: 3.
3 Read Ahl 1986 if you mean to read any of the scholarship. Cf. the new essays by W. J. Dominik, P. Hardie, D. E. Hill and D. McGuire in Boyle 1990, Boyle in Boyle and Sullivan 1991: 217–22 and bibliography to Vessey 1973. Burck 1979b is a fine survey essay; Vessey 1982 may be taken as a standard opinion. (*Contrast* the audacities of Vessey 1986.)
4 E.g. Suetonius, *Life of Vespasian* 1.
5 For evasive deferral, or 'sublation', with a *nondum* ('not yet'), cf. Virg., *Georg.* 3 Proem, Prop. 2.10, Calpurnius' first word, and so his whole *œuvre*. So too *Theb.* 12.1's first word, and so the programme for this last book: '/nondum cuncta' ('Light at the end of the tunnel, dear Reader. You're nearly there, now. Announcing: a final(e) book of totalization to cap even the eleven you have just known!'). Let's see if this titular phrase for book 12 re-echoes round your cranium as you read on past the narrative's final *aposiopesis* –
6 Contrast the responsively agitated picturing of Virgil's epic heroism in daring the main of the imagination you will find in Horace's tribute, *Odes* 1.3, where the writing of the *Aeneid* is teamed with acclamation of Augustus' heroism in the previous poem as Horace's first and most powerful introduction to his vision of the seams of imperial order, the dyarchy of power with culture.
7 See Coleman 1988: *ad loc.*
8 Juvenal, *Satire* 7.82–7.
9 R. Ogilvie quoted by Ahl 1986: 2808.
10 On the politics of imperial representation, see Ahl 1984, 1986. For Statius' adversions to Ovid and Lucan's editorial figuration see Vessey 1986: 2974ff., Ahl 1986: 2835 n. 36 and Vessey 1973: 61.
11 Vessey 1982: 572.
12 Cf. Ahl 1986: 2814 and *passim*.
13 Davies 1989: 23ff., 'The *Thebais*'.
14 On the embroiling of Argos with Theban metaphoricity see Zeitlin 1990: 145ff., 'The Middle Term: Argos'. Statius makes great play of the

'Tantalid' connection of Argos, itself the tragically cursed scene of fraternal hatred between Atreus and Thyestes. His Polynices *becomes* an Argive for his Theban enemies Eteocles, then Creon, and for Jocasta.

15 New tattered fragments in Lloyd-Jones and Parsons 1983: frr. 52–79.

16 See Ziegler 1966: 20ff.

17 See Stahl 1985: 48–71, especially 63ff. and 182, 'Will the same lasting praise be granted to the *Aeneid*? Or will it suffer the fate of Ponticus' or Lynceus' or Homer's *Thebaid*?'

18 Vidal-Naquet 1986: 186.

19 Apollodorus 3.5.7–7.1 is the fullest ancient summary.

20 Racine, Preface to *La Thébaïde*.

21 Earlier version, Zeitlin 1986.

22 Zeitlin 1990: 134, 145. Cf. Euben 1990: especially 99f., 133, Vidal-Naquet 1986.

23 Barthes 1977: 61, 62f. Cf. Zeitlin 1982: 25f., 'Two sons must "fight not so much to settle the differences between them . . . but instead to establish through violence a definitive difference – victor-vanquished – by means of which they can be distinguished each from each" [Fineman . . . on Girard]. But Eteokles and Polyneikes, by their mode of death, which I have termed reciprocal and reflexive, fail to establish that difference between victor and vanquished, for each is victor over the other but each is also vanquished by the other. This is exactly the meaning of their conflict, unlike other conflicts between brothers . . . namely, that issue from an incestuous union cannot establish any difference between its offspring, but can only produce sons who embody the principle of difference, unreconcilable except through their inevitable identical end'.

24 Wills 1983: 160f.

25 Henderson 1989: 97.

26 Lynn-George 1988: especially 230–76, 'The Homeless Journey', is the most sophisticated, heart-felt, exploration of the tensions surrounding the 'closure' of the *Iliad*. Ahl 1989b shows briskly how simplificative the notions of narrativity that have generally been applied to the reading of ancient epic have been, how simplistic the claims for 'closure'.

27 Hanson 1989: Introduction, 13.

28 Juhnke 1972: 74ff.

29 Cf. 'consanguineas acies sulcosque nocentes', 4.436, 'blood-link lines, ploughed Guilt'.

30 Eteocles–Polynices, Menoeceus–Haemon, Euneos–Thoas, Jupiter–Neptune –Pluto, Mars–Apollo, Hercules–Bacchus–Apollo, Mars–Mercury, Sleep– Death, Castor–Pollux, Boreads, Belidae, Minos–Rhadamanthys, Ismenus– Asopus, Amphion–Zethus, Cadmus–Europa, Jupiter–Juno, Apollo–Diana, Athena–Hercules, Cydon + sister, Argia–Deipyle, Antigone–Ismene, Furies, Fates, Muses, Nymphs . . .

31 See especially Bonds 1985. On 'The Death of Tydeus', see Vessey 1973: 283–94.

32 Foucault 1979: 217.

33 Cf. Henderson 1988: 157 n. 26, Schetter 1960: 37ff., Zwierlein 1988: 68ff.

34 See Vessey 1970a, Kytzler 1986 for the reverberations of the 'Coroebus' myth through the poem.

35 Cf. Segal 1971a: 61.

36 *Rep.* 571c, 619b. For the 'Oedipal' construction of Greek tyranny, see Vernant 1982. On the cultural atopia of cannibalism, see Detienne 1979: 53–67, 'Gnawing His Parents' Heads'.

37 *genae*, 'cheeks', can only be cordoned from *genae*, 'sockets', by a dictionary, e.g. *OLD, s.v.*: (1), (2).
38 Holland 1932: 171, quoted by Tylee 1990: 230f.
39 For the (traditional) 'con-fusion' of *una* in *urna*, see 3.148f., 'felices quos una dies, manus abstulit una, / pervia vulneribus media trabe pectora nexi' ('Lucky sons! Lost to one day, one foe, and joined for ever – by a dirty great pole stuck right through your medals, a Highway for wounds').
40 The night-attack in *Thebaid* 10 is to recover Tydeus' body. This remakes *Il.*10, where Tydeus' son is abroad. You will recognize here the Statian meshing of Fighting with Mourning: the squires '*rummage*, locate (fail to) retrieve' the corpses of Tydeus and Parthenopaeus (359, 'scrutari campum', 370, 'quaeritur'). *Floodlighting* from the Moon/Diana helped (371, 'monstravit funera'), but Hopleus dies '*hugging*' Tydeus (403, *tenens*), and then, like a cornered *mother* lioness (414ff.), Dymas invokes the Theban paradigm of *Ino and Palaemon* for pity (425) before '*falling upon*' Hopleus' body by way of 'burial' (440, 'pe-ctus / iniecit puero'). Redoubled horror-show from *Aen.* 9's Nisus and Euryalus, as the foursome '*hugs*' death (442, 'complexibus').
41 Burian 1985: 149, q.v.
42 Pointon 1990: 134.
43 See Colace 1982.
44 See Thomas 1983: especially 103ff.
45 See Hardie 1990a for this. The chief, paraded, intertextual episodes are listed handily in Lesueur 1990: xviiiff. Juhnke 1972: 315–70 tabulates 'Homerparallelen zu Statius' *Thebais*' in full.
46 Cf. Götting 1969: 50–62 for comparison with Homer and Virgil. On self-reflexivity in the latter see chapter V above, pp. 99–103.
47 Simon 1987.
48 Lynn-George 1988: 250, 252.
49 Ahl 1986: 2897.
50 See Hardie 1990b for the Ovidian Thebes of the *Metamorphoses*, an important resource for Statius.

X

FLAVIAN VARIANT: MYTH. VALERIUS' *ARGONAUTICA*

Martha A. Malamud and Donald T. McGuire, jr

VALERIUS FLACCUS, AUTHOR OF THE *ARGONAUTICA*

Philip Hardie has recently drawn attention to the importance of imitation in Flavian poetry, particularly the imitation of more than one source, as a means of allowing the author to comment upon and interpret his sources at the same time he constructs his own text.[1] Allusion and imitation are, of course, techniques common to all classical literature, but the Flavian period in particular was notable for its rewriting of earlier texts, and among the major Flavian authors Valerius Flaccus is the most overt and insistent rewriter of them all.

Valerius' *Argonautica*, which took shape sometime between 80 and 92 CE, is stamped by its subject matter as an experiment in rewriting, for it is a Roman, post-Virgilian version of a widely known and imitated Hellenistic epic, the *Argonautica* of Apollonius of Rhodes.[2] Apollonius' *Argonautica*, which blended epic metre and subject matter with the Hellenistic traits of elaborate structuring, extensive allusion and self-allusion, and *doctrina*, is itself a text which demands to be read in conjunction with, and as a reaction to, other texts.[3] Apollonius' *Argonautica* helped to redefine epic, giving it a place in a highly literate, cosmopolitan society that was very different from the culture of Archaic Greece that produced the *Iliad* and the *Odyssey*. Virgil recognized the revolutionary implications of Apollonius' treatment of epic, and used the *Argonautica* as one of the major sources for his own recasting of epic, the *Aeneid*.[4]

Simply by the choice of subject matter, then, Valerius has situated himself within a certain tradition; he stands in relation to Apollonius as Apollonius to the Homeric poems, but by consistently reading Apollonius through a Virgilian lens, he claims Virgil as a model as well. The creation of such a reflective text may be meant to imply that he is heir to the Alexandrian tradition of epic – it also suggests that his epic is an imitation of an imitation.

In Jorge Luis Borges' surrealist short story 'Pierre Menard, Author of the *Quixote*', the narrator describes the peculiar literary output of a novelist with whom he was acquainted. Menard was the author of a number of slight works – to choose one example which marks its author as a true philologist, the narrator includes in his catalogue of Menard's works 'a manuscript list of verses which owe their efficacy to punctuation' (Borges 1964: 38). However, the narrator claims that Menard's real masterpiece was both invisible and unfinished – 'the ninth and thirty-eighth chapters of the first part of *Don Quixote* and a fragment of chapter twenty-two' (Borges 1964: 39). Menard's self-imposed task is not to write a contemporary *Don Quixote*, or to transcribe it:

> He did not want to compose another *Quixote* – which is easy – but *the Quixote itself*. Needless to say, he never contemplated a mechanical transcription of the original; he did not propose to copy it. His admirable intention was to produce a few pages which would coincide – word for word and line for line – with those of Miguel de Cervantes.
>
> (Borges 1964: 39)

Menard, 'a Symbolist from Nîmes, essentially a devotee of Poe, who engendered Baudelaire, who engendered Mallarmé, who engendered Valéry, who engendered Edmond Teste' (Borges 1964: 40–1), is evidently the belated product of an overwhelming literary tradition; his absurd project (to arrive somehow at the *Quixote* without either copying it or transforming it) makes him a caricature of the author in confrontation with a literary predecessor.

Among the hindrances that Menard faces in his impossible task is that of history:

> To compose the *Quixote* at the beginning of the seventeenth century was a reasonable undertaking, necessary and perhaps even unavoidable; at the beginning of the twentieth, it is almost impossible. It is not in vain that three hundred years have gone by, filled with exceedingly complex events. Amongst them, to mention only one, is the *Quixote* itself.
>
> (Borges 1964: 41–2)

And yet, despite, or perhaps because, of this problem, the fragments that Pierre Menard does produce turn out to be more subtle, ironic, and complex than the 'real' *Quixote*:

> In spite of these . . . obstacles, Menard's fragmentary *Quixote* is more subtle than Cervantes' . . . Cervantes' text and Menard's are verbally identical, but the second is almost infinitely richer. (More ambiguous, his detractors will say, but ambiguity is richness.)
>
> It is a revelation to compare Menard's *Don Quixote* with

Cervantes'. The latter, for example, wrote (part one, chapter nine):

> . . . truth, whose mother is history, rival of time, depository of deeds, witness of the past, exemplar and adviser to the present, and the future's counselor.

Written in the seventeenth century, written by the 'lay genius' Cervantes, this enumeration is a mere rhetorical praise of history. Menard, on the other hand, writes:

> . . . truth, whose mother is history, rival of time, depository of deeds, witness of the past, exemplar and adviser to the present, and the future's counselor.

History, the *mother* of truth: the idea is astounding. Menard, a contemporary of William James, does not define history as an inquiry into reality but as its origin. Historical truth, for him, is not what has happened; it is what we judge to have happened.

(Borges 1964: 42–3)

Menard's solution, to reproduce Cervantes' exact words, but in so doing to change their significance entirely, is patently absurd, but we offer his *Quixote* as an object of contemplation here, at the beginning of this essay, because it exemplifies one of the issues at the heart of Valerius Flaccus' *Argonautica*: the relationship between production, reproduction and imitation within a textual tradition. Pierre Menard's discovery, that the same story retold hundreds of years later takes on an entirely new significance, is a useful one for the reader of Valerius Flaccus to keep in mind, for Valerius, in taking up the *Argo* myth, is also retelling a story, one that had already been told not once, like the *Quixote*, but many times. Valerius shows his awareness of the importance of context in interpreting a text by his method (which Virgil had already used with great effect in the *Aeneid*) of creating a textual universe in which different, sometimes conflicting versions of the same story appear to exist simultaneously; in which characters take their cues and even at times their dialogue from other texts; in which the inadequacy of the mythic narrative is continually suggested by the blatant artifice of the text. Pierre Menard took on a single text and reproduced (parts of) it exactly. Valerius takes on an entire textual tradition and uses his poem to reflect different bits and pieces of it. In both cases, it is the author's engagement with his predecessor(s), and his readers' continual awareness of that engagement, that make the text signify.

In the rest of this essay we will first briefly examine the Roman topos of the *Argo* as first ship, and then focus on one episode, the abduction of Hylas, which can serve as a model of Valerius' use of myth and his method of dealing with earlier texts. In this episode, rather than

194

attempting to 'tell the myth of Hylas', Valerius instead constructs a situation where variant versions of the myth are put into confrontation with one another. Appropriately enough for a myth that inscribes a tale of loss, in which echoes and reflections are substituted for reality, the effect of Valerius' manipulation of his sources is to collapse the myth, to deny it any authoritative form.

THE MYTH OF THE *ARGO*

> illa rudem cursu prima imbuit Amphitriten.
> quae simul ac rostro ventosum proscidit aequor,
> tortaque remigio spumis incanuit unda,
> emersere freti candenti e gurgite vultus
> aequoreae monstrum Nereides admirantes.
> (Catullus 64.11–15)

That ship first probed the untouched sea in its journey. As it cut through the windy water with its prow and the waves, swirled by the oars, foamed and flashed, then in wonder at the omen the watery Nereids lifted their faces from the shining whirlpool of the sea.

In the Roman poetic tradition established by Catullus, the *Argo* is the first ship (*prima*), the symbol of human enterprise and daring, but of human violence and corruption as well.[5] One of the key features of Catullus' treatment of the *Argo* myth is that, although he insists upon the primacy of the *Argo* at the beginning of his account of the marriage of Peleus and Thetis, he undercuts his own claim later in the poem, when he shows the wedding guests admiring a bedspread upon which is embroidered the story of Ariadne abandoned by Theseus. This tale is clearly set in the past relative to the story of Peleus (Catullus introduces it with the word *olim*), yet ships are prominent in the story – Theseus sails to Crete; he takes Ariadne by ship to the island of Naxos, and then sails off without her. The text's attempt to fix an origin for human violence is revealed to be only a fiction; as the poem progresses we find that past, present and future are equally implicated in an endless cycle of destruction.[6]

The first lines of Valerius' epic indicate that he is following the Catullan tradition of the *Argo* as first ship:

> prima deum magnis canimus freta pervia natis
> fatidicamque ratem, Scythici quae Phasidis oras
> ausa sequi mediosque inter iuga concita cursus
> rumpere flammifero tandem consedit Olympo.
> (*Argonautica* 1.1–4)

We sing of seas first crossed by the great children of the gods, and a prophetic ship which boldly went to the shores of Scythian Phasis and burst a path through the middle of the clashing rocks before it settled on starry Olympus.

As Martha Davis has pointed out, the combination of *prima*, 'first', as the first word of the poem, with *ausa*, 'dared' (the first word of line 3), suggests that the *Argo* earns its place in heaven because of its position as the original ship, first to dare to enter a new element.[7] But, again like Catullus, Valerius at various points in the poem undercuts the *Argo*'s claim to be the first ship by introducing evidence that contradicts this version of the myth. For example, in their very first adventure the Argonauts arrive at the island of Lemnos, where they meet the Lemnian women, who have recently committed their famous crime, the slaughter of their male relatives. The crime occurs in the first place because the men of Lemnos had sailed to Thrace and brought back captive women; they have already returned and been slain by their wives before the Argonauts arrive at the island.

In both Catullus and Valerius, as the *Argo* sails, it comes upon traces of earlier voyagers – even for the first ship, it turns out that there is nothing new under the sun. By the time Valerius inherits it, the myth of the *Argo* has become a trope for the impossibility of discovering an origin; for Valerius it seems also to be a metaphor for the impossibility of creating a truly original text. For Valerius, as for Pierre Menard, to create a text is to reproduce an earlier tradition.

Valerius' poetic technique relies upon this presumption. For example, at various points in the narrative, characters seem to act upon motivations that are never explained in Valerius' own text – the audience are apparently supposed to rely on their knowledge of other versions of the *Argo* story to understand what is going on. A minor example of this (but relevant because it is part of the Hylas tale we will be considering shortly) is the following. As the Argonauts debate whether to abandon Hercules and Hylas, Meleager, who is a persistent trouble-maker, gives an emphatic speech urging them to set sail immediately (*Arg.* 3.649–89). This excites all the Argonauts, but, says Valerius, *Calais* is more eager than any of them to depart (*Arg.* 3.690–2). This makes little sense in the context of the narrative, where Calais' sudden zeal is unmotivated, but readers who are familiar with Propertius' treatment of the Hylas story would know that in his poem Calais and his brother Zetes attempted to rape Hylas just before his abduction by the Nymph (Propertius 1.20.25–30). Valerius does not mention this detail, but it perfectly accounts for Calais' unseemly haste to escape before the return of Hercules.

This is only one example of many places in the *Argonautica* where

Valerius makes it clear that he is sailing in the wake of his literary predecessors, in the same way that his Argonauts, bold sailors in the first of all ships, sail belatedly in the wake of earlier travellers. Traces of earlier texts intrude themselves again and again. The *Argo* myth which seems at first glance to be about origins, exploration, and innovation, becomes in Valerius' hands a vehicle for exploring the endless repetitions and variations of a profoundly derivative literary world.

HYLAS AS AN OBJECT OF DESIRE

Near the beginning of Book 1, Mopsus, one of two seers assigned to the *Argo*, prophesies a number of the disasters that await the Argonauts; among them is the loss of Hylas, to which he alludes in the following words:

> subita cur pulcher harundine crines
> velat Hylas? unde urna umeris niveosque per artus
> caeruleae vestes?
>
> (*Arg.* 1.218–20)

> Why does lovely Hylas cover his hair with a sudden veil of reeds?
> Why the urn on his shoulder, the blue robes on his snowy limbs?

Cur? Unde? Why indeed? No doubt the Argonauts listening to these obscure words asked themselves the same questions, for Mopsus' prophecy (as is typical of oracles) has been framed so that it can only be understood by those who already know what it means. Valerius' contemporary audience/readers would have no trouble understanding the prophecy, since the myth of Hylas was enormously popular in both literature and art, but the Argonauts, as characters ignorant of their own future and presumably unacquainted with the Graeco-Roman artistic tradition, would be more confused. Mopsus' prophecy reveals his knowledge of the future, but it also reveals Valerius' knowledge of the literary past, and suggests that one of his strategies is to create situations in which the reader must confront the relationship between the *Argonautica* and earlier texts, much as Virgil relies on his readers' familiarity with a number of variant versions of the fall of Troy and the founding of Rome to create the characteristic and disturbing ambiguity of the *Aeneid*.

There were a number of earlier versions of the Hylas myth – in retelling it, Valerius takes his readers over well-travelled terrain. In addition to Apollonius' version of the story in his *Argonautica*, Valerius would very probably have been familiar with the versions of Theocritus, Nicander (now lost but summarized in Antoninus Liberalis) and Propertius. Virgil, indeed, mocks the ubiquity of the myth in

Georgic 3.3–6 ('cetera quae vacuas tenuissent carmine mentes,/ omnia iam vulgata . . . /cui non dictus Hylas puer?', 'all other subjects that might have occupied idle minds in song have already been published – to whom has the story of the boy Hylas not been told?'), though one of the singers of this hackneyed theme is Silenus in Virgil's own sixth *Eclogue*.[8]

Mopsus' prophecy assumes the version of the myth that is attested in Apollonius and Theocritus, in which Hylas goes off to seek water, for in Mopsus' prophecy Hylas has a pitcher (*urna*), and both Greek poets specifically mention that the boy was carrying a pitcher when he was seized by the Nymph or Nymphs (Theocritus 13.39; Apollonius, *Arg.* 1.1207; 1235–7).[9] As both Robert Colton and George Osmun have pointed out,[10] this is noteworthy because Mopsus, in specifying the pitcher, differs from Valerius' own version of the Hylas episode in *Argonautica* 3, where Valerius differs from all other sources and has Hylas go off hunting a stag rather than searching for water. We will discuss possible reasons for the hunting variant below; what we would like to emphasize here is the complexity of the confusion implicit in Mopsus' brief reference to Hylas. On the level of the narrative, he makes a prophecy that must be obscure to the Argonauts. It is, however, apparently clear to the informed audience/readers of Valerius' poem, who are assumed to be well acquainted with Apollonius' *Argonautica* and aware that Hylas was lost while fetching water. As it turns out, though, it is precisely that familiarity with the Apollonian source material that encourages Valerius' readers to deceive themselves, for the Hylas story as Valerius presents it is not quite the same as the one Mopsus' prophecy implies; the pitcher which is a signal of Hylas' fate to the reader is absent from the text when Hylas finally meets his fate.[11] It seems that the confusion that Mopsus generates with his prophecy arises from the fact that his knowledge is based not on a reading of signs and omens, as Idmon's was, but on a reading of Apollonius' *Argonautica*.

The disjunction between Mopsus' prophecy about Hylas and the tale as Valerius actually tells it in Books 3 and 4 suggests that one of the salient features of Valerius' treatment of this myth (and of myth in general in the *Argonautica*) is his refusal to create a seamless, univocal account. Other versions of the myth that differ from the one that the author chooses to tell are available not only to the reader, but apparently to some of the characters in the poem as well.

Let us summarize the myth of Hylas. Though different versions vary in detail, treatment and emphasis, there are certain invariants. All agree on the setting of the story (the coast of Mysia, near the city of Cius). In each, Hylas, the young companion of Hercules, becomes separated from the rest of the Argonauts, stops by a pool in the woods, is spotted by a Nymph (or Nymphs) who falls immediately in love with him, and is drawn into the pool. Hercules, maddened by grief, searches for his beloved companion and cries his name until the woods echo, but fails to find him and free him. Meanwhile the Argonauts set sail and depart, leaving Hercules behind. The identity and number of the Nymphs, the reasons for Hylas' visit to the fatal pool (or river), the reaction of Hercules and the motivation of the Argonauts' departure all vary; what remains constant is the constellation of the young boy, the Nymph or Nymphs and the pool, the grief of Hercules and the echoing cry of Hylas' name. Hylas exists primarily as an object of desire in this myth: the sight of his beauty causes his abduction, and the boy is replaced by an echo of his name.

In Apollonius' version, Hylas is barely described, and his emotions are left entirely to the reader's imagination; he is merely the beautiful object of the Nymph's desire:

> But the water Nymph was just rising out of the beautifully flowing spring, and she saw him nearby flushed with beauty and sweet grace. For the full moon shining from the sky struck him. And as for her, Cypris startled her heart and in her helplessness she could scarcely gather her wits back.
>
> (Apoll., *Arg.* 1.1228–33)

The same is true of Theocritus' account, where the setting is a highly erotic, feminized landscape; where the shock of desire felt by the Nymphs is explicitly mentioned, but the boy himself is barely described – he appears like a star, falls out of sight, and is briefly depicted struggling in the laps of the Nymphs, again the object of desire rather than the desiring subject. In both the Greek accounts, part of the erotic charge in the Hylas myth seems to come from the passivity and ignorance of the boy, and the surprise of the Nymph's (or Nymphs') sudden attack.

Propertius treats the scene quite differently in his poem 1.20. His inclusion of the rape attempted by Zetes and Calais has several significant effects: it extends sexual aggression from the female Nymphs to Hylas' male companions, making Hylas the object of desire to both sexes, and not simply the victim of an overwhelming female force. It also sets up a contrast between male force and female seduction – Hylas is able to escape from the attack of the Boreads, but he is seduced by the erotic landscape, and has in effect already surrendered sexually before the Nymphs seize him:

> hic erat Arganthi Pege sub vertice montis
>   grata domus Nymphis umida Thyniasin,
> quam supra nullae pendebant debita curae
>   roscida desertis poma sub arboribus.

> et circum irriguo surgebant lilia prato
>   candida purpureis mixta papaveribus.
> quae modo decerpens tenero pueriliter ungui
>   proposito florem praetulit officio,
> et modo formosis incumbens nescius undis
>   errorem blandis tardat imaginibus.
>
> (Propertius 1.20.33–42)

[The spring] Pege was here, under the peak of Mt Arganthus, a watery home pleasing to the Thynian Nymphs. Over it, beneath the lonely trees, hung dewy apples entrusted to no one's care. And all around in the well-watered meadow rose shining lilies mixed with crimson poppies; now, plucking them with his soft nail like a child, he preferred the blossom to his appointed task, and now, unknowing, leaning over the lovely waters, he delays his wandering with the seductive reflections.

The ripe fruit hanging from the trees, the loneliness of the scene and the combined scarlet and white of the lilies and poppies are all characteristic features of eroticized landscapes, and Hylas' response sets him apart from the portrayals of Hylas in the Greek writers in that it implicates him in the economy of desire. Picking flowers has a clear sexual connotation in Latin and Greek poetry. As early as the Homeric *Hymn to Demeter* we see Proserpina out gathering flowers just before her rape in the vale of Enna; Catullus describes Lesbia's devastating effect on him by reversing the genders of the *topos* in his famous image likening himself to the flower grazed by a passing plough (Catullus 11.21–4); the landscape of Ovid's *Metamorphoses* is bright with flowers – the narcissus, the hyacinth, the anemone – that were once beautiful youths transformed after a fatal erotic encounter.[12] The straightforward voyeurism of the Greek texts, where it is the innocence and ignorance of the victim that pique our interest, is made more complex by Propertius. His Hylas cannot be as ignorant and innocent as his earlier counterparts, for he has just fended off an attempted rape and is thus to some extent aware of his sexual nature. His plucking of the flower seems to signal an attempt at a transition from the role of passive victim to active agent, an attempt doomed to fail, for Hylas will become the victim of the powerful Nymph, and will not make the 'natural' transition from sexually passive young boy to sexually aggressive man.[13]

It is also Propertius who makes explicit something latent in the Greek accounts, the fact that Hylas, as he bends over the pool, is confronted with his own reflection. Like Ovid's Narcissus, he is captivated by what he sees. Propertius' language is decidedly ambiguous here. It is unclear exactly how Hylas is *nescius*: is he unaware of the fate awaiting him, or ignorant of his own reflection? Nor is it entirely obvious whether his *error* refers to his being lost in the woods or to his confusion at the sight of his own reflection (after reading Ovid's *Metamorphoses*, it is hard to avoid projecting the confusion of Narcissus back upon Hylas; it is probable that Ovid used this scene as a model for the Narcissus story). The final ambiguity in Propertius' presentation of Hylas is contained in lines 47–8:

> prolapsum leviter facili traxere liquore:
> tum sonitum rapto corpore fecit Hylas.

Lightly they pulled him as he fell through the yielding water, and Hylas made a sound as his body was taken.

Hylas' echoing cry (imitated in the Latin by the echoing syllable in *tum sonitum*, just as the waters of the pool are suggested by the repetition of liquid *l*s and *r*s in line 47), is, like his plucking the flower, ambiguous: is it a cry of fear as the Nymphs seize his body, or a cry of pleasure?

HYLAS AT THE POOL

As we noted above, Valerius' use of Mopsus' prophecy at the outset of the *Argonautica* is not entirely straightforward. On the one hand it notifies the audience that the familiar tale of Hylas and the Nymphs would be included in this Roman version of the epic; on the other hand, the expectations aroused by the vision Mopsus presents of Hylas with his urn in hand turn out to be misleading. Hylas indeed appears and is lost to a Nymph, but Valerius makes considerable alterations to the various versions of the Hylas myth available to him.

Valerius' innovations are numerous. One of his techniques throughout the poem is a variation on a strategy of Virgil's: in the *Aeneid*, careful and consistent allusions to earlier epics – the *Iliad*, the *Odyssey* and Apollonius' *Argonautica* – create a pervasive and somewhat subversive sub-text to the heroic tale of the founding of Rome. Jason, the dubious hero, is clearly one of the models for Aeneas, though the 'Odyssean' and 'Achillean' aspects of the hero are given more obvious prominence. In the same way that Virgil projects the world of Greek epic on to the backdrop of the founding of Rome, using the conflicts and contradictions this engenders to problematize the notions of heroism and of history, so Valerius 'reads' the Greek *Argo* myth through the *Aeneid*. As the Greek Jason is one of the models for Aeneas, so now in the Roman *Argonautica*, Aeneas anachronistically becomes a model for Jason (and Hercules, as we will show below), and the effect is somewhat disconcerting. The Hylas passage affords several examples of this technique in action. In a passage that recalls Juno's use of the promise of a bride to incite Aeolus to raise the winds against Aeneas in

201

Aeneid 1, Valerius makes his Juno the motivating factor behind the loss of Hylas. In *Arg.* 1.487–546, Juno appears unexpectedly, not as the patron of Jason, but as the bitter enemy of Hercules – she is the implacable Virgilian Juno rather than the capricious but generally benign Hera of Apollonius' *Argonautica.*[14]

The malevolent nature of the goddess is summed up in the casual explanation Valerius gives for her arrival on the scene: 'tempus rata diva nocendi' ('the goddess thought it was time to do harm', *Arg.* 3.488). First sending Pallas to stir up civil war in Phasis, she then launches into a complaint against Hercules that is a composite of *Aen.* 1.37–49 and her similar, even more emphatic speech in *Aen.* 7.293–323.[15] After outlining the reasons for her anger against Hercules, Juno notices a company of Nymphs out hunting, and appears to one of them, Dryope, who had stopped to watch Hercules, also hunting. Assuring the Nymph of the boy's extraordinary beauty, she promises him to her, and then engineers Hylas' separation from Hercules by sending a stag to lure him into the woods alone. This action again recalls both *Aeneid* 1 and *Aeneid* 7: in *Aeneid* 1, Juno's bribe to Aeolus and the subsequent shipwreck are followed closely by Aeneas' own stag hunt, and then by his encounter with his mother, Venus, disguised as a Nymph huntress; the hunting imagery set up in *Aeneid* 1–4 becomes one of the dominant metaphors for the fatal love of Dido. In *Aeneid* 7, Juno's servant Allecto brings on war between the Latins and the Trojans by luring the young Ascanius to kill Silvia's remarkable pet stag.

The description of Hylas' fatal encounter at the pool is carefully constructed. As Hercules looks on in approval, the stag leads Hylas far away to the pool, and then bounds away; thwarted of his prey, the boy turns to the pool instead:

> credit Hylas praedaeque ferox ardore propinquae
> insequitur; simul Alcides hortatibus urget
> *prospiciens.* iamque ex oculis aufertur uterque,
> cum puerum instantem quadripes fessaque minantem
> tela manu procul ad *nitidi* spiracula *fontis*
> ducit et *intactas* levis ipse superfugit *undas.*
> hoc pueri spes lusa modo est nec tendere certat
> amplius; utque artus et concita pectora sudor
> diluerat, gratos *avidus* procumbit ad amnes.
>
> (*Arg.* 3.549–57)

Hylas believes it and, fierce with ardour for the prey so close at hand, he follows; at the same time Hercules watches and spurs him on with encouraging shouts. And now both [the boy and the stag] are carried out of his sight, when the four-footed beast leads the boy, pressing on its trail and threatening it with the weapon in his weary hand, far away to the fountain of a shining spring, and it lightly leaps over the untouched waters. In this way the boy's hope is deceived, nor does he struggle to go further; as sweat had flooded his limbs and his stricken breast, he throws himself greedily on the pleasant waters.

In these few lines, Valerius delineates an erotic structure quite different from the Apollonian account, in a way that suggests that in addition to recalling the Virgilian theme of the erotic hunt, he is working from Ovid's *Metamorphoses* as well, a text which dwells almost obsessively on the eroticism of the hunt, spinning out variant after variant on the basic tale of the young boy or girl who has a fatal encounter with the force of love while out hunting.

Ovid's account of Narcissus (and the related tale of Salmacis and Hermaphroditus, as we will argue below), which Valerius appears to read as a variant of the Hylas story, is one model for Hylas' encounter at the pool. The general situation is similar – the boy, exhausted by hunting, stretches out by the waters of the pool – and there are suggestive repetitions of Ovidian vocabulary as well. Compare Ovid's description of the pool:

> *fons* erat inlimis, *nitidis* argenteus *undis*
> quem neque pastores neque pastae monte capellae
> contigerant . . .
>
> > (*Met.* 3.407–9)

There was a clear pool, silver with shining waters, which neither shepherds nor the goats fed on the mountain had touched.

Valerius' pool (*fontis*) is also shining (*nitidi*) and untouched (*intactas*, from the same root as *contigerant*); both poets also include the word *unda*, wave, in their brief descriptions of the pool.

Hylas, then, has passed from a Virgilian hunting scene to an Ovidian *locus amoenus*, from being hunter to being prey. But he is not the passive victim of sudden desire that Theocritus and Apollonius describe; instead, the language of the scene suggests that Valerius is developing the erotic situation along the lines suggested by Propertius in 1.20 and elaborated by Ovid in the *Metamorphoses*. In Valerius' account, for example, erotic language is specifically applied to Hylas, who is *ferox ardore* (fierce with desire) as he chases his prey; who arrives at the untouched waters (*intactas undas*) of the fountain and disturbs them; who throws himself greedily (*avidus*) into the pleasing stream (*gratos amnes*). Hylas' role as hunter and his symbolic violation of the untouched waters of the spring place him in an ambiguous role, potentially both victim and aggressor.

One of Valerius' major innovations in his handling of this central scene of the myth is his elimination of any reference to the emotions aroused in the watching Nymph by the sight of Hylas. Compare the accounts of Apollonius, Theocritus and Propertius. In Apollonius, the Nymph is just as surprised at Hylas' beauty as he is by her sudden attack:

> For the full moon shining from the sky struck him. And as for her, Cypris startled her heart and in her helplessness (*amēkhaniēi*) she could scarcely gather her wits (*thumon*) back.
>
> (Apoll. *Arg.* 1.1231–3)

In Theocritus, as Hylas leans down to fill his pitcher, the Nymphs are shocked with desire ('desire for the Argive boy startled their tender hearts', Theocritus 13.48–9), and in Propertius, almost the same thing occurs:

> cuius ut accensae Dryades candore puellae
> miratae solitos destituere choros.
> (Propertius 1.20.45–6)

> The Dryads, inflamed by the shining beauty [of his shoulder], in wonder abandoned their usual dances.

Only Valerius eliminates the Nymph's reaction to the sight of the beautiful boy. Instead, the motivation for the rape is displaced to the opening of the episode, where the loss of Hylas is ascribed to Juno's wrathful interference; even there, we are not shown Dryope's reaction to the news that Hylas is hers. Instead of the passionate desire of the Nymph, we are presented with a cold-blooded business transaction, as Juno constructs her revenge against Hercules by giving Hylas to Dryope.

Thus Valerius, while keeping the general framework of the myth, has completely reversed the erotic economy. Hylas, the victim of rape, is characterized by language of desire that suggests he is also a sexual aggressor, while at the same time the desire of the Nymph, stressed in every other account (and elaborated at length in Ovid's description of Echo) is simply eliminated. (This elision of desire is oddly paralleled by Valerius' treatment of Hercules' relationship with Hylas, as we will discuss below.)

As Hylas leans forward over the pool to drink, the verb Valerius uses to describe his action, *procumbit*, echoes Ovid's use of the same verb (*procubuit*) to describe Narcissus as he leans down to drink; Ovid's choice in turn is very likely an echo of Propertius' use of a related verb, *incumbens* (1.20.41). This moment, in all of the earlier accounts, is the decisive one: in Apollonius, Theocritus and Propertius, Hylas' leaning forward results immediately in his being grabbed by the Nymph. Similarly in Ovid, Narcissus' action results in his immediate infatuation with his reflection. In this narcissistic model of eros, the act of looking into the pool both reveals the presence and stimulates the desire of the lover.

Again, Valerius' treatment of this detail is significantly different. In place of the moment of revelation supplied by the other texts, Valerius substitutes a simile:

> stagna vaga quasi luce micant, ubi Cynthia caelo
> prospicit aut medii transit rota candida Phoebi,
> tale iubar diffundit aquis; nil umbra comaeque
> turbavitque sonus surgentis ad oscula Nymphae.
>
> (*Arg.* 3.558–61)

Just as still waters glitter with wandering light, when Cynthia looks down from heaven or Phoebus' shining wheel crosses the middle of the sky, just so he spread radiance across the waters; the shadow and the hair and the sound of the Nymph rising to kiss him disturbed him not at all.

This simile does a number of things simultaneously. First, the moon-beam striking the water reminds us of Apollonius' account of the rape, where Hylas is revealed to the Nymph by the full moon ('for the full moon shining from the sky struck him', Apoll., *Arg.* 1.1231–2). Valerius, however, includes the image of the sun shining on water as well, the subject of one of Apollonius' most effective similes describing Medea's love for Jason:

And her heart raced swiftly in her breast, as a sunbeam trembles in the house, leaping up from water just poured out in a basin or pail.

(Apoll., *Arg.* 3.755–8)

For readers aware of this scene, the reference heightens the eroticism of the moment; it also creates a peculiar time-warp – the reader is reminded of the encounter between Medea and Jason in an earlier text, a meeting which in the world of Valerius' *Argonautica* has not yet taken place. The future is reflected in the dazzling light shining from the surface of the pool, but the characters remain unaware of it.

Apollonius is not the only source for Valerius' simile: Ovid's tale of Salmacis and Hermaphroditus (constructed to be a warped mirror of the Narcissus story) has a number of elements in common with the Hylas story, in particular the conjunction of the Nymph and the boy, the reflecting pool, and sun and moon imagery. Salmacis is both a Nymph and a spring.[16] At the beginning of the episode, the mirror-like qualities of the spring are introduced as part of the characterization of Salmacis, an unathletic Nymph who refuses to hunt and sits instead by her pool, using it as a mirror as she tries out different ways of doing her hair:

> saepe Cytoriaco deducit pectine crines
> et quid se deceat, spectatas consulit undas.
>
> (*Met.* 4.311–12)

Often she swept back her hair with a boxwood comb, and asked the mirror-like waves (literally, the 'gazed-upon waves') what became her.

Like Hylas in Propertius' poem, Salmacis plucks flowers by the side of her pool, and it is while engaged in this activity that she first sees Hermaphroditus:

> saepe legit flores. et tum quoque forte legebat
> cum puerum vidit visumque optavit habere.
>
> (*Met.* 4.315–16)

Often she gathers flowers. And it happened by chance at that time that she was gathering flowers when she saw the boy and having seen him decided to have him.

Her eyes as she watches his naked form gleam like sun reflected in a mirror:

> tum vero stupuit nudaeque cupidine formae
> Salmacis exarsit, flagrant quoque lumina Nymphae,
> non aliter quam cum puro nitidissimus orbe
> opposita speculi referitur imagine Phoebus.
>
> (*Met.* 4.346–49)

Then truly Salmacis was stunned, and blazed with desire for his naked beauty; the Nymph's eyes shone also, just as when Phoebus, brilliant with his pure orb, is reflected back in the image of a mirror held opposite.

Salmacis' eyes are like the sun reflected in a mirror; earlier, Hermaphroditus' blush as she confronts him and asks her to marry him is compared to the red colour of an eclipsed moon: 'aut sub candore rubenti,/cum frustra resonant aera auxiliaria lunae', ('or like the moon blushing under her whiteness, when the bronze instruments that aid her echo in vain', *Met.* 4.332–33).[17] The cluster of similar elements (the youth out hunting, the reflective pool, the sun simile, the sexually aggressive Nymph) suggests that Valerius may well have had Ovid's reflected sun and eclipsed moon in mind when he created his simile of sun or moonlight reflected in water as a model for the erotic encounter between Hylas and the Nymph.

What happens to Hylas after the simile ends further parallels the Salmacis story. The dazzling radiance Hylas casts on the waters (or perhaps the dazzling effect of the simile) seems to blind him, for as he gazes into the pool he fails to notice the Nymph rising to seize him:

> nil *umbra* comaeque
> turbavitque *sonus* surgentis ad oscula Nymphae.
>
> (*Arg.* 3.560–1)

The shadow and the hair and the sound of the Nymph rising to kiss him disturbed him not at all.

Hylas' failure to notice the Nymph as he gazes at the surface of the pool suggests that she and he are in some way identical – she appears here in place of Hylas' reflection, immediately after a simile that describes reflected light and alludes to Ovid's simile of a mirror reflecting the rays of the sun. Furthermore, the description here, particularly the word *umbra*, suggests that she is herself a sort of inverted reflection of Hylas. Here the primary meaning of *umbra* is shadow, and it contrasts with the *iubar*, radiance, cast by Hylas, but *umbra* can also be used to mean image or copy as well. Certain peculiarities of the scene also suggest that she is a double of Hylas: as he bends down (*procumbit*), she rises up (*surgentis*); he is *avidus*, greedy, in line 557, and she has greedy hands (*avidas manus*) in line 562.[18] Most strikingly, as she rises from the pool to claim him, she is described not as a human being, but as an *umbra* and a *sonus* – a shadow/shade and a sound. As we shall see, Hylas too will be reduced to an *umbra* and a *sonus* of his former self.

Valerius seems to be composing his own variation on an Ovidian theme here. His treatment of Hylas and Dryope recalls Narcissus and Echo (the one fascinated by his own reflection, reduced in the end to an image of his own grief; the other an echo with no voice of her own); the suggestion that the Nymph and Hylas are becoming assimilated through their encounter at the pool also recalls the plight of Hermaphroditus, who becomes literally indistinguishable from Salmacis – the two become one androgynous unit (*Met.* 4.373 79).[19] But this violent incorporation of the masculine into the feminine does not result in the erotically satisfied Aristophanic androgyne that one might expect. Hermaphroditus' fate is presented as both a rape and an emasculation, and his bitter curse endows the pool with the power of emasculating any man who touches its waters:

> quisquis in hos fontes vir venerit, exeat inde
> semivir et tactis subito mollescat in undis!
>
> (*Met.* 4.385–6)

Whoever comes as a man into these waters, let him leave them a half-man; let him weaken [*mollescat*, a verb suggesting effeminacy] instantly when he touches the waves!

The similarities between Hylas and Hermaphroditus help us to see what may be one of the underlying issues of the Hylas episode in Valerius'

Argonautica: sexuality, and in particular, pederasty. The myth of Hylas is predicated upon the existence of a pederastic relationship between Hercules and Hylas; his attraction as an object of desire results from his extreme youth and his concomitant passivity. In the Graeco-Roman 'model' of sexuality, it was inappropriate for adult male citizens to take the passive role in an erotic relationship – this was reserved for women, boys, and slaves.[20] The myth of Hylas dramatizes the inevitable loss that such a pederastic relationship entails – the beautiful youth must either grow up and be unavailable to the lover, or else die, which would make him equally unavailable. Hylas is only one example of many doomed, beautiful youths whose loss is celebrated in Greek and Roman literature.

What makes Valerius' treatment of the myth rather peculiar is his elision of the erotic relationship between Hercules and Hylas. They are never referred to as lovers, and Hylas appears to be extremely young, a little boy: his hands are too small to carry Hercules' club (*Arg.* 1.110–11) and he has to struggle to keep up with Hercules' footsteps (*Arg.* 3.486, an image that brings to mind the young Ascanius following in the footsteps of Aeneas as they leave Troy). This suggests a father–son relationship rather than an erotic one, and indeed immediately after Hylas has disappeared into the pool, Hercules is referred to as *pater*, father (*Arg.* 3.565). When Hercules is explicitly said to feel love ('urit amor', *Arg.* 3.736), the erotic overtones are immediately undercut (or at least made problematic) by a simile comparing him to a lioness grieving for a lost cub (*Arg.* 3.737–40): again the parental model is substituted for the erotic. The culmination of this rewriting of the relationship between the two comes at the opening of *Argonautica* 4, when Jupiter looks down from heaven and takes pity on the *pios amores*, the pious love, of his son (*Arg.* 4.2). The Virgilian overtones of this phrase are immediately reinforced by what follows: the sleeping Hercules is visited by a vision of the lost Hylas, in a scene modelled on Aeneas' vision of his wife Creusa, lost as she tried to follow Aeneas out of Troy (*Aen.* 2.771–95).

ECHOES AND GHOSTS

There are a number of parallels between Aeneas' vision of Creusa and Hercules' vision of Hylas. Both Aeneas and Hercules are shown wandering in a seemingly endless search for their lost loved ones; both cry out the name of the beloved again and again:

> ausus quin etiam voces iactare per umbram
> implevi clamore vias, maestusque Creusam
> nequiquam ingeminans iterumque iterumque vocavi.
> (*Aen.* 2.768–70)

And then indeed I dared to throw my voice through the gloom; I filled the streets with shouting, and sadly, vainly, repeating again and again, I called Creusa.

> rursus Hylan et rursus Hylan per longa reclamat
> avia; responsant silvae et vaga certat imago.
> (*Arg.* 3.596–7)

Through the vast pathless space he calls 'Hylas!' and 'Hylas!', again and again; the woods reply, and a wandering image/echo imitates him.

> ille graves oculos et Hylan resonantia semper
> ora ferens . . . procumbit.
> (*Arg.* 4.18–19)

Lifting his heavy eyes and his lips always echoing 'Hylas!' . . . he falls forward.

Like Creusa's ghost, the image of Hylas tells Hercules to stop grieving, explains what has happened to him, and urges Hercules to continue on his heroic journey. Creusa's appearance before Aeneas is modelled on a famous scene in *Iliad* 23, when the ghost of Patroclus appears in a dream to the sleeping Achilles; Valerius shows his awareness of the Iliadic source by restoring a detail that Virgil omitted. Whereas Creusa appears to Aeneas while he is awake and wandering through the streets of Troy, the image of Hylas stands by the head of the sleeping Hercules ('stansque super carum tales caput edere voces', *Arg.* 4.24), just as Patroclus comes and stands over the head of Achilles ('the ghost came and stood over his head and spoke a word to him', *Il.* 23.68). The effect of this reminder of the Iliadic source of the scene is to undermine the aura of *pietas* that has been building up; the reference to the love of Patroclus and Achilles reinserts the pederastic relationship suppressed in Valerius' treatment of Hylas and Hercules.

In a peculiar play on Creusa's speech, the ghost-Hylas concludes his address with the following request:

> tu semper amoris
> sis memor et cari comitis ne abscedat imago.
> (*Arg.* 4.36–7)

You remember our love always, and don't let the image of your dear comrade disappear.

Creusa, by contrast, ends her speech to Aeneas by reminding him to take care of their *son*: 'iamque vale et nati serva communis amorem' (*Aen.* 2.789, 'And now farewell, and preserve your love for our common son'). Hercules and Hylas, of course, have no son; indeed, as Valerius

209

has configured the relationship, Hylas, who appears to be modelled on Ascanius, takes the place of the son. It is therefore entirely logical for Hylas to mimic Creusa by praying that Hercules remember him, since he takes on the role of son in the poem, but the reader, once Creusa has been brought to mind, is likely to be forcefully reminded that the pederastic relationship between Hercules and Hylas is rather different from Aeneas' relationship with his wife and his son.

By characterizing the relationship between Hercules and Hylas as one of *pietas*, Valerius is able simultaneously to give it a veneer of moral respectability and to call it into question. For, as is typical of Valerius, the cloak of *pietas* has visible holes in it. The elaborate development of erotic themes and imagery from the *Aeneid* and the *Metamorphoses* throughout the Hylas episode make it impossible to read Hylas as simply the foster-child of Hercules, despite the lip-service paid to piety in the text; the more Hylas is likened to Ascanius and Hercules to Aeneas, the more preposterous the episode becomes. The echoes of the *Aeneid* and the *Iliad* in the scene where Hylas' ghost appears create a sort of cognitive dissonance in the reader – Valerius shows both his knowledge of epic and his mastery of the Alexandrian technique of layering source material, but instead of bringing the *Iliad*, the *Aeneid* and the *Argonautica* into a single focus as members of different generations of a harmonious tradition, the double quotation provides conflicting paradigms, as Hylas oscillates between the roles of wife, son, and lover.

DOMITIAN AND EARINUS

This is the moment to raise a further question – one often shunned (and certainly impossible to answer with any certainty): does Valerius' treatment of the Hylas episode, his literary reworking of the story and its epic (and lyric) models, have any bearing on contemporary imaging at the Flavian court? Is Valerius alluding, however indirectly, to Domitian?

In answering, we might return to Valerius' phrase describing Hercules' love for Hylas at the start of *Argonautica* 4, *pios amores*, for by using this particular term and focusing on the issue of *pietas* Valerius locks the love affair between Hylas and Hercules into a system of imagery that Virgil used three generations earlier as a model for the Augustan principate. *Pietas* in subsequent generations of epic was always to be measured – at least in part – against the *pietas* displayed by Virgil's Aeneas; and such a comparison could not exclude the resonances Virgil created between his epic hero and that hero's imperial Roman counterpart, Augustus.

The idea of reading Valerius' Hercules against Valerius' own *princeps* is attractive on several levels, for the account of Hercules' love for Hylas finds a close counterpart at the imperial court in Domitian's long-standing enjoyment of his favourite eunuch Earinus. True, the dating of the *Argonautica* is too vague to claim any absolute correspondence between the epic and one of the few known facts about Domitian's private life; but Valerius' narrative does seem to have been published during the same brief span of time in which Martial published his own several poems to Earinus and in which Statius published his own notorious lyric commemoration of Domitian's boy, *Silvae* 3.4, a poem in which Statius compares Earinus specifically to Ganymede, Endymion, and . . . Hylas himself.[21]

There is, in addition, more concrete evidence that supports our seeing a link here between Domitian and Hercules, for Domitian seems to have been the first *princeps* to issue portraits of himself in the likeness of Hercules.[22] There are a few surviving pieces of statuary and stonework identified as Domitian in the guise of Hercules, or Hercules as Domitian – a marble bust in the Boston Museum of Fine Arts;[23] another bust in Compiègne;[24] and an elaborate carnelian ringstone in Munich.[25] There is, in addition, a colossal basalt statue of Hercules in Parma which, though it does not seem to bear any particular resemblance to Domitian, did occupy a prominent place in Domitian's throne room at Rome.[26]

The best evidence for the link between Domitian and Hercules is found in Martial's ninth book of epigrams (the same book that contains Martial's poems to Earinus), where we learn that Domitian dedicated a temple to Hercules along the Via Appia and had his own face imposed on the cult statue. Martial writes in poem 65 of this book:

> Alcide, Latio nunc agnoscende Tonanti,
>   postquam pulchra dei Caesaris ora geris,
> si tibi tunc isti vultus habitusque fuissent,
>   cesserunt manibus cum fera monstra tuis,
> Argolico famulum non te servire tyranno
>   vidissent gentes saevaque regna pati;
> sed tu iussisses Eurysthea: nec tibi fallax
>   portasset Nessi perfida dona Lichas;
> Oetaei sine lege rogi securus adisses
>   astra patris summi, quae tibi poena dedit;
> Lydia nec dominae traxisses pensa superbae
>   nec Styga vidisses Tartareumque canem.
> nunc tibi Iuno favet, nunc te tua diligit Hebe;
>   nunc te si videat Nympha, remittet Hylan.
>   (*Epig.* 9.65.1–14)

Hercules, recognizable to the Thunder-god of Latium, now that you sport the attractive features of our divine Caesar, if that same face and figure had been yours when wild monsters yielded to your

211

hands, the world would never have seen you work as a slave for the tyrant of Argos or endure his brutal regime. You would have given the orders to Eurystheus; and that liar Lichas would not have brought you the deadly gifts of Nessus; you would have safely reached the starry realm of your supreme father without the requirement of your Oetaean cremation – instead your suffering gave you this reward. You never would have spun any Lydian wool for a domineering mistress, or seen the Styx or the dog of Tartarus. Even Juno likes you now; your own Hebe now loves you; and if that Nymph should catch sight of you, she'll give back Hylas.

This connection between Hercules and the *princeps* is significant in iconographic terms, for though Hercules certainly populates the literature and propaganda of the Julio-Claudian era, the Julio-Claudian rulers shied from any visual connections between their own person and the hero – perhaps, as Palagia argues,[27] because the assimilation of a ruler's features to Hercules was too obvious a throwback to the absolute monarchies of the Hellenistic world. We might find further reasons for Octavian to steer clear of Herculean iconography in the fact that Octavian's greatest opponent, Antony, claimed descent from Hercules and frequently drew on symbolism from the Hercules myth. As in many other aspects of their portraiture and self-representation, the Julio-Claudian successors here might have been following Octavian's example.[28]

Valerius' uses of the Hercules story thus take on a different slant from those found in the epics of the Julio-Claudian era: for in writing under a *princeps* who fashions himself in his public art as a new Hercules, Valerius can, in his own representations of Hercules, take advantage of Hercules' new iconographic presence at the imperial court, and configure his Hercules in ways that would correspond to Domitian himself.

In this context the paradoxes and dissonances of the Hylas episode, the attempts to force the love affair between Hylas and Hercules into a framework defined by *pietas*, and the increasing impossibility of accepting this innocent and idealized definition of their relationship recall some of the noteworthy moments at which Domitian seems to have assumed a superficial semblance of piety – the best example, of course, being his public ban of castration, a ban which never precluded his enjoyment of his own *castratus* Earinus.

THE REFLECTIVE TEXT

The image of the reflecting pool is central to this essay, for it can function as a metaphor of Valerius' poetic technique. In concluding, then, we will return to the simile of the light reflecting off the surface of the pool, a simile which reveals so much about Valerius' use of literary precedents. One of the curious features of the simile is its placement: it is interposed in the text at the very moment that we expect Hylas to see a face revealed in the water – either the face of the Nymph waiting to seize him, or, as the consistent references to the Narcissus story seem to suggest as an alternative, his own face. Instead of this revelation, we get a deferral: a beam of light (*iubar*) replaces the face; a simile is substituted for the expected sight. Rather disconcertingly, the simile describes the very phenomenon it exemplifies – the glare cast by sun or moonlight on to water dazzles the eye, making it impossible to see anything but refracted light. In Apollonius' version, the light of the moon reveals Hylas; in Valerius' adaptation, the dazzling light cast by Hylas conceals whoever is in the pool. The association of Hylas with an echo appears in every version of the story, and in Antoninus Liberalis' version it is even stated that he was transformed into an echo by the Nymphs who stole him. In Valerius' *Argonautica*, the echo appears when Hercules roams the woods crying Hylas' name:

> rursus Hylan et rursus Hylan per longa reclamat
> avia; responsant silvae et vaga certat imago.
> (*Arg.* 3.596–7)

'Hylas', he calls, 'Hylas', he calls, again and again on the long, path-less trail; the woods answer, and a wandering echo imitates him.

Appropriately enough for a description of an echo, the repetition of *Hylan* itself echoes Virgil's brief mention of Hylas in the sixth Eclogue:

> his adiungit, Hylan nautae quo fonte relictum
> clamassent, ut litus 'Hyla, Hyla' omne sonaret.
> (*E.* 6.44–5)

To these [stories] he added the sailors calling for Hylas, aban-doned at that fountain, until the whole shore echoed 'Hylas, Hylas'.

But the disappearance of Hylas and his replacement by an echo is not, as we have seen, the end of the story in Valerius. He returns as an *umbra*, a ghost (*Arg.* 4.41), and thus becomes both a *sonus* and an *umbra*, the two terms used to describe Dryope at the moment she meets Hylas at the surface of the pool ('nil umbra comaeque / turbavitque sonus surgentis ad oscula Nymphae', *Arg.* 3.560–1).

At the moment that Hylas and Dryope meet, they vanish, replaced by echoes and shadows. This myth, an almost textbook example of voyeurism in its Greek variants, becomes in Valerius' poem a paradigm of the frustrated gaze, on a number of different levels. Hylas fails to see

213

the Nymph, who seizes him.[29] The supremely erotic moment of the other versions, when the Nymph sees Hylas and is filled with desire, is simply omitted in this account – we may assume it has occurred, but we do not 'see' it. Hercules too is a frustrated viewer – Hylas vanishes from his loving gaze at the beginning of the hunt:

> simul Alcides hortatibus urget
> prospiciens. iamque ex oculis aufertur uterque.
> (*Arg.* 3.551–2)

At the same time the son of Alcaeus, looking on, cheers him on with shouts. And now each of them is taken from his sight.

Despite the sharpness of his vision, he fails to see him afterwards:

> sed neque apud socios structasque in litore mensas
> unanimum videt aeger Hylan nec longius acrem
> intendens aciem.
> (*Arg.* 3.570–2)

But, sick with grief, he does not see him among his friends or the tables built by the shore, nor, sending his sharp gaze even further, does he see his soulmate Hylas.

In the end, when the sleeping Hercules receives his vision of Hylas, Valerius uses the ambiguity of the passive voice of *video* to suggest the unreliability of a dream vision:

> ecce puer summa se tollere visus ab unda . . .
> stansque super carum tales caput edere voces.
> (*Arg.* 4.22–4)

Look, the boy seemed to raise himself from the surface of the water . . . and standing above that dear head, he seemed to say these words.

Ironically, Hylas' last words to Hercules are to warn him not to let the *cari comitis . . . imago*, the image of his dear companion, slip away from him; this is precisely what happens when Hercules tries vainly to grasp the dream image.

The frustration of the viewer extends beyond the level of the plot. It is reflected in our own experience as readers. As we have seen, the voyeuristic scene where the Nymph observes Hylas and falls in love with him is absent in Valerius; a Narcissus-like encounter between the boy and his reflection is set up as a substitute, but just as we are not shown the Nymph seeing Hylas, so we do not see Hylas seeing himself or the Nymph. A simile describing the dazzling reflection of light on the surface of a pool is substituted, a simile that thwarts our gaze too. For we, the readers of the poem, are spectators as well, leaning over Hylas' shoulder and peering into the water along with him. Instead of a revealed object, we are confronted with a simile which interferes with our desiring gaze, momentarily blinding us as Hylas was blinded by his own radiance.

The frustration of vision, the confusion of identities and the allusions to and departures from earlier versions of the Hylas story in Valerius' *Argonautica* suggest a parallel between the myth of Hylas and the creation of Valerius' own text. The myth is a tale of loss, in which echoes and dreams are substituted for the beloved object; in Valerius' version, the echoes, reflections and dreams enact on the level of metaphor the textual allusion and imitation that project the illusion of poetic reality. Hylas dissolves when he touches the surface of the pool, replaced by an echo and a ghost, much as the narrative of the *Argo* story breaks down into echoes and variations on earlier works when one looks closely at the reflective surface of Valerius' text. Valerius' Argonauts sail through seas choked with precedents, crowded with *doppelgängers*. Their unmapped unknown is for the author a well-charted world of familiar texts; for the reader, the *Argonautica* is an endless voyage into the familiar made strange.[30]

NOTES

1 Hardie 1990a: 3–5.
2 The myth of the *Argo* is an ancient one. The ship, already associated with Jason, is mentioned in *Odyssey* 12.70ff.; Apollonius' *Argonautica* is the earliest full-scale epic treatment of the myth to survive from antiquity, but both the voyage and the disastrous love affair of Jason and Medea are frequently mentioned in Greek tragedy.
3 Bing 1988 provides an excellent introduction to these aspects of Hellenistic poetry.
4 Unfortunately we cannot know how much Valerius borrowed from Varro of Atax's earlier Roman rewriting of the *Argonautica* (from the mid-first century BCE), of which only fragments remain.
5 Davis 1990: 48–51; Boyle in Boyle and Sullivan 1991: 270–2; Lefèvre 1971: 11–16; Konstan 1977: 1–18.
6 Catullus' isolation of the *Argo* as the first ship is a logical extension of the notion of the *Argo* as the original cause of suffering, which appears in the opening lines of Euripides' *Medea*:

> How I wish the *Argo* had never reached the land
> Of Colchis, skimming through the blue Symplegades,
> Nor ever had fallen in the glades of Pelion
> Smitten fir-tree to furnish oars for the hands
> Of heroes who in Pelias' name attempted
> The Golden Fleece! For then my mistress Medea
> Would not have sailed for the towers of the land of Iolcus . . .
>
> (*Medea* 1–7, tr. Warner)

7 Davis 1990: 47.

8 The myth was also popular with Martial, who mentions Hylas in a number of his poems (*Epig.* 5.48; 6.68; 7.15; 7.50; 9.25; 9.65; 10.4; 11.43).

9 Antoninus Liberalis says that Hylas went in order to get water from the spring, but does not mention the pitcher; Propertius changes the story, for his Hylas, though he sets out in search of water, carries no pitcher and prepares to draw water from the spring with his hands ('tandem haurire parat demissis flumina palmis', Propertius 1.20.43). Statius, Valerius' contemporary, mentions the urn, but the Nymph has seized it from Hylas' hands in *Silvae* 3.4.42–3.

10 Colton 1979: 107–8; Osmun 1983: 56.

11 Not only does Hylas have no pitcher in *Argonautica* 3, but when he reappears in Book 4 to Hercules, instead of wearing the blue robes specified by Mopsus ('caeruleae vestes', *Arg.* 1.220), he is clad in saffron weeds ('frondibus in croceis', *Arg.* 4.23).

12 Segal 1969 offers a good introduction to the erotic landscape in Ovid's *Metamorphoses*.

13 The Nymph Salmacis plucks flowers (*Met.* 4.315–16) before she rapes Hermaphroditus; see the analysis in Nugent 1990a: 168–9.

14 The Juno in Seneca's *Hercules Furens* rivals Virgil's Juno in ferocity, and is very probably another source for Juno's appearance here as Hercules' foe.

15 Cf., e.g., *Arg.* 3.514, 'en ego nunc regum soror – et mihi gentis / ullus honos'? and *Aen.* 1.46–8; *Arg.* 3.520, 'mox et Furias Ditemque movebo', and *Aen.* 7.313, 'flectere si nequeo superos, Acheronta movebo'.

16 Nugent 1990a: 163–5 has a very useful discussion on the confusion in the text between the Nymph and her pool as part of her analysis of gender and erotic discourse in the tale of Salmacis and Hermaphroditus.

17 See Nugent 1990a: 173–5 for a discussion of Ovid's characterization of Salmacis' desire as reflexive and specular and Hermaphroditus' as based on touch; she suggests that the rape itself is a (failed) fusion of two different discourses of desire.

18 Even Dryope's name (only Valerius calls the Nymph Dryope) links her to Hylas, whose father Theiodamas was the king of the Dryopians.

19 For analysis of the rape of Hermaphroditus, see Nugent 1990a and Richlin 1992.

20 The literature on this topic is vast. See Richlin 1983; Keuls 1985; Halperin 1990; Winkler 1990.

21 For an analysis of this poem that finds deep irony and criticism in Statius' representations of Earinus, see the Appendix to Ahl 1984b, written by J. Garthwaite, 111–24.

22 The most recent discussion of this can be found in Palagia 1986: especially 144–6.

23 Vermeule 1981: 300–1.

24 Daltrop, Hausman and Wegner 1966: 100.

25 Palagia 1986: 145.

26 Andreae 1981: 178, 180 and plate 397.

27 Palagia 1986: 145.

28 Zanker 1988: 44–7; cf. Plutarch, *Antony* 4.

29 It is possible that Valerius intends the adjective *avidus* (greedy), which characterizes both Hylas and Dryope, to reflect the blindness of desire (playing off of the similarity between *avidus* and *video*). For this sort of word-play in Latin poetry, see Ahl 1985 and Snyder 1980.

30 We would like to thank the following colleagues for their help with this project: F. M. Ahl, A. J. Boyle, Jeffrey Henderson, J. Pollini, A. Richlin, and the participants in the Pacific Rim Roman Literature Seminar, held at USC, September 1991.

XI

FLAVIAN VARIANT: HISTORY. SILIUS' *PUNICA*

Marcus Wilson

Lucan in his *Pharsalia* successfully negotiates the contradictory demands of history and poetry, modifying both to create a work at once faithful to history's particular facts and passionately committed to poetry's universal truths.[1] Silius Italicus never attempts any such reconciliation. In the *Punica*, each historical situation is treated as an occasion for poetic invention, for the imitation of scenes from the *Iliad*, the *Aeneid*, Ovid's *Fasti* or *Metamorphoses*.[2] History is, as it were, mythologized, wrenched not just in language but in event into the epic mode. The epic imagination is everywhere victorious over historical probability. History is there only to be transmuted. Silius had been consul in 68 CE, witness to and participant in the civil and military turbulence of 69 CE, had governed the province of Asia under Vespasian and was for many years a prominent forensic orator.[3] Martial lists him as one of the more influential men in the city and law courts ('proceres urbisque forique', 6.64.9) and Pliny associates him with the leading figures of state ('fuit inter principes civitatis', 3.7.4). On his retirement he might have seemed well placed to take up the writing of history. Instead he preferred to defy it. Re-appropriating from prose historiography the story of the most significant foreign war fought by the Roman nation, he restored it to poetry, its original home. The opening lines of the *Punica* imitate the first paragraph of Livy's account of the Hannibalic war.[4] This is especially clear in lines 13 and 14 where Silius' 'propiusque fuere periclo / quis superare datum' ('they came nearer to destruction who finally prevailed') follows closely the thought and loosely the expression of Livy's 'et adeo varia fortuna belli ancepsque Mars fuit ut propius periculum fuerint qui vicerunt' ('so varied were the fortunes of war and uncertain the fighting that they came nearer to destruction who were finally victorious', 21.1.2). From the outset Silius invites consideration of the relation his epic version of the war bears to the Roman prose historiographical tradition.[5] At the same time he indicates how far from it he stands. The war he will describe is not between Romans and Carthaginians but between the descendants of Aeneas

(*Aeneadum*, 2) and the tribe of Cadmus (*gens Cadmea*, 6); he writes not as a historian with one eye on his sources but as bard under the inspiration of Calliope (*Musa*, 3); his gaze is not limited to earthly sights but extends to the heavens (*caelo*, 1); Italy is Hesperia (4); Scipio Africanus is a Trojan leader ('Dardanus . . . ductor', 14–15); the first echo is of the *Aeneid* (*arma*, 'arms', 1). Through epithets and nomenclature Silius refashions the identity of places and persons. In looking ahead at the start of the poem to Scipio's historical conquest of Carthage (14–15) the reader is forced simultaneously to look back to the mythical origins of the Roman race in Troy. An authority more than human is claimed for the narrative, and the years 219–201 BCE are rediscovered not from the perspective of Augustan or even Flavian Rome but of eternity. In Silius' hands epic narrative offers an alternative to prose historiographical narrative as a vehicle for drawing out the significance of past events, one which imports a radically different (if archaic) cultural ideology: different concepts of time, of causality, of human psychology and human identity. The *Pharsalia* and the *Punica* cannot be classed together. The former is a compromise, a historical epic. Silius' epic is uncompromisingly anti-historical.[6]

Compare their treatment of the causes of war. Early in the first book of the *Pharsalia* Lucan states his intention of expounding the causes (*causas*, 67) of the civil war of 49–45 BCE. Despite the talk about Fate (70, 94), the personification of Rome (84–6) and the imagery of cosmic dissolution (72ff.), it can be seen that he emphasizes first the antecedent events which led up to the outbreak of war: the formation of the First Triumvirate (85ff.); the defeat and death of Crassus at Carrhae (104ff.); the death of Julia, Caesar's daughter, wife of Pompey (111ff.); the personal rivalry between Pompey and Caesar, especially over Caesar's military successes in Gaul (120ff.). He then turns his attention to deeper social causes ('publica belli / semina', 158f.): the influx of wealth and resultant shifts in moral outlook and behaviour (160ff.); the resort to violence (174ff.) and bribery (178–80) for political ends; the growth of usury (181f.). Historians ancient and modern might debate Lucan's particular interpretation, but they would recognize the terms in which he is thinking. How should they respond, though, to Silius' account in his first book of the origins (*causas*, 17) of the second Punic war? He shows no interest in exploring the details of what was allowed or what was forbidden under the treaty between the two powers, no interest in explaining Carthaginian resentment at the loss of Sicily and Sardinia or the size of the tribute paid to Rome as a result of the defeat in the previous war. He turns, instead, to the story of Dido (21ff.) and to the goddess Juno's legendary favouritism towards Carthage and prejudice against Rome (26ff.). Silius takes as his source not Livy, not Polybius, but Virgil, whose own inquiry into cause in the *Aeneid* ('Musa, mihi causas memora', A. 1.8) also centred on the role of Juno, and who had depicted Dido pledging ceaseless enmity between her descendants and those of Aeneas (A. 4.622–9), even prophesying the advent of Hannibal (A. 4.625) as avenger of her fate. Silius' personal literary universe has its own rules which supplant those considerations of cause and effect that govern the understanding of historians. Juno drives the action of the poem from her igniting of Hannibal's aggressive instincts near the beginning of Book 1 ('iuvenem facta ad Mavortia flammat', 55) until her reluctant withdrawal from the field of Zama just before the end of Book 17 (604). That the seeds of war were sown in the legendary rather than historical past is a message underscored by opportune reminders of Dido's tragedy which arise in the course of the poem. It is at her temple in Carthage that the young Hannibal takes his oath of lifelong hostility towards the Roman people (1.8ff.); scenes of her life and death figure conspicuously on Hannibal's shield (2.406–25); her suicide is again recounted by her sister Anna in Book 8 (81–103; 124ff.) prior to Silius' description of the battle of Cannae. The source of Juno's anger is itself explained by Proteus, who recalls the story of the judgment of Paris to the terrified Nereids in Book Seven (437ff.). In the *Punica* there is little causation of the type approved by historians. Silius' epic Muse has her own ways of comprehending events: by aetiology and the ascription of divine instigation and purpose. This is a work rich in aetiological explanations. The Pyrenees are named after Pyrene, a maiden ravished by the drunken Hercules (3.417–41); Saguntum was named after Zacynthus, companion of Hercules who was buried there after dying from the bite of a poisonous snake (1.273–90); Lake Trasimene takes its name from the young man seized by the Nymph Agylle and carried off to live with her in its depths (5.7–23); Falernian wine was a return gift to Falernus for his hospitality to Bacchus (7.162–211); the worship of Anna in Italy comes about through her transformation into a Naiad in the waters of the river Numicius (8.44–201). The song of Teuthras at Hannibal's feast in Capua is aetiological in character, tracing the lineage of Capys, founder of the city, back to Jupiter (11.288–97). There is a fabulous story behind almost every name or place: Hannibal's wife Imilce is descended from Milichus, son of a Nymph Myrice and a lustful satyr (3.97–107); Baius, one of Ulysses' companions, conferred his name on Baiae (12.113–15); Sardinia, previously called Ichnusa, was renamed by Sardus, a descendant of Libyan Hercules, after himself (12.358–60). The poet records, explores, invents legendary associations which determine the identity and significance of persons, places and events. His presentation of the origins of the war is entirely in keeping with this procedure. Often the association is with a deity. Thus the world and its inhabitants are persistently linked to the actions of the gods. The greatest Roman heroes have their divine pedigree unequivocally announced: Fabius Maximus belongs to a family which traced its founding to Hercules (2.3; 6.627–36; 7.35, 592), Paulus is descended from gods (8.293f.; 341f.); Scipio Africanus when in the underworld is told by his deceased mother the secret of his parentage, that his true father is not, as he thought, Publius Cornelius Scipio but Jupiter (13.634–47), a point forcefully reiterated in the very last lines of the poem:

> nec vero, cum te memorat de stirpe deorum,
> prolem Tarpei mentitur Roma Tonantis.
>
> (*Pun.* 17.653f.)

> When Rome asserts your divine lineage as child
> Of the Tarpeian Thunderer, she speaks no lie.

The gods have no inhibitions when it comes to involving themselves in human affairs.[7] They intervene frequently and at times in mutual contention. Jupiter is responsible for the injury suffered by Hannibal at Saguntum (1.535–40); the wound is healed by Juno (1.548–52); Venus sends Vulcan to set fire to the foliage along the banks of the river Trebia (4.675ff.); at Lake Trasimene the other gods avert their gaze (5.201), leaving Bellona to range over the carnage (5.220ff.); Pallas and Mars alight on the battlefield at Cannae (9.438ff.) and commence combat; Pallas prevents Hannibal from facing Scipio in a personal duel to the death (9.484f.) by veiling him in cloud and transferring him to a different place; when Hostus throws his spear at Ennius in Sardinia Apollo ensures that it misses and that Hostus dies, his head pierced by an arrow (12.403–14); Hannibal is beaten back from the walls of Rome by the gods of the city led by Tarpeian Jupiter (12.605ff.; 655ff.; 707–25); the plague at Syracuse is blamed (at least in part) on divine animosity (*invidia divum*, 14.583) and anger (*ira deum*, 14.617); Neptune excites a sea-storm to prevent Hannibal turning his fleet back to Italy (17.236ff.); at Zama, Juno fashions a false image of Scipio to draw Hannibal away from a direct confrontation with the Roman general (17.524ff.) and then impersonates a shepherd in order to postpone his return to the deciding conflict (17.567ff.). One of the most important causative factors in Livy's version of the war, Roman class politics, is pushed almost out of sight by the shift into epic mode. Flaminius in Livy (21.63) wins election to a second consulship after alienating the Senate, thereby gaining the favour of the masses; Minucius, according to Livy (22.25–6) is granted equal powers with Fabius only after an acrimonious political controversy at the end of which Varro, then praetor, proposes the novel arrangement so as to curry popular support for his own political ambitions. Contrast the *Punica*, where it is Juno who instigates both Flaminius' and Minucius' appointments to the command (4.708–10; 7.511f.). Similarly, Jupiter stage-manages the selection of Fabius as dictator (6.609ff.), and clinches the choice of Scipio as commander in Spain by delivering a favourable portent (15.143–7) in the form of a triple thunderbolt. Where history views change in terms of human institutions and aspirations, epic (as Silius writes it) subordinates these to divine control.

The gods manipulate minds as well as events. The second Punic war is itself Jupiter's way of strengthening the Roman character and restoring it to a love of virtue and glory (3.163–5; 573–583). On the other hand, the resolute discipline of Hannibal's soldiers is undone at Capua by the action of Venus, who directs her children to fire arrows into their hearts instilling in them the love of pleasure (11.385–9; 410ff.). The human actors are subject to the direction of powerful outside forces revealed by epic narrative, hidden from historians: Virtue and Pleasure vie for the soul of Scipio (15.20–128); the goddess Fides takes possession of the inhabitants of Saguntum, filling them with a burning passion for herself ('sui flagrantem inspirat amorem', 2.517); they are next driven to self-destruction by Tisiphone disguised to resemble Tiburna (2.553ff.). Later, Fides and Fury again compete, this time for the minds of the Capuans (13.281–95). At the battle of Ticinus, the young Scipio, having witnessed his father's wounding, is about to kill himself in despair, but Mars diverts his rage against the Carthaginians ('bis transtulit iras / in Poenos Mavors', 4.458f.). Hannibal begins his march to Italy after being prompted by Mercury who appears to him in a dream (3.168–214). Scipio is given the idea of attacking New Carthage by a dream in which he is exhorted by his (human) father's ghost (15.180–99). The idea of marching to join forces with Livius Salinator against Hasdrubal is planted in Claudius Nero's mind by Oenotria, the very soil of the homeland ('Oenotria Tellus', 15.522ff.; 'Latiae telluris imago', 15.546), which then purposefully confuses the invading troops and gets them lost (15.617–25). Before Cannae Hannibal's confidence is uplifted by the visit of Anna under instructions from Juno (8.28–38; 226–31); his failure to advance upon Rome immediately after Cannae is the result of a dream Juno sends (10.348–71); his decline of Marcellus' challenge to single combat at Nola is again Juno's work (12.201f.). It is Mars who makes the Roman army more bellicose (9.486–90), and Pan who causes it to put aside its ferocity (13.316–28).

Like Ovid in his *Metamorphoses*, Silius is engaged in the work of transformation, the transformation not of things but activities and events. In particular he transforms the nature of war.[8] Battlefield tactics count for little, so everything comes down to individual courage and prowess. Emotions rather than plans govern the fighting, especially rage over the death of a comrade, as when Asbyte seeks revenge for Harpe (2.121); Mopsus for his sons (2.138f.); Mago for Isalcas (5.302ff.); Brutus for Casca (7.652); Paulus for Servilius (10.225ff.); Scipio for

Marius (13.234ff.); Hannibal for Asbyte (2.209ff.) or Sychaeus
(5.586ff.); as when Pedianus slays Cinyps, who is discovered wearing
armour stripped from the dead consul Paulus (12.236f.). Above all,
soldiers are inspired by their leaders' speeches or example, dispirited
and weakened when their leaders fail. At the battle of Lake Trasimene
Hannibal is for some time absent from combat after his brother Mago
is wounded (5.344ff.). This brings an opportunity for Flaminius to
dominate the action in a successful counter-attack (5.376ff.). The tide
of battle fluctuates ('variis . . . casibus', 530f.) until Mago and Hannibal
return to the field reasserting Carthaginian superiority. When Flaminius
falls Roman resistance ceases instantaneously ('nec pugna perempto /
ulterior ductore fuit', 658f.). The soldiers think no longer of fighting
but want only to follow Flaminius into death, to share his fate and
enhance his memory by their own destruction. They allow themselves
to be cut down above his body, constructing a tomb for their leader
from their piled corpses ('sic densae caedis acervo, / ceu tumulo,
texere virum', 665f.). Similarly, at the battle of Cannae, all the
determination of the Romans collapses the moment the consul Paulus
is slain:

> postquam spes Italum mentesque in consule lapsae,
> ceu truncus capitis, saevis exercitus armis
> sternitur, et victrix toto fremit Africa campo.
>
> *(Pun.* 10.309–11)

> Their consul dead, the Romans' hopes and courage failed.
> As if headless, the army by fierce arms is crushed
> And on all the field Africa roars triumphant.

Even Fabius, a strategist in avoiding battle, once the fighting starts leads
by example ('exemplo laudis furiata iuventus', 7.617), instilling in
younger Romans a craving for his approbation ('volebant / spectari
Fabio', 7.620f.). Carthage is described as wholly dependent on Hannibal
('uni nixa viro', 17.150, 197f.). At Zama, according to the poet's
explicit statement:

> sub tanta cunctis vi telorumque virumque
> in ducibus stabat spes et victoria solis.
>
> *(Pun.* 17.399f.)

> Despite both sides' power in weaponry and men,
> On the leaders alone success and hope relied.

In the course of the battle Scipio seeks out Hannibal because he knows
the fortunes of Carthage ride on those of this one man ('unus . . .
unus', 17.512–16). Commanders on both sides become in action the
sorts of Homeric heroes with whom they are sometimes compared (e.g.

223

Fabius with Nestor, 7.596f.; Hannibal with Achilles, 7.120–2). In the *Punica*, anachronism is a principal source of meaning.

Silius reshapes the battles of the war in accordance with ritualized forms that go back to the *Iliad*, forms like the *aristeia* and the duel.[9] Thus the narrative will frequently focus on the successive feats of a single warrior who (at least temporarily) holds supremacy against all antagonists: Asbyte (2.56ff.); the elder Scipio (4.230–47); Fabius (7.587ff.); Paulus (10.1–30); Laelius (15.451–70); Hannibal (4.324–54; 17.444–78). There are duels to the death between Hannibal and Theron (2.233ff.), the elder Scipio and Crixus (4.259ff.), Mago and Appius (5.302ff.), Brutus and Cleadas (7.634ff.), Nero and Hasdrubal (15.780ff.). Other duels are inconclusive or narrowly thwarted: between Hannibal and Flaminius at Trasimene (5.607–14), interrupted by an earthquake; between Taurea and Claudius at Capua (13.143ff., attested by Livy also, 23.47); between Hannibal and Scipio Africanus at Cannae (9.428ff.) and again at Zama (17.509ff.), forestalled in both instances by divine interference. Often duel, *aristeia* and speech are put together in various combinations, perhaps the best example being that in Book 1 (376–534) involving Murrus and Hannibal at Saguntum. There is more than mere adherence to literary tradition in Silius' use of these conventions. In his Preface he declared his intention of recording 'how many and how great' ('quantos . . . et quot . . . viros', 1.4f.) were the men Rome summoned to her defence in this war ('ad bella', 4). These epic conventions are uniquely adapted to the task of highlighting the physical and moral excellence of the heroic individual in battle.

In the *Punica* warfare closes the distance separating mortals from immortals. They fight alongside one another in the same battles, as when Rome's citizens are joined by Jupiter in repelling Hannibal's attack on her walls (12.587–732). At the battle of Cannae, which occupies the centre of the poem, as the human armies clash, so simultaneously do the gods fight amongst themselves:

> nec vero, fati tam saevo in turbine, solum
> terrarum fuit ille labor; discordia demens
> intravit caelo superosque ad bella coegit.
>
> (*Pun.* 9.287–9)

> Nor amid this savage storm of fate was the strife
> confined to earth; into heaven irrational
> contention entered, impelling the gods to war.

Mars, Apollo, Neptune, Venus, Vesta, Hercules, Cybele, Faunus, Quirinus and Pollux take up arms against Pallas, Ammon and, of course, Juno (290–9). Heaven is left deserted as they all descend to battle ('vacuo descensum ad proelia caelo', 303). On the other hand, mortals rise above normal human limits, even contending with forces of nature, as Hannibal does with wind, rain and lightning (12.610ff.; 656ff.); as the elder Scipio does with the river Trebia (4.638–701); and the Roman soldiers do at Cannae, where they are opposed by Volturnus (9.491ff.) or at Trasimene, where not even the violent shaking of the earth stops them hurling their missiles at the enemy (5.627–9). In an extended simile in Book 1 (433–6) Hannibal at Saguntum is likened to the god of war riding his chariot through the land of the Thracians. Mars is again pictured riding through Thrace in his chariot in another simile in Book 17 (486–90). At Zama, though, it is not Hannibal who is the image of Mars but Scipio.

Nowhere is Silius less historical than in his treatment of death in battle. He is not interested in the casualty statistics provided by Livy and other historians. Death has a life of its own in the narrative and is astonishingly inventive. Allius is doubly killed, struck by two spears simultaneously; they clank as they meet in his heart (4.566–9). Three Carthaginian brothers tackle three Italians, also brothers, slaying and being slain by them (4.355–95). Cupencus has one blind eye and dies with a spear through the other (4.541). Tyrrhenus the bugler, while sounding the call to battle, has his windpipe punctured by a javelin; his groan is sustained by the instrument as a dying musical cadence (4.169–74). In a sea battle off the coast of Sicily Polyphemus, killed when his body is pinned to the rowing bench by a spear, continues to make rowing motions (14.532–8). In the same fight Bato commits human self-sacrifice (14.458–61): he stabs himself in the chest and, while dying, catches the blood in his hands and pours it between the sacred horns of Ammon. Graphic descriptions of violent death were a literary inheritance from Homer. Yet here more than anywhere else Silius is indebted to post-Virgilian models, especially Ovid and Lucan. He appeals to the mind's eye, inviting the reader to picture the improbable, the incredible. Dismemberment offers some striking instances: Ascanius' head, when it is cut off, falls at his feet, but the rest of his body keeps running (13.246–8); Draces' head, when it is cut off, continues its jabbering pleas for mercy (15.470); a Roman ship pulls away with Lilaeus' hand still clutching it, though severed (14.489–91); Larus' hand is lopped off by Scipio's sword, but hangs on to its favourite battle-axe (16.66f.). Other deaths are no less pictorial and spectacular: Ufens is carried off by an elephant after being skewered by a bayonet fastened to its tusk (9.581–6); another elephant lifts Mincius with its trunk, waves him about in the air, then dashes him to the ground (9.627–31); as Dorylas falls mortally wounded from the battlements of Saguntum, the arrows from his quiver rain down around him (2.129ff.); Sciron, half in, half out of the water, endures a slow death, his body transfixed by the sharp beak of a battleship (14.481–4); Hampsicus,

225

after being hunted like a bird as he leaps from branch to branch of a tall tree, dies dripping blood from on high (7.667–79). Tunger's skin is black, he dresses in black armour, drives black horses and in his chariot looks like Pluto, 'the ruler of eternal darkness' ('aeternae regnator noctis', 7.688); but, on seeing Cato about to behead him with a sword, for the first and last time in his life, he turns pale (7.680–704). Death frequently enacts paradoxes, metaphors, ironies. Caicus, speared by Hannibal's javelin, rolls down a steep embankment, thereby returning the weapon to its owner (1.304–9); in a grotesque reunion, Mopsus plummets from a lofty tower on to his dying son's limbs (2.145–7); some, like Bibulus and Siccha (7.621ff.; 9.388), though surrounded by enemies intent on killing them, perish by accident; a spear, falling short of its mark, has its power to kill restored by the victim rushing to meet it (4.140–2). Death imitates art, both visual and literary; and on the killing fields of Italy resides a hideous kind of beauty. Pedianus, having ripped the helmet from dying Cinyps' head, stands, his fury abating, in mute admiration of his victim's face (12.241–52).

Most of those who fall in battle spring to life in the narrative just as death draws near. Only by their deaths are they known. Death becomes thereby a self-commemorative act, not the antithesis of life so much as its ultimate expression. It brings an opportunity to convert the moment of annihilation into an unrivalled moment of self-assertion. At the Ticinus, Quirinius, certain he is going to die, musters all his boldness to win a glory he will not survive to enjoy ('certusque necis petit omnibus ausis, / quod nequeat sentire, decus', 4.197f.). At the Trebia, Fibrenus refuses to waste death (*perdere mortem*, 4.605) when he can use it to buy fame (*famae*, 606). Flaminius at Trasimene offers to teach his soldiers to die (*disce mori*, 5.638). After the battle Hannibal exclaims upon the character displayed by the Roman corpses:

> 'quas mortes!' inquit. 'premit omnis dextera ferrum,
> armatusque iacet servans certamina miles.
> hos, en, hos obitus nostrae spectate cohortes!
> fronte minae durant et stant in vultibus irae'.
>
> (*Pun.* 5.670–3)

> 'What deaths!' he said. 'Every hand still grips its
>   sword.
> Each body lies there armed, continuing the fight.
> Come, my men, examine these deaths. Threatening glares
> Stiffen on their brows and their faces express rage'.

In death their animosity lives on. Bruttius tries to put his death to good use in preventing the capture of a military standard ('iniecta morte tegebat', 6.32). Laevinus uses his time of dying to kill (6.41–53), as do others in the poem (4.589f.; 14.553f.). Marcellus, surrounded by the enemy, with no avenue of escape, is eager to carry with him to the shades a great reputation for death ('magnum secum portare sub umbras / nomen mortis avet', 15.372f.). The people of Saguntum by choosing not to survive procure an everlasting honour (2.612f.; 696ff.).[10] At the battle of Cannae Scaevola declares that 'virtue is a meaningless word unless the moment of death is sufficient for the birth of renown' ('virtus futile nomen, / ni decori sat sint pariendo tempora leti', 9.376f.). The casualties of war in the *Punica* quit life snatching at immortality.

'I take up the arms by which the glory of Aeneas' descendants raises itself to the heavens' is Silius' opening proclamation ('ordior arma, quibus caelo se gloria tollit / Aeneadum', 1.1f.). Jupiter in justifying the war to Venus points out that the hardships involved will produce men whose fame will not be unworthy of heaven ('nomina nostro / non indigna polo referet labor', 3.585f.). He refers to Paulus, Fabius, Marcellus and Scipio (586–92). According to the speech of Virtue in Book 15 (75–8) nature has condemned debased souls to the obscurity of Avernus, but the gate of heaven lies open ('caeli porta patet') for those who cherish the divine seed with which mortals are endowed. Even Hannibal accepts that some men are destined for eternal fame and divine honours (3.136f.). In the course of the narrative each of the major Roman heroes is attributed a moral and military ascendancy that puts him on a par with the gods. It is fitting that Fabius should lift up his sacred head into heaven ('emerito sacrum caput insere caelo', 7.19); later, the Roman soldiers venerate him with libations (7.749f.). Paulus by the grandeur of his death wins honour reaching up to the stars ('misitque viri inter sidera nomen', 10.308). Marcellus, after victory at Nola, is called the peer of Mars (12.278f.); after the capture of Syracuse he rivals the gods in temperament ('aemulus ipse / ingenii superum', 14.680f.). The Roman Senate, meeting to consider action over Saguntum, 'matches the gods in virtue' ('aequantem superos virtute senatum', 1.611). The Saguntines themselves obtain a glory that will last for ever ('in saecula', 2.511; 'aeternum', 2.613); the poet apostrophizes their 'celestial souls' ('sidereae . . . animae', 2.696f.). Similar language is used of earlier Roman heroes like Brutus (13.721f.), Camillus (13.722) and Regulus (6.546–9). Among the attendants of Virtue is Triumph leading the way to the stars ('producit ad astra Triumphus', 15.100). Scipio chooses Virtue over Pleasure (15.121–3) and in the final scene of the *Punica* rides in triumph, assured of perennial esteem (17.625), the equal of Quirinus and Camillus (651f.), the successor to Bacchus and Hercules (647–50).

Two contrasting mythical paradigms condition Silius' handling of relations with the gods in the *Punica*: the apotheosis of Hercules and

227

the gigantomachy.[11] The way these operate in the case of Hannibal is complex. On the doors of Hercules' temple are depicted his labours (3.32ff.), culminating in the scene on Oeta where the flames carry off his noble soul to the stars ('ingentemque animam rapiunt ad sidera flammae', 3.44). Hannibal visits the temple and 'sates his eyes with the multi-faceted portrait of virtue' displayed there ('oculos varia implevit virtutis imago', 3.45). He seems for a time intent on following in Hercules' footsteps in traversing first the Pyrenees (3.415ff.) and then the Alps (2.356f.; 3.91f., 496–9; 4.4f., 63–5). However, in climbing the Alps, Hannibal departs from the path of Hercules (3.513–15) and, in his determination to breach the physical barrier, breaches also a moral one. He pushes his way higher than those mountains piled up by the Giants in their assault on the heavens (3.494f.), until he seems to be trespassing with his army on sacred domains ('sacros in fines', 501) in contravention of nature ('natura prohibente', 502) to make war on the gods ('divisque repugnent', 502). There are subsequent allusions in the poem to the gigantomachy, in Book 9 as the battle of Cannae commences (9.305–9) and, above all, in the action of Book 12. In attacking Rome Hannibal aims to expel Jupiter from the Capitol ('cernas / et demigrantem Tarpeia sede Tonantem', 516f.); he is resisted by the gods collectively, who take up defensive positions atop the city's seven hills (606–11; 622–5; 709ff.); Jupiter complains to Juno that Hannibal wants to smash his way into the gods' homes and is, as it were, forging his own thunderbolts against them (12.697–700); sounds of the battle remind Typhoeus, buried deep underground, of his own war with heaven (659f.); Juno urges Hannibal to yield to the gods and desist from gigantic warfare ('cede deis tandem et Titania desine bella', 725). At the end of the poem Hannibal persists in his defiance, claiming the fame of his own deeds will outlast Jupiter's occupancy of the throne of heaven (17.606–10). Scipio, when visiting the dead, suggests that Hannibal might be suitably punished in the same manner as Tityos (13.872f.). Hercules was prominent in putting down the revolt of the Giants (12.143f.); thus Hannibal comes now to be associated with Hercules' adversaries. That this should be the case was foreshadowed at the beginning of the war by the Carthaginian attack on Saguntum, a town established by Hercules (1.273, 369, 505, 661; 2.582) over the sufferings of which he is profoundly disturbed (2.475ff.; 9.292f.). In the fighting there Hannibal destroys the image of Hercules in the form of Theron, a priest of Hercules' temple, who comes to battle dressed in the skin of a lion and armed with a club (2.149–59, 237–60). Numidian soldiers burn the lion skin and club; the body is left as food for vultures (2.267–69). In Scipio Hercules is reborn. Like Hercules Scipio is begotten by Jupiter; Scipio's mother occupies a place of honour in Elysium alongside Alcmena (13.632f.). Like Hercules Scipio is offered the choice of Virtue or Pleasure for his guide in life, and like Hercules he chooses Virtue (15.18–123). Both while living visit the world of the dead and both are adjudged worthy of heaven in recognition of their exceptional accomplishments on earth. The particular role of Hercules with which Scipio is associated at the end of the poem is that of vanquisher of the seditious Giants on the battlefields of Phlegra ('cum Phlegraeis, confecta mole Gigantum, / incessit campis', 17.649f.).[12]

Silius' restoration of the gods to the narrative of Rome's past cannot be lightly dismissed as mere literary conservatism. The connection between mortal and immortal is the foundation stone of his whole poetic edifice.[13] It is the dimension of the past which history misses, which epic alone is qualified to reveal. The responses of Scipio and the Sibyl on seeing the ghost of Homer contain important clues to Silius' ideas on the scope and function of epic. Homer, according to the Sibyl, embraced in song not just the earth and sea but also the heavens and the world of the dead ('carmine complexus terram, mare, sidera, manes,' 13.788). Epic does not just uphold the immortality to be won through virtue; it collaborates in achieving it. As the Sibyl says: 'Homer took Troy up to the heavens' ('tulit usque ad sidera Troiam', 791). In the same way Ennius will raise Roman leaders to the sky ('attolletque duces caelo', 12.411).[14] Scipio, in order to praise Homer, addresses Achilles:

> 'felix Aeacide, cui tali contigit ore
> gentibus ostendi! crevit tua carmine virtus'.
>
> <div align="right">(<i>Pun.</i> 13.796f.)</div>

> 'Achilles, you were lucky that such a voice showed
> You to the world! Through his poem your virtue grew.'

Achilles is immortalized by poetry ('aeternus carmine Achilles', 14.95). In the quest for immortality epic is an active partner, itself the vehicle of undying eminence. Like Homer and Ennius before him, Silius seeks to elevate his heroes to the heavens. The task of the poet, as he conceives of it, is no mean one: to interlace the human with the divine.

Chronology is indispensable to history. Livy, writing in prose about the war, assiduously records annual events which mark the transition from one year to the next: the holding of elections; the performance of ceremonies to appease the gods; the distribution of responsibilities, legions, commands. Most important is the election of consuls by whose names the year will, in future, be differentiated from other years. The forward movement in time brings with it also a sense of causal connection; later situations arise out of earlier ones. Ultimately a continuity is asserted between past and present. This is implied even in Livy's title: *From the Founding of the City* (*Ab Urbe Condita*). Time in the

Punica assumes a radically different significance. It is an obstacle that needs to be overcome; that must be conquered in order to attain everlasting fame, glory, honour (*laudes, gloria, decus*). Addressing Scipio (13.772–5), the ghost of Alexander the Great criticizes slow-moving warfare ('lenti . . . Martis') as discreditable (772); virtue exercised too slowly ('pigra . . . virtus') will never excel (773f.); Scipio should anticipate time ('praecipita tempus') to achieve greatness, for black Death always hovers near (774f.). Epic, as Aristotle remarked (*Poetics* 1449b13f.), does not observe limits in time. Silius takes full advantage of this freedom. He goes much further than Livy in allowing thematic relevance rather than temporal duration to determine the amount of narrative allocated to particular incidents. The phase of the war that ends with the battle of Cannae occupies one-fifth of Livy's version, over half of the *Punica*; of the eighteen years covered by the poem's action, ten books out of the *Punica*'s seventeen are devoted to the first four. Where he wishes, Silius expands events (e.g. the major battles; the siege of Saguntum). Elsewhere he compresses or omits.[15] For instance, the two separate embassies which, according to Livy, approached the Carthaginians, one before and one after Saguntum's fall (21.9–11, 18), are conflated by Silius into one (2.1–24, 270–390). Silius is deliberately imprecise about time. He does not signal the passing of the year in any systematic manner. Elections are mentioned only irregularly; for some years (e.g. 215 and 206 BCE) there is no indication at all of who held the consulship. Where he does notice time it is usually in the form of stylized evocations of sunrise and sunset involving personifications of dawn (*Aurora*: 1.576ff.; 5.24ff.; 15.251, 439f.; 16.135ff., 229f.), the sun (*Titan, Phoebus*: 4.480ff.; 5.55ff.; 6.1ff.; 7.205f.; 10.537f.; 11.267ff., 369f.; 12.648f.), evening (*Hesperus:* 11.267ff.; 12.646 f.) or night (*Nox*: 1.556f.; 13.254; 15.284, 542, 612, 809f.). These descriptions depict time in terms of repetition and cyclicity rather than linear progression. Time is tied to the motions of the heavens and to the gods who, by their presence or absence, bathe the earth in light or plunge it into gloom.

Epic reopens the borders closing off the present from the future and the past.[16] By visiting the dead Scipio can converse with persons who lived long ago and view the souls of Romans as yet unborn (13.850–67). Similar things happen in dreams. Scipio encounters his father's ghost twice, once when he visits the underworld (13.650ff.) and again in a dream (15.181ff.). Before leaving Spain, Hannibal, in his dreams, is crossing the Alps and attacking Rome (1.64ff.); towards the end of the war he suffers from a nightmare in which he is pursued by Romans who died at Trasimene and Cannae (17.159ff.). Flaminius claims to be haunted at night by an army of Roman corpses from the Trebia (5.127–9). The night before Cannae, Romans in their sleep see the ghosts of Gauls breaking out of their tombs (8.641f.). Through prophecy and prediction events are described prospectively rather than retrospectively as in history: by Juno (1.45ff.), the priestess of Dido's temple (1.125ff.), Bostar reporting the oracle of Ammon (3.700ff.), Mars (4.472ff.), Proteus (7.476–93), a delirious soldier at Cannae (8.659ff.), Paulus (9.57ff.), Hanno (11.570ff.), envoys returning from the Delphic oracle (12.324ff.), the Sibyl (13.505–15, 874–93), Pleasure (15.125–8), Jupiter (3.584–629; 9.542–50; 17.373–84) and the narrator (2.699ff.). Omens warn of disasters ahead of time, for instance the battles of Ticinus (4.103–35), Trasimene (5.59–104) and Cannae (8.624–55; 9.252–66); the death of Marcellus (15.363–5); the treachery of Syphax (16.264ff.). Other signs tell of coming success: the Roman siege of Capua (13.114ff.); the alliance with Masinissa (16.119ff.); Scipio's leadership (15.138ff.); Rome's eventual victory (17.44–7; 52–5). The third Punic war is foreshadowed (7.492f.; 17.373–5) just as the first is repeatedly recalled (1.61f., 621ff.; 2.304ff., 340–4, 432–6; 4.78–80; 5.246; 6.140–550, 658–97; 11.527; 13.730ff.). Hannibal's ignoble death by poison in 183 BCE is excluded from Livy's third decade by chronology, but that is no obstacle to its inclusion in the *Punica* (2.699ff.; 13.874ff.). Silius is persistent in associating his narrative with the Muse (invoked at 1.3; 3.222; 5.420; 7.217; 9.340; 12.390; 14.1), a divine source of knowledge standing outside of any particular time. By the frequency and ease with which his verbs oscillate between past and present tenses, the narrator seems to travel back and forth between the time of the events themselves and the time of the reader's reading about them, treating them as both completed and still in progress.[17] In the poem's conclusion Silius forsakes narrative in the third person and past tense to address Scipio directly: 'Hail, invincible parent' ('salve, invicte parens', 17.651). It is as if they are contemporaries.

Time is also bridged by art.[18] Romulus is an infant under the care of the she-wolf in a scene engraved on the shield of Flaminius (5.143–5). The shield of the Gaul, Crixus, shows Rome occupied by his ancestors (4.152f.). Mucius Scaevola's hand roasting in the flames is depicted on the shield of his descendant at Cannae (8.385–9). Scipio's shield at the battle of Zama carries portraits of his father and uncle (17.396–8). Hannibal, whose whole life is pledged to the prolongation of past passions and grudges, to fulfilling Dido's curse and Hamilcar's ambitions, is presented with a shield on which the sources of his motivation are displayed: Dido is there as foundress of Carthage; then, abandoned by Aeneas, she commits suicide; along with other scenes from the previous war, Hamilcar rides jubilantly across the countryside of Sicily; Hannibal swears his childhood oath of undeviating hatred for Rome (2.406–36).[19] Architecture too keeps the past alive. Hercules' labours are recorded on the doors of his temple (3.32ff.). Dido's temple, constructed on the spot where she died (1.85f.), lies in deep shadow surrounded by yews and pines, and accommodates marble statues of Belus, Agenor, Phoenix and Dido herself, Aeneas' sword at her feet, reunited with Sychaeus (1.83–91). The temple in which the Roman Senate meets is like a museum; it is adorned with captured chariots, helmets, shields, blood-stained weapons, the beaks of ships, the bolts of city gates, mementoes of earlier campaigns against Carthage, Pyrrhus, the Gauls (1.617–29). In the *Punica* there is a struggle for supremacy between rival images of the past. Book 6 closes with an extraordinary antithetical pair of ecphrases. Hannibal finds, in the porticos of a temple at Liternum, scenes representing Roman victories in the first Punic war (6.653ff.), including one where Hamilcar is exhibited in bonds as a prisoner of war (689–91). Hannibal's initial response is creative, to counteract these scenes of the past with contrasting scenes of the future. He imagines the pictures that will be set up on buildings in Carthage to commemorate his own victories over the Romans (700ff.). The climax will be Rome aflame and Jupiter cast down from the Tarpeian rock (712f.). Hannibal's second response is destructive. He orders his men to 'wrap these memorials in flames and turn them into ash' ('in cineres monumenta date atque involvite flammis', 716). Instead of Rome he burns the images of Rome. Hannibal fears the power of art, and not without reason. When he and his army surrender to pleasure in Capua there are no detailed reports in the *Punica* of sexual or drunken debauchery. Silius stresses, rather, the Capuans' predilection for theatrical entertainment (11.428f.) and for music (430–8). Teuthras sings for Hannibal a lengthy celebration of the power of song:[20] by song Amphion raised walls for Thebes (443–5); Arion charmed the creatures of the sea (446–8); Chiron shaped the mind of Achilles and could soothe the anger of the sea or dismal Avernus (449–52); Orpheus moved wild animals, rivers, forests, mountains, the sea and the dead (459–74). As Orpheus by his song turned the tide to launch the *Argo* (469–72), Teuthras by his song turns the tide of war against Hannibal. At the end of his performance the narrator announces that:

> sic tunc Pierius bellis durata virorum
> pectora Castalio frangebat carmine Teuthras.
> (Pun. 11.481f.)

> Thus Pierian Teuthras' Castalian song
> Broke the Carthaginians' war-hardened resolve.

In Scipio's triumphal procession at the end of Book 17, the world is transfigured into art and brought to Rome (634–42). Rivers such as the Ebro (641) and the Baetis (637–9), mountain ranges like the Pyrenees (640f.) and places like Gades and Calpe (637f.) pay homage to their conqueror. Personifications of Spain, now pacified ('iam lenis'), and of Carthage 'stretching her humbled arms towards the sky' ('victas tendens Carthago ad sidera palmas') march before his chariot (635f.). Artistic vision overrides historical reality. Though Hannibal escaped capture, he is paraded in his absence:

> sed non ulla magis mentesque oculosque tenebat,
> quam visa Hannibalis campis fugientis imago.
> (Pun. 17.643f.)

> But no likeness held their eyes and attention more
> Than that of Hannibal fleeing across the plains.

Scipio's triumph is not so much part of the war as the first attempt after its conclusion to create, by artistic means, an image of its significance and hence is a precursor of the *Punica* itself.

Pliny regards Silius Italicus himself as something of an anachronism: a Neronian in the age of Trajan; the last surviving Neronian consul ('ultimus ex Neronianis consularibus', 3.7.10). Certainly Silius was of an older generation than Statius and Valerius Flaccus. He was, in fact, born more than a decade before Lucan. Also, unlike many other poets like Martial and Statius he did not require patronage; on the contrary, he bestowed it. Because of his wealth, his age, his retirement from public life and eventually from Rome itself ('ab urbe secessit', 3.7.6), he largely escaped the financial, social and career pressures under which poets commonly wrote. Few other men have so possessed the will and the means to immerse themselves in another world of their own choosing. Silius lived not in Domitian's Rome but with Cicero, Virgil and other poets and artists of the past, surrounded by books, statues and portraits ('multum ubique librorum, multum statuarum, multum imaginum') in each of his many villas ('plures . . . villas possidebat', 3.7.8). This is what Pliny finds most remarkable about him. Silius made of art a religion, of Virgil's tomb a temple ('monimentum eius adire ut templum solebat', 3.7.8).[21] His retirement was from a time as well as a place. From Silius' world contemporary politics are banished. It appears from Pliny's letter that Silius abstained from political involvement in later life. Because he sought to exercise no power he was subject to no resentment ('sine potentia, sine invidia', 3.7.4). He does not even go to Rome to congratulate the new emperor on his accession ('ne adventu quidem novi principis inde commotus est', 3.7.6). In the *Punica* also he keeps his distance. Unlike Lucan, Valerius and Statius he does not take pains to mention the reigning emperor early in the first book of his epic.[22] He delays introducing Flavian Rome into the poem until late in Book 3 (594–629) and even then avoids doing so in his own voice as narrator. Instead, adopting a Virgilian device (*A.* 1.254–96), he presents his own era in the form of a prediction put into the mouth of Jupiter.[23] By this means Flavian Rome enters the *Punica* under a different aspect: not as the time in which the poem is composed but as part of the future awaiting Rome after the war with Hannibal is finished. The Flavian emperors themselves are transformed, mythologized, depoliticized. They become a 'warrior tribe' (*bellatrix gens*, 596). All the emphasis is placed on their activities (real or projected) at a great distance from Italy and Rome: Vespasian in Thule (597), Caledonia (598), Judaea (600), Africa (599), on the Rhine (599); Titus in Palestine (605f.); Domitian in Germany (607f.), Bactria (613), on the Danube (617) or the Ganges (612), now far to the north ('Arctoo . . . axe', 614), now far to the east ('Eoos . . . triumphos', 615). They are conquerors and rulers of foreign lands; the role of the emperor in domestic politics is passed over in silence.[24] Even the brief compliment to the emperor at the end of Book 14 (686–8) refers only to actions affecting the provinces. Silius reinvents Domitian as an incarnation of the themes around which the *Punica* turns. A triumphant military hero (614f.), he also has artistic credentials both as orator ('eloquio', 618f.) and poet ('huic sua Musae / sacra ferent', 619ff., 'to him the Muses will bring their offerings');[25] virtually a composite of Scipio, Cicero and Virgil. He re-establishes links between earth and heaven by his reconstruction of the Capitoline temple of Jupiter ('et iunget nostro templorum culmina caelo', 624) and is one of a long line of Romans going back to the Hannibalic war who are said by Jupiter to be deserving of admission to heaven (585f.; 611; 625–9). Silius is as antihistorical in dealing with his own age as he is with every other. The historical Domitian never was deified.

The example of Lucan focused attention on the differences and similarities between epic and history. Silius Italicus seems to have reflected upon these and realized that implicit in the epic and historiographical modes of narrative are contrasting ideological assumptions about time, cause and effect, human psychology and the role in human affairs of the divine. Whereas Lucan had tried to resolve these, Silius accentuates and exploits the discrepancy, using epic to transform history, Homer and Virgil to rewrite Livy. The result is a poem that induces in the reader simultaneously a sense of strangeness (with respect to historical events) and of recognition (in that the episodes echo familiar epic models). The situation of the narrative between history and epic, tending continually to move in the direction of the latter, reflects Silius' view of human nature. Silius' chief philosophical preoccupation concerns the transcendence of mortal limitations. This calls for a particular approach to narrative, one which attempts repeatedly to draw the reader away from history, with its human perspective on human events, into epic, where the divine is made conspicuous and heroism reaches superhuman heights. As history approaches epic, mortals approach immortality. Silius' theme demands that what is credible in normal human terms be exceeded, that 'reality' be transgressed, that common sense be contravened. Some readers baulk. Opinions of the *Punica* surviving from antiquity are sharply divided. The poet Martial thinks highly of it (4.14; 7.63); Pliny, who day-dreamed about writing history (5.8), disapproves (3.7.5).[26] Pliny's reaction shows what scholars have subsequently demonstrated over and over again, that the *Punica* is liable to discompose the prosaic mind.[27]

NOTES

1 Lucan 'skillfully shaped history into epic form without betraying either history or epic . . . His extraordinary ability to reconcile the demands of both genres is everywhere evident' (Ahl, Davis and Pomeroy 1986: 2502f.).
2 On the relation of the *Punica* to Homer see Juhnke 1972; to Virgil see Albrecht 1964: 166–84 and Ahl, Pomeroy and Davis 1986: 2493–501; to Ovid see Bruère 1958; 1959.
3 Pliny is the source for Silius' consulship (3.7.9) and proconsulship of Asia (3.7.3), Martial for his career as advocate (7.63.7–8) and Tacitus for his role in 69 CE (*Hist.* 3.65.2).
4 On the opening lines of the poem see Albrecht 1964: 16–24; for their relation to Livy 21.1, see Pomeroy 1990: 124.
5 It remains the case that: 'Agreements between Silius and Livy in passages of considerable length occur so often as to put the poet's use of the historian beyond doubt' (Nichol 1936: 17). This is not to deny Silius' use of other sources. See also Matier 1981 and Spaltenstein 1986: xivff.
6 I am talking of 'history' here primarily as a narrative mode, though this is not entirely separable from the question of historicity. Feeney 1991:250ff. has a useful discussion of relations between history and epic. Ahl, Davis and Pomeroy 1986: 2501–4 provide an instructive comparison of the *Punica* with the *Pharsalia*.
7 The presence of the gods in the *Punica* is still viewed by some scholars as an irremediable blemish; see Duff 1927: 369; Gossage 1972: 195; Vessey 1982: 95. Contrast Mendell 1924: 105; 1967: 141f.; Matier 1989: 6. See also the discussions of Burck 1979a: 286–90; Kissel 1979: 11–57; Feeney 1991: 302–12.
8 Silius' treatment of Rome's early defeats are dealt with in detail by Niemann 1975.
9 Silius 'relates battles, not as matters of strategy but as conglomerates of individual combats' (Duff 1927: 369).
10 The Saguntum episode has attracted much comment, for instance Vessey 1974b; Küppers 1986: 164ff.; McGuire 1990: 33–41.
11 Hercules' importance in the *Punica* is well established by Albrecht 1964: 82f.; Bassett 1966; Kissel 1979: 153–60; Liebeschuetz 1979: 170–3. the poem has been called a 'philosophisch gefärbten Gigantomachie in historischem Gewande' (Albrecht 1964: 143).
12 Noted by Albrecht 1964: 84f.
13 Cicero's *De Re Publica* and especially the *Dream of Scipio* is an important influence on the thought of the *Punica*, as noted by Heck 1970; Liebeschuetz 1979: 179; Colish 1985: 289.

14 Matier 1989: 5 has revived some of the emphasis on Silius' relation to Ennius earlier propounded by Mendell 1924: 98ff.; 1967: 142ff. See also Häussler 1978: 148ff.

15 For the following examples I am indebted to the very useful article of Wallace 1968.

16 Newman 1986: 532 has popularized the term 'vertical time'.

17 This feature of style is not, of course, unique to Silius Italicus.

18 Frank 1974: 840–4 discusses art in the *Punica*, but not in depth.

19 Hannibal's shield is discussed in detail by Vessey 1975; Küppers 1986: 154–64.

20 On this song see Burck 1984: 24–8.

21 On this Vessey 1974a: 111f. is persuasive.

22 Luc., *Phar.* 1.33ff.; Stat., *Theb.* 1.17ff.; V. Fl., *Arg.* 1.7–21. Writers seem to have been expected to acknowledge the emperor near the start of their work. Quintilian apologizes for neglecting to do so (*Inst.* 4, *pref.* 5).

23 That Roman poets used prediction by a character to avoid saying something in their own voice is reiterated by O'Hara 1990: 123–7. On Jupiter's speech generally, see Schubert 1984: 45–70.

24 The context of Jupiter's speech is not wholly auspicious: it is delivered while Hannibal is camped on the summit of the Alps, poised at the top of the world, a danger to the gods and to the peoples of Italy below.

25 On Domitian's literary activities, see Coleman 1986.

26 Both Martial and Pliny have been suspected of ulterior motives: Vessey 1974a: 110; McDermott and Orentzel 1977: 32–4; Matier 1989: 3. Martial's admiration is considered sincere by Mendell 1924: 95; 1967: 140 and Matier 1989: 4.

27 'The hostility and malice of most modern English critics is simply beyond belief' (Matier 1989: 4).

XII

EPIC IN MIND: CLAUDIAN'S
DE RAPTU PROSERPINAE

Peter Connor

Claudian manifestly entertained lofty ideals about the supereminent nature of epic, as his first Preface demonstrates.[1] In it the poet states his belief that the difficulties involved in composing epic require an apprenticeship in writing. He likens, in an epic simile, the writer's gradual acquisition of expertise through practice and experience to the growth in expertise of ocean-going vessels: just as sailors launched at first on timid voyages that hugged the shore-line, later attempting the waters of bays enclosed by jutting arms of land, and finally assuming a bold spirit to burst upon the open sea and conquer its dangers, so the poet must grow in courage and skill as the ultimate danger and the ultimate prize beckon. Skill, an acquired and carefully nurtured skill, is especially stressed. The Preface begins with words that seem to promise an attack on the first builder of ships; for the first builder of ships is usually reckoned to be a villain.[2] But no. Invention is the key concept, pursuit of an idea, giving space to ingenuity:

> qui dubiis ausus committere flatibus alnum
> quas natura negat praebuit arte vias.
> > (*DRP*, pref. 2–3)

Who dared commit the alder to doubtful blasts and by his art showed paths which nature denied.

We might note, in passing, an important link with the words of Jupiter at the beginning of Book 3:

> provocet ut segnes animos rerumque remotas
> ingeniosa vias paulatim exploret egestas
> utque artes pariat sollertia, nutriat usus.
> > (*DRP* 3.30ff.)

So talent-giving need might stimulate dulled minds and bit by bit explore the far-off ways of things, and so that shrewdness might produce the arts and practice nourish them.

237

The practice of literature and the practice of life are in theory conjoined.

Virgil had long toyed with the notion of writing epic poetry, and he came to realize how that epic should be conceived.[3] But when he began his poem, like Homer his model, he briefly invoked the Muses for inspiration, and charged on. Even Ovid in *Amores* 1.1 and the young Virgil of *Eclogue* 6 are blithely prepared to make an immediate start.

For all his audaciousness and high ambition, Claudian on the other hand is notably self-conscious. Whilst the epic bard like Demodocus sings to and for all,[4] Claudian adopts the style of Horace at the beginning of the Roman Odes:

> gressus removete profani.
>
> (*DRP* 1.4)
>
> Do not tread here, you uninitiate.

And he has a more vehement sense of inspiration than that expressed by Horace in, for example, *Odes* 3.25. When Claudian's god of poetic inspiration (Phoebus) arrives, there is the bright light we expect in epiphanies, but the temples reel and snakes hiss savagely: a violent concept of divinities. Hecate menaces, and even Bacchus, who has perhaps an unthreatening appearance, smooth-cheeked, ivy-crowned, attractive gold claw-knot at his neck, is reeling drunk. The awesomeness of scale is thus deflated by this Bacchus and there is introduced a lack of consonance often found in Claudian.

Claudian continues now to invoke the underworld gods as he sets out his themes: how Dis fell in love, how Proserpina was raced off, and how mortals were given the gift of corn and so were able to dismiss acorns as food.

Along with the grandiose invocation and the grandiose scheme of his epic comes an impressive command of language and of solemn rhythms, to be noted especially in 1.20ff. We will find, however, that Claudian limits himself to this one epic sound, and its adequacy requires our consideration.

1

It would seem to be the case that if the would-be epic poet takes as subject a myth-story usually told in a succinct and summary form, usual with myths, then the events have to be brain-stormed, thought through, fleshed out: imagination is required to summon up the thought-patterns of the participants, the causes, the motives.[5] This must often be quite the opposite of that epic-material which is mighty in scale both of events and time, where successful narrative demands thematic organization and careful selection involving pruning of incident.

Take, for example, the arrival of Pluto's chariot. In the three main accounts previous to the time of Claudian, and with which Claudian must be in competition, this incident is not established in a motive-context; it just occurs:

Homeric *Hymn to Demeter*, 16ff.

The wide-pathed earth yawned . . . and the lord, Host of Many, with his immortal horses sprang out upon her.

As Richardson says: 'the transition . . . is sudden and rapid'.[6]

Ovid, *Fasti* 4.445ff.

Here her uncle saw her, and swiftly carried her off on his dusky steeds into his own realm.

Ovid, *Metamorphoses* 5.356ff.

Pluto left his gloomy realm to examine the foundations of Sicily threatened by the volcanic heavings of the Titans in case light was let in to the underworld and terrified the shades of the dead. He caught sight of Proserpina and, smitten by Cupid, he bore her off as fast as he could go.

Claudian's Pluto has to fight his way out of his realm,[7] and his purpose in doing so is fully examined. He has a mission; the rape is not on the spur of the moment, as appears in earlier accounts. His dissatisfaction with the single life and as a result having no offspring are both established in this poem, and the divine agreements have been entertained at length.[8]

For Claudian much of the requirements of his epic-needs had been prepared by certain interests of Hellenistic mythological fiction which allowed its heroes and heroines room for their deepest thoughts and emotions, often in soliloquies.[9] We sense and experience the thoughts and feelings of Pluto (as austere and unsympathetic as we might find them). So the epic began with an echo that needs no comment, with blazing anger:[10]

dux Erebi quondam tumidas exarsit in iras.
(*DRP* 1.32)

Erebus' Lord, one time, blazed out in swelling bouts of anger.

239

Extreme emotions are appropriate. However, our topic for the moment is the ascent of Pluto from the underworld. As in the earlier versions Pluto's ascent is by way of Sicily,[11] and Claudian too like Ovid finds it fitting to detail the geography of Sicily and its subterranean prison-house of the Titans in a mixture of geomorphology and mythology.[12] The Titans here and at the beginning of Book 1 are an important part of epic texture.

Epic narrative is such that it must evoke a broad canvas, marshalling episodes which shape a complex of action across a number of actors, rather than presenting a simple linear account in the picaresque manner of the Homeric *Hymn to Demeter* or Ovid's story of Pluto and Proserpina and Ceres, or that crystal-like account of the love of Apollo for Cyrene in *Pythian* 9, or the powerful narratives of visual and dramatic action developed by the playwrights in their messenger speeches. Claudian's epic narrative technique is to establish weighty persons involved in weighty and interlocking incidents. By 1.160 Claudian has sketched in most of the actors, and each component of the narrative is held temporarily in 'suspense'. The location too is an actor.[13]

Pluto is seen by Ovid as awesomely powerful,[14] not just in that his steeds brush aside the naive and foolhardy futility of Cyane's attempt to block their path with her body, but in the aggressive way he smites open a track to the underworld:

> haud ultra tenuit Saturnius iram
> terribilesque hortatus equos in gurgitis ima
> contortum valido sceptrum regale lacerto
> condidit; icta viam tellus in Tartara fecit
> et pronos currus medio cratere recepit.
>
> (Ov., *Met.* 5.420ff.)

The Saturnian held in check his wrath no more: urging on his dreadful steeds, he buried in the whirlpool's depths his regal sceptre hurled with powerful arm; earth, so struck, made a path to Tartarus and in mid-crater received the headlong chariot-team.

Claudian's Pluto bursts on an idyllic world with as much startling suddenness as does the Pluto of the *Hymn to Demeter*, with a thundering crash, the collapse of towers, and towns uprooted. Not, however, because he was clear and into open air, but because he bullocks his way along labyrinthine tracts beneath the earth, where not rock alone but Enceladus too tries to block his path by twining his snakes in the chariot wheels. Enceladus resists because now he has Pluto as well as the whole of Sicily crushing him down. None the less the chariot-wheels scythe through his limbs:

immania findunt
membra rotae pressaque Gigas cervice laborat
Sicaniam cum Dite ferens temptatque moveri
debilis et fessis serpentibus impedit axem:
fumida sulphureo praelabitur orbita dorso.

(*DRP* 2.158ff.)

The wheels cut through the monstrous limbs, and Gigas toils
because his neck is squashed and carries Sicania and also Dis; he
feebly tries to move and with his tired snakes impedes the wheels:
the smoking chariot slides over the sulphurous back.

Pluto is on his way to take Proserpina, but for a moment he has his
share of battling the Giants. Jupiter and his Olympians had tackled
them victoriously once; now it is the turn of Jupiter's brother, Pluto.
The baroque character of the description, as if it were the verbal
equivalent of the Great Altar at Pergamum, is specially noticeable here,
with the atmospheric effects of that final line. He is not, however, out
and away, for a continued task lies ahead of him: just like a sapper who,
through a tunnel dug beneath the foundations of a city wall, enters the
city seeming to spring from the earth.[15] The unusual comparison works
like a good epic simile: it has its own life and interest and it relates well
to its context: a war context. Jupiter may have agreed; but here is an
enemy infiltrating with stealth. In any case wrathfully (wrath again)
Pluto strikes open a way with his beam-like sceptre. This is an impressive
show of force, the effect of which is cosmic: the earth shudders and
resounds; Vulcan and his Cyclops are frightened, even they, used to
creating din and upheaval.

Nor are we finished. To fine-tune our sense of the mighty blow and its
effect on nature, we are reminded of the draining of the lake of
Thessaly when Neptune pierced a passage through the mountains and
the waters ran away to their proper location, the sea.

Nor are we finished still. The gaping cleft in the ground ('immenso
. . . hiatu', 'with enormous gaping chasm', *DRP* 2.187),[16] which is what
other versions limit themselves to, creates fear among the stars so great
that in haste they scurry past their natural course; the sun is blotted out
by the horses' dark breath, though the horses themselves, alarmed at
the brightness, move on only when lashed by the importunate Pluto.

Claudian rarely soft-pedals with his description, but the picture of
the horses, their bloodied bits, their foul breath that pollutes and
darkens the day, is a gothic *tour de force*, a pictorial elaboration typical of
so much of Claudian's concept of his task. According to the tale of the
survivor, Electra, which we read later in the poem, some strange things
happened as the island shook and the sun grew dark and horses' hoofs
beat and wheels rushed; but if she was talking about what is described

so violently at this point, it was no *Picnic at Hanging Rock*, and Electra's account indicates a gap in the poet's coordination of the incident in these two places in the poem.

Pluto's anger, which I have stressed somewhat, provides another instance of a certain inconsistency. The action begins with the wrath of the Lord of Erebus (1.32f.), and though we learn that he is *indocilis flecti* ('hard to budge', *DRP* 1.69) – in any mood, I suppose – it takes but little persuasion on the part of Lachesis (*DRP* 1.55–67) to mollify him: 'erubuitque preces' ('shamed by her prayers', *DRP* 1.68).

Still, anger and the gigantomachy are woven as a leitmotif throughout the books as we have them. Electra's first response to Ceres' questioning about the course of events is to take up the possibility put to her that the Titans are responsible:

> regnatne maritus
> an caelum Titanes habent? . . .
>
> (*DRP* 3.181f.)

Is my husband king? or do Titans possess the heavens? . . .

Would that they had, is Electra's reply:

> acies utinam vesana Gigantum
> hanc dederit cladem!
>
> (*DRP* 3.196f.)

Would that the Giants' frenzied battleline had wreaked this disaster!

Because the destruction would be common to all.

We return to these turbulent monsters yet again when a little later (3.332ff.) Ceres, searching for suitable trees to fashion torches, chose the grove where Jupiter set up the trophies of his victory over the Giants. Once again we are treated to the full-blown baroque of his description.[17] Virgil touches baroque themes and styles, as a comparison of his Cacus episode with the robber-baron of Livy's story (1. 7) would clearly show;[18] but the whole of his large epic exhibits many varieties of language.[19] Claudian may have a more limited range of grandiose language effects; but it is well mastered and well sustained.

It is appropriate to mention here the most succinct incident of this epic: the rape itself.

> diffugiunt Nymphae: rapitur Proserpina curru
> imploratque deas.
>
> (*DRP* 2.204f.)

The Nymphs scatter: Proserpina is snatched up on the chariot, and implores the goddesses.

No other statement is so blunt; and it may be that Claudian designs the central event subordinate to both the marriage and the wandering of Ceres. Pluto, however, has not escaped. The deed is not yet over, because Athena and Diana, in a sisterhood of virginity, stand their ground, not with action alone but with the insistence of their several questions.

Jupiter's thunderbolt puts a swift end to their opposition; but a stillness is interposed in the action by their address of lament to Proserpina, which brings into epic the non-epic evocation of the sympathy of nature mourning at the death of the poet-shepherd, well known from Theocritus and Virgil:

> te iuga Taygeti, posito te Maenala flebunt
> venatu maestoque diu lugebere Cyntho.
>
> (*DRP* 2.244f.)

For you the peaks of Taygetus, for you Maenalus' peaks will weep, their hunting set aside, and by sad Cynthus you will long be mourned.

It brings before us poignantly again the paradox inherent in the deep structure of the myth that Pluto is carrying off an immortal and not the shade of a dead woman, though it must be recalled that, according to Claudian, Proserpina appeared to Ceres in dreams as dead, not as the imperious queen of the underworld.

2

Please consider now the opening of Book 3, where Jupiter summons all the gods and holds a council. This is, of course, a fundamental element of epic poetry. At this council, Jupiter is pre-eminent and delivers to all, under pain of the most dire penalties, an indisputable warning that the identity of the rapist-charioteer must not be revealed to Ceres. In Claudian's hands Jupiter escapes the bickering and unruly answering-back which is his lot in *Iliad* councils. The regulation extends to the closest members of Jupiter's own family, amongst whom Juno and Athena are specially mentioned:

> natus licet ille sororve
> vel coniunx fuerit natarumque agminis una,
> se licet illa meo conceptam vertice iactet:
> sentiet iratum procul aegide, sentiet ictum
> fulminis et genitum divina sorte pigebit
> optabitque mori.
>
> (*DRP* 3.57–62)

Be it son or sister, or wife or one of my band of daughters, or if she boast she was born from my brow, she'll feel from far away my weapon's wrath, and the strike of thunder, and regret that she was born divine, and will wish to die.

The pronouncement is delivered with proper solemnity. Indeed the whole of Jupiter's oration is couched in a high-toned grand style, since here, within the poem itself, is inserted the theme of the awarding to humans of the gift of corn through Ceres, following the (partial) restoration of her daughter.[20] Claudian had sign-posted this impressive theme in the Preface to Book 1. There is no sign that Jupiter is panicked into restoring Proserpina and granting the gift of corn as he is rather in the Homeric Hymn.[21]

As Hinds notes, concerning the difference of narrative manner between Ovid's story in the *Metamorphoses* and the *Fasti*, it is the higher purpose of didactic-epic that marks off the *Fasti* narrative.

So Juno and Athena are present, no doubt, to hear the special admonition. Yet as the gods gather there is no mention of them, or of any gods like them. Compare in *Iliad* 4 the first such council. No time is spent on travelling. The gods are already seated, and their argument begins forthwith. Hera and Athena are particularly rumbustious:

He spoke, but Athena and Hera muttered against him; they sat together plotting evil for the Trojans. Athena was silent, spoke not a word, angry with her father Zeus; and savage wrath gripped her.

(Hom., *Il.* 4.20–3)

The council is the deliberative gathering of the Olympians. By contrast the gods detailed at length by Claudian may perhaps well be 'the gods from the whole universe' we hear about in line 2, but those specifically mentioned are all Hellenistic types: divinities of rivers, seas and lakes, with special mention of Nereus, Phorcus, Glaucus and Proteus. Jupiter, of course, needs to enjoin secrecy on all divinities; therefore a comprehensive meeting of this magnitude (in numbers) is required. But it should be noted that Claudian does rather stress the picturesque and even the emotional aspects of this assembly:

fluvios umentibus evocat antris.

(*DRP* 3.5)

He calls the rivers from their watery caves.

plebeio stat cetera more iuventus
mille amnes. liquidis incumbunt patribus udae
Naiades et taciti mirantur sidera Fauni.

(*DRP* 3.13–17)

The other youths, a thousand rivers, like the Plebs, stand round about. On their liquid sires watery Naiads lean and Fauns, in total silence, wonder at the stars.

The lesser gods stand around, as happens to the young men at assemblies of Claudian's own time. The notion of all keeping their status-driven positions can be seen also in the council of gods of *Metamorphoses* 1.166ff., though Ovid has a cheekier point in mind, likening the divine assembly to the Roman political gatherings of his time.

Ovid too includes the lesser gods: they dwell apart from the gods of higher rank. Where the top gods live is actually, Ovid avers, rather like the Palatine in Rome, and the acquiescence of all assembled on this occasion prompts Ovid to compare Jupiter's pleasure with that of Augustus:

> nec tibi grata minus pietas, Auguste, tuorum
> quam fuit illa Iovi.
>
> (Ov., *Met.* 1.204f.)

Nor was the reverence, Augustus, of your people less pleasing to you than that was to Jove.

Ovid keeps us alert with a little mockery about the political situation, and we see perhaps the source of the total obsequiousness imagined by Claudian, though he gives it a more solemn purpose.

Claudian's Jupiter wins *pietas* ('reverence', 'loyalty') too; he too begins by expressing his cares on behalf of mankind:

> abduxere meas iterum mortalia curas
> iam pridem neglecta mihi.
>
> (*DRP* 3.19f.)

The affairs of mortals, which I have long neglected, once more have captured my concern.

Compare Ovid:

> non ego pro mundi regno magis anxius illa
> tempestate fui, qua centum quisque parabat
> inicere anguipedum captivo bracchia caelo.
> (Ov, *Met.* 1.183–5)

I was not more distressed about world-rule that time when all the snake-foot Giants set themselves to fling their hundred hands to capture heaven.

Ovid's council is heralded with the simple statement 'conciliumque vocat' ('and he summons a council', Ov., *Met.* 1.167), and, though travelling along the Milky Way is briefly described, no divine-type is singled out and none is called by name.

Although the shape of things in Claudian's assembly is epic, there is some lack of consonance, again, between the unswerving awesomeness of Jupiter and his pronouncements and a certain playfulness about the character of his audience, and, as in so many instances, Claudian seems to wish to tease out a particular flavour from each scene, neglecting its relation to the next.[22] Of course it makes sense that all divinities are summoned, since not a word about the identity of the culprit must be whispered, and also the stress on water deities may rise from Ovid's version of this myth in the *Metamorphoses*. For there it is Arethusa who, on her journey through the underworld from Elis to Sicily, caught sight of Proserpina as queen of the dead and, having quickly become a Sicily-lover with a burning passion to protect the good name of her new country (where she found safety), she told all.[23]

In this third book, epic episodes continue with the sequence of dreams and visions that haunt Ceres. In Ovid's versions, Ceres either is at a tea-party hosted by Arethusa (Ov., *Fast.* 4.423f.) or she quite simply hears the fading cries of distress uttered by Proserpina (Ov., *Met.* 5.396ff.; cf. *Hymn to Demeter* 39). Claudian puts Ceres in Phrygia visiting her mother and indulging in an ecstatic religious orgy or two, or so Proserpina says (*DRP* 3.102f.). Whilst Ceres is away, Proserpina fills the void of her mother's absence by embroidering a cloth as a gift for Ceres on her return: a nice Penelope-like touch.[24] Meanwhile hideous dreams begin to warn of disaster and we can deduce that Ceres is feeling guilty.

Dreams are a feature of epic, where they often play an important role at a critical stage.[25] In Homer the dream assumes, if it can be phrased this way, the likeness of a person, as in Penelope's dream (Hom. *Od.* 1) or the dream of Achilles, when Patroclus appears as he was alive, not gory in death (Hom., *Il* 23.65ff.). Patroclus comes to give instructions, as do all Homeric dream-persons.[26]

Claudian's dreams have, as we might by now expect, a more baroque character, smacking of ghosts and ghostly happenings. Ceres is the recipient of several dreams which increase in intensity and clarity of import. Initially, a spear seems to pierce her body and then her clothing becomes black (just that); next the dream expands to the laurel over Proserpina's room, axed and laid in the dust and grime: an explanation asked of the Dryads (tree-Nymphs) produces a kind of gothic horror which could hardly be called an interpretation:

Dryades dixere gementes
Tartarea Furias debellavisse bipenni.
(*DRP* 3.78f.)

The Dryads moaned and said the Furies had destroyed it with an axe of Tartarus.

We now escalate beyond Proserpina's favourite tree to a vision of the girl herself confined in chains, which leads us to a description of the change in her appearance (compare the ghost of Hector in *Aeneid* 2.268ff.: 'quantum mutatus ab illo', 'how greatly changed . . . '), which leads in turn, because Ceres has great difficulty in recognizing her daughter in this vision, to a series of questions asked first by Ceres and then by Proserpina, which assists a little the perception that, though the portents are portents of death, something slightly different from death has been envisaged (the gods are, after all, immortal) and the girl might be able to return to the world above. By implication, I suppose, Ceres would understand that she is in the world below:

> his, oro, miseram defende cavernis
> inque superna refer. prohibent si fata reverti,
> vel tantum visura veni.

(*DRP* 3.106–8)

From these caverns rescue me, I beg, and return me to the world above. If fates block my return, come at least to see me.

The ascending intensity demonstrates quite clearly the rhetorical basis of this passage, and it might become apparent from my discussion that Claudian's larger ambition to produce an epic rests unequivocally on a strong desire to produce impressive examples of epic episodes. The reader responds quickly to the impression that Claudian, deeply familiar with the canonical components of epic, has ensured their appearance in his work. Claudian's poem soon begins to resemble several school exercises placed together end on end:[27] a list ticked off as each item was completed: *concilium*: yes; dream: yes; and so on.[28]

This impression is strengthened by the quite ornate way each episode is teased out for as much as it is worth, to the extent of including aspects that do not seem to belong to epic proper, as we have seen in both the *concilium*-episode and in the dream-episode that opens Book 3.

An interesting set-piece scene is that of Proserpina's embroidery. Claudian's Proserpina is girlish, as she is in other versions, and delights in girlish pastimes like picking flowers with blithe avidity, but she is also right for marriage, as the mention of the divine suitors shows: an aspect not found in other versions of this story. That she balances on the edge of captivating maturity is the reason for the fortress-like 'prison' in which she is kept whilst her mother is away.[29] We might also note that on the threshold of maturity, and with the requisite capacity for making the decision, Proserpina has inclinations to remain, like her aunts Athena and Diana, a virgin. Her maturity of figure anyway is such that dressed in the appropriate clothing and weapons she is difficult to tell apart from either Athena or Diana (*DRP* 2.36ff.).

In other words we find here a fuller picture of Proserpina, whereas in other versions she is just a slip of a girl who is raced off.[30] Claudian's is the Hellenistic mode (coming *via* Euripides at least) which asks questions about what people are like and how they behave, what they are likely to say and do, and how they might have reacted to some of the events which in normal mythological accounts are given in quite summary form. That is, not that kind of Hellenistic mode that cleverly alters details for our scholarly delectation.

As she embroiders (1.246),[31] Proserpina charms the house with her melodious song. The subject of her song is not revealed; but the subject of her embroidery is: the picture is a cosmogony, the origin of the world from the whirling atoms as the seeds separated each to its own place.[32] So we have the five zones of the world, with the extremes of cold, the temperate zones and the burning central zone. The poet keeps his eye firmly on an ecphrasis of the embroidery by relating the red colours for the equatorial zone, cold colours for the frozen north and south; gold are the stars and the seas purple. Realism is stressed as the waves swell with water, seaweed crashes on the rocks, and finally the waves run softly up the sand which seems to drink in the water.[33]

Further, it strikes me, this intriguing passage is the equivalent of the bard's song. In the *Odyssey* and in the *Aeneid*, bards sing at a banquet. This motif, of course, amounts to a tantalizing brief encounter with a song inside the song we are already hearing. What do the epic bards sing of? Demodocus sings of the travails of Odysseus; Iopas sings of the creation of the universe or natural history.

When the bard sings in the *Aeneid*, we want to hear more. So, the embroidery of Proserpina has that same attention-grabbing quality, and since it is the equivalent, as I suggest, of the bard's song, it holds its place fitly in an epic context. The description is compelling, and captures for us also the sense of the passing time and Proserpina's lonely activities. It is part of the suspense, part of the ominous time lag between the departure of Ceres and the fatal flower-picking expedition. When, therefore, in the final lines of Book 1, with the mention of night (time is important in epic)[34] we find that Allecto is marshalling Pluto's chariot at the threshold ready for the morning's foray, there is a beautifully caught moment of impending doom. On this occasion too the detail of the horses' names, Orphnaeus, Aethon, Nycteus and Alastor,[35] and their special equine qualities sustain the atmosphere of impatient waiting. The ripe gothic imagination lingers here only over 'the rotting pools of sluggish Lethe', whence dark oblivion drips from their slumbrous lips:[36]

> stagnaque tranquillae potantes marcida Lethes
> pigra soporatis spumant oblivia linguis.
>
> (*DRP* 1.282f.)

They drink the putrid pools of the still Lethe and dull oblivion foams from their sluggish tongues.

The full details of the arrival of the divine visitors is delayed until the narrative of Cyane in Book 3, a technique paralleled in the *Hymn to Demeter*, where the account of the rape itself is held back until line 405, when none other than Persephone tells how it happened. We did, however, hear that Proserpina's needle-work was interrupted by their appearance at the door (*DRP* 1.270ff.) and that she blushed in a fittingly epic way:[37]

> non sic decus ardet eburnum
> Lydia Sidonio quod femina tinxerat ostro.
> (*DRP* 1.274f.)

The ivory-glory does not shine so bright when dyed by a woman of Lydia with Punic purple.

We might turn now in this analysis of epic ingredients to the moments before the flower-picking party sets off. First, in epic manner, the day dawns (*DRP* 2.1ff.), or rather is on the point of dawning:

> tremulis vibratur in undis
> ardor et errantes ludunt per caerula flammae.
> (*DRP* 2.2f.)

Brightness quivers on tremulous waves and straying flames play on blue seas.

And then comes the description of each goddess. Since this is an expedition, the reader is reminded of the gathering for the hunt in *Aeneid* 4. There, the assembling huntsmen and Aeneas and Dido are described and a leisurely comparison is established between Aeneas and Apollo – leisurely in the sense that a lengthy simile is offered. There are, however, notable differences in the presentation of the two scenes. Claudian gives the impression that no detail must be omitted; the divine attributes of Athena and Diana, goddesses we have encountered before, are again enumerated:

> haec tristibus aspera bellis
> haec metuenda feris.
> (*DRP* 2.20f.)

Athena cruel in grim wars, Diana feared by beasts.

A sort of comprehensiveness is the goal. The reader must pause and regard each of the divine members of the party, and we might be distracted from even our slow introduction by the detail of Delos (and its story) woven on Diana's dress:

motoque in stamine Delos
errat et aurato trahitur circumflua ponto.
(*DRP* 2.34f.)

On her flowing dress Delos wanders, and moves along surrounded
by a golden sea.

But this is merely a brief encounter with pictured garments, since next
our attention is turned to Proserpina and the dress she wears. The poet
adopts the typical classical view that the more lifelike the figures, the
more skilful the artist:

nulli sic consona telae
fila nec in tantum veri duxere figuras.
(*DRP* 2.42f.)

Never such harmony of thread in cloth; nor forms so fashioned
like to life.

Of greater interest is the subject matter: Sun and Moon, offspring of
Hyperion, as babies nursed by Tethys (wife of Ocean), who quiets their
infant sobbing and is flooded with light from their infant rays: as the
Sun wails, a mild flame spills from his mouth;[38] the Moon sucks the
breast of Tethys. This is a totally captivating version of this mythological
pair, and Claudian has written it with restrained precision and point. It
does nevertheless distract attention from the broader narrative.

Next we hear in detail of the Naiads in the company of Proserpina,
again a concentration of water deities,[39] but at least we are introduced
to Cyane, who plays an important part in Ovid's two narratives and who
is specially picked out by Claudian too in the moments of frenzied
inquiry immediately after the rape. The Nereids are compared to bands
of Amazons whose activities are described, and also to Maenads along
the Hermus, and of course the beneficence of the river-god in gold and
water is added.

Whilst the company is thus assembling, Aetna, who has plenty of time
to spy them, does so and encourages Zephyrus, who is thereabouts
anyway but clearly not yet active in promoting a top-class spring day. He
needs encouragement. And so Aetna details all the natural wonders she
would like to occur.

Dixerat: she finished speaking, as of course any epic speaker does.
Zephyrus sets to work, fertilizing the ground with nectar which drips
from his wings,[40] leading the poet to exclaim in wonderment:

Parthica quae tantis variantur cingula gemmis
regales vinctura sinus? quae vellera tantum
ditibus Assyrii spumis fucantur aeni?
(*DRP* 2.94ff.)

250

What Parthian belt fit to bind a regal breast is decked so variously with gems? What fleeces dipped in the rich foam of Punic cauldrons are so deeply dyed?

This is strange, because there is a tradition that 'ordinary' nature is far superior to man-made luxuries, even those that depend on natural objects (gems and dyes).[41] The comparisons continue with colours: peacock and rainbow. None of these can match the Zephyr-induced beauty of this winding vale.

There is more: the plain, the hills, the copious water and the trees. Here we are told that the pine is for ships and the cornel for spears, that the oak is special to Jove, the cypress stands over graves, the holm-oak is full of hives and the laurel (of Apollo) is prescient. Claudian gives every sign of being at the mercy of every poetic practice from every genre that preceded him.

Contrast with this Virgil's description of the gathering for the hunt: whilst we seize in the mind's eye the extent of the gathering hunters and assistants with nets and dogs, and the description of the garments of Dido and Aeneas, where quite lengthy similes compare the leaders with Apollo and Diana and their noisy bands of followers, we are not distracted or suborned by detail that seems extraneous. All relates to the thronging clamour of the scene and its atmosphere. The air of excitement is felt throughout, and the visual impact is a part only of the poet's total apprehension of the scene. Even Dido's delay, her (bashful) moments of lingering, add to the tingle of expectancy in the air: from the first moment the whole troupe is keen to be off.

This atmosphere cannot be found in Claudian. He sweeps his vision all too slowly and unselectively around the assembling group, stops at each section and permits leisurely consideration at every stop. There is no urgency, but an all-embracing lushness. The eagerness of Pluto and his team champing at the gates of Hades, impatient for the signal, is totally forgotten. With Claudian the selection of material does not enhance the surge of the narrative. In this opening we are at a standstill.[42]

Also effectively at a standstill, when we reach it, is the chariot scene; though calculation warns that those horses are getting the hell out of there. Pluto carries off Proserpina. Her hair streams behind her (2.247ff.), her hands beating her arms and also (I presume) thrust out to the heavens imploring her father: a picture quite like that on the façade of the recently discovered tomb at Vergina which has a dramatic painting of Proserpina, arms flung high and wide in terror and Pluto intent on his violent task.[43] The action is dramatic but frozen, caught at the story's most violent moment, which is a characteristic of visual representations because of the action and because it is pivotal to the whole story.

Claudian, as we might expect, looks into the incident and imagines what words might have been uttered in that chariot: Proserpina, perplexed, cries out in pain and anger. Ovid reports that she called out to her mother and her companions (but more often to her mother, *Met.* 5.396f.); or gives us her simple words ('io, carissime mater/auferor', 'o, dearest mother, I am carried off', *Fast.* 4.447f.). In the Homeric Hymn she calls to her father (20f.), but he is busy receiving sacrifices and does not hear. Finally her mother hears the shouts ringing in the mountains (38f.). Claudian's Proserpina delivers a speech; to which Pluto makes a reasoned and apparently persuasive reply.

Proserpina's words to the skies are nicely placed because she immediately and directly addresses her father, Jupiter, and he lives up there. Her questions are purposeful, energized, not merely plaintive (as happens with questions at other times). Calling on her father betokens a keen perception on her part, for he, as we have seen, engineered the whole thing. Perhaps too Proserpina saw the thunderbolt and heard, as she was whipped away, the words of Jupiter to Athena and Diana as they tried to rescue her. However, in her final call, to her mother, she cannot avoid describing the eunuch Galli:

> seu tu sanguineis ululantia Dindyma Gallis
> incolis et strictos Curetum respicis enses.
> (*DRP* 2.269f.)

Or if you dwell on Dindyma that wails with bloodied Galli and gaze on the Curetes' unsheathed swords.

And her last words, adjective-rich –

> comprime ferales torvi praedonis habenas
> (*DRP* 2.272)

Restrain the savage robber's deadly reins

– slacken the tension of the original strong demand: 'compesce furentem', ('stop his frenzied lust', *DRP* 2.271). Just as the chariot-reins are funereal ('ferales . . . habenas'), so Pluto's cloak is dingy (*ferrugineo*). Claudian loses no opportunity to point to underworld gloom. The effect of the dingy cloak tenderly wiping dry the maiden's tears sharpens again the lavish pictorial pathos of the contrasts.

Pluto himself has quite another vision of his realm. There is a purer light, an Elysian sun, soft meadows and (Proserpina's favourite pastime is assured) flowers that bloom everlastingly, and so on. Proserpina will in addition be queen and receive the obeisance of all. Pluto has had his right of reply, and the next stage is prepared because there has to be a wedding to legitimize matters, and this cannot occur with a hollering bride. Within the tableau the action, fierce though it must have been, is on hold.

Then comes the wedding. In Claudian's world of this myth there is a necessary sequence of events. Prosperina cannot be picking flowers, then carried away, and then be queen of the underworld (as spotted by the fleeing Arethusa) without there being a wedding. Normally the wedding is part of the ellipse of the mythological narrative. So what did the wedding mean to the denizens of the gloomy shades? Exactly the same as a wedding on earth, which enthralls the guests. But first, the horses. It cannot just be accepted that they have done their job and that's that:

> occurrunt properi lecta de plebe ministri:
> pars altos revocant currus frenisque solutis
> vertunt emeritos ad pascua nota iugales.
> > (*DRP* 2.317ff.)

From the chosen youth attendants rush in haste: some withdraw the lofty chariot, and from the loosened curbs they turn the wearied horses to pastures that they know.

Our interest is caught by visualizing how delightful for all the present occasion must have been (even Pluto smiled). Of course *all* must be happy; therefore no new arrivals, for they may not be overjoyed; therefore 'death walked not on earth':

> > mors nulla vagatur
> in terris.
> > (*DRP* 2.355f.)

No death wanders abroad on earth.

And that means, further, no queues at the Styx. Therefore:

> impexamque senex velavit harundine frontem
> portitor et vacuos egit cum carmine remos.
> > (*DRP* 2.359f.)

The aged ferryman has wreathed his uncombed brow with reeds and singing plies his fruitless oars.

Amazingly the epithalamium is short (*DRP* 2.367–72), though displaying a possible lack of tact about Ceres' grandchildren in the last line.

3

On catching sight of the old nurse Electra (a nice intimate touch, this),[44] Ceres is led to ask a great many questions ending with inquiries about her servants, especially Cyane and the Sirens:

quo mille ministrae?
quo Cyane? volucres quae vis Sirenas abegit?
(*DRP* 3.189f.)

Where have the thousand servants gone? Where has Cyane? What power has driven off the winged Sirens?

Familiarity with Ovid's versions of the Ceres/Proserpina story, I suppose, makes us relish the account of the end of Cyane, because for some reason she is important in the household and certainly in the story.[45] In Ovid she boldly attempts to block the careering advance of Pluto's horses and later (Ov., *Met.* 5.469f.) Proserpina's bra is found floating on her waters to provide the clue to the mystery, and symbolize the loss of her maidenhood.[46]

Claudian's version is immediately enthralling in this context. The story (the aetiology) demands, of course, that Ceres is left ignorant for some time so that she can mourn, punish the world with winter, and provide agricultural benefits after the (partial) recovery of her daughter.[47] Therefore Cyane breathes her last before she can reveal all. She changes into water, which suits the metamorphic interest of Ovid, and it is entirely that mode of Ovidian epic and story-telling that captures our interest here. Claudian is giving us a fresh and lively confrontation of nurse and mother (though we do not forget this is epic). If Claudian is competing with Ovid he performs well, exhibiting a remarkable restraint. Cyane is spotted in the fields, already half dead, about her are blackened flowers (the object of the outing). The questions put to her are vigorous and succinct, instinct with pressing uncertainty of the moment:

quis vultus equorum?
quis regat?

(*DRP* 3.249f.)

What did the horses look like? Who their driver?

Cyane cannot answer but melts away totally into water. Claudian details only her hair, her feet and her arms; and then in a touch of delicate realism the newly created water washes the inquirers' feet: they are of course standing right at the spot.

When, however, at the end of the nurse's speech we get a detail of the Sirens' whereabouts, it sounds so much like keeping the accounts straight (a book-keeping account) that it seems superfluous.

Immediately then as she shouts against Olympus in search of her daughter she is likened, in epic simile, to the Hyrcanian tigress roaring on the loss of her cub to a horse-riding hunter, but checked by her own reflection in the mirror held out to her. This little picture really does constitute a distraction, and not only because the hunter appears to escape safely with his victim.

Actually the vignette is fascinating in being a version in writing of an identical scene in mosaic, roughly contemporary, at Piazza Armerina, in Sicily.[48] This little detail, coupled with the reference to impregnation by the wind, points clearly to the writer's wish to break the bounds of the tighter requirements of the task. When we read next –

> haud aliter toto genetrix bacchatur Olympo
> (*DRP* 3.269)

> Not otherwise the mother rages over all Olympus

– we realize we are no better off.[49] Ceres launches into another set of short questions (*DRP* 3.272ff.). In the Homeric *Hymn to Demeter*, Demeter/Ceres closes up; she avoids Olympus and the gods and wanders unknown among men; she sits without speaking because of her sorrow. In *Metamorphoses* 5.438ff., she just goes off without speaking. Claudian does, however, have Ceres conclude on a strong note, where the tone is fierce and the ferocity is impressive:

> insultate mihi, caelo regnate superbi,
> ducite praeclarum Cereris de stirpe triumphum.
> (*DRP* 3.328f.)

> Trample on me. Reign arrogant in heaven. Celebrate a glorious triumph over Ceres' daughter.

4

This review of an important sample of episodes from the *De Raptu Proserpinae* effectively demonstrates that Claudian has his eye fixed determinedly on producing an epic flavour. The episodes find their parallel or rather their origin in the famous epics before him, so Claudian overtly stands proud in the tradition and draws attention to that fact. His command of language in epic style is impressive too. He sustains his rhythms and his diction, though it must be said that his range is not broad, since he seems unwilling to attempt racy, pared-down narrative (though initially his narrative is robust and swift-moving) and his episodes, after the impressive start, tend to appear very much as discrete episodes. A count of line-length of episodes in Book 1 reveals that, whilst there is no strict symmetry, the various sections start to come out at much the same length. One occasionally notices a little fireworks in metrical effects, for example; but Claudian is content normally to shape his rhythm with a one-word enjambment, an effect that Virgil manipulated with such flexibility.

Claudian likes full-blown baroque description, so his words are colourful and extreme. Virgil, as we have already noted, utilized baroque language and description; but he essayed a greater range of styles, and his flexibility of language and rhythm seems endless. Claudian stays with the baroque, largely because in his competition with the authors of the epic canon, immersed in and following the aesthetic dictates of the time, he seeks out *amplificatio*.[50] This takes control.

Claudian's sense of the requisite scope of epic is just, if, for example, we accept Hind's distinction in narrative technique between Ovid's two versions of this myth.[51] It is the larger view of the task of epic that matters. Here the larger view is proclaimed to be how corn was given to man; not just a quick aetiological poem, but a deliberative essay in which the deep significance is presented and explored.

This theme does not emerge strongly in the unfinished poem, but even so there appear to be conflicting elements: namely that mankind already has the gift of corn, of agriculture, and it is Ceres' sorrow that causes it to be lost. Further Ceres promises Sicily that she will endow its land with a fruitfulness that needs no husbandry. It was, according to Jupiter, exactly this golden-age plenty that destroyed the fibre of mankind, and required him to set man to work to give him strength of purpose and true dignity. The hard primitive life was imposed as remedy for slackness caused by just such a condition as Ceres promises.

This conflict arises from trying to place a chronology on events when in mythic thought Ceres is always quintessentially the goddess of corn and, in this way of thinking, no time exists when she was not. This conflict can be detected also in the *Hymn to Demeter*, as Richardson explains.[52]

Still Claudian has expressed his lofty aims, and he strove to adhere to them according to his own lights.

5

Notwithstanding Claudian's aims, the versions of Ovid exercised pervasive influence, and the poem becomes a thick narrative giving weight to every imaginable aspect of the story.

The story touches an unusually poignant note when Ceres discovers her house empty and eventually encounters the old nurse Electra, from whom she, and we the readers, finally learn of the events immediately leading to the momentous rape of the girl. Amongst the numerous descriptions of episodes, where the poet had clearly consulted his imaginative reconstruction of events, this section (*DRP* 3.146–259) is perhaps the most enthralling, simply because there is something more reflective, less tensely animated, than the baroque extravagance of much of the rest of the poem. Elsewhere the action, often hurried and violent, is stilled into a tableau; here at no point does Ceres rant and rave as one might have expected, given the tenor of her appearances previous to this. True, she rends her garments and tears her hair; but her actions are slow with shock as she wanders the rooms, empty now, and observes Proserpina's unfinished weaving.

There is, of course, a considerable inconsistency to note. Hades had been attacking like an enemy, as we saw, but there is no point in the story where he attacked the house. The scene of a certain destruction, then, is not motivated by the incidents of the rape, though we must suppose that no servants would wish to feel the wrath of Ceres if she suspected delinquency, so they clearly made their prompt escape.

Ceres is stunned. Without wild complaint she kisses the loom and clasps to her bosom her daughter's spindles and the wool she was weaving. This impressive picture of her devastation, which is itself held, slow and deliberative, is heightened by the simile which follows in which a herdsman, returning from a time away, wanders through the pastures emptied by savage beasts and plaintively calls in vain to his vanished animals.

On catching sight of Electra, Ceres turns over again the gigantomachy theme in her rapid questions: Typhon, Alcyoneus, Enceladus and Briareus are named and described; the question cannot be put simply. At the end of all this Electra recounts what transpired to bring Prosperpina and company to the flower-filled meadows. Since Claudian envisaged the enticing of Proserpina by means of the guile of Venus, the reader has surely been wanting to discover exactly how events worked out, so on the whole this incident satisfies and offers a clue to the essential quality of this poem.

Recent important studies of late antique art and poetry have charted the growth of a new aesthetic, product of an artistic vision which sees with different eyes, and of a new style. A process over the third to fifth centuries CE (though some would see the roots implanted in the second century) culminates in a style that later delivers western medieval art and the Byzantine art of the East. The artistic ideals of the classical world are abandoned. And yet throughout this process, in the visual arts classical values are not dormant. Regularly they supply the formative power behind impressive works, for example the Junius Bassus sarcophagus of the mid-fourth century, and during these centuries one has to note 'the dialogue between the classicizing and the late antique style'.[53] Occasionally classical values reappear in full bloom, as in the diptych of the Nicomachi and the Symmachi, where a classical style harmoniously incorporates a statement about pagan religious tenets, themselves altered in the new age. This work has been called 'academically dry and pathetically nostalgic';[54] but George Hanfmann has proposed a different vision: 'it proclaims that the old religion is decent, dignified, and beautiful'.[55] Amongst the multiplicity of styles of these centuries of the late Roman empire, classicism was never completely eclipsed; for the classical tradition was not 'a distant ideal that could be "revived" or imitated at will: it was simply the only tradition that was known to work'.[56] The continuing attraction of the classical tradition can undoubtedly be seen in the collection of sculpture in an Athens house first built in the mid-fourth century CE.[57]

In this climate, Claudian's *De Raptu Proserpinae* is very much a child of its time rather than an oddity. It must be viewed as one amongst many classicizing artefacts.[58] Since, however, it draws on its classical forebears, a reader's careful consideration must weigh its relations with its (mighty) antecedents as well as the controlling aesthetics of the day.

The story of Demeter/Ceres and Persephone/Proserpina is elemental in a deeply mythopoeic way and is rich in incident. Claudian has opted for the grand and portentous as he raises the story to epic status, but the incidents have previously been cast in story form (Ovid), and to minds influenced by Ovid's narrative of the myth, and the story-telling of Apuleius and Petronius, the unfolding of the plot grips most. We might finally have to realize that, though we believe that Claudian must be credited with a mastery of epic style, we should nevertheless admit preference for the intimate details of the mythic story.

NOTES

1 On the hierarchy of genres, see recently Lyne 1989: 14 and n. 51.
2 First builder of ships: see McKay 1972: 53f.; Boyle in Boyle and Sullivan 1991: 271f.
3 On Virgil's realization of how his epic should be conceived, see Otis 1964: 38ff.
4 See, for example, Rutherford 1985: 138; 141ff.; Segal 1971b.
5 More than by simply inventing little incidents as the girdle floating on the lake: Ov., *Met.* 5.462; Proserpina's footprints erased by pigs: Ov., *Fast.* 4.455ff.
6 Richardson 1974: 147.
7 Pluto's difficulty in finding a way out is perhaps equivalent to the epic theme of 'struggle and journey'. See Hardie 1986: 135. Hardie also describes the stylistic consequences: 'to depict struggle, a manner is appropriate which includes pathos, hyperbole, savage realism, in short a style which tends to the baroque'. This is worth noting when considering Claudian's style in *DRP.*
8 Hinds 1987: 110.
9 For example the full psychological elaboration of Atalanta in Ov., *Met.* 10.560–680. See also Fordyce 1961, on poem 2b.
10 Clay 1989: 249 points out instances of the epic wrath of Demeter, including the Homeric Hymn.
11 Hinds 1987: 53 for pre-Ovidian accounts of a Sicilian location. See also Richardson 1974: 76f.; 148ff.

12 Ovid's geography of Sicily: Ov., *Met.* 5.346ff.; Ov., *Fast.* 4.420ff.

13 Hall 1969: 205 on 1.194.

14 Note that in Ov., *Met.* 5.420 Pluto is angry because Cyane attempts to block his path.

15 Hall 1969: 221 on *elusos* in l.165.

16 Richardson 1974: 147.

17 For an analysis of the description of this grove, see Roberts 1989: 26ff.

18 See Hardie 1986 and 1983.

19 For Virgil's poetic diction, see Lyne 1989: 1–19, and the further references he adduces.

20 For the combination of two separate stories concerning famine and the gift of corn, see Richardson 1974: 259f.

21 *Hymn to Demeter* 310ff.

22 See Roberts 1989: 55 for an evaluation of the episodic nature of late antique poetry: 'magnifying the constituent parts at the expense of the whole'.

23 On the council, see Gruzelier 1988: 61ff.

24 For embroidered fabrics, Gruzelier 1990: 307.

25 Kessels 1978: 53f. See also Grillone 1967.

26 Kessels 1978: 55.

27 Roberts 1989: 39ff. discusses literary training.

28 Hall 1969: 205. A non-epic passage is the inquiry into the causes of volcanoes (1.171ff.), considered an interpolation by some, but accepted as genuine by Hall 1969: 205.

29 The house too is given a comprehensive description (*DRP* 1.237ff.); Gruzelier 1990: 311, one is left 'less with a picture in mind than an impression'.

30 Richardson 1974: 147, on line 11.

31 Gruzelier 1990: 307.

32 Cf. Silenus in *E.* 6.24ff. or Orpheus in *DRP*, pref. 2.

33 Galand 1987: 87f.

34 James 1978.

35 Ov., *Met.* 5.402f. implies their names: 'raptor egit currus et nomine quemque vocando / exhortatur equos.'

36 On the supposed awkwardness, which I reject, see Hall 1969: 210.

37 Cf. *Il.* 4.141f.; *A.* 12.67.

38 In the Homeric *Hymn to Demeter* 74ff., Helios gives Ceres the information about Proserpina; see Richardson 1974: 156f. on lines 26ff.

39 See Richardson 1974: 149 on the presence of Oceanids. An Orphic version has the rape occurring 'in the regions about Oceanus'.

40 See Hall 1969: 217 on *maritare*.

41 Curran 1975.

42 Virgil's hunt also ended with an erotic incident. The setting for the rape rests on an established motif in which an amorous encounter opens with a girl picking flowers in a meadow: see Bühler 1960: 77–82; 109–15; Bremer 1975.

43 See Kämpff-Dimitriadou 1979: 35; Pollitt 1986: 193 fig. 204; Trendall 1981.

44 Electra is one of Proserpina's companions in the Homeric Hymn 418.

45 Cyane is the spring at Syracuse into which Persephone/Proserpina vanishes with Hades, cf. Richardson 1974: 181.

46 See, for example, Fordyce 1961, on *zona* in Catullus 2b.

47 Cf. *Hymn to Demeter* 302ff.

48 Gentili 1959: pl. 33.

49 Demeter is likened to a Maenad also in the Homeric Hymn 385f.
50 Galand 1987.
51 See, however, Anderson in chapter VI above, pp. 110–12.
52 Richardson 1974: 259f.
53 Roberts 1989: 97.
54 Ibid., 68 n. 7.
55 Hanfmann 1980: 89.
56 Brown 1980: 23.
57 Camp 1989.
58 The criticism of Cameron 1974: 157 must therefore be severely tempered.

XIII

AFTER ROME: MEDIEVAL EPIC

John O. Ward

In the one thousand years that separate Claudian's poetry from the *Africa* of Petrarch,[1] the epic enjoyed what can only be described, given its ancient pedigree and the considerable length of a typical poem, as an extraordinary vogue. Whether we cite the Viking sagas, or the French epic articulation of 'two great themes, feudal relations (between the king and his vassals) and the theme of defence and extension of Christianity against the Saracens' (Keller 1987: x, citing Marguerite Rossi), or the apotheosis of tragic destruction in the Germanic *Nibelungenlied*, or the frontier adventures of the Cid, or the Latin poetry dealt with in the present chapter, we can only conclude that the epic form, surprising as it may seem, continued to appeal to medieval writers and their audiences.

Of all these manifestations of the epic form, however, perhaps the most difficult for us to comprehend today is the medieval Latin epic. Enjoying a considerable revival from the ninth century onwards, and a peaking of interest, perhaps, in the so-called and much-discussed 'Renaissance of the Twelfth Century' (Ward 1990), the Latin epic nevertheless strikes modern readers as an odd fish in the sea of medieval culture. Tied to an influential pattern forged by Virgil and his successors, and located in a world that progressively lacked many of the cultural features that gave late Roman republican and early imperial epic its relevance and resonance, the medieval Latin epic has seemed to some but a pale, atavistic and anachronistic reflection of its Roman forebear. It is, nevertheless, important to resist such first impressions. Latin reading audiences in the Middle Ages were small by Roman standards, but they frequently contained society's intellectual leaders and were spread across a geographical area in some ways as extensive as in Roman times. These audiences had too many practical concerns to sustain the fireside antiquarianism of which they are often accused. Indeed, it is important to ask whether the medieval Latin epic *was* the tired product of antiquarian schools in the after-glow of Graeco-Roman culture, or whether it was linked to certain vital threads in the neo-

Latin culture of the central Middle Ages in western Europe, and catered to a cultivated audience of persons closely involved with the management of current social and political problems. I hope to confirm in what follows the impression that 'epic' remained a vital and frequently practised form of expression for the centuries that followed the fall of the Roman empire, a form of expression suited to the exploration of the largest and most perplexing of contemporary problems. My major illustration will be the frequently discussed late Carolingian poem known as the *Waltharius,* and the links that I believe exist between the composition of this poem and the problems late Carolingian bishops were encountering in connection with the new marital legislation and attitudes of the Carolingian church. In brief, I propose that the author of this poem was consciously reshaping older Germanic material to suit new clerical tastes and attitudes. His purpose was partly poetic, to express older Germanic heroic themes in Virgilian hexameters, that is, to reduce Germanic legend to a pleasurable and entertaining form suited to the new Latin reading classes of the Carolingian empire, and partly utilitarian, to provide the leading clergy of the day with a form of this legendary material that would suitably underline a view of the relationship between aristocratic men and women that the upper clergy wished to impart – for quite practical reasons – to their lay contemporaries.

OVERVIEW

Ironically, perhaps, in view of the oral origins of the genre, most of the epics with which the historian has to deal have come to his/her attention because they were at some past time written down. Recording, as Bowra long ago noted, in almost every case deforms the original, unless that original has become so polished and refined by ages of reciting as to sustain recording without much loss or deformity (Bowra 1952: 42). The epics with which this chapter is to deal are, happily, exempt from this problem and its consequences. Less useful as an index to popular or folk culture/mentality than the kinds of epics which Bowra treats, the epics that fall within the purview of the present study are yet a closer indication of the thinking and literary practice of the emerging literate elite whose influence was to become so marked in western European civilization from at least the time of the Carolingians onwards. Having been composed as written documents in the first place – though oral recitations were probably intended in many cases as a mode of audience consumption (cf. Auerbach 1965: 204) – the epics with which this chapter deals set up and conform to their own compositional patterns. Deriving much, or little, as the case may be, from whatever epic pattern happened to influence their authors, they are yet not to be evaluated, necessarily, either in function, content or style, in strict accordance with that antecedent epic pattern: behind their composition lies, in most cases, some link with the literary or political world in which their authors lived and wrote; this link is the subject of my inquiry, and central to a proper understanding of it is the fact of controversy.

Controversy and conflict have, in fact, frequently surrounded the history of epic writing, whether between Christian and pagan ethical norms, between imitation and innovation, between the goals and standards of *moderni* and *antiqui* or between rivals working in a common field. Despite the feelings of some modern critics, epic seems never to have flourished as a purely school exercise, unrelated to larger contemporary issues and controversies, safely locked away in institutions and practices that could stand still in time, theme, style or content. The influence of Virgil's *Aeneid* on the medieval Latin epic and the role of the schools in keeping this influence current cannot, of course, be downplayed, and the present chapter will draw attention to several examples of 'Virgilian' influence upon medieval epic writing. Nevertheless, new Latin composition in epic fulfilled such a variety of forms that the Virgilian model was at best a sub-text rather than a strict model for *imitatio*. This is evident in the teaching of the medieval schools which did not, despite some misconceptions, lock writers into any kind of imitative straitjacket. It is certainly true that commentators on the *Aeneid* and the pseudo-Ciceronian *Ad Herennium* repeat the equation between *seria/magna/altiloqua vocabula* ('serious, important, lofty words') and epics such as the *Aeneid*, but, equally, they admit that mixing of the *genera dicendi* ('levels of style') is possible and desirable, that is, lofty words can be found in comedy and the bucolic genre, humble words in tragedy. The aim of the technical manuals in the art of poetry (*artes poetriae*) that came into existence from the late twelfth century onwards was *not*, in fact, to inculcate any rigid equation between styles and subject matter, even if some of their remarks may have helped to reinforce such an equation in their schools. The treatise writers are not centrally concerned with consistency of style across large-scale works such as epics; they do not treat 'the organisation of the poem as a whole, the system of relations, correspondences, antitheses, and balancing of various elements which serves to illuminate or intensify the meaning and effect both of the individual elements themselves and of the total poetic framework of which they each form a part' (Fenik 1959: 1) . 'What they teach is more suitable for short pieces, declamatory in nature and ornamental. Such pieces, the *praeexercitamina* or *progymnasmata,* are typical classroom exercises for which there are numerous examples.'

It seems clear in fact that neither the *artes poetriae* nor the theory of

the *tria genera dicendi* had much influence on the selection and treatment of epic topics. Medieval ideas of epic were fed by numerous
sources and reflect more the environment and purpose which affected
textual production in general during the Middle Ages than the impact
of any particular technical training; the latter affected the ways by
which the authors of epics chose to secure certain word or image effects
at close range, in accordance with the privileged Graeco-Roman discourse model. In his *Alexandreis*, for example, Walter of Chatillon chose
an ancient theme rather than one of his own creation or one that
involved a great deal of adaptation or experimentation. Such a choice
was largely his own, and if he needed guidance in making it he would
have turned to Horace's *Ars Poetica* rather than to the medieval manuals
written by his contemporaries. Between the prose version of Quintus
Curtius and the general resource provided by Virgil's treatment of
Aeneas' adventures, Walter inserted his own work, which provided him
with an opportunity of indulging his skill in the kind of speeches and
descriptions that Matthew of Vendôme and those like him taught.
Nevertheless, and here again he was operating somewhat beyond the
range of the manuals, he chose to stress certain aspects of what he
thought arose out of a consideration of the Alexander story: virtue,
kingship, good government, royal chastity in the face of temptation; at
the end he chose a combination of pagan apotheosis, Christian
expostulation at the pettiness of mere human endeavour and craven
address to his patron. In this latter emphasis he differed considerably
from his major source: Quintus Curtius allows his account to linger on
after Alexander's death, and the hero's last words deal not with plans to
extend his empire to the heavens but with practical problems of
rulership and ethnic integration on earth.

It would be mistake, therefore, to confuse the part with the whole
and to deduce from the way medieval writers handled the phrase, the
metaphor or the conceit their handling of the whole. How particular
the latter can be to their own cultural environment is perhaps best
indicated in a more extensive analysis, and here we must proceed from
the general to the particular, for there would be little point here in
attempting any exhaustive treatment of the full range of medieval Latin
epic. Suffice it to say that the latter covers the full range of elements
often pointed to in the classical and late antique epic, the vatic
('prophetic', 'messianic'), satiric (critical of the *mores* of the time),
celebratory (affirming 'the serious, ecclesiastical, feudal and political
cult forms and ceremonials') and the carnivalistic (overturning, upset-
ting, undermining the same).[2] If such texts as the epyllion-length
elegiac *Mathematicus* of Bernard Silvestris, with its Virgilian 'sub-text',
to some extent undermine the certainties of the day, and other
comparable-length elegiac 'mini-epics' stress a carnivalistic overturning

of the formal and the authorized (Embrico and Walter of Compiègne), others stress the celebratory element. This latter aspect is uppermost in such works as Avitus (bishop) of Vienne's biblical epic *De Spiritalis Historiae Gestis* (c. 470 CE), as, indeed, in the longer historical and epic poems that crown the Carolingian Renaissance and usher in the Ottonian period. The latter are continued by a spate of eleventh- and twelfth-century Latin epic philosophical, biblical, cosmic, didactic and historical poems.[3] The celebratory element is, perhaps, uppermost in these medieval Latin epics, though vatic/satiric elements are not absent from such texts as the *Anticlaudianus*, and an entire sub-genre developed to satisfy and express the satiric urge.[4] Carnivalistic elements are largely excluded, since most writing emanated from and celebrated the first of Bakhtin's two worlds: 'the serious official, ecclesiastical, feudal and political cult forms and ceremonials' (Bakhtin 1984: 5).

A number of points should be made about this spate of medieval epic. In the first place, it is certainly not true that the allegorical imperative so often encountered by modern observers of medieval literary theory dissuaded medieval writers from the composition of circumstantial epic, or reflected a mentality that was adverse to such epic composition. Rather, the allegorical impulse extended and deepened the medieval interest in epic: it led to adventurous new attempts to render existing epics meaningful and it led, in its own right, to the composition of wholly new types of epic, for example the biblical epic of Avitus of Vienne already referred to, or of Sedulius,[5] or the cosmographical epic of the twelfth century. In fact, to dismiss late antique and medieval Latin epic in the way that several recent writers suggest[6] is to render null the work of numerous writers, from Claudian (c. 400 CE) to Alan of Lille, whose link with Claudian is more than accidental: his celebrated epic *Anticlaudianus De Anterufino* parodies the *In Rufinum* of Claudian. Just as the latter is a poem ascribing to its subject all the vices, so Alan's poem describes how the virtues adorn nature's perfect man. Indeed, 'the twelfth century . . . offered an environment more hospitable to the philosopher poet than that environment would be again during the Middle Ages' (Lynch 1988: 23).

There is, in fact, no particular reason why the 'epic way of seeing', which fed the imaginations of the poets of the Renaissance, should not also have fed the imaginations of the medieval poets. The epic way of seeing involved a perception of the larger design, an ability 'to experience movement [not] as aimless wandering through an uncharted labyrinth [but] to understand that the journey has been directed all along', a viewing of the past 'as if it were a future, a future to which [the poet historical] and his heroes are granted access only in extraordinary moments of prophetic vision during which the scroll of fate is unrolled and the divine plan is for an instant revealed' (Fichter 1982: 9,7,1). For the lesson of the ancient epic was that history alone could not provide the key to the larger design: it revealed an aimless and barbaric pattern redeemed only by personal sacrifice and faith in a secular vision of an apocalyptic new order beyond the ravages of time and circumstance. The medieval allegorical imperative, in fact, was peculiarly adapted to the epic vision, in so far as the latter was a matter of seeing the grand design behind the obscuring cloud of particularity and circumstance.

Even to run through the subject matter of the immense mass of epic and epic-like Latin verse produced in the Middle Ages would require volumes (for example, those of Raby!) and to explain it as a literary phenomenon would require a monograph. To set it aside as 'the product of the schools' is to mistake fact for explanation. Certain aspects of the period in question need to be kept in mind: until the middle of the twelfth century, the only language of literacy was Latin. As in Roman antiquity, all bureaucratic and governmental preferment depended upon, indeed presupposed, a measure of fluency in written and, to a lesser extent, spoken Latin (Guibert of Nogent, *Memoirs* 3.4). As is clear from the cases of Claudian, Prudentius and Silius Italicus, precocious Latin literacy was a favoured mode of social ascent for ambitious provincials and the less well born or connected in society. So it was in the Middle Ages (Ward 1979). Despite the complaints of the twelfth-century goliardic poets, command of Latin literacy, rhetorical skills and a sprinkling of lore handed down only in Latin (often occultic) was a favoured road to influence at court for many: indeed, the goliardic laments concerning the futility of classical Latin literacy are as much proof of the competitive nature of this phenomenon as they are arguments against its existence.

Given these circumstances, the exercise of epic and related skills was a reflection as much of the ubiquity of demand for court panegyric as of literary fashion and an urge for cultural status. The composition of such literature reflects, too, the phenomenon of the 'over-trained courtier-bishop' discussed recently by Jaeger 1985. The thirteenth century was to reduce and streamline the kinds and standards of Latin literacy necessary for court and bureaucratic preferment, as it was to regularize and routinize that very preferment itself. The spread of vernacular literacy also worked to problematize and diffuse the circumstances that produced the remarkable efflorescence of Latin epic writing in the preceding centuries.

From these generalities, it is necessary to come down to a few examples that the reader can begin to get the feel of in some detail. To illustrate the particular concerns of the present chapter, we happen to have to hand an early and in some ways quite precocious example of a medieval innovative 'Virgilian' epic, the celebrated *Waltharius*, a Christian Latin (monastic) hexameter poem 1,456 lines long, probably written during the later ninth century, in the Rhineland/Swabia/Bavaria region of the fading Carolingian empire. This epic, together with the lesser but in some ways comparable *Gesta Ottonis* of the nun Hrotsvit, writing at Gandersheim in Saxony in the third quarter of the tenth century CE, have been much discussed in scholarly literature, but are still capable of yielding relatively unprobed insights. The rest of the present chapter will be devoted to these insights.

THE *WALTHARIUS*

The *Waltharius* deals with legendary episodes remembered from the fifth-century CE conflict between the Huns and the Burgundians. Some of these episodes survive in vernacular fragments, versions, and even a later Latin chronicle, but the *Waltharius* is the only complete, systematic presentation that we have. It is also the earliest, apart perhaps from the Anglo-Saxon *Waldere* fragments. The relationship between the *Waldere* fragments and the Latin poem have been explored by Marion Learned (Learned 1970: 180–1), who concludes that the *Waltharius* is a tenth-century adaptation of an Alamannic alliterative poem 'either contemporary with that of the *Waldere,* or slightly later'.[7] The author of the *Waltharius* alone preserves 'a strictly consistent grouping of historical events and characters' and provides 'the most consistent treatment' of 'the hero's career' (Learned 1970: 178–9). Nevertheless, he 'chose for his Latin poem the central episodes of his original (chief among which was the combat), and omitted such as did not harmonise with his conception of epic treatment'. His main purpose seems to have been skilful translation into epic form rather than literary creation' (Learned 1970: 181).

Subsequent discussion has added little that is certain to this picture, and there seems no point here in attempting further speculation. It is perhaps more useful, and, indeed necessary, given the fact that Learned's estimate (1970, originally 1892) is now practically a century old, to examine what is actually involved in this act of 'translation' of a Germanic folk/vernacular poem or series of poems into Latin epic. Can it be dismissed as simply an act of 'translation . . . rather than literary creation'? Is it *possible* to 'translate' from one such medium to another *without* some act of literary creation? Or are our standards somewhat lower than those shared by critics in 1892? It seems worth while to take these questions a little further, and the remainder of the present chapter will attempt to do so.

A summary of the story of the *Waltharius* will be useful. The narrative divisions follow Kratz 1984: xv-xvi. **1–418**: Attila, king of the Huns, sweeps through western Europe. To avoid warfare, tribute and three young hostages are given to him: Walther, son of Alpher, king of Aquitaine; Hagen, a young nobleman in the service of Gibicho, king of the Franks; and Hiltgunde, daughter of Heiric, king of the Burgundians, and betrothed to Walther since childhood. The girl and the young warriors gain favour at Attila's court, the warriors excelling in arms and winning triumphs for the Huns. On the death of Gibicho, his son Gunther succeeds to the Frankish throne and abrogates the treaty with the Huns, upon learning which Hagen escapes to join him. To prevent Walther from similar conduct Attila, at the suggestion of his queen Ospirin, offers him the pick of Hunnic noblewomen for his wife. Walther declines, but continues to lead the Huns in triumph, winning a great battle. In the feast which follows Walther, desiring to escape, gets the whole court drunk, and he and Hiltgunde leave, taking with them treasure obtained by Hiltgunde on Walther's instructions. **419–1061**: They journey to the land of the Franks, where their arrival is reported to King Gunther, who – against Hagen's advice – takes Hagen and eleven other warriors to capture what he claims to be treasure sent by his father to the Hunnic court. Walther has occupied a narrow pass in the rocks and can only be attacked in an extensive series of individual engagements. Hagen refuses to participate. Walther kills all eleven assailants, including Hagen's nephew. Only Gunther and Hagen remain. **1062–1456**: After much persuasion Hagen is induced to join Gunther in the final fight, which takes place on open ground. Everyone is wounded, Gunther the most seriously, but Walther himself loses his right hand. He is reconciled with Hagen and returns with Hiltgunde to Aquitaine, where he makes a public declaration of his betrothal vows. After his father's death he rules Aquitaine 'happily' (*feliciter*) for thirty years.

Certainly the theme of the *Waltharius* is heroic,[8] and is announced as surely as Aeneas announces his grief stricken-tale of Troy in *Aeneid* 2. For Virgil, a *queen* (Dido) bids Aeneas *renew* his dreadful grief, and to tell how the Greeks plundered the ill-fated *kingdom* of Troy. For the author of the *Waltharius*, a *king* (Attila) rules a *kingdom* and is indefatigable (*impiger*) to *renew* ancient triumphs.[9] The *Waltharius* author adopts the natural opening, Virgil uses the artificial, but the allusion to *Aeneid* 2 is not to be lost on the attentive reader: Horace in his *Ars Poetica* links *impiger* with *iracundus* ('wrathful'), *inexorabilis* ('implacable') and *acer* ('fierce') (in the case of Achilles, Horace, *AP* 121): just as the *Danai* plundered the *opes Troianas*, so Walther is to plunder the Hun treasures (*Waltharius* (henceforth cited as *W.*) 261ff.), and Attila, *impiger* at *W.* 12, becomes *efferus ira* at line 380, when Walther, *lux Pannoniae* ('beacon of Pannonia', *W.* 121ff., 376–7), the Trojan Horse for the Huns, betrays his lord (Attila) – just as Hector, *lux Dardaniae* ('beacon of Dardania', *A.* 2.280), disappoints Aeneas by announcing doom (in a dream), rather than providing a remedy against it.

The *Waltharius* author is careful to hint at a Trojan link – Hagen is described as 'veniens de germine Troiae' ('coming from Trojan stock', *W.* 28) – but does not permit the allusion to be more than a hint of dramatic irony: it is not thematically *structuring*; the heroic world and its audience are much more straightforward than the late Roman republican audience for the *Aeneid*, and the *Waltharius* author has no wish to obscure his theme. He has chosen, in the main, to highlight heroism on the battlefield: the central episode, dominating 70 per cent of the poem, is Walther's battle for defence of treasure and *sponsa* (*W.* 428–1446),[10] and the ethos of the poem is faithful to the lay aristocratic world of the early Middle Ages, and its values. An appreciation of this is essential to any understanding of the deeper motives lying behind the composition of the work.[11]

The poem assumes lordship as the fundamental basis of society ('if to be angry with one's lord is ever right . . . ', *W.* 633). Walther is keen to retain the treasure he and Hiltgunde have taken from the Huns and to increase it from the spoils of his combat with Gunther's twelve companions ('to seek a noble death by wounds is better than, / my wealth lost, to survive, a lonely wanderer', *W.* 1217–18);[12] so too does Gunther covet the treasure (*W.* 470ff., cf. 483), for treasure is the essential lubricant of lordship. Thus Hagen, in a famous passage, like a kind of Greek choric figure, expostulates against the ruling thirst for gold and riches: 'O vortex mundi, fames insatiatus habendi, gurges avaritiae, cunctorum fibra malorum . . . O saeva cupido' ('O whirlpool of the world, voracious lust of having! Abyss of avarice, the root of every evil! O dreadful one . . . ', *W.* 857ff.)[13] – the bottom line, as it were, of lordship; at one point (*W.* 618) Walther's offer of 'a hundred arm-rings made of bright red metal' (later raised to two hundred at *W.* 662!) to Gunther is recommended by Hagen, for with it 'you can reward your band of men (*tecum comitantes*)'. With this treasure – though his title to it does not emerge clearly from the poem – Walther can set up as a lord, buy retainers and found his power. In a related way, Walther must retain Hiltgunde, as well as the treasure, because Hiltgunde is (a) beautiful (and hence likely to produce children), (b) well born, (c) devoted to Walther, as a future wife should be, and, (d), perhaps the strongest argument, betrothed to him. With her he can found lineage.

Loyalties and obligations, however, pull in different directions in the poem. Hagen, for example, finds himself – like Raoul de Cambrai in a later age – torn between his loyalty to Gunther as lord, and to Walther as comrade; to this tension is added the tension between comradeship towards Walther, and hostility occasioned by Walther's slaying of his, Hagen's, nephew (the tie of kinship, 'carum nepotem', 'my darling nephew', *W.* 1112). All these tensions come to a great climax in Walther's speech to Hagen, perhaps the core of the poem. Turning away from Gunther, who had just addressed him as *hostis atrox* ('cruel foe'), Walther speaks directly to Hagen: 'ad te sermo mihi, Hagano, subsiste parumper' ('my words are meant for you now, Hagen. Stay a moment!'). With a directness perhaps peculiar to this clerical reworking, Walther asks why Hagen, whom he expected to be the first to welcome himself and Hiltgunde, should have turned hostile 'nullis nempe malis laesus' ('that now, harmed by no crimes', *W.* 1239ff.). To this speech Hagen makes what seems to us a weak rejoinder, claiming that it was Walther who first began hostilities, though he should have recognized Hagen's *arma* (*W.* 1270). This is a peculiar response as Hagen made every effort to dissuade the insane Gunther from the hostile course of action the latter proclaimed upon learning of Walther's return (*W.* 466ff., 479, 487, 530 ('male sana mente gravatus', 'burdened by an insane mind'), 619, etc.); having failed, and given the hostility inevitable in Gunther's first approach to Walther through the warrior Gamalo (*W.* 601), it was only to be expected that Walther would resist the demands of Gunther and resort to arms. It was, in fact, Gamalo who initiated combat: 'consumare etenim sermones nunc volo cunctos / aut quaesita dabis aut vitam sanguine fundes' ('for now I wish to end all talk, and you will give / the things I seek or pour your life out with your blood', *W.* 666–7). Whereupon, he positioned his shield and hurled his spear at Walther.

The dilemma for Walther is a very personal one. Should he surrender Hiltgunde and the treasure (*W.* 602) because Gunther was 'supreme king' in the West, because Gunther was the first to meet him on his return from the Huns, because Gunther's father supplied so much of the treasure in the first place? If we find such reasoning bizarre, we should remember the celebrated incident of the Vase of Soissons in Gregory of Tours (*The History of the Franks* 2.27), or the extraordinary lengths to which Attila went to secure justice – according to his own understanding of the word – in regard to 'booty'. Or was Walther to stand up for his own independent rights as a king and lineage-founder/continuer, and fight for his booty? When it actually comes to *fighting* Hagen, Walther obviously feels vassalic loyalty has gone too far: he is, no doubt, prepared to recognize that the mainspring behind the hostile Frankish reception of himself and his betrothed was Gunther's 'luckless' arrogance; he is, doubtless, prepared to accept that Hagen has done all in his power to prevent the events that have taken place, but has failed. Yet, that Hagen should actually *fight* Walther is the balancing point between ties, and that is the theme of Walther's address at *W.* 1239ff. If he had accepted Walther's offer at this point, Hagen would have undoubtedly had a breach with Gunther on his hands. However, by plunging on with the pre-ordained, at it were, course of action, Hagen involves each of the heroes in the demeaning and critical wounds they each receive from each other: 'illic Guntharii regis pes, palma iacebat / Waltharii nec non tremulus Haganonis ocellus' ('King Gunther's foot was lying there, and also Hagen's twitching eye', W. 1402–3). Only then, when the damage has been done, do the remaining combatants come to some agreement. In the end it is the pact and the tie of friendship/comradeship that prevails: 'his dictis pactum renovant iterato coactum' ('when this was said, the men renew again their pledge', W. 1443): neither lordship nor vassalage prevail as such, only a kind of forced compromise rendered inevitable by the unresolvable balance of conflicting forces and emotions. In the *Waltharius* poet's mind, perhaps, the element that might, indeed *should* have been otherwise was Gunther's 'luckless' arrogance. Yet that very element was an intrinsic part of the Germanic warrior/retinue-band/treasure-orientated survival ethos; its unfortunate aspects could only be gradually expunged from society by the process of civilization, and in that process the *Waltharius* was meant to play its part.

It should be clear by now that the poet of the *Waltharius* did not shrink from the problematizing of values that is, perhaps, peculiarly associated with the epic form. His main interest, however, or the area in which he perhaps hoped to contribute most of novelty, concerned another type of loyalty, that based on the bethrothal of a man and a woman. In this connection it should be pointed out that Hiltgunde occupies a rather special place in the poem. She is a *fida amica*, and a *sponsa*, and *cara* ; she is the only companion who does not do the dirty on Walther, and her support is crucial to his success. She is the only person in the poem to whom he can 'pandere cuncta ... cordis mysteria' ('show you all the secrets of [my] heart', W. 247). It is, after all, Hiltgunde who provides Walther with the crucial treasure, through her own good offices. She is also Walther's truest vassal: she calls him *domne, mi senior* ('O lord, O my master'); his *iussi* ('orders') are *placiti* ('pleasing'), she is at one point 'viri genibus curvata' ('stooping to his knees', W. 248), while at another 'obsequitur dictis virguncula clara iubentis' ('the lovely girl obeys his words as he commands', W. 1225).

The stage has, in fact, been carefully set by our author to focus on Hiltgunde. An initial twenty-one lines are devoted to the Hunnic negotiations with the Franks (W. 13–33), within which four lines mention Gunther (W. 15–16, 29–30) and two describe Hagen (W. 27–8). Fifty lines describe the encounter between the Huns and King Heriricus, within which six and a half mention and describe Hiltgunde: we are told that she was an only daughter, of high birth capped by beauty, heiress to her father's hall and wealth (W. 36–9). Here is a woman firmly embedded within the patriarchal, propertied feudal nexus. Hiltgunde was the 'pulcherrima gemma parentum' ('her parents' loveliest jewel', *W.* 74), not the least because she was so entirely eligible on all counts and could be expected to secure for her parents a rich connection. We are reminded of the Germanic lawcodes' ferocious protection of the patriarchal right to dispose of daughters' bodies. All of which leads to a puzzle: why would Heiric resign so precious a daughter to the Huns? The act underlines the absolute nature of patriarchal power and prerogative in Germanic society: Hiltgunde was valued property, whether to make an alliance with another house, or to ward off destruction (*W.* 59–63).

The final Hunnic negotiations are conducted with Alpher, and only sixteen lines are allocated to them, within which a solitary phrase describes Walther: 'primaevo flore nitentem' ('resplendent in the flower of youth', *W.* 79, and cf. *dilectum*, 90), a neutral phrase of undistinguished Virgilian context (*Aeneid* 7.162). Three lines (*W.* 80–2), in fact, advance our understanding of the fate of Hiltgunde: she has been betrothed by pact to Walther ('iusiurandum . . . inter se dederant' '[the kings] had sworn an oath among themselves'). Such an arrangement (*desponsatio*) was normal and binding upon the parents of the girl: 'young men, on the other hand, could escape with relative ease from unwanted engagements'.[14] Indeed, in one celebrated ninth-century case a marriage was annulled in an ecclesiastical court simply because the husband, a count, had had previous pre-marital intercourse with a relative of his wife. Naturally ninth-century churchmen were more than keen to tighten up the legal and procedural technicalities for the conduct and preservation of valid marriages: strict betrothal and due execution of the obligations it called for were essential.

The prominence given these betrothal arrangements by the *Waltharius* author is significant. Apart from the *Waltharius* itself, only the *Novalician Chronicle* and the Graz Middle High German fragment mention these arrangements.[15] The former is entirely derivative from the *Waltharius*, but the latter, perhaps, reflects 'doubtless the remains of a MHG. *Epic of Walther and Hildegunde*' (Learned 1970: 182). In the *Waltharius* the betrothal arangements match the episode in Attila's hall (Learned 10–11, 139ff.), where, in the *Waltharius*, the betrothal arrangements are broached for the first time since the exiles left their native lands. Learned 10–11 are mentioned in no other version of the Walther material, although in the thirteenth-century Old Norse and Polish versions – independently related to the source for the *Waltharius* – it seems that Walther meets Hiltgunde at a feast held by Attila and persuades her by wooing to accompany him in his escape plans. In the Old Norse *Thidhreksaga*, Hiltgunde, confronted by Walther's announcement at a sumptuous banquet and war-dance held in Attila's court that he intends to escape and that she should accompany him, requests him not to make fun of her since she is not with her kinsfolk, but confesses that she has loved him since she first saw him at the age of four and will gladly fly with him. There is no mention of any betrothal and the reference to possible mockery of her by Walther suggests there has been no betrothal: Walther's proposal to return together is seen as a proposal of concubinage (against which Hiltgunde's kinsmen would naturally protest). Walther's reply, stressing their lineage, is intended to allay Hiltgunde's fears: they are both sufficiently noble and well connected to marry in due time in the proper way; again this would be less meaningful if the couple had been already betrothed.

It seems likely that the early Germanic versions of the saga made Hiltgunde, and Walther's relationship that of a simple love story: exiles meet at a Hun banquet, mutually deplore their lot and decide to escape (elope?) together. Alone the Graz fragment – which some feel records a very old version of the original story – complicates this version of events, but interestingly. Hagen's departure from the Hunnic court is presented – in so far as the fragmentary relics can be satisfactorily made out – as an amicable and public event; there seems to have been some suggestion that Walther should leave with Hagen, abandoning Hiltgunde, so to speak. Hagen reminds Walther that this would be perfidious: (a) Hiltgunde is of such noble birth that in normal circumstances she would be 'an empress with a crown' (*mit krōne ein [k]eyserinne*); (b) she has waited so long already for Walther (implying a bethrothal); (c) she *is* in fact betrothed to Walther: Hagen was there at the ceremony, but has to remind Walther of it. Walther is satisfactorily recalled to his senses and exclaims with remorse that he will henceforth be faithful to Hiltgunde (Carroll 1952: 141, 157–8).

There are some points of interest in this version of events. Walther had forgotten about, or chosen to ignore, the betrothal. Hiltgunde seems not to want to mention it openly (as if the insult is too deep for *her* to allude to it). Hagen assumes the role of upholder of marital law and order, an interesting reversal of his role in the *Nibelungenlied* . This latter poem, too, is a tale 'of spousal troth kept beyond the grave, of mutual faith between vassal and lord passionately maintained till death' (Clark 1973: 206), yet in it Hagen plays a major and an ultimately destructive role: he sets Siegfried up in Gunther's eyes and this leads to Siegfried's covert role in Gunther's wooing of Brunhilde, which leads to Siegfried's death – on Hagen's advice – which leads to Hagen's embattled display of vassalic loyalty to Gunther (when asked by Kriemhild for the whereabouts of the Nibelung treasure), which leads to his own death – at the hands of the outraged wife of Siegfried (Kriemhild). In the *Waltharius*, Hagen plays only the shadow of this role, although it is the pivot for the plot's resolution. In the Graz fragment, Hagen's role is pivotal once again: in the *Waltharius* Hagen plays no such role.

273

A further curious point arising from the Graz fragment's version of events is this: how was the betrothal made in the presence of Hagen? Were Walther and Hagen childhood friends among the Franks or the Aquitainians? We are not told in any source. Finally, it seems that in the original form of the saga, as reflected in the Graz fragments, there must have been no mention of the betrothal earlier than the events to which Learned has assigned 10 and 11, for otherwise, why would Hagen have to vouch his own authority for it?

It is therefore possible that the betrothal element, mentioned for the first time in Attila's palace (Learned 10–11), is a (later) variant of the love-story version, effected because the latter gave offence to some audiences who may have worried because of the lack of legitimization for the alliance between the hero and the heroine. Is it too far-fetched to see in this the advance of (clerical) culture and civilization? In the older Germanic ethos it may have seemed perfectly natural for Walther to carry off Hiltgunde, take her with him, seize her or however else the act of abstracting her from Hunnic tutelage was described. Later sensibilities – whether Latinized or simply Germanic aristocratic/patriarchal – might have felt this procedure a little too disrespectful of Hiltgunde's nobility and parentage, a little too lacking in the social niceties that should surround successful marital alliances.

At any rate, the *Waltharius* author has further improved the respectability of the situation and makes the betrothal a central feature of his preliminary arrangements. His initial presentation of Hiltgunde and her context is fuller than that of either of her two male partners in exile, and Hiltgunde remains central to the poet's concerns: more attention is given to her in the early days of the exile at the Hunnic court than to the two boys, who are dealt with collectively and somewhat perfunctorily: they display strength and intelligence leading to military command, as one might have expected of heroes. But Hiltgunde, 'puella . . . virgo . . . moribus eximiis operumque industria habundans . . . provida' ('the girl . . . the maiden . . . abounding in good character and diligence . . . prudent', *W.* 94, 110–13), and autonomous: 'nam quicquid voluit de rebus, fecit et actis' ('for she did what she wished concerning things', *W.* 115: Hiltgunde is virtually a queen herself). Carefully arranging the saga events to suit his purpose, the *Waltharius* author has Hagen escape *alone* and *secretly* ('nocte fugam', *W.* 120), following Gibicho's breach of the pacts formed initially between the westerners and the Huns. Strategically this permits a dialogue between Attila and Ospirin, his queen, in which the latter advises Attila as to how he can keep Walther from doing what Hagen has done, and hence to keep up the flow of Hunnic *triumphos* (*W.* 12 and 108). It is noteworthy that a woman here provides this key advice – even to the very words to use – and that the advice turns on the role a woman can play: Walther is to be married to

274

a Hunnic noblewoman and hence tied to a Hunnic existence. The author thus keeps the betrothal and the woman-focus central to his version of the poem, and it is perhaps significant that none of these developments are extant in any other known version of the saga.

Walther's reply to Attila's execution of his wife's plan is also worth attention. The poet gives nothing away except to hint that Walther has other secret plans – presumably to escape (*W.* 143–4). His direct-speech reply is a masterpiece of clerical casuistry: marriage would impede a warrior's duty and hence it is in Attila's best interest to keep Walther a single warrior, on call all the time.

The poem moves swiftly to a first climax, weaving a tapestry found in no other extant version of the story and changing modes significantly: a passage rehearsing the characteristics of traditional heroic prowess and strewn with carnivalesque grotesqueries (*W.* 185–207) builds Walther's military reputation to a height ('vir inclitus', 'the famous man', *W.* 217) ; the poet then, aware of the different registers inherent in Virgil's refashioning of the epic code, switches into a slow-moving, delicate personal mode, which scholars have done well to note carefully (for example Westra 1980). To Westra's analysis should be added certain observations drawing out more clearly the poet's purpose, which we may define as to stress the innate, irrefragible sanctity of the betrothal vow, with its inevitable consequences, and to build a portrait of Walther as *fortis*, but also as respectful in his approach to women.

Events compel the fulfilment of the betrothal vow – without Hagen's intervention – and the fulfilment expresses innate tendencies within the characters' make-up. The context is entirely believable: the action is slowed to nothing and behavioural details are dwelt upon carefully (for example *W.* 219–20). The word *offendit* (*W.* 221) expresses much: the encounter with Hiltgunde is a chance one (Kratz translates 'found'); it upsets Walther (who may not have thought to include Hiltgunde in his plans);[16] it upsets Hiltgunde (who may have been 'offended' that Walther has apparently made no mention of their betrothal since their arrival in the territories of the Huns, and who would undoubtedly, given her relationship with Attila's queen, have been consulted over Ospirin's plan to marry Walther to a Hunnic noblewoman). All this is, at least, implied by the word *offendit* . The words 'cui post amplexus atque oscula dulcia' ('he first embraced and kissed her sweetly', *W.* 222) stress Walther's capacity for fondness towards women and, since he would doubtless not have taken such liberties with a girl unrelated to him or to whom he was not betrothed, are probably intended to imply that Walther wishes to communicate to Hiltgunde his awareness of the betrothal obligations.

The next lines –

'ocius huc potum ferto, quia fessus anhelo.'
illa mero tallum complevit mox pretiosum
porrexitque viro, qui signans accipiebat
virgineamque manum propria constrinxit

(*W.* 223–6)

'Bring drink here quickly; I am gasping with exhaustion.'
At once she filled a precious beaker with strong wine
And gave it to the man, who, as he took it, crossed
Himself, and pressed the maiden's hand with his

– move from traditional heroic male/female relations (attendant, attractive female brings refreshment to weary warrior), through a reminder of Christian duties ('signans') to a renewal of the affection exemplified earlier ('virgineamque manum propria constrinxit' (see *W.* 222)), couched in a peculiarly feudal form, hinting at loyalty and ties between the two. At this point the relationship becomes complicated: in lines evocative of the more powerful passage from *Aeneid* 4 in which Dido upbraids Aeneas for ingratitude and treachery (and the *Waltharius* author had Dido in mind, Westra 1980: 54 on *W.* 222, Kratz 1977: 129), Hiltgunde treats Walther as if he *were* Aeneas, planning to run out on her, in *Aeneid* 4 physically, in Hiltgunde's mind for another (Hunnic) woman, in the reader's mind one *or* the other. The poet underlines Hiltgunde's concern by shifting from the military *vir* to a word that implies a domestic power/sexual relationship between the two: (*h*)*erilem* (*vultum*). The word, popular in Latin comedy, means (in this case) 'the (her) master's'. As with Dido, who had Aeneas' right hand (*A.* 4.307, 314) and had begun marital procedures (*A.* 4.316), Hiltgunde felt Walther was committing an act of betrayal. The slow-motion continues – 'Walthariusque bibens vacuum vas porrigit olli' ('then Walther drained the cup and gave it back to her', *W.* 228) – and the poet suddenly plays the ace: 'ambo etenim norant de se sponsalia facta' (*W.* 229). Both *knew* of the betrothal arrangements, *but* the one had not mentioned them, and perhaps had not *wanted* to do so, while the other, because of her sex, *could* not mention them.

Walther then challenges/makes his appeal to/provokes/excites (all of which are implied by the word *provocat, W.* 230) Hiltgunde, and the phrase 'caram puellam' ('dear girl', *W.* 230) confirms earlier hints (*W.* 222) and indicates the hero's intention *now* to execute his obligations: they have both been in exile for a long time; for how long are they to ignore 'quid nostri forte parentes / inter se nostra de re facere futura' ('what our parents arranged among themselves about our future state', *W.* 232–3)? Walther's question, which softly attempts to push aside his male responsibility for the fact that the betrothal arrangements have *not* so far been mentioned, invites Hiltgunde to *share* responsibility for this fact. She does not respond as Walther expects: taking a cue, perhaps, from the extensive discussion of irony in Quintilian's *Institutio Oratoria* (9.2.40; 9.2.44ff.), the author of the *Waltharius* makes Hiltgunde believe that Walther is here feigning: what he *really* means is 'we should not any longer mention this matter of betrothal; circumstances have rendered it null'. Hiltgunde's response ('quid lingua simulas quod ab imo pectore damnas'?, 'why feign in speech what you condemn deep in your breast?', *W.* 237) is thus the direct equivalent of Virgil's 'dissimulare etiam sperasti, perfide, tantum / posse nefas tacitusque mea decedere terra' ('you, whose word is nothing, did you hope to cover up for your unspeakable behaviour and to sneak away from my land?', *A.* 4.305). Walther (Aeneas) is to marry another (leave the land) and abandon Hiltgunde (Dido) 'as if it were a disgrace now to take up such a bride' (*W.* 239, presumably since a more respectable, Hunnic, bride has been offered). The poet has in fact deliberately left it vague whether Walther refused (*W.* 167) the Hunnic bride because he planned to run away *and* take with him his betrothed, or just the former; nor are we told how much Hiltgunde knows or suspects of Walther's options and plans. However, in the event, trust is re-established as certainly as it is betrayed in the case of Dido and Aeneas: Walther, 'sapiens, heros magnanimus' ('wise . . . great-hearted hero', *W.* 240, 292), reveals that only Hiltgunde's close relationship to Ospirin placed a guard on his mouth: having tried and found good her loyalty he can reveal his intention to flee *and* the fact that he could have done so long ago 'si non Hiltgundem solam remanere dolerem' ('were I not grieved that Hildegund be left alone', *W.* 255).

There are two curious aspects to the above sequence of events and emotions. First, the line from the *Waltharius* just cited should read something like 'were we not betrothed' (though *sola* could mean 'alone, unmarried'); second, the ensuing events reveal that even though Walther could have escaped alone, he could do so in a far more stylish manner with Hiltgunde's help (*W.* 263ff.). Indeed, Hiltgunde's pledge of loyalty is absolute (*W.* 248–51, 256–9), and our final impression is that the girl has *not* wavered from *her* correct path in regard to her betrothal vows, whereas Walther, to whom the initiative in furthering the betrothal arrangements properly belonged by social convention, had let himself get carried away, and put his own fame, comfort and future slightly ahead of the strict alacrity with which he should have furthered the vows of betrothal once it became possible or desirable on other grounds to leave the Hunnic camp. Certainly at the end of the poem, Hiltgunde is the only principal actor who emerges unscathed.

The central emotional episode of the poem is therefore devoted to the re-establishment of trust between the two principals, a trust which has been ruptured by their separate experience in the Hun camp and the separate need/desire to 'get on' there. In passing up fame and good fortune among the Huns, Walther and Hiltgunde are deliberately turning the clock back and putting (a) hatred for a foreign land (*W.* 340, 354, 401, n. 19 above), (b) love of the fatherland, and (c) 'quid nostri forte parentes / inter se nostra de re fecere futura' (*W.* 232–3) before success in the new world. The poet neatly distances his couple from the ill-fated Dido and Aeneas by having Walther purposely give the bridle of the horse carrying their wealth (and future happiness) to Hiltgunde's right hand (*W.* 332): Hiltgunde had obtained all this for them both and symbolically she shall retain control of it. It is now Attila and Ospirin who are cast in the role of abandoned Dido, as opposed to the equal *comites*, Hiltgunde and Walther, both on foot, leading their ladened horse.

The Virgilian allusions in the *Waltharius* thus play an important role at the major points of the medieval poem. It is, in fact, essential to have in mind the 'meta-' or 'sub-' text of *Aeneid* 4 in order to grasp the full meaning and gist of what is going on, for example in the central episode just discussed. Betrayal is at the core of the matter, but it is never stated directly in the text. To have made explicit Walther's intention to abandon Hiltgunde would have irretrievably flawed the hero's character, reducing him henceforth to the role of a penitent. Aeneas was to survive his betrayal because it occurred in a context which was essentially a deviation from the path of his destiny: Walther's destiny, on the other hand, was to rediscover his loyalty to Hiltgunde, not to betray it. Hence the *Waltharius* poet could not reproduce or imitate the Virgilian oratory in *Aeneid* 4: he achieves his goal by the devices of parallelism (where his characters seem to play roles parallel to those of Aeneas and Dido) and inversion or reversion (where his characters seem to invert or reverse the relationship that exists between Dido and Aeneas). Thus Aeneas and Attila are both parallel but reversed in being called upon/wishing to renew griefs/triumphs: Attila, who is *impiger renovare* at the beginning of the poem (*not* grief-stricken, as in the case of Aeneas, who is being asked to 'recall' *unpleasant* memories, but joyous in 'anticipation' of *pleasant* victories, *W.* 12), has later on become *efferus ira* (i.e. grief-stricken, *W.* 380), and is described in language taken from Virgil's description of Aeneas' grief in Books 4 and 5 of the *Aeneid*. Aeneas, on the other hand, passes in the course of Book 4 from grief and anger to calm restoration of congruence between his actions and destiny: he thus *reverses* Attila's passage from joy to grief. Again, Attila and his queen are both *united* (unlike Aeneas and Dido) and abandoned (like Dido);[17] they are thus Dido-like (parallel, abandoned), in their un-Dido-likeness (their being united as a couple). The young couple too, instead of *breaking* their trysts like Dido and Aeneas (which would have put them in a parallel relationship

278

with Virgil's couple), rediscover and renew the trysts, thus proceeding along their destined path and subverting the parallelism that exists at one point (*W.* 227, 237ff.).[18]

This may sound overly complicated, and I do not intend to imply that the *Waltharius* poet plotted every element in the pattern of the intertwined relationships just suggested, or that his text was intended to read the way Virgil's does. However, it is beyond dispute that the *Waltharius* poet knew the *Aeneid* and wished to recall it at various points to his reader's mind or auditor's ear: once *Aeneid* 2 and 4 and the *Waltharius* are thus set in mind together, the coincidences and oppositions suggested above automatically multiply.[19] Unwittingly perhaps, the *Waltharius* poet has absorbed the fusion of the Callimachean and the heroic that some have thought marks the success of the *Aeneid*,[20] this 'polyphonic way of writing' (Conte 1986: 157). Consequently, the registers of resonance between the two texts are *available* and *accessible*, whether precisely intended at each point in the *Waltharius* or not. They are also enriching. They hint of the perilous path of destiny versus the abyss of deviation, of the power of 'illicit' sex versus duty, of passion versus order, cultivation of the self versus duty towards society, state and family, of the perils of contrasting paths of duty (Walther's duty towards the Huns and to Hiltgunde), of the fragility of social conventions: the Hunnic world promotes Walther and Hiltgunde, but not as they would have been promoted in their homelands, and the whole network of patronage and promotion can collapse in a moment; Walther, new friend of the Huns, emerges from the Hunnic camp their enemy and finds himself also an enemy in his homeland, etc. Life is a lottery; no one wins all (Aeneas loses Dido, Walther his right hand, Hiltgunde a 'whole' husband). The best one can do is to be aware of the choices and their consequences, of models and guidelines and of the dimensions of one's own character and of the characters and situations of other persons. Armed thus, the good person, with God on his/her side, will come out on top. If this is the message of the *Waltharius*, it is powerfully reinforced by the kaleidoscopic parallelisms and reversions set in motion by the juxtaposition of the medieval poem and its classical 'sub-' text.

Faithful to his purpose, the *Waltharius* poet sacramentalizes the couple's journey to the Rhine: they are forty days in the wilderness, and during the whole time Walther made no assault upon Hiltgunde's chastity, despite the presumably numerous opportunities and their necessarily close cohabitation during the journey ('namque fugae toto se tempore virginis usu / continuit vir Waltharius laudabilis heros', 'and that praiseworthy hero Walter, all the time / they fled, refrained from carnal use of Hildegund', *W.* 426f.). Why should the poet introduce such an idea? Because, in the first place, it would certainly have been

assumed by his audience that the couple *would* have made love together, had the poet not specifically stated that they did *not*, and,
second, the poet was keen to castigate such conduct: 'marriage in
Carolingian times became a serious affair' (Wemple 1981: 89). Incest
was progressively condemned and marriage by way of *public* ceremony
was increasingly insisted upon; concubinage was considered an inferior
form of union and progressively frowned upon; trial marriages, with
their unfortunate consequences for women, were condemned as concubinage, and episcopal condemnation of sexual promiscuity and pre-
marital sex became more pronounced. Indeed, women who participated
in 'trial' or 'informal' marriages were prone to acquire – among
ecclesiastics at least – the reputation of being sorceresses.

The *Waltharius* thus clearly reflects the ninth-century, in which 'the
continuance of aristocratic lineages could no longer be entrusted to a
succession of wives or to simultaneous wives'.[21] 'Marriage became
exclusively a social institution "by which families of the same standing
among the aristocracy perpetuated themselves". Thus, fewer women,
only those whose unions were approved by their parents and in-laws
and sealed with a *dos* provided by their husbands or husbands' kin,
qualified to occupy the lofty position of wife' (Wemple 1981: 96).

Contrary to the official ecclesiastical position announced in some
Carolingian synods (e.g. Nantes 895 CE), Walther and Hiltgunde are
inseparable equals on their 'liminal' return journey, he 'rex inclite . . .
viro forti similis' ('outstanding, hero-like ruler', *W.* 452ff.), she 'puella
. . . incredibili formae decorata nitore' ('a girl adorned with stunning
radiance of beauty', *W.* 456) . . . 'virguncula clara' ('beautiful young
maiden', *W.* 1225), though their roles are different: she is to lead the
horse, keep second place ('hunc . . . assequitur calcemque terit', *W.*
456f.), and encourage her man in battle, while he is to bear and use
arms for protection and hunting; he is to sleep and she to stand guard,
singing herself awake (*W.* 504, 1181), and he is to be bold in the face of
danger, while she is to be fearful ('sonum . . . muliebrem', *W.* 543, 892,
'sexus enim fragilis animo trepidare coegit', *W.* 1211). Yet, they stand
side by side (*W.* 542), united by gentle caresses ('attactu blando', *W.*
506, 'placido tactu', *W.* 534), terms of affection and respect ('mi cara',
W. 508, 'mi senior', *W.* 545, 'fida amica', *W.* 550) and frequent
recalling of their betrothal (*W.* 571, 1174). The two face the world as
equal partners. Outside the charmed *munt* offered by betrothal, Hiltgunde is but an object of carnal lust (*W.* 546–7), a chattel (*W.* 602 (the
girl suddenly finds herself mentioned as part of the treasure), 819).

Nevertheless, the poet reminds his audience from time to time of
Walther's failings: pride verging upon vainglory, and, perhaps, the
conventional *chanson de geste* view of women as domestic stalwarts or
courtly ornaments to whom to boast on return from war (*W.* 561–5,

980).[22] It is also undeniable that the core of the poem concerns the traditional martial prowess of males: carnivalistic military exploits occupy a substantial section of the poem (*W.* 666–1061), interspersed with suitable battlefield dialogue and a choric outburst of a vatic/satiric nature from Hagen (*W.* 857ff.). An interlude (*W.* 1172–1280) is inserted to build up momentum for a final crisis and serves two purposes: first, it underlines the 'fraternal' horror of the foreshadowed fight between Walther and Hagen – 'solus enim Hagano fuerat suspectus et illud / oscillum regis subter complexibus actum' ('for only Hagen was a threat to Walter – and / that kiss the king gave him along with an embrace', *W.* 1140–1)[23] – and second it underlines Walther's chivalry towards women: treating Hiltgunde as a conversational partner (*W.* 1174 – contrast *W.* 104), allowing her to sleep (*W.* 1184–5).

The interlude leads into the final triangular battle (*W.* 1280–1396) which serves to allocate to each of the three combatants their *insignia*, their 'punishments': 'insignia quemque notabant' ('marks of honour branded each', *W.* 1401), *insignia* which originate, as in the *Nibelungenlied*, in a dispute over treasure (*W.* 1404). Gunther, the king, loses his leg, from the knee to the thigh. Walther, the hero, loses his right hand. Hagen, the vassal, loses his right eye, his teeth and his lips. These 'injuries' are in many respects unique to the *Waltharius* version of the story.

Walther is excessively conscious of shame/honour/pride (*W.* 561–5, 980), and hence loses the means to that in which he principally glories: his sword hand ('Waltharius manu fortis'). Nevertheless, he *does* keep his treasure, he *does* protect his betrothed's chastity (*W.* 545–54), he *does* 'console her (when sorrowful, *maesta*) with pleasant talk' (*W.* 1174), he *does* marry her, and he *does* live happily ever after. Arguably, he comes off better than the other two. His superiority comes out most clearly, in fact, in his attitude towards women: contrast the neglect Hagen's nephew shows for his wife with Walther's detailed consideration for Hiltgunde.

Nevertheless, there is more to Walther's loss of a right hand, his spear hand (*W.* 339), than meets the eye: recall the right hand that Aeneas gave to Dido, ultimately to betray her; remember the right hand which Aeneas invoked at the height of the battle in *Aeneid* 10 (773) and before he hurled his spear at Mezentius, the right hand into which Walther entrusted the bridle (*W.* 332 'virgineae . . . dextrae'), the key to his future happiness: Walther has lost *his* right hand because he *did* contemplate betrayal. Hiltgunde thus becomes the only truly loyal character in the poem.

Hagen too has conceded too much to conventional notions of rank, honour and manhood (*W.* 1080, 1085, 1095, 1109–10), breaching his 'sponsam / Walthario plerumque fidem' (*W.* 1090 and cf. 1113 (note how 1278 cancels out 1113); cf. too *pactum, W.* 1443). It is this, rather than the desertion of Walther involved in his escape from the Huns, that forms his major failing and results in his fateful combat with Walther. Yet Hagen is far superior to Gunther because he *realizes* what he should do; he sees the faults of Gunther, yet does not speak decisively against the role he is being asked to play because he is a client and Gunther is his lord (*W.* 1094, 1098–9, etc.). He thus loses an eye because he *saw* but did not act accordingly: he does not need an *eye* if he pays no attention to what it shows him. Similarly, since he was prepared to *act* against *plighted* (pledged, *spoken*) troth (to Walther), what need has he of a properly functioning mouth? If you pay no attention to what is said in faith, and you are prepared to speak against it when the going is tough, what need is there of a mouth?[24]

Gunther has few virtues by modern standards, but he *is* king. This is his greatest virtue, his headship of the pyramid of lordship. This inspires all his actions and earns for him survival, but the worst of the injuries, the one most likely to weaken his image as a king and hence to injure his pride: 'consedere duo, nam tertius ille iacebat' ('two sat, because the third of them was lying down'), as the poet, somewhat wickedly, says.

Nevertheless, despite his preoccupation with warfare, and males, as the saga demanded, the poet of the *Waltharius* places Hiltgunde in the foreground of his story: she and her betrothal dominate both beginning and end of the tale, as well as its chief emotional episode. The two final episodes are in this regard telling. In the first (*W.* 1424–46), the male survivors engage in an incredible display of carnivalesque, grotesque humour: at once the 'varios pugnae, strepitus ictusque tremendos' ('the crashing tide and awesome blows of battle'), the pomp and seriousness of males locked in lofty struggle, collapses into drunken play: 'inter pocula scurrili certamine ludunt' ('amid their drinking [they] play a game of taunting jokes') – all in the space of a line! For Hiltgunde, however, as the final episode makes clear, there is no play, only duty: 'even the champion of women, Hincmar of Rheims, while stressing equality of men and women before the law, referred to women as the weaker vessel and upheld the notion that a husband was the ruler of his wife' (Wemple 1981: 103). So it could be said of the author of the *Waltharius.* Hiltgunde is timid, as a member of the *sexus fragilis* should be (*W.* 1209, 1408); she obeys her lord (*W.* 249, 1225). It is Walther who 'commands' ('sponsus praecepit eidem', *W.* 1409); he is *sponsus ac senior* to the *virgo* (*W.* 1419–20). The poet sets his seal of approval on this arrangement of roles in his Epilogue: Hiltgunde, who, because of her sex, is exempt from the trials and failings of men (*W.* 1209, 1407), and who is thus able to be the ritual celebrant at the final ceremonies marking each hero's punishment (*W.* 1407ff.), secures the proper and tranquil reward appropriate to nature, role and sacrifices: 'publica Hiltgundi fecit sponsalia rite' ('declared in public he would marry Hildegund', *W.* 1448.), followed by thirty years of happy, successful, married life, as, indeed, was foreshadowed early in the poem (*W.* 39). For Hiltgunde, there are *publica sponsalia* rather than *pactum*, and no carnivalesque ribaldry: just thirty years of 'happy married life', the very opposite of male mateship enshrined in the notion of *pactum* and *scurrile certamen.* Hiltgunde is thus a classic illustration of our recent textbook accounts of Carolingian attitudes towards women and marriage (Wemple 1981: 105, 123; Brundage 1987: 173–5).

Thus there are no absolute heroes in the *Waltharius*, only a heroine who is matched to the best of a flawed lot – Walther, through whose experiences the trying situations and conflicting loyalties of the man's world are reconciled. Walther *is* the best of the heroes, the least *flawed*, but he *is* still flawed. The pattern of values and moral suasions in the poem as we have it confirms the view that the *Waltharius* is *not* simply an aristocratic vernacular epic in Latin; it is not simply *translated.* It has been carefully and symmetrically recrafted by a skilled Latin-speaking Christian cleric in imitation of Prudentius, Statius and Virgil; it has *not* been designed to ridicule pagan sin in a Christian manner, or to joke on the misguided values of the characters (Kratz 1977: 137; 1984: xxiii) or to criticize the values associated with the epic tradition. It was no doubt written to entertain upper clergy, and through them, perhaps, the lay aristocracy, and to reduce the tendency or need for both groups to read or hear read pagan Latin literature, or, worse, bardic songs and epics in the vernacular. Yet it seems also to have been written as an exercise in the exploration and probing of public and private values in the aristocratic world of the day, whether secular or ecclesiastical, and to suggest that the role of no one in life is perfect or straightforward: each character is constrained by his/her social stereotype, whether that of king, female, betrothed, vassal, captive, recipient of trust, friend or similar. No one can, of course, escape the primary ethical system of the day, which stressed valour, shame, honour, material success. This ethical system is *not* criticized or satirized in the poem, but exposed for what it is. If there *is* a message in the poem, it is, first, the general desirability of girls like Hiltgunde (whose best fate (not a perfect one, for who would, in an ideal world, want a husband with no right hand?) is a man like Walther), and second, the need for warrior aristocrats to respect and treasure such girls. The poet makes clear that Walther's real treasure is Hiltgunde, not the baggage carried by his destrier. The Germanic saga has been carefully rewritten to suggest a new model of male/female relations, one based on male respect for females, on female subservience and fidelity from betrothal to death, on marital indissolubility, on continence before marriage.

Is it too far-fetched to connect this rewriting with the 'moral and social revolution' effected by church legislation in Carolingian times within the field of marriage and attitudes towards sexual relations? Certainly the author of the *Waltharius* would have been duly scandalized by events such as those associated with King Lothair II and his wife Theutberga, and just as certainly he would have seen eye to eye with Archbishop Hincmar of Rheims, who (like the poet) 'sought to harmonise Germanic tradition with Christian teaching' (Brundage 1987: 136). The traditional dedicatory Preface of the *Waltharius*, whether it records an act of authorship or simply the gift of another's book, commends the book to a bishop who is to be entertained, but also improved (*W.* 14 (?)). It was the bishops in the ninth century who, individually and in synod, bore the particular brunt of Carolingian and late Carolingian marital and sexual reform. During the ninth century, 'clerics were thought to be definitive problem-solvers' (Bishop 1985: 59) in the area of marriage, and this required the resolution of many thorny problems peculiar to the clerical condition. Effecting a balance between the Christian notion of the equality of the sexes (St Paul, Galatians 33.28) and the notion of woman as the gateway for Satan was the chief problem: celibacy, monogamy, marital restrictions were the chosen formulae to effect this balance. Nevertheless, in searching themselves, the canons and the Bible for counsel, ninth-century bishops avoided the worst conclusions of Roman Christian misogyny: 'it is notable that in this era neither disgust at feminine corruption nor admiration of wifely subordination *per se* is known to have entered into the calculations of any ecclesiastical marital advisor. There was, it is true, some discussion of husbandly headship, but it seemed to imply responsibility rather than privilege. But women who were resisting actual or potential wrongdoing by their husbands and who consulted churchmen about it, found not lectures about their duty of womanly deference to their husbands' wills, but encouragement in their fights . . . the ninth-century tendency was to maneuver [the basic Christian tradition] in the direction of an egalitarian and reciprocal view of marriage' and to control the disgust 'churchmen who had themselves forsaken sexual life' felt 'at its continuation in others' (Bishop 1985: 83–4).

This spirit distinguishes ninth-century episcopal attitudes towards marriage, and it is one of the major inspirations behind the *Waltharius* poet's 'rewriting' of his saga materials. The poet was, no doubt, fascinated by an element of the story of little concern to the original bards and singers, who must have chosen to celebrate, in the main, prowess, and, perhaps, the foundation of the house and lineage of the son of Alpher. For the late Carolingian poet, on the other hand, the saga events have become a *Magic Flute*-like Trial, a testing of the devotion that should be inseparable from a betrothal, a tale of heroism, no doubt, but one in which the warrior's closest companion, partner and, indeed, saviour, is woman. The poet has thus effected a union between the heroic world of the freelance warrior leader and the emerging seigneurial world of the post-Carolingian age, a world in which, as Georges Duby (1983) and others have amply shown, lineage, property, rank and title were increasingly protected by a more rigid aristocratic/ecclesiastical attitude towards marriage and a progressive reduction of the role of woman to that of obedient subordinate, but vital partner and legitimate/licensed *procreatrix*.[25] The heroic epic has thus been rewrought to create space for the *Romance* and to explore the tensions between convenient social arrangements protecting male privilege/hegemony, and the chaos of external events theatening them.

THE *WALTHARIUS* AND THE *GESTA OTTONIS*

A curious confirmation of the approach taken in this chapter to the *Waltharius*, and a further confirmation of the vital utility of the epic form for medieval writers, is to be obtained from a brief consideration of the *Gesta Ottonis*, an epic poem in hexameters by Hrotsvit, a canoness in the north German (Saxon) abbey of Gandersheim, who has been described recently as 'the first poet of the Saxons, the first female German poet, the first dramatist of Germany, the first female German historian, and the first person in Germany to employ the Faust theme' (Wilson 1985: 2; 1988: ch. 5, especially 122ff.). Hrotsvit was writing c. 965–8 CE; at the least, some forty years after the poet of the *Waltharius*, and, at the likeliest, some three-quarters of a century later. Her epic was in some senses occasioned by political factors, and its commission fell to her somewhat unprecedented lot by, it seems, the chance of politics and the prominence of Ottonian aristocratic, cloistered women. Nevertheless, the work, which is some 1,517 lines in length, significantly about the length of the *Waltharius*, is set within a complex of works, the symmetry and meta-textual architecture behind which have been carefully and illuminatingly explained by Katharina Wilson (1985: 3–12; 1987: ch. 7), and also by Vynckier (1987: 187), who comments on the ternary aspects of the *Gesta Ottonis* (henceforth *GO*), following, among others, Peter Dronke (1984: 61–4 citing Kuhn, and cited by Wilson 1985: 9), for whom Hrotsvit 'achieved the boldest and most elaborate compositional design in Carolingian or Ottonian literature and art'.

The agenda which, behind or in addition to the above political and symmetrical compositional exigencies, determined Hrotsvit's own peculiar adaptation of heroic epic seems to have been her concern with balancing, on the one hand, the inherited Latin (male) panegyric epic form and current acceptance of female fragility/inferiority with, on the other, her own conviction that female heroism deserved 'equal-time' celebration at long last. The prefaces to her *Gesta* emphasize the conventional humility-*topos* themes – a female set within 'an unknown forest . . . the forest of these royal (i.e. male) deeds', becomes 'silent'; her 'homely simplicity . . . unsupported by any authority', her 'uncultured style' (versus the male 'festal eloquence of choice expression'), matches, indeed, expresses 'the weakness of my sex and the inferiority of my knowledge' (Hill 1972 (henceforth Hill): 119).[26] The execution of her task, however, reveals Hrotsvit's selective adaptation of her assignment. 'I, bidden to undertake a complete chronicle of illustrious achievements' ('magnificarum prolixitatem rerum iussa ingredi, regalium multiplicitatem gestorum'), she writes, could find no adequate model or source of information for much of what she felt bidden to cover. This, in itself, is a hint that her task proposed more than a conventional summary of male royal achievement, for which, clearly, there must have been ample evidence to hand, one way or another, for someone with court connections. In fact, by her own statement (Hill: 120, 137), Hrotsvit deliberately avoids 'a complete chronicle of illustrious achievements' and goes out of her way to point out that, though others later will write such chronicles, her own efforts were unprecedented. Her choice of the Latin hexametric verse epic form provides her with the creative pretext for this pose, and with a model rather different from the model she claims (Hill: 120) she lacked: the comparable-length Latin hexametric verse epic dealing likewise with male/female relationships that we have just been exploring: the *Waltharius*. It is my contention that the latter poem seriously influenced Hrotsvit's conception of her task and that this conception demonstrates again the creative, and, for the context of the time, pragmatic way in which medieval authors dealt with their Latin epic inheritance.

The substance of the *GO* is, in fact, a curious mirror for princes, emphasizing at the outset an Old Testament notion of triumphant, hereditary, warrior, Christian judicial kingship which may have had as one of its sustaining motivations the particular political strategy of Hrotsvit's abbess Gerberga. It is anxious to set Germanic kingship not only in a context of sovereign, holy, Old Testament, Roman messianic kingship, but also in a strange antithetical relationship to her own persona, as her first lines make clear:[27]

> Potent (*pollens*) ruler of the empire of the Caesars,
> Otto, who because of the nourishing compassion (*pietate*) of
> the eternal ruler,
> [Otto], outstanding in the realm of augustal honour,

[Otto, you who] surpass all the former *augusti* in compassion
(*pietate*),
[Otto, you whom] many peoples living in every region fear,
[Otto, you whom] the Roman world also endows with varied
duties/gifts (*muneribus*),
Do not spurn the slender gift/duty (*munus*) of this song.
(Kratz 1987: 204–6).

A second invocation follows, like a liturgical refrain, thirty-five lines
later:

Otto, prefulgent mini-gem of Roman rule,
Splendid flower of the ever-to-be-venerated *augustus* Otto [I],
Upon whom the high-throned ruler and his eternal son
[Potent (*pollens*)] bestowed a[n] [potent (*pollens*)][28] empire
at the summit of things,
Do not spurn the web/woven thing/text (*textum*) of an
insignificant nun.

At approximately thirty-five-line intervals, we find recurrences of this
lofty invocatory rhetoric, but this time abandoning the launching pad
of the humble nun. As Hrotsvit's account unfolds, the reader observes
that dynastic historiography has been 'opened up' to reveal a larger
space for the royal women whose fecundity and talents contributed a
large share to the story of lineage-maintenance that is being chronicled.
Just as the partnership between *vilis monialis* ('humble nun', Winterfeld
1965 (henceforth Win.): 203.5) and *pollens imperii regnator caesariani*
('powerful ruler of the empire of the caesars', Win: 202.1) produced
the unprecedented *GO*, so the partnership between male rulers and
female consorts produced the illustrious line of Romano-German
augusti whose latest manifestation Hrotsvit was celebrating in her epic.
   A second section of the poem begins now (at Win. 209.236) with a
resolving account of the revolt of the youngest brother of Otto I, the
very revolt that had placed Abbess Gerberga II, niece of the same Otto,
in so compromised a position. The account of treason and its resolution, concluded in the Canossa-like penitence of Henry before his
brother Otto, ends at line 467 (Win., p. 215), having explicitly distanced
itself from male epic by eschewing details of wars and battles, as things
more appropriate to 'the toil of qualified men' than to a woman in a
monastery. Hrotsvit then reverts with the death of Edith, Otto I's first
queen, in 946 CE, to the theme of the first section, the role of chaste
(i.e. monogamous) and benevolent women in lineage-maintenance,
leading up to the centre-piece account of a woman worthy of rule in her
own right, Adelaide, who, by the death of her husband Lothar in 950 CE,
would have come to rule Italy, had not the marquess of Ivrea, Berengar,

usurped the rule and imprisoned Adelaide, who had refused to marry his son Adalbert (Hill: 31). A 'complete chronicle of illustrious achievements' (Hill: 119) might well, had it been written in conventional terms, have left details of Otto I's second wife Adelaide's obscure Italian adventures prior to her second marriage unsung, but not so Hrotsvit, who devoted almost 200 lines to the subject (*GO* 475–665), some 20 per cent of the surviving 912 lines of the poem, or 12 per cent of the original 1,517 lines. This central episode, this 'unusually large part of the epic' (Vynckier 1987: 195, citing Strecker) has long provoked scholarly allusions to the *Waltharius*, with *its* dramatic central escape episode. An evil ruler steals Adelaide's treasure with his greedy right hand, just as in the *Waltharius* the heroine plunders the treasure of the Hunnic queen, a bishop (as in the ninth-century Carolingian environment discussed above) offers the queen solace in (marital) distress and the 'virtuous queen' (*regima piissima*)[29] makes a daring escape, assisted by only one maid and one priest.

The climactic episode occurs when the raging Berengar, in full chase of Adelaide, 'passed through the very grainfield in whose winding furrows the lady whom he was tracking down was hidden under the protecting curtain of blades of growing grain' (Hill 132). The substitution in the original of the goddess Ceres for the word 'grain' completes the picture of pious and chaste female autonomy, 'shaken with no little fear', preserved against rampaging male rapacity, with its extended spear (*extenta hasta*) penetrating and seeking to part the grain fronds (*culmos*) that protected the woman and her capacity to produce legitimate heirs from unauthorized ravaging. As Hiltgunde's chastity was finally sacrificed to Walther's need for legitimate offspring, so too Adelaide's body was judged worthy to be 'carried beneath the royal roof of Otto I's bed chamber' (Win.: 221.596). Otto's messages 'of very sweet love' (Win.: 222.642) and protestations of *firma fides* (Win.: 222.643), together with the symbolic reversal of Adelaide's grief in her royal city of Pavia (Hill: 133), complete the rehabilitation of the queen, as Walther's actions rehabilitated Hiltgunde.

Hrotsvit ceased her labours in March 968 as if her intentions were complete (Win.: 228.1511, 'his ita finitis et summatim replicatis', 'now that my recital has been completed and its story cursorily recounted', Hill: 137), though much remained that *could* have been told ('now there remain to be recorded further deeds of this same monarch', Hill: 137, and cf. Dronke 1984: 77). What was Otto to have made of such a submission, assuming that he saw it? What indeed would Gerburga have made of it? If there *was* a message in the text, aside from the local one of mitigating any wrath Otto may have felt at the revolt of his brother Henry, it was *not* that male heroism *per se* should triumph. Rather, it was a reaffirmation of the sanctity of just, Christian sovereignty, joined to a reaffirmation of the value of partnership, and recognition of the role that the female played in preserving this sanctity. It was a role beset, indeed, with vulnerable fragility (symbolized by the episode of the grain stalks), but one that should be honoured for what it was. It was a manifestation of the 'high place in the history and culture of the Ottonian Reich' women occupied, 'despite the fragility and levity of their sex, which clerical writers in the patristic tradition imputed to them as a matter of course'.[30]

Is it not likely that such a theme took some inspiration, of language and content, from the *Waltharius*? There is nothing improbable in the possibility from a geographical point of view: the author of the earlier poem may have worked in the neighbourhood of the Worms–Strass-burg–Metz triangle around the year 910 CE, or, according to 'recent research' (Wilson 1988: 157; Schaller 1987: 99 n. 77), the last decades of the ninth century. If we accept the dedication to a Bishop Erchamboldus (*W.* 6) as the dedication of the author (rather than of a secondary redactor), then it is not implausible to identify this Erkam-bold with a known Bishop of Eichstätt in Bavaria by that name who presided in the years 884–912. Eichstätt was presumably a cultural centre much influenced by an Anglo-Saxon tradition of educated nuns, which may have some bearing upon the emphases this chapter has sought to trace in the *Waltharius*. Gandersheim, where Hrotsvit wrote, is closer to Lorsch than to Eichstätt (by about a third of the distance), and other identifications, varying widely in date, for both Erkambold and the author of the *Waltharius* have been not implausibly proposed, but neither Bavaria nor the Rhineland is an improbable location for contacts with a well-connected Ottonian abbess, nor is either difficult from the point of view of manuscript survival. It is perhaps, again, no accident that the same region and the same careful adaptation of the Latin, Virgilian epic form to contemporary needs and problems, are in question when we consider a mid-eleventh-century masterpiece of Salian culture, the *Ruodlieb*, a highly original reworking of elements of the epic tradition, with overtones of Romance and the *speculum principis* tradition. The *Ruodlieb* also displays a keen interest in women and marriage. Kratz (1977: 139) has described it 'as an imitation and a rival of the *Aeneid*' and links it with the *Waltharius*, in that both writers were 'striving to extend the capabilities of Latin epic by exploring ways of making it a suitable vehicle for the expression of Christian values'.

No more illuminating example, therefore, of the function of the epic in medieval Latin culture (the subject of the present chapter) could be located than that of the *Waltharius*, the harbinger of the Ottonian epic, as well as the swansong of the Carolingian. Both the *Waltharius* and the *Gesta Ottonis* demonstrate the malleability of the epic genre and the way that, in reduced form, it was called upon to play a crucial role in the social and intellectual aspirations of Europe's leading intelligentsias, both male and female. This malleability formed the fertile epic legacy of the Carolingian and Ottonian era to later days, and what these later generations made of the legacy is, in part, indicated by such diverse masterpieces as the *Mathematicus* and *Cosmographia* of Bernardus Silvestris, the *Alexandreis* of Walter of Chatillon and the *Anticlaudianus* of Alan of Lille. Fed by such different streams as Germanic heroic (oral) song and the moving phenomenon of Virgilian epic, the written Latin epic of the medieval period maintained its hold as a major literary form for influencing and entertaining the leading writers and thinkers of medieval Europe. The latter's continued capacity to consume such epic fare derived from the vitality of the Latin-based educational curriculum of the earlier medieval period and the political hegemony of the clerical class. If the 'Virgilian revolution' in late Roman republican antiquity amounted to the renovation of heroic song in a cultivated, urban context, a 'profound reformulation of the ground-rules for epic verse' (Boyle p. 104 above), then there is no more eloquent testimony to its impact and success than the long line of Latin epic and epic-type writings that followed it, from the time of Lucan to that of the *Alexandreis* and beyond. Of this long line, the *Waltharius* forms perhaps the clearest illustration of the use to which contemporaries put the epic genre, and it is no accident that to understand certain crucial episodes within the late Carolingian poem, the reader needs to have in mind the Virgilian antecedent, especially *Aeneid* Books 2 and 4.

NOTES

1 See Schaller 1987: 99 n. 78; Bergin and Wilson 1977. The *Africa* seems to have been completed initially between the years 1338 and 1343 CE and is defined (Bergin and Wilson 1977: xv) as 'the earliest Renaissance epic rather than as a medieval artifact'. Its imitative nature and failure to catch the imagination of contemporaries should be borne in mind when comparing it and its successors with the epics mentioned in the present chapter.

2 See Newman 1986: 212–15, 243; Quinn 1979: 84; Bakhtin 1984: 5.

3 Raby: I, 356–60, 395–9, 405–8; II, 7–22, 34–83, 84, 102, 106–14, 118–21, 126–41, 150–1, 154–62, 164–8.

4 The goliardic poetic form. See Morris 1972: 121ff.

5 Springer 1988 describes Sedulius' *Paschale Carmen* (425–50 CE) as a Virgilian biblical epic that 'was required reading in schools throughout the middle ages and a source of inspiration for Latin and vernacular biblical epics well into the seventeenth century' (p. 1). Sedulius was, in fact, only one of a number of Christian poets in the fourth, fifth and sixth centuries who, after the *Edict of Toleration*, experimented with Latin hexametric verse as a medium for biblical narratives. See chapter I above, p. 13, Roberts 1985 and Springer 1988: 5–7. Virgil and the *Aeneid* were a powerful influence on these poets, partly because of the 'practice popular in the early church of quoting from pagan poets like Virgil to make apologetic points or to

illuminate scripture passages' (Springer: 13), and partly, of course, because of the place Virgil had come to occupy in the pagan educational curriculum.

6 E.g. Newman 1986; Fichter 1982. It is common for books on the history of epic to skip the medieval contributions: Murrin 1980, duBois 1982; Martindale 1986; Nimis 1987.

7 Carroll 1952: 128ff., 167ff. and 1953 deal with the differences between the *Waltharius* and the original (epic and ballad) forms of the Walther legend.

8 Carroll 1953: 41; Norman 1969: 265 considers the *Waldere* was probably 'a secular epic under clerical influence . . . unlikely to have been less than a thousand lines long'. In regard to the theme of the *Waltharius*, note the (general) assertion of Giamatti 1984: 4, 'The epic is often concerned with exile and the way back, and woman is always at the center.' Compare Walther's longing for his homeland with Aeneas' 'longing' for *his* fatherland and his 'longing' for Pergamum (*A.* 4.340–4; Conte 1986: 180).

9 The italics in my text at this point are designed simply to draw the reader's attention to parallelisms between the opening of the *Waltharius* and that of *Aeneid* Book 2. Kratz 1977 deals with other examples of the medieval poet's interest in Virgil (Kratz 1977: 129, the banquet given by Dido in honour of Aeneas (*A.* 1.637–756, *W.* 305–9 etc.), and with the medieval poet's interest in Statius and Prudentius.

10 Although only one-third of the poem is devoted to actual military (battle-field) feats.

11 Vynckier's view of the *Waltharius* as a 'crafty *vituperatio* of the unchristian *modus operandi* of the Germanic warrior caste' (Vynckier 1987: 183–4) reduces to nonsense by far the largest part of the *Waltharius*.

12 All references to the *Waltharius* in the present essay are to the edition of Kratz 1984, from which most of the English renderings for Latin passages have been taken.

13 A curious expostulation in view of Hagen's role in the *Nibelungenlied*. Kratz 1977: 131–2, 137 sees this expostulation also as central to the poem, because, for him, the theme of the poem 'is the condemnation of avarice'. I find this a somewhat narrow, didactic, approach to the author of the poem's creative purpose. See Kratz 1980: 47 and Schaller 1987: 91. Cf. *Aeneid* 3.56–7.

14 Wemple 1981: 32–3 and cf. pp. 37, 93. Ennen 1989: 28ff., 33ff., 41–61. The endowed marriage, public and contractual, was the normal form of marriage among the early medieval Germans.

15 Learned 1970: 65–6, 133, 182–3, Magoun and Smyser 1950: ch. 5. I owe thanks to Professors Clunies-Ross and Clifton-Everest of the University of Sydney for their kind assistance with the Norse and MHG versions of the *Walther-saga*.

16 Though he *says* (*W.* 255) that he *did* include her . . .

17 Cf. Bate 1978: 7–8 on *W.* 383–401: Attila's hang-over, appropriately, is described in the language of Dido's love-sickness.

18 Walther = Aeneas vs Hiltgunde = Dido (at, for example, *W.* 227, 237ff.) becomes, as it were, Hiltgunde + Walter = Aeneas + Destiny, vs Attila [and Ospirin] = Dido.

19 Bate 1978 thinks the Virgilian echoes are in part parodies (pp. 7–8): 'the use of these echoes from well-known Virgilian passages would be certain to provoke laughter from an educated, late tenth century audience or reader' and are unique to the Latin epic (as distinct from its vernacular antecedent). Walsh 1986 picks up Bate's views and likens the *Waltharius* to a 'cento' of

'well-remembered phrases . . . as part of a literary entertainment'. He speaks of 'parody', 'humorous borrowing' from, 'sportive adaptation of' Virgil, but his case is helped neither by the examples he cites nor by his erroneous statistics. I find myself, however, less confident about what a tenth-century Frenchman or German would have found comic (humorous, sportive, entertaining). The uses of Virgil in the *Waltharius* to which Bate, for example, draws attention function quite obviously in purposeful ways, whatever their comic element may or may not have been taken to be. Thus the echoes in the *Waltharius* of the dialogue in the *Aeneid* between Juno and Venus serve only to strike a note of far-reaching destiny and divine negotiation behind mere human action, as valid for the *Waltharius* as for the original Virgilian context; what more natural, also, than that the banquet which in the *Aeneid* functions to *divert* Aeneas, to thwart fate and destiny, and in the *Waltharius* serves to *reorientate* the hero and heroine, *permitting* the consummation of fate and destiny (the betrothal), should be described in linking language? Bate's rather limited view of the *Waltharius* poet's 'Virgilianism' needs to be tempered by the comments of others: Katscher 1973: 56–7, 114ff.; Kratz 1977: 129; Schaller 1987: 91,99. Less masterly uses of Virgil by ninth-century Carolingian poets are discussed by Kratz 1987: 202–3. See Alfonsi 1977, who points out the Camilla-like parallels inherent in the picture of Hiltgunde in the *Waltharius* (pp. 6–7), and (p. 14) comments on 'la presenza di tutte le voci della poesia vergiliana' in the *Waltharius*, which is 'più che un "Eneide", un "episidio" dell'Eneide sviluppato a dimensione di poema eroico'. The analogies between Lausus/ Mezentius and Hagen P[B]atavrid (cf. Strecker 1951: n. to *W*. 864ff. and the comments of Boyle 1986: 96ff., 121ff.) are, again, allusive rather than exhaustively parallel. The *furor/pietas* theme of the *Aeneid* expounded illuminatingly by Boyle 1986: ch. 4, was probably lost on, or inconceivable for, the *Waltharius* author, but 'the most pervasive and arresting theme of the entire *Aeneid*' (Boyle 1986: 111), the tragedy and wastage involved in maintaining the worth of empire and fame (lineage and *dominium*, perhaps, in the case of the *Waltharius* poem) might *not* have been lost on the medieval author.

20 Newman: 1986: 199. A. J. Boyle (in a paper delivered to the Department of Latin, Sydney University, 1990) has also argued that Virgil took much from neoteric epyllion. See also chapter V above, pp. 80f., 86–8, 90.

21 As in Merovingian times: Wemple 1981: 51–7, 95–6. I comment further on the date of the *Waltharius* below.

22 Cf. *The Song of Roland*, 1720 and 1960f.

23 Cf. the epic battle between Hildebrand and Hadubrand (*Hildebrandslied*, c. 800 CE). Note too the fratricidal theme of Statius' *Thebaid*, (1.1, 'fraternas acies'); on Statius' *Thebaid* and the *Waltharius* poet see Kratz 1977: 128.

24 A promising approach to the comic, bathetic aspects of the punishments and their immediate aftermath is Bakhtin's notion of techniques of debasement and of grotesque realism (Bakhtin 1984: 235, 370). Certainly, the mutilation passages in the *Waltharius* intrude upon the closed, official, formal world of Germanic warrior-heroism, but there may lurk here a more fundamental aspect of the relationship between literature and society, intellectual and folk, than a simple urge to make fun of one formal, official, system, merely to replace it with another.

25 The *Waldere* fragments record a sample of Hiltgunde's oratory of encouragement to Walther: the *Waltharius* has no monopoly, therefore, of the idea

that Hiltgunde played a valuable role for Walther. The context of the *Waldere* fragment A, however, is one of narrowly military exploits.

26 For the original Latin see Winterfeld 1965: 201–2; Dronke 1984: 64–7, 75–7. Compare *W.* 1209 and elsewhere, for the *Waltharius* author's emphasis upon the 'fragility' of the female sex.

27 My translation attempts to follow the Latin fairly literally. In general see Leyser 1979: part 3.75–107.

28 *Pollens* can be translated at either point here.

29 Have we here, as it were, a female Aeneas leaving a *terra periculorum* for her new promised land?

30 See Leyser 1979: 51. On the 'great spate of early medieval [monastic] foundations for women' in Saxony and elsewhere in Germany, see Leyser 1979: ch. 6; Wilson 1987: ch. 2 and 1988: 148–51. Compare the thrust of the female-authored 'second and later *Life of Queen Mathilda*' (Leyser 1979: 67) with that of the *GO*.

XIV
AFTER ROME: RENAISSANCE EPIC

Philip Hardie

The history of Renaissance Latin epic remains to be written.[1] That bold chronicler would have to master a vast and unflagging output that does not begin to dry up until well into the sixteenth century, and not before it had helped to fertilize the soil for those Renaissance vernacular epics that today enjoy the status of classics, Tasso's *Gerusalemme Liberata*, Camoens' *Lusiads* and Milton's *Paradise Lost*. Relieved by time and space of the responsibility to be exhaustive I here focus on two moments in that history, one from the heroic beginnings of humanism, the other from the period of high classicism by a contemporary of Raphael and Michelangelo.

PETRARCH'S *AFRICA*

Predictably, posterity has judged Petrarch's *Africa*[2] to be a noble failure, a misguided attempt to revive the supreme genre of antiquity on its own terms. Such a view seems to be endorsed by Petrarch's own doubts about the value of his enterprise, by his unwillingness to make public his drafts, and by the naked fact of the epic's incompletion. But the question of what achievements are truly valuable and the difficulty of acquiring lasting fame are central themes of the *Africa* itself; the poem has become a too successful advertisement of its own 'faults'. The failure to complete is itself as much a literary gesture as a biographical misfortune; in the *Secretum* Petrarch is impelled to voice again Virgil's wish for the cremation of his poetic offspring. Recent criticism of other works of Petrarch has taught us to value the incomplete as an expression of his restless search for goals that always receded;[3] the *Africa* too may be understood not as a frigid attempt to resuscitate an alien and outmoded form, but as a monumental expression of that same search for an identity, personal and cultural, that produced the *Canzoniere* and the *Secretum*.

Ever since Homer a central aim of composers and interpreters of epic has been to make the remote past of immediate relevance to the

294

present. In this respect 'epic' is a suitable label for the humanists' effort to revive the classical past and make it live at the centre of the cultural and educational life of Europe. As a work of scholarship and imitation the *Africa* is impressive enough. The epic's primary narrative brings Scipio Africanus from his crossing to Africa through the battle of Zama to his triumph in Rome; Livy, for whose text Petrarch did so much, is accordingly the main source.[4] Cicero and Virgil, Petrarch's *due occhi* of the language, are also important presences, both simultaneously in the dream of Scipio Africanus, which takes up almost the entirety of the first two books of the epic. The primary model is the dream of Scipio Aemilianus at the end of Cicero's *Republic*; but, far more than the *Somnium Scipionis* reheated, the Petrarchan dream is a remarkably alert combination of the series of Latin works into which the Ciceronian *Somnium* inserts itself. The parade of heroes past and future draws on the speech of Anchises in *Aeneid* 6, itself indebted to the Ciceronian dream, while Petrarch's positioning of his eschatological dream at the opening of his epic is a structural echo of the positioning of the dream of Homer at the opening of Ennius' *Annales*, a passage imitated by both Cicero and Virgil.[5]

Virgil is the dominant but by no means exclusive epic presence.[6] Homer was for Petrarch in the period of his life when most work was done on the *Africa* a truly bloodless ghost. As for Ennius, Petrarch does what he can with the testimonia and fragments, and that something is not a little. Of the later Latin epicists Lucan is of great importance:[7] for the conception of a historical epic largely dispensing with divine machinery; for the explicit moralizing, especially in the account of the causes of the war, 1.71ff. (like the Civil war, the war with Hannibal is the result of *invidia*, 'envy'); for the magnification of Zama as a battle that affects the world like Pharsalia (both battles narrated in a seventh book);[8] for the Caesarian energy of Scipio, first seen at a point of crossing, the Pillars of Hercules, as Caesar is precipitated into Lucan's poem at the edge of the Rubicon; for the depiction of Roman *virtus*, as in the speech of the elder Scipio, 1.285ff., one of the several examples in the parade of heroes of Roman commanders prepared to sacrifice themselves for the greater good; for the obsession with *umbra* and *nomen*, transferred to the particular historical anxieties of post-antique Petrarch.[9]

Petrarch is highly self-conscious about his imitation of the ancients: in two famous letters to Boccaccio, *Fam.* 22.2 and 23.19, he discusses his goals and anxieties, summed up in the precept 'the imitator must take pains that what he writes is like but not the same'. The similarity between imitation and model should be as that between son and father, or as that between honey and the flowers from which the bees produce it, not the likeness of a painted portrait, which is the mimicry of apes, not of poets. Petrarch is obsessively cautious of reproducing the actual words of other poets, though aware that in this he is more self-critical than ancient poets, including Virgil. The danger comes with those authors whom he has read most deeply, Virgil, Horace, Livy, Cicero, who have become so 'fixed in his marrow' that their words are likely to emerge from Petrarch's subconscious as his own, *aliena* mistaken for *propria*. Petrarch tells cautionary tales against himself of phrases in the *Bucolicum Carmen* that, on rereading, were found to be borrowed plumage. Recent publication of notes from Petrarch's own hand copied into an early manuscript of the *Africa* reveals just this *labor limae* applied to the verbal texture of the epic as the author worries away to eliminate excessive verbal dependence on ancient models.[10]

This is a fairly mechanical way of preserving a measure of independence; the wider question of Petrarch's creative imitation remains. Thomas Greene in an important study of Renaissance imitation writes that 'the *Africa* is marred by failings that from our perspective can be attributed to a double incapacity: first, to grasp the alien substance of ancient epic in its artistic fullness; and second, to gauge lucidly the character of the writer's own poetic vocation'.[11] That this may perpetuate a long-standing prejudice about the relative inferiority of the Latin epic to the vernacular poems is suggested in a superb article by Giuseppi Velli, who analyses with great acumen and learning such imitative features as *oppositio in imitando* and contamination of models in the *Africa* and other works, and shows how Petrarch embraces 'the two moments of, firstly, historical "reconstruction", and, secondly, of a realization in accordance with the spiritual needs and intellectual problems peculiar to Petrarch'; Velli questions whether the distinction between Latin and vernacular works has not hindered a full appreciation of Petrarch's literary discourse.[12] My general discussion of the *Africa* aims to give a macroscopic sense of Petrarch's canny combination of fidelity to model with pertinence to his own poetic and cultural interests; at the level of the microtext almost everything remains to be done.

Petrarch is perhaps particularly Ennian in the insistence with which, directly and indirectly, he introduces his own person into his epic. Modern discussions of self-referentiality in the traditionally 'objective' epic may help us to see this as something other than an anachronistic injection of the self-awareness of the 'first modern man'.[13] The first two words of the carefully constructed Prologue already emphasize the poet's person: 'et mihi conspicuum meritis belloque tremendum, / Musa, virum refers' ('to me also, Muse, you will tell of a man outstanding by his merits and fearsome in war').[14] Now the address to the Muse is traditionally the place for the epic poet to use the first person singular; Petrarch's *mihi* occupies the same position as in Horace's translation of the first line of the *Odyssey, Ars Poetica* 141, 'dic mihi, Musa, virum' ('tell me, Muse, of the man'). But the *et* makes the difference, stressing the poet's own hopes at the same time as it places him in a position of dependence and supplementarity. 'To me also' – as well as to whom? There is more than one answer: doubtless as well as to Ennius, who sung of his patron's exploits; but the conjunction of appeal to the Muse with mention of a 'man' is Homeric, while the particular qualities of this man, 'outstanding by his merits and fearsome in war', are more reminiscent of Virgil's Aeneas than Homer's Odysseus.[15]

In the two dreams that frame the action of the whole epic, Scipio in Books 1 and 2 speaks with his father; Ennius in Book 9 speaks with Homer. Both authority figures have the prophetic power to call up the poet of the *Africa*, Petrarch himself. It is as if Virgil had written himself in to the speech of Anchises, a model for both the Petrarchan dreams. The elder Scipio introduces Petrarch (2.443) as 'a second Ennius', vehicle for the praise of Africanus, in the course of a homily on the transience of glory, and looks forward to the 'third death' of Scipio, the final death of his fame (after his first, literal, death, and his second 'death', the decay of his tomb and epitaph). The vision of Ennius is far more particular. Taking a hint from the allusion to the Ennian dream of Homer in Cicero's *Somnium Scipionis* Petrarch has Ennius tell Scipio of the waking dream in which he saw the ragged figure of Homer, who uses of himself the words *qualis erat* that Aeneas applied to the mutilated figure of Hector (*Aen.* 2.274), a line that Servius says is Ennian.[16] As we work our way further into the realities/unrealities of this waking dream, Homer answers Ennius' interrogation on the cause of his blindness with a distinction between outer and inner sight; with this inner sight he is mysteriously able to share Ennius' direct vision of the youth Petrarch seated among the laurels of Vaucluse. The mechanism of the epic vision allows the great poets of the past that direct access to the poet of the distant future which the latter for his part so eagerly desired to his predecessors;[17] only at the end are the relative positions equalized, as Ennius approaches Petrarch with the futile eagerness of the Virgilian Aeneas, 'with the desire to gaze on him and speak with him' (9.269); this latter-day Marcellus[18] is on the point of being called into premature life, as Ennius' greeting barely penetrates Petrarch's hearing and he slowly lifts his eyes to address Ennius, when he, and we, are summoned back to the 'reality' of the narrative by the morning reveille, and the active shape of Scipio replaces the dreaming Petrarch in Ennius' gaze (284–9).

Where the elder Scipio dwelt on the impermanence of fame in the future, the anxiety of Ennius – and of Petrarch – is how to maintain contact with the past. It is the power of Petrarch's epic poetry to persuade us of the immediate reality of Scipio at Zama (just as the blind

Homer has nevertheless a lynx-like power of visualizing the whole wide world, 9.188ff.). But elsewhere Petrarch is acutely aware of the great divide that separates him from antiquity; in this respect Ennius is a figure of the poet, as one conscious of his role as the transmitter of a *peritia fandi* 'a verbal skill' (9.45) that has been transferred from one home to another. Ennius describes his epic mission thus:

> vestigia Famae
> rara sequens, quantum licuit per secula retro
> omnia pervigili studio vagus ipse cucurri,
> donec ad extremas animo rapiente tenebras
> perventum primosque viros, quos Fama perenni
> fessa via longe ignotos post terga reliquit.
>
> (*Africa* 9.133–8)

Following the sparse footsteps of Fame, with unsleeping application I made my wandering way where possible backwards through all the centuries, until my hurrying spirit brought me to the remotest shades and those great men whom Fame, exhausted by her ceaseless travelling, left forgotten far behind her.

This is a picture of the fourteenth-century poet's voyage in search of antiquity, not of the journey that Ennius had to undertake to rediscover Homer; it is also the journey undertaken both literally and figuratively by Petrarch as he climbed the Capitol in 1341 CE:

> ipse ego ter centum labentibus ordine lustris
> dumosam tentare viam et vestigia rara
> viribus imparibus fidens utcumque peregi.
>
> (*Africa* 9.404–6)

I myself after the lapse of fifteen hundred years trusting in my unequal abilities to attempt that path through the scrub following those sparse footsteps, achieved it in my fashion.

Petrarch's own strenuous attempt to realize a Homeric visualization of absent places is reserved for Hasdrubal's tour of Rome at 8.862–951. The Virgilian model is Aeneas' tour of the site of Rome in *Aeneid* 8, an imaginative recollection of a time before there was a city by a poet living amidst the full splendour of ancient Rome; Petrarch strives to recapture that splendour from a reality that is merely a name or a shadow.[19]

Petrarch's sense of distance, his desire to reach out to the unreachable, may be responsible for the initially disconcerting way in which the *Africa* takes to an extreme the *Aeneid*'s tendency to present persons and events indirectly, through vision, flashback, or prophecy.[20] The nine books are framed by dreams, the dream of Scipio in 1 and 2, and the

298

dream of Ennius in 9. Books 3 and 4 are taken up with songs and conversation during Laelius' visit to the palace of the African King Syphax; these correspond to the Song of Iopas and Aeneas' auto-narrative in 1–3 of the *Aeneid,* and give us the remoter history of Africa and Rome, and the life of Scipio to date;[21] in 8, after the battle of Zama, the Roman victors take time off for a rather medieval debate on the relative ranking of the world's great generals, Alexander, Pyrrhus, Hannibal – and Scipio.

Ennius is also privileged as a poet by his close association with the subject of his verse; he relates the secrets of his dream of Homer to Scipio as a way of passing the journey from Carthage to Rome. Ennius is 'the constant witness and companion of Scipio's deeds' (9.11). Petrarch uses this relationship to comment on his own most ambitious and intimate aspirations as poet, and here in particular draws past events into the present. The bond between Ennius and Scipio is an ideal-ization of Petrarch's relation to King Robert; Scipio's interrogation of Ennius on poetics evokes the *viva voce* examination of Petrarch on the same topics conducted by Robert as a preliminary to the laureation. The *Africa* concludes, as did the original version of Ennius' *Annales,*[22] with the triumph of the victorious general, with his triumphant poet at his right hand, both wearing laurels (9.398–402). This is immediately followed by the reference to Petrarch's own poetic triumph at the *laureatio* of 1341, which in a very real sense was a triumph for the present poem, in prospect at least, and furthermore a triumph earned by his narrative of the triumph of Scipio. In this association of poetic with political-military success Petrarch was both making a claim for the place of poetry and scholarship in the future and reviving an authentic-ally ancient claim, of which the beginning of *Georgic* 3 is the clearest example, Virgil as poet-in-triumph celebrating the triumphs of Caesar.[23]

Bernardo speaks of 'Petrarch's peculiar bent for fusing apparently disparate images'.[24] As *triumphatores* Scipio and Ennius begin to merge into one another. Ennius is an obvious figure of the later poet Petrarch; but how far does Scipio himself merge into the poet's own ambitions and anxieties? From the time of the earliest commentaries on the *Canzoniere* the identity of Laura has been questioned: real woman, or figure for Petrarch's poetic activity and desire for fame, embodied or disembodied Muse? Scipio is the historical embodiment of supreme virtue, but he also tends to become a figure for Petrarch's own search for a form of virtue that satisfies both humanist and Christian re-quirements.[25] Both Laura and Scipio reveal clearly the inseparability of Life and Literature for Petrarch. Bernardo skilfully plots a further complication in the meaning of Scipio, whereby as a figure of Virtue he is inseparable from the figure of Laura as figure of Glory, the 'shadow' of Virtue. Bernardo adduces a number of passages from other works of

Petrarch where the link is made between Scipio, the epic subject, and Laura, the lyric subject, as for example in *Bucolicum Carmen* 3, where Dane/Laura tells Stupeus/Petrarch of the mountain where grows the laurel, the mount on which Ennius, Virgil and others crowned themselves with the laurel. The *Africa* ends with the triumph of Scipio, the *Trionfi* with Laura at the head of the Triumph of Eternity. Both Scipio and Laura function as *loci* for Petrarch's anxieties as to the possibility of reconciling the demands of this world and the next. Petrarch tells us (*Canzoniere* 3) that he first set eyes on Laura on a Good Friday; it was likewise on a Good Friday (*Ep. Posteritati*) that he received the inspiration to write the *Africa*. There is here surely rather more self-fashioning than unadorned autobiographical truth.

The tension between pagan epic and Christian truth is dramatized in *Bucolicum Carmen* 1, cast in the form of a dialogue between Silvius (Petrarch) and Monicus (his brother, the monk Gherardo). The latter enjoys a supra-pastoral tranquillity in the retreat of his cave, to which, like Tityrus in Virgil's first Eclogue, he invites Silvius, forced to a life of eternal wandering because of *amor* for the great models of epic, Virgil and Homer. Monicus suggests as an alternative the biblical poetry of the shepherd David. This separation of the classical and the Christian is for the most part a truthful characterization of the *Africa*. The poem has a threefold invocation, first to the Muses (1.1–10), and second to Christ (10–18), before turning third to Robert of Sicily. Christ is offered 'pious songs' from Parnassus, presumably to be understood as the present poem (rather than putative Christian poems in the future), but the poet is uncertain as to Christ's reception of his songs, and suggests as an alternative offering his tears. The poem is 'pious' presumably in that it does not contradict Christian truth, rather than being more directly Christian. The elder Scipio's revelation to his son of the decline of Rome after its zenith under Augustus does not include a prophecy of the rise of Christianity; and it is not easy to reconcile his Ciceronian description of an astral after-life with Christian schemes. The perspective beyond the pagan frame is only opened up overtly in the allegorical scene in Book 7 in which Roma and Africa present their pleas to the Thunderer (never explicitly called Jupiter, though on one level it is he) before the battle of Zama. There are models in Virgil, Lucan and Claudian, but Petrarch uses this very classical scene to very unclassical ends. The Livian view of Zama as the victory that gives mastery of the world is transumed into the Christian view of a providence that favours Roman empire as the vehicle for the universal church. Africa's and Roma's claims for the godlikeness of their respective protégés, Hannibal and Scipio (7.552ff., 632ff.), are 'corrected' by God's prophecy of the Incarnation. God's indifference to the pleas of both matrons is contrasted with his fervent attachment to another

300

woman, the Virgin Mary (723–4). Nevertheless the pagan and the Christian tend to leak into each other: Jonathan Foster suggests a general resemblance between the careers of Scipio Africanus and Christ, both youths said to be of divine parentage, who manifest great *pietas* towards their father, noted for their continence, and at the last tried and found guilty by an ungrateful nation.[26] Petrarch was at least aware of the possibility that his pagan epic might be read in a Christian light, as *Seniles* 2.1 makes clear by its defence against the charge that the dying speech of Mago, 6.885–918 (the only part of the poem to be widely circulated during Petrarch's lifetime), is anachronistic in its use of Christian motifs.[27]

In *Seniles* 4.5 Petrarch, in line with a dominant medieval and Renaissance tradition, allegorizes the *Aeneid* as the story of the moral perfection of Aeneas. His own epic hero Scipio is another example of the perfect man, held up for our imitation. Scipio himself is too perfect to provide an interesting study in the struggle between reason and the passions, and this may be one reason for the relative lack of action in the first four books of the poem, taken up almost entirely with speeches about the past and future; even in Book 5 Scipio plays a relatively minor role, to emerge decisively on to the stage only in the last four books, which narrate the war in Africa itself. Psychomachia is, however, the central subject of Petrarch's reworking of the story of Dido and Aeneas into the tragic history of Sophonisba and Masinissa in Book 5, presented far more unequivocally than in Virgil as a conflict between Virtue and Pleasure; Scipio himself is our interpreter in the speech to Masinissa at the centre of the book (386–437). Here Scipio also draws the parallel between external and internal warfare: Masinissa has won glory through the defeat of Syphax, but the greater glory is to be won through conquest of the self. In the allegorization of the *Aeneid* Petrarch had taken the sack of Troy as a figure of the state of war inside the city of the mind in the benighted state of this life.[28]

Kallendorf uses the Sophonisba episode as evidence for his contention that the *Africa* can only be appreciated as a specimen of epideictic rhetoric, a poem of praise and blame that leaves no space for moral or poetic complexity. Such an epic would be truly unreadable for many moderns. Kallendorf speaks of Petrarch's 'condemning Sophonisba . . . to the punishment of hell',[29] but this is a distorted summary of the way in which at the beginning of Book 6 Sophonisba is assigned to the Fields of Mourning. For many earlier critics the contrast between Scipio's high moral line and the interminable agonizing of Masinissa over his choice between love and duty (his last monologue to Sophonisba occupies over 150 lines) has suggested rather the psychological and moral interest of that conflict between love for the earthly Laura and the duty of a Christian that lies at the centre of the *Canzoniere*. It would be perverse to deny that the *Africa* is above all a panegyric of Scipio, but it is far from being as monolithic as Kallendorf would make out. There are generic complexities: consider the remarkable, and very unclassical, listing of the beauties of Sophonisba at 5.20–63, suggesting the metaphorical and hyperbolical conceits of Petrarchan lyric.[30] As the Sun sinks in the west to usher in the night in which Masinissa must resolve to abandon Sophonisba, he takes pity on the mortal as he remembers his own thwarted passion for Daphne: '**laurea**que ante oculos stabat sua sacra' ('his own sacred laurel hovered before his eyes', 5.480). In the contrary pulls of Book 5 we sense also Petrarch's reliving of the painful beguilement that Virgil's story of Dido exercised on Augustine, another of Petrarch's great role-models.[31] And we have seen above how Petrarch's uncertainty and second thoughts as to the value of fame, glory and poetry strike a remarkably Virgilian chord. The awareness that above and beyond all of this stands the more dogmatic certainty of a Christian age qualifies but hardly weakens the complexity of Petrarch's epic persona.

FROM PETRARCH TO VIDA

In Renaissance Italy classicizing epics were a natural vehicle for the panegyrical relation of the exploits of rulers who had themselves been brought up on a diet of the *Aeneid* and other Latin epics. This chronicle type of epic flourishes particularly in the fifteenth century, and in the early sixteenth century Vida is still found composing a *Juliad* on the deeds of Pope Julius II. A typical, if superior, example is the *Hesperis* of Basinio Basini,[32] thirteen self-consciously Homerizing books celebrating the wars of Sigismondo Malatesta against the Aragonese house of Naples in 1448 and 1453; the narrative of the two campaigns, which begins when Jupiter sends Mercury to rouse Sigismondo into action, is punctuated by a three-book fantasy in which Sigismondo travels to the Fortunate Isle, where he is favoured with the love of Psyche, daughter of Zephyrus (a cover for Isotta), who acts as his guide through visions of a Temple of Fame and of the after-life. Basini is buried in the Tempio Malatestiano, that ultra-classicizing version of a Christian church built for Sigismondo by Alberti.

The taste for panegyrical epic when combined with the adoration of Virgil provided a surefire formula for success in the case of Maffeo Vegio's *Aeneid* 13. Completed in 1428, this was the most enduring of several attempts to provide a satisfactory ending to the *Aeneid* and was regularly printed in editions of Virgil until well into the sixteenth century.[33] It is a book of speeches, processions and pageants, a set of displays perhaps more in tune with Renaissance tastes than our own, and it reveals a reading of Virgil normative in the early Renaissance.

302

Aeneas emerges as the *vir perfectus* of the medieval and Renaissance tradition; his translation to the stars is the proper reward for an epic hero of this sort. Turnus is unequivocally the guilty party, although this does not rule out the possibility of compassion. The topics of praise of Aeneas and blame of Turnus are focused in the central speech of Drances (329–73), here a far less devious speaker than he had been in Book 11.

With the sixteenth century comes a relative shift to the production of religious epics which stand in a tradition going back to the earliest Christian attempts to appropriate pagan cultural goods for Christian use, as the Israelites had taken for their own use the spoils of the Egyptians. Indeed the spate of new epics was in part prompted by a renewed interest in such early Christian works as Juvencus' *Evangeliorum* and Sedulius' *Carmen Paschale*; Aldus Manutius brought out a collection of ancient Christian poets in three volumes in 1501–4.[34]

VIDA'S *CHRISTIAD*

Two early sixteenth-century biblical epics enjoyed especial success. The first is Jacopo Sannazaro's three-book poem on the Nativity of Christ, the *De Partu Virginis*, finally published in 1526.[35] While the main narrative covers only the time from the Annunciation to the Nativity and focuses on the humility of the Virgin, the universal implications of this short segment of time are brought out through ecphrasis and prophecy, especially the prophecies of David, from Limbo, and of Proteus as related by the river Jordan, which come at the end of the first and third books respectively. Sannazaro is more famous today as the author of the *Arcadia*; as well as drawing on the *Aeneid*, the *De Partu Virginis* makes heavy use of the fourth Eclogue, above all in the scene of the shepherds at the manger.

Girolamo Vida's *Christiad* in six books, published in 1535, was written by the future bishop of Alba, who ended his career as zealous enforcer of the counter-Reformation; this product of his earlier years is the consummate expression of the Humanist Maronolatry.[36] In its imitative practice the *Christiad* differs widely from Petrarch's *Africa*. There is significant and recurrent use of Lucretius, and Lucan's Erictho episode is used for the hyperbolical account of Christ's casting out of the devils into swine, the centre-piece of John's account of His ministry (4.439–531), but Vida's obsessive fidelity to Virgil deservedly earned him the sobriquet of the 'Christian Virgil'. In the Renaissance debate about imitation of the ancients Vida stands firmly with those who sought excellence through a scrupulous fidelity to the ancient models. Much praised and read in the Renaissance for his success in getting inside the skin of Virgil, he has been excoriated by later centuries as a mechanical imitator. His name survives as a ghostly presence for students of English literature as a precursor of Milton;[37] classical Latinists used to the study of imitation at once detailed and creative may find it easier to appreciate this kind of poem.

The epic is a fitting companion piece to Vida's hexameter *De Arte Poetica* (1527), which is as much a critical appreciation of the *Aeneid* as it is a prescriptive work on how to write epic;[38] it ends with a hymn to Virgil (3.554–92) in which Vida expresses his own devotion in the language that Lucretius had used of his dependence on Epicurus. In the first book a potted history of Latin literature points to a fatal degeneration in post-Augustan poetry. The ensuing dark age has been interrupted by the recall of the Muses under the Medici. Vida tells us that the *Christiad* was undertaken at the behest of the Medici Pope Leo X, who is said to have adapted Propertius' announcement of the *Aeneid*: 'cedite Romani scriptores, cedite Graii / nescio quid maius nascitur Aeneide' ('give way writers of Rome and Greece, something greater than the *Aeneid* is coming to birth'). As Virgil decked himself in the spoils of Homer and improved on his model, so we may read behind Vida's professions of modesty the ambition of taking a loftier Christian flight with the feathers of Virgil.

The architecture of the *Christiad* is Virgilian in scope and control. The main action occupies the space of a few days, from a point shortly before the Entry into Jerusalem to the Ascension, with a coda on Pentecost. True to his own precept in the *De Arte Poetica*, (2.66–8) Vida launches the reader at a point near to the end; the narrative begins: 'iam prope mortis erant metae finisque laborum' ('and now the goal of death was at hand to end his labours', 1.15). In the *De Arte Poetica* he has in mind a plot like that of the *Aeneid*, where the hero must face many unexpected diversions before the journey from Sicily to the promised land of Italy may be completed. Christ, of course, is not that kind of wanderer, and the diversions that the reader will be led through take the form of catalogue, ecphrasis, song and flashback. The description of the Temple in 1 and the Song of Simon in 2 relate the Six Days of Creation and episodes from the Old Testament; the prophecies of the Father at the ends of 1 and 6, reworking the speeches of Jupiter in *Aeneid* 1 and 12, look forward to the universal triumph of the church seated in a Christian Rome and to the celebration of Christ on the banks of the rivers of Cremona.[39] The central Books 3 and 4, a third of the poem (and two books, as with Aeneas' narrative to Dido), are taken up with narratives of the life of Christ related before the tribunal of Pilate, the Latinus-like just man unable to calm the storm of hatred: in 3 Joseph tells of the birth and early life of Jesus, up to the beginning of the Ministry; in 4 John is inspired to tell of First Things, the Trinity and the Falls of Angels and of Man, before taking up the story of Jesus' life from the time of the Baptism and concluding with Christ's prophecy of the Second Coming. Like Milton, Vida skilfully imitates Virgil's telling of a spatially and temporally limited story in such a way as to include reference to the widest canvas of universal history, cosmological and human.

The *De Arte Poetica* discusses imitation in a section on the choice of words (*dictio*). Petrarch was anxious not to imitate *verbatim*; for Vida the *verba ipsa* are fair game (3.215). The possibility of an imitation that goes beyond a frigid classicizing correctness is opened up by a congruence between the terms Vida uses for talking about imitation and about figurative language. Borrowed words are 'spoils', *exuviae* (3.213), an image used earlier of metaphorical words used to dress up the basic subject (3.47) and also of Virgil's 'plundering' of Homer (2.551); metaphor and imitation are both viewed as acts of metamorphosis or of expropriation. At 3.234ff. imitative 'theft' is compared to Aeneas' 'translation' of 'the throne of Asia and the *penates* of Troy' to Latium, on whose soil they flourished more greatly than in their native home; this is one of the many places in *De Arte Poetica* where Vida hints at the interconvertibility of the themes and poetics of epic in a way that anticipates some modern critical approaches. Vida speaks of imitation where 'dictis nihil ordine verso / longe alios iisdem sensus mira arte dedere' ('using the same words with no change in order they produced quite other senses through their wonderful art', 3.225–6); the language is close to Quintilian's definition of the trope of allegory (*Inst. Or.* 8.6.44 'presenting one thing in the words, another in the sense'). To see imitation as a kind of trope opens the way to a much more dynamic and pleasurable reading of the *Christiad*.

Vida's ideal reader is one who from early childhood has immersed himself in Virgil, alive to echoes at the smallest verbal level.[40] Yet this patchwork technique coexists with allusive manipulation at the thematic level. An example: in Book 2 we attend an epic banquet whose host is also an epic bard versed in astronomical lore; this banquet is the Last Supper, and the biblical Iopas is Simon. A description of the regal trappings of the feast that echoes Dido's banquet in *Aeneid* 1 is followed by mention of a baleful presence: 'una inter dirus Iudas / dissimulans sedet et vultu mentitur amorem' ('in their midst sits the accursed dissembler Judas wearing a mask of love', 2.649–50). We remember the dissimulating traitor at the banquet of Dido, Amor himself, who also puts on a feigned countenance, as Venus instructs him to: 'tu faciem illius . . . / falle dolo et notos pueri puer indue vultus' ('counterfeit his [Ascanius'] face and put on the familiar features of the child, child as you are', *Aen.* 1.683–4). Here the *verba ipsa* are mostly not reproduced, as they are in another allusion to the same Virgilian passage. At *Aeneid* 1.716 the disguised Cupid embraces Aeneas before making for Dido: 'et magnum falsi implevit genitoris amorem' ('and satisfied the greedy love of a father not his own'). The last four words with one change are repeated at *Christiad* 3.917: 'implebat veri genitoris amorem' ('satisfied the love of His true Father'). Joseph, recounting the childhood of Christ, tells of His obedience to His mother and to himself at the same time as He 'satisfied the love of His true father'. It is Joseph who is the *falsus genitor*, who has taken the place, as foster-father, of the child's true, heavenly, Father, just as Cupid takes the place of the true son of Aeneas at the Carthaginian banquet; but at the same time recollection of the Virgilian original points to the similarity between *this* divine child sent down from above and the child Cupid sent down by Venus. In the line before, Vida plays with another line from the Virgilian scene: 'carae et mandata facessere matris' ('he carried out His dear mother's instructions', 3.916), alludes to *Aeneid* 1.689, 'paret Amor dictis carae genetricis' ('Cupid obeys his dear mother's words'). But where obedience to the pagan goddess of love will lead to the destruction of human relationships, the infant Christ's obedience to His 'mother' symbolizes harmony in the human family and also the coming reconciliation of God and Man.

This cunning use of details in the Virgilian text contributes to wider thematic structures. Let us start with the importance of love, *amor*, in the *Christiad*. It is love that prompts the Father to sacrifice his son for mankind (2.863); God is Love in the person of the Holy Ghost (4.40–2), the Spirit that fills the Virgin at the Annunciation and the disciples at Pentecost, and which the poet Vida calls down for his own inspiration.[41] Love draws the disciples to Christ (4.809), and the Magdalene at the Tomb is afflicted with the same wound as Dido (6.351); in a parody of the motif Satan rebukes Judas for his attachment to Christ in terms appropriate for the deluded elegiac or Lucretian lover (2.95ff.). The final interview with the Father, in which the Son asks for the gift of the Spirit for the disciples (6.815–97), is modelled on the Virgilian seduction of Vulcan by Venus, and the discreet eroticism of that passage, of the marriage of Sky and Earth at *Georgic* 2.325–35, and of the less explicit Lucretian discussions of sexual love, is shed over a surprisingly large number of passages in the *Christiad*. As well as an epic of *pietas* in the Virgilian manner, Vida offers us a vision of an epic world where love is creative rather than destructive, as in the *Aeneid*.

Second, the theme of the god unrecognized, the subject of local episodes in the *Aeneid*, becomes a central theme of the *Christiad*. Not only that, but the wider issue of knowledge and ignorance, truth and falsehood is the source of the major dichotomies of the poem, frequently concretized in literal and figurative uses of a contrast between light and darkness (life/death, Heaven/Hell, insight/blindness). At several points mention is made of puzzles and enigmas: Christ is the interpreter of the 'arcane signs' carved on the marble of the Temple (1.587–80, 691–2), aniconic hieroglyphs of the Creation and types of the Crucifixion; Christ Himself uses indirect language ('nunc caecis vera involvens ambagibus ultro', 'now deliberately wrapping the truth in dark puzzles', 4.1031, echoing Virgil's description of the Sibyl's speech, *Aen.* 6.99–100), and talks of the secret meaning of Jewish ritual, hidden to its practitioners:

> nec priscos tollo ritus, legesve refigo.
> quippe alia arcanis longe sententia dictis
> indeprensa latet. longe altera sacra teguntur
> nube sub obscura verborum.[42]
>
> (*Christiad* 1.811–14)

I do not abolish the ancient practices or unmake the laws. For a quite different meaning lies undetected under those mysterious words, and a quite different religion is concealed in the dark mist of words.

But the *Christiad* does not veil its subject in allegory; the failure to understand signs and prophecies as a result of mental blindness or darkness is a recurrent theme within the narrative, but Vida does not dramatize the knowledge and ignorance of the Christian reader in the way that Milton does. For Vida the crucial point is that his reader lives after the events narrated, and is in the position of Cleophas who says, after the Supper at Emmaus:

> atque equidem, memini, nuper media urbe canebat,
> obscura sed verborum rem ambage tegebat.
> nunc autem manifesta patent, nunc omnia aperta,
> nube palam ablata, nec spes fovistis inanes.[43]
>
> (*Christiad* 6.520–3)

Indeed I remember that he recently prophesied these things in the heart of the city, but veiled his message in dark and puzzling words. *But now* all lies open to view, freed from the cloud, and your hopes were not vain.

However, the way in which the poem negotiates its relationship to its great pagan model the *Aeneid* may be described as allegorical; there is an analogy between the surface and depth of a parable or a type, and the Virgilian *verba* reused to express a Christian *res*. Vida is a precursor of Milton in the way that he transvalues and inverts the main Virgilian themes in order to bring out the lines of a truly Christian heroism and a truly Christian mission.[44]

In both the *Aeneid* and the *Christiad* the hero is a unique suffering individual but also a man of supra-individual importance. Aeneas' story is also the story of every Roman leader and of Rome itself; it is, of course, easier for the hero of the Christian poem to be the representative of the race; Christ becomes Man as much as He is incarnated as a man. Christ is unique, alone, but also all in one (or one for all). There is much play on *unus* and *omnes*, or *multi*, in this poem. The Virgilian tag *unum pro multis* ('one for many'), used at *Aeneid* 5.815 by Neptune of the necessary sacrifice of Palinurus for the salvation of the Trojan race, is inevitably a favourite of Vida's. It is used more truly than he knows by Caiaphas in his speech for the prosecution, at 2.249, and with (by now) full understanding by the virtuous dead at 6.174. At 1.880 an allusion to the Palinurus prophecy in the mouth of the Father refers not to Christ but to Judas – 'unus erit tantum', 'there will be but one . . . '. This is the first of a number of hints that Judas is a parodic double of Christ, culminating in the manner of his death at the beginning of Book 5, a freely chosen act of expiation, as is also the death of Christ narrated at the end of the book; but Judas' death is a journey from light into darkness and annihilation. The universal significance of the localized history is also brought out by the repeated appeal to an audience of *seri nepotes*, 'descendants in ages hereafter', for whom the life of Christ is both exemplary and existentially determinative. Pentecost enables a universal and timeless presence of Christ ('ego praesens adero omnibus', 'I will be present to you all', 6.640).[45] In the penultimate line this significance is expressed aetiologically: 'protinus hinc populos Christi de nomine dicunt / Christiadas', 'from that time they call the peoples of Christ Christians [literally "sons of Christ"]' (6.984–5), as the Romans are called by Virgil *Aeneadae*.

The epic values of the *Christiad* are a revaluation of the pagan values. Virgil is challenged in the opening invocation of the poem, a seven-line sentence corresponding to the seven-line sentence that opens the *Aeneid*:

> qui mare, qui terras, qui caelum numine comples
> spiritus alme, tuo liceat mihi munere regem
> bis genitum canere, e superi qui sede parentis
> Virginis intactae gravidam descendit in alvum,
> mortalesque auras hausit puer, ut genus ultus
> humanum eriperet tenebris, et carcere iniquo
> morte sua, manesque pios inferret Olympo.

Nurturing Spirit, who fills sea, earth and sky with your power, grant that by your gift I may sing of the twice begotten king who came down from the seat of His celestial father into the womb of the immaculate Virgin, and who as a boy drew the breath of mortality, that He might avenge the human race and by His death

snatch man from the shadows of his evil prison and lead the pious
dead to Heaven.

Replacing the Virgilian first-person *cano* is an invocation to the Holy
Ghost in language that reworks the Lucretian invocation of Venus at
the beginning of the *De Rerum Natura*. Vida carefully avoids calling his
hero *vir*, 'man' (unlike Milton's 'one greater man'), and instead
chooses the noun *rex*, 'king'. The nature of Christ's kingship is, of
course, one of the chief areas of misunderstanding of His mission; in
truth He is far from being one of the earthly kings, traditional subject
matter of epic. In both Virgil and Vida the substantive (*vir*, *rex*) is
followed by a relative clause describing a journey, and a final clause
describing the purpose of the journey. In the case of Vida the purpose
is another journey that with the first journey completes a circle: Christ
is the king who descends from His Father's throne in order to lead back
the human race in a reascent to Heaven. It is the second leg of the
journey that corresponds to the journey of Aeneas and his Trojans from
Troy to Italy (and which had often enough been allegorized as the
spiritual journey of the Christian virtuous man).[46] In each author the
final word of the sentence also marks the final goal of the epic: for
Virgil *Romae*, for Vida *Olympo*. The imperial city is replaced by a
kingdom not of this earth; but in this most emphatic of positions Vida
chooses a pagan word. In *Olympo* we have an emblem of the fusion of
antique form and Christian content that is Vida's goal as a poet.

The heroism and labours of Christ differ qualitatively from those of
Aeneas.[47] The *pax* that is as much the goal of this epic (4.893ff., 6.631)
as of the *Aeneid* is a peace not of this world; Christ's triumph leads to
the heights of Heaven, not of the Capitol (the analogy with Roman
triumph, introduced in Satan's speech in the infernal council at
1.190–2, becomes insistent in the last book, culminating in the simile at
6.701–7, which compares the reception of the ascending Christ by the
angels to the return to Rome of a triumphing consul). In the *Aeneid* the
theme of triumph reverses the theme of exile; in the *Christiad* the one
rather complements the other. At the beginning of the narrative
(1.18–24) the crowd that accompanies Jesus as he returns to Jerusalem
is described in language that alludes to Virgil's description of the
Trojan survivors gathering round Aeneas to go into exile (*Aen.*
2.796–800). But this group of 'exiles' is travelling *towards* a city,
Jerusalem, that will put its leader to death. Earthly cities are irrelevant.

At 5.694–702, after the attempt of the Angels to launch an armed
rescue of Jesus on the largest scale has been frustrated by the Father, a
simile compares their agony as they watch the Crucifixion to the
distress felt by the partisans of the worsted combatant in a duel. Botta
may be right to see an allusion to the regrettable popularity of duelling

in sixteenth-century Italy, but Vida's ideal reader will not miss the echoes of the confrontation of Turnus and Aeneas in *Aeneid* 12. The effect is twofold: first, this is a conflict that is *not* to be decided by superior force of arms (Vida's war in Heaven is much more of a farce than is Milton's); second, and shockingly, Christ is implicitly compared to the loser in the *Aeneid*, Turnus. But, as we have seen, this is an epic where defeat and disgrace are paradoxically the means to triumph, where the youthful victim of a *funus acerbum*, 'premature death', is true victor.

This power of Jesus' mission to make all things new is expressed in the repeated use of *longe alius*, 'far other'. The seductress Mary comes to see Jesus with amorous designs, but when she looks on his divine beauty, 'alias longe concepit pectore flammas' ('a quite different fire was kindled in her breast', 1.345). At 6.546–9 Christ on the road to Emmaus plays with both the spatial and figurative sense of *alius*: 'non illum . . . agnovimus ante / quam . . . parvamque subivimus urbem, / namque iter ulterius fingentem, seque ferentem/longe alias sedes petere' ('we did not recognize him until we entered the small town, for he made out that he was journeying further and said that he was heading for a quite different place'). For those who have ears to understand, this onward journey is qualitatively other than the journey of Cleophas and Amaon to a human city. *Longe alius* expresses both the making different of history at the Incarnation and the Christian epic poet's transformation of his beloved classical models.

NOTES

1 Partial surveys of the field in: Belloni 1912: chs 4 (fifteenth-century historical and encomiastic epics), 11 (religious epic), 12 (mythological epics); Zabughin 1921: ch. 5 (chronicle-type courtly epics of the fifteenth century); Zabughin 1923: ch. 4 (religious epics of the sixteenth century); van Tieghem 1944: ch. 6.

2 The standard edition is by Festa 1926a, rev. Fraenkel 1927. The older edition by Corradini 1874 includes useful notes on sources and parallels. Important new work on the text has been done by Fera 1984, who promises a new edition. English translation with basic notes: Bergin and Wilson 1977. The best modern study is Bernardo 1962; see also Kallendorf 1989: ch. 2, with extensive bibliographical notes. Still useful are Carlini 1902 and Festa 1926b.

3 For an excellent recent characterization of the man in his works see Mann 1984.

4 For a comparison of the use of Livy in the *Africa* and in Silius Italicus' *Punica* (a work not available to Petrarch) see von Albrecht 1964.

5 Petrarch's immersion in all the classical texts available in his day makes of him an almost mediumistic imitator of Ennius. One wonders how far the wish to animate an improved reconstruction of Ennius lies behind the *Africa*. See Suerbaum 1972a.

6 On Petrarch's relation to Virgil: de Nolhac 1907: ch. 3; Seagraves 1976; some good close analyses of individual passages in Foster 1979.

7 Detailed parallels in Bruère 1961.

8 There are several lacunae in the poem, and it is not certain that the poem was not projected in more than nine books.

9 Lucan's simile at *Phar.* 1.135–43 comparing Pompey to a mighty but moribund tree is reworked at *Africa* 2.318–22 in the comparison of Rome in decay to an aged lion still king of the forest.

10 Fera 1984.

11 Greene 1982: 99.

12 Velli 1976: 190, 198.

13 Despite Petrarch's evident disdain for Dante there is perhaps a regret that he could not introduce himself into his epic as an immediate spectator in the way that Dante is involved at first hand in his epic. See Bernardo 1955.

14 On the Prologue see Carrara 1931; Velli 1965.

15 The pair suggests, though it does not make explicit, the peace/war dichotomy of *Aen.* 1.544–5: 'quo iustior alter / nec pietate fuit, nec bello maior nec armis' ('[a king] than whom none was more just in doing his duty, none was greater in warfare'), while the phrasing echoes Virgil's own Proem: 'insignem pietate virum' ('a man outstanding in piety', *Aen.* 1.10), 'belloque superbum' ('proud in war', *Aen.* 1.21).

16 Homer's language of escape to an audience at 176, 'huc ego vix tandem reserato carcere Ditis' ('I come here at last having barely unlocked the prison of Hades'), is paralleled in Boccaccio's appeal to Petrarch's epic to go public, *ad Africam* 32: 'tristesque domos et carceris umbras / linque fuga celeri' ('fly swiftly from your gloomy abode and prison shades').

17 An access that Petrarch conjures up in the letters in the *Familiares* addressed to Homer, Cicero and Virgil.

18 Petrarch as Marcellus: with *Aen.* 6.861, 870–1 cf. *Africa* 9.220–1, 274.

19 See the highly suggestive essay by Smarr 1982.

20 Greene 1982: 93 speaks of 'the necromantic superstition at the heart of the humanist enlightenment'.

21 The *Africa* is closely and intricately related to the *Vita Scipionis* in the *De Viris Illustribus*: see Bernardo 1962: chs 2, 6.

22 Could Petrarch have known that? Or that the first edition of the *Annales* also in a sense ended with poetry, with the Temple of Hercules and the Muses?

23 The *laureatio* speech takes as its text another passage from the *Georgics*, 3.291–2: 'sed me Parnasi deserta per ardua dulcis / raptat amor' ('but sweet love snatches me over the empty heights of Parnassus'); later in the speech Petrarch quotes Statius, who he believed was the last ancient poet to have undergone the *laureatio* that he was reviving for himself. On the *laureatio*: Wilkins 1943; Suerbaum 1972b. The *laureatio* speech is edited by Godi 1970.

24 Bernardo 1962: 51 n. 4.

25 This may be understood as obedience to the imperative of imitating an *exemplum*. In the *Vita Scipionis* Petrarch boasts of having adopted Scipio's own habit of modelling his personal life on past greats – imitation of imitation!

26 Foster 1979.

27 Bernardo 1962: 61–2. Smarr 1982 discerns other hints of a Christian under-sense, for example in the image of the serpent of the Carthaginians (2.103ff., 6.544ff.) pointing to Scipio's victory over Hannibal as a figure of Christ's victory over sin.

28 Petrarch tends to present the struggle between Rome and Carthage in schematic, dualistic, terms, so that the whole war comes to be seen in terms of psychomachy, *fraus* vs *virtus*; see especially 2.62ff. for the line-up of Virtues and Vices.

29 Kallendorf 1989: 40.

30 In general compare the way in which the recurrent use of elegiac language and motifs in *Aeneid* 4 suggests an alternative view of the world to the dominant epic one.

31 The threads are drawn tighter in *Secretum* 3, where Augustinus compares Petrarch's love of Laura to the sixteen years during which Hannibal plagued Rome; Petrarch will have been well aware that Virgil's Dido functions as a prefiguration of Hannibal.

32 Basini 1794.

33 Most conveniently available in Brinton 1930, who also prints the English translations of Gavin Douglas (1515) and of Thomas Twyne (1584). More scholarly is the edition of Schneider 1985. For critical discussion, Zabughin 1921: 281ff.; Hijmans 1971–2; Kallendorf 1989: ch. 5. Vegio was also the author of an *Astyanactis*, a supplement to the *Iliad* on the fate of Astyanax; an *Antoniad* on St Antony, and a mythological epic on the Golden Fleece.

34 An excellent survey and discussion of biblical epic in Lewalski 1966: ch. 3. See also Roberts 1985; Kirkconnell 1952, with a catalogue of biblical poems.

35 A new critical edition by Fantazzi and Perosa 1988.

36 The English reader is well served by di Cesare 1964, 1974. English translation: Drake and Forbes 1978.

37 For Milton's praise of Vida see *The Passion* 26: 'Loud o'er the rest Cremona's trump doth sound.'

38 Edited with parallel English translation and commentary by Williams 1976.

39 Vida's inclusion of himself in the prophecy seems to allude to Ennius' vision of Petrarch at the end of the *Africa*: with *Christiad* 6.881–2 cf. *Africa* 9.404–9.

40 Vida's practice is described thus by his sixteenth-century commentator Bartolomeo Botta: 'decerptis apum more vergiliano ex poemate verborum flosculis, ac sententiarum' ('bee-like plucking flowerlets of words and thoughts from Virgil's poem').

41 As in the case of *Paradise Lost* there is a strong convergence between the experience of the poet and the experience of his characters, above all in the parallelism between the poet's mental flight through the heavens at 2.324–30 and the rapture of John at 4.4–9 and the rapture of the disciples at Pentecost, 6.953ff. The description of the inspiration of the disciples at 6.928ff. is close to the account of poetic inspiration in the 1517 version of *De Arte Poetica*, 2.591ff.

42 The last four words of the Latin are reminiscent of Ennius' account of poetic 'veiling' in Petrarch's *Africa* 9.93–4.

43 See also the Magdalene's reaction to the type of Jonah sculpted on the Tomb of Christ, 6.361–2: 'veterum agnosco non vana futuri / signa' ('I recognize the ancients' signs, full of the future').

44 Not that this is new to biblical epic: see Brooke 1987: 286.

45 Cf. *Aen.* 4.386 (Dido's threat): 'omnibus umbra locis adero', 'I shall be present everywhere as a shade'.

46 On 1.59 Botta comments that by his use of the first speech of Aeneas at *Aen.* 1.198–207 Vida points to an interpretation of Aeneas' journey as a pilgrimage through the 'sea' of this world; 'unde quidam versus illos sic mutavit, "per varios casus per tot discrimina rerum tendimus in caelum"',

'consequently some have altered those verses "through varied fortunes and many dangers we journey to heaven"' (for *caelum Aen.* 1.205 has *Latium*; the same substitution is suggested by Vegio, *De Perseverantia Religionis* 1.5).

47 Cf. *Paradise Lost* 9.31–2: 'the better fortitude Of patience and heroic martyrdom'.

REFERENCES

Ackerman, R. (1896) *Lucans Pharsalia in den Dichtungen Shellys.* Zweibrücken.
Ahl, F.M. (1976) *Lucan: An Introduction.* Ithaca/London.
—— (1984a) 'The Art of Safe Criticism in Greece and Rome', *AJP* 105: 174–208.
—— (1984b) 'The Rider and the Horse: Politics and Power in Roman Poetry from Horace to Statius', *ANRW* 2 32.1.40–110.
—— (1985) *Metaformations: Soundplay and Wordplay in Latin Poetry.* Ithaca/London.
—— (1986) 'Statius' "Thebaid": A Reconsideration', *ANRW* 2 32.5.2803–912.
—— (1989a) 'Uilix Mac Leirtis: The Classical Hero in Irish Metamorphosis', in Rosanna Warren (ed.) *The Art of Translation: Voices from the Field*: 173–98. Boston.
—— (1989b) 'Homer, Vergil, and Complex Narrative Structures in Latin Epic', in Marcovich 1989: 1–31.
Ahl, F. M., Davis, M. A. and Pomeroy, A. (1986) 'Silius Italicus', *ANRW* 2.32.4:2492–561.
Albrecht, M. von (1964) *Silius Italicus.* Amsterdam.
Alfonsi, L. (1977) 'Considerazioni sul Vergilianesimo del *Waltharius*', in G. Varanini and P. Pinagli (eds) *Studi filologici letterari e storici in memoria di Guido Favati*: 3–14. Padua.
Allen, W. jr (1940) 'The Epyllion: A Chapter in the History of Literary Criticism', *TAPA* 71: 1–26.
—— (1958) 'The Non-existent Classical Epyllion', *Studies in Philology* 55: 515–18.
Anderson, W. S. (1969) *The Art of the Aeneid.* Englewood Cliffs.
—— (1973) 'The *Heroides*', in J. W. Binns (ed.) *Ovid*: 49–83. London.
Andreae, B. (1981) *The Art of Rome.* New York.
Arkins, B. (1982) *Sexuality in Catullus.* Hildesheim.
Assouline, P. (1990) *An Artful Life. A Biography of D. H. Kahnweiler, 1884–1979.* Tr. Charles Ruas. New York.
Auerbach, E. (1965) *Literary Language and its Public in Late Latin Antiquity and in the Middle Ages.* New York.
Austin, R. G. (ed.) (1963) *P. Vergilii Maronis Aeneidos Liber Quartus.* Oxford.
—— (ed.) (1977) *P. Vergili Maronis Aeneidos Liber Sextus.* Oxford.
Badian, E. (1972) 'Ennius and his Friends', in *Ennius, Entretiens Hardt* 17: 149–208. Geneva.
Bakhtin, M. M. (1981) *The Dialogic Imagination: Four Essays.* Ed. M. Holquist. Tr. C. Emerson and M. Holquist. Austin.
—— (1984) *Rabelais and his World.* Tr. H. Iswolsky. Bloomington.

Baldwin, B. (1982) 'Literature and Society in the Later Roman Empire', in Gold 1982: 67–83.

Bardon, H. (1943) *L'Art de la composition chez Catulle*. Paris.

—— (1952) *La Littérature latine inconnue. I. L'Epoque républicaine*. Paris.

—— (1956) *La Littérature latine inconnue. II. L'Epoque imperiale*. Paris.

Barlow, C. W. (1938) *Epistolae Senecae ad Paulum et Pauli ad Senecam <Quae Vocantur>*. Horn, Austria.

Barthes, R. (1977) *On Racine*. New York.

Basini, B. (1794) *Basini Parmensis Poetae Opera Praestantiora* I. Rimini.

Bassett, E. L. (1966) 'Hercules and the Hero of the *Punica*', in L. Wallach (ed.) *The Classical Tradition. Studies in Honor of H. Caplan*: 258–73. Ithaca/London.

Bate, A. K. (1978) *Waltharius of Geraldus*. Reading.

Belloni, A. (1912) *Il poema epico e mitologico*. Milan.

Bergin, T. G. and Wilson, A. S. (eds and trs) (1977) *Petrarch's Africa*. New Haven/London.

Bernardo, A. S. (1955) 'Petrarch's Attitude toward Dante', *Proc. Mod. Lang. Assoc.* 70: 500–17.

—— (1962) *Petrarch, Scipio and the Africa*. Baltimore.

Bilinski, B. (1954) *Rôle idéologique de la tragédie romaine sous la république*. Wroclaw.

Bing, P. (1988) *The Well-Read Muse: Past and Present in Callimachus and the Hellenistic Poets*. Göttingen.

Bishop, J. (1985) 'Bishops as Marital Advisers in the Ninth Century', in J. Kirshner and S. F. Wemple (eds) *Women of the Medieval World*: 54–84. Oxford.

Boës, J. (1986) 'Le Mythe d'Achille vu par Catulle: Importance de l'amour pour une morale de la gloire', *REL* 64: 104–15.

Bonds, W. S. (1985) 'Two Combats in the *Thebaid*', *TAPA* 115: 225–35.

Bongie, E. B. (1977) 'Heroic Elements in the *Medea* of Euripides', *TAPA* 107: 27–56.

Borges, J. L. (1964) 'Pierre Menard, Author of the Quixote', in D. Yates and J. Irby (eds), *Labyrinths*: 36–45. New York.

Bowra, C. M. (1948) *From Virgil to Milton*. London.

—— (1952) *Heroic Poetry*. London.

—— (1966) *Poetry and Politics 1900–1960*. Cambridge.

Boyle, A. J. (ed.) (1976) *The Eclogues of Virgil*. Melbourne.

—— (1977) 'Virgil's Pastoral Echo', *Ramus* 6: 121–31.

—— (ed.) (1983) *Seneca Tragicus*. Berwick.

—— (1986) *The Chaonian Dove: Studies in the Eclogues, Georgics and Aeneid of Virgil*. Leiden.

—— (ed.) (1988) *The Imperial Muse: To Juvenal Through Ovid*. Berwick.

—— (ed.) (1990) *The Imperial Muse: Flavian Epicist to Claudian*. Bendigo.

Boyle, A. J. and Sullivan, J. P. (eds) (1991) *Roman Poets of the Early Empire*. Harmondsworth.

Braga, D. (1950) *Catullo e i poeti greci*. Messina/Florence.

Bramble, J. C. (1970) 'Structure and Ambiguity in Catullus LXIV', *PCPS* 16: 22–41.

Bremer, J. M. (1975) 'The Meadow of Love', *Mnemosyne* 28: 268–80.

Bright, D. F. (1987) *The Miniature Epic in Vandal Africa*. Norman/London.

Brinton, A. C. (1930) *Maphaeus Vegius and his Thirteenth Book of the Aeneid*. Stanford.

Brisset, J. (1964) *Les Idées politiques de Lucain*. Paris.

Brooke, M. (1987) '*Interpretatio Christiana*: Imitation and Polemic in Late Antique Epic', in M. Whitby et al. (eds) *Homo Viator: Classical Essays for John Bramble*: 285–95. Bristol.

315

Brooks, R. A. (1953) '*Discolor Aura*: Reflections on the Golden Bough', *AJP* 74: 260–80. Rpt Commager 1966: 143–63.

Brown, P. (1980) 'Art and Society in Late Antiquity', in Weitzmann 1980: 17–27.

Bruère, R. T. (1958) '*Color Ovidianus* in Silius *Punica* 1–7', in N. Herescu (ed.) *Ovidiana*: 475–99. Paris.

—— (1959) '*Color Ovidianus* in Silius *Punica* 8–17', *CP* 54: 228–45.

—— (1961) 'Lucan and Petrarch's *Africa*', *CP* 56: 83–99.

Brundage, J. A. (1987) *Law, Sex and Christian Society in Medieval Europe*. Chicago.

Büchner, K. (1982) *Fragmenta Poetarum Latinorum*. Leipzig. Rev. of Morel 1963.

Bühler, W. (1960) *Die Europa des Moschos*. Wiesbaden.

Burck, E. (ed.) (1979a) *Das römische Epos*. Darmstadt.

—— (1979b) 'Die Thebais des Statius', in Burck 1979a: 300–51.

—— (1984) *Silius Italicus: Hannibal in Capua und die Rücheroberung der Stadt durch die Römer*. Mainz.

Burian, P. (1985) 'Logos and Pathos: The Politics of the Suppliant Women', in P. Burian (ed.) *Directions in Euripidean Criticism: A Collection of Essays*: 129–55. Durham, NC.

Cairns, F. (1984) 'The Nereids of Catullus 64.12–23b', *GB* 11:95–101.

—— (1989) *Virgil's Augustan Epic*. Cambridge.

Cameron, A. (1970) *Claudian: Poetry and Propaganda at the Court of Honorius*. Oxford.

—— (1974) 'Claudian', in J. W. Binns (ed.) *Latin Literature of the Fourth Century*: 134–59. London.

Camp, J. Mck. (1989) 'The Philosophical Schools of Roman Athens', in S. Walker and A. Cameron (eds) *The Greek Renaissance in the Roman Empire*: 50–5, pls 8–12. London.

Carlini, A. (1902) *Studio su l'Africa di F. Petrarca*. Florence.

Carrara, E. (1931) 'Sulla soglia dell' *Africa*', *Studj Romanzi* 21: 117–37.

Carroll, B. H. (1952) 'An Essay on the Walther legend', *Florida State University Studies* 5: 123–79.

—— (1953) 'On the Lineage of the Walther legend', *Germanic Review* 28: 34–41.

Cizek, E. (1982) *Néron*. Paris.

Clark, J. (1973) *A History of Epic Poetry (Post-Virgilian)*. New York. Rpt of 1900 edn.

Clausen, W. (1964) 'Callimachus and Latin Poetry', *GRBS* 5: 181–96.

Clay, J. S. (1989) *The Politics of Olympus: Form and Meaning in the Major Homeric Hymns*. Princeton.

Colace, P. R. (1982) 'Il Nuovo Callimaco di Lille, Ovidio e Stazio', *RFIC* 110: 140–9.

Cole, T. (1969) 'The Saturnian Verse', *YCS* 21: 3–73.

Coleman, K. M. (1986) 'The Emperor Domitian and Literature', *ANRW* 2.32.5: 3087–115.

—— (1988) *Statius Silvae IV*. Oxford.

Colish, M. L. (1985) *The Stoic Tradition from Antiquity to the Early Middle Ages*, vol. I. Leiden.

Colton, R. (1979) 'Some Greek and Latin Poets on the Abduction of Hylas', *CO* 20: 107–8.

Commager, S. (ed.) (1966) *Virgil: A Collection of Critical Essays*. Englewood Cliffs.

Conte, G. B. (1984) *Virgilio: Il genere e i suoi confini*. Milan.

—— (1986) *The Rhetoric of Imitation: Genre and Poetic Memory in Vergil and Other Latin Poets*. Ed. Charles Segal. Ithaca/London.

Cornell, T. (1986) Rev. of Skutsch 1985, *JRS* 76: 244–50.

Corradini (ed.) (1874) 'F. Petrarca: Africa', in *Padova a F. Petrarca nel quinto centenario della sua morte*. Padua.

Courtney, E. (ed.) (1970) *C. Valerii Flacci Argonauticon Libri Octo.* Leipzig.

Croce, B. (1902) *Estetica come scienza dell'espressione e linguistica generale,* Trani. Tr. D. Aimslee (1909). London.

—— (1936) *Poesia.* Bari. Tr. G. Gullace (1981) *Poetry and Literature.* Carbondale.

Curran, L. C. (1969) 'Catullus 64 and the Heroic Age', *YCS* 21: 171–92.

—— (1975) '"Nature to Advantage Dressed": Propertius 1.2', *Ramus* 4: 1–16.

Curtius, E. R. (1953) *European Literature and the Latin Middle Ages.* Tr. W. R. Trask. London.

Daltrop, G., Hausman, U., and Wegner, M. (1966) *Die Flavier: Das römische Herrscherbild.* Berlin.

Davies, M. (1989) *The Epic Cycle.* Bristol.

Davis, M. (1990) '*Ratis Audax*: Valerius Flaccus' Bold Ship', in Boyle 1990: 46–73.

de Battaglia, O. F. (ed.) (1930) *Dictatorship on its Trial.* Tr. Huntley Paterson with an Introduction by Winston S. Churchill. London.

Degrassi, A. (1957) *Inscriptiones Latinae Liberae Rei Publicae.* Florence.

Deroux, C. (1973) 'L'Identité de Lesbie', *ANRW* 1.3: 390–416.

Detienne, M. (1979) *Dionysos Slain.* Baltimore.

di Cesare, M. A. (1964) *Vida's Christiad and Vergilian Epic.* New York/London.

—— (1974) *Bibliotheca Vidiana. A Bibliography of Marco Girolamo Vida.* Florence.

Drake, G. C. and Forbes, C. A. (1978) *The Christiad: A Latin–English Edition.* Carbondale.

Dronke, P. (1984) *Women Writers of the Middle Ages.* Cambridge.

duBois, P. (1982) *History, Rhetorical Description and the Epic from Homer to Spenser.* Cambridge.

Dubrow, H. (1982) *Genre.* London/New York.

Duby, G. (1983) *The Knight, the Lady and the Priest: the Making of Modern Marriage in Medieval France.* Tr. B. Bray. Harmondsworth.

Duckworth, G. E. (1962) *Structural Patterns and Proportions in Vergil's Aeneid.* Ann Arbor.

Duff, J. Wight (1927) *A Literary History of Rome in the Silver Age.* London.

—— (1964) Third edn, London.

Dyck, A. R. (1989) 'On the Way from Colchis to Corinth: Medea in Book 4 of the "Argonautica"', *Hermes* 117: 455–70.

Earl, D. C. (1961) *The Political Thought of Sallust.* Cambridge.

—— (1967) *The Moral and Political Tradition of Rome.* London.

Eliot, T. S. (1919) 'Tradition and the Individual Talent', in *Selected Essays* (Third edn, 1951): 13–22. London.

—— (1944) 'What is a Classic?', in *On Poetry and Poets* (1957): 53–71. London.

Ennen, E. (1958) *Les Arts poétiques du XIIe et du XIIIe siècle.* Paris.

—— (1989) *The Medieval Woman.* Tr. E. Jephcott. Oxford.

Euben, J. P. (1990) *The Tragedy of Political Theory: The Road not Taken.* Princeton.

Fantazzi, C. and Perosa, A. (eds) (1988) *J. Sannazaro: De Partu Virginis.* Florence.

Feeney, D. C. (1986) 'Epic Hero and Epic Fable', *Comp. Lit.* 38: 137–58.

—— (1991) *The Gods in Epic. Poets and Critics of the Classical Tradition.* Oxford.

Fenik, B. (1959) 'Parallelism of Theme and Imagery in *Aeneid* II and IV', *AJP* 80: 1–24.

Fera, V. (1984) *La revisione petrarchesca dell'Africa.* Messina.

Ferguson, J. (1985) *Catullus.* Lawrence, KA.

Festa, N. (ed.) (1926a) *F. Petrarca: Africa.* Florence.

—— (1926b) *Saggio sull'Africa del Petrarca.* Rome.

Fichter, A. (1982) *Poets Historical: Dynastic Epic in the Renaissance.* New Haven.

Floratos, C. (1957) *Über das 64. Gedicht Catulls.* Athens.

Fordyce, C. J. (ed.) (1961) *Catullus: A Commentary*. Oxford.

Forsyth, P. Y. (1975) 'Catullus 64: The Descent of Man', *Antichthon* 9: 41–51.

—— (1987) 'Catullus 64.400–402: Transposition or Emendation?', *EMC* 31: 329–32.

Foster, J. (1979) 'Petrarch's *Africa*: Ennian and Vergilian Influences', *Papers of the Liverpool Latin Seminar* 2: 277–98.

Foucault, M. (1970) *The Order of Things: An Archaeology of the Human Sciences.* New York.

—— (1979) *Discipline and Punish.* New York.

Fowler, A. (1979) 'Genre and the Literary Canon', *New Literary History* 11: 97–119.

Fraenkel, E. (1927) Rev. of Festa 1926a, *Gnomon* 3: 485–94.

—— (1954) 'The Giants in the Poem of Naevius', *JRS* 44: 14–17.

—— (1935) 'Naevius', *RE Supp.* 6: 622–40.

Frank, E. (1974) 'Works of Art in the Epics of Valerius Flaccus and Silius Italicus', *RIL* 108: 837–44.

Fränkel, H. (1932) 'Griechische Bildung in altrömischen Epen', *Hermes* 67: 303–11.

—— (1935) 'Griechische Bildung in altrömischen Epen II', *Hermes* 70: 59–72.

Friedrich, W.-H. (1968) 'Vorwart', in O. Ribbeck (ed.), *Die römische Tragödie im Zeitalter der republik.* Rpt Hildesheim.

Frye, N. (1971) *Anatomy of Criticism.* Rpt of 1957 edn, Princeton.

Galand, P. (1987) 'Les "fleurs" de l'ecphrasis: autour du rapt de Prosperpine (Ovide, Claudien, Politien)', *Latomus* 46: 87ff.

Galinsky, G. K. (1975) *Ovid's Metamorphoses: An Introduction to the Basic Aspects.* Berkeley.

Garbarino, G. (1973) *Roma e la filosofia greca dalle origini alla fine del ii secolo A. C.,* vol. 1. Turin.

Gentili, G. V. (1959) *La Villa Erculia di Piazza Amerina. I mosaici figurati.* Rome.

Georgii, H. (1891) *Die Antike Aeneiskritik.* Stuttgart. Rpt 1971 Hildesheim.

Giamatti, A. B. (1984) *Exile and Change in Renaissance Literature.* New Haven.

Giangrande, G. (1972) 'Das Epyllion Catulls im Lichte des hellenistischen Epik', *AC* 41: 123–47.

Godi, C. (1970) 'La *Collatio laureationis* del Petrarca', *Italia Medioevale e Umanistica* 13: 13–27.

Gold, B. K. (ed.) (1982) *Literary and Artistic Patronage in Ancient Rome.* Austin.

Goldberg, S. M. (1989) 'Poetry, Politics, and Ennius', *TAPA* 119: 247–61.

Gorler, W. (1987) '*Obtrectatores*', in *Enciclopedia Virgiliana*: 807–13. Rome.

Gossage, A. J. (1972) 'Statius', in D. R. Dudley (ed.) *Neronians and Flavians: Silver Latin I*: 184–235. London/Boston.

Götting, M. (1969) *Hypsipyle in der Thebais des Statius.* Wiesbaden.

Granarolo, J. (1967) *L'Œuvre de Catulle: aspects religieux, éthiques et stylistiques.* Paris.

Gransden, K. W. (1984) *Virgil's Iliad. An Essay on Epic Narrative.* Cambridge.

Grant, M. (1970) *Nero.* London.

Greene, T. M. (1982) *The Light in Troy: Imitation and Discovery in Renaissance Poetry.* New Haven/London.

Grilli, R. (1965) *Studi enniani.* Brescia.

Grillone, A. (1967) *Il sogno nell'epica latina.* Palermo.

Gruen, E. S. (1990) *Studies in Greek Culture and and Roman Policy,* Leiden.

Gruzelier, C. E. (1988) 'Temporal and Timeless in Claudian's *De Raptu Proserpinae*', *G & R* 355: 56–72.

—— 'Claudian: Court Poet as Artist', in Boyle 1990: 299–318.

Gutzwiller, K. J. (1981) *Studies in the Hellenistic Epyllion.* Königstein.

Hague, R. H. (1983) 'Ancient Greek Wedding Songs: The Tradition of Praise', *Journal of Folklore Research* 20: 131–43.

Hainsworth, J. B. (1991) *The Idea of Epic.* Berkeley/Los Angeles.

Hall, J. B. (1969) *Claudian De Raptu Proserpinae.* Cambridge.

Halperin, D. (1990) *One Hundred Years of Homosexuality.* New York.

Hanfmann, G. M.A. (1980) 'The Continuity of Classical Art: Culture, Myth and Faith', in Weitzmann 1980: 75–99.

Hanson, V. D. (1989) *The Western Way of War: Infantry Battle in Classical Greece.* London.

Hardie, C. (1966) *Vitae Vergilianae Antiquae.* Oxford.

Hardie, P. (1983) 'Some Themes from Gigantomachy in the "Aeneid"', *Hermes* 111: 311–26.

—— (1986) *Virgil's Aeneid: Cosmos and Imperium.* Oxford.

—— (1990a) 'Flavian Epicists on Virgil's Epic Technique', in Boyle 1990: 3–20.

—— (1990b) 'Ovid's Theban History: the first "Anti-*Aeneid*"?' *CQ* 40: 224–35.

—— (1993) *The Epic Successors of Virgil. A Study in the Dynamics of a Tradition.* Cambridge.

Harkins, P. W. (1959) 'Autoallegory in Catullus 63 and 64', *TAPA* 90: 102–16.

Harmon, D. P. (1973) 'Nostalgia for the Age of Heroes in Catullus 64', *Latomus* 32: 311–31.

Hatto, A. T. (ed.) (1980) *Traditions of Heroic and Epic Poetry. Vol. I: The Traditions.* London.

Häussler, R. (1978) *Das Historische Epos von Lucan bis Silius und seine Theorie.* Heidelberg.

Heck, E (1970) 'Scipio am Scheideweg. Die *Punica* des Silius Italicus und Ciceros Schrift *De re publica*', *WS* 4 156–80.

Heinze, R. (1919) *Ovids elegische Erzählung.* Leipzig.

Henderson, B. (1903) *The Life and Principate of the Emperor Nero.* London.

Henderson, J. (1988) 'Lucan/The Word at War', in Boyle 1988: 122–64.

—— (1989) 'Not "Women in Roman Satire" but "When Satire writes 'Woman'"', in S. H. Braund (ed.) *Satire and Society in Ancient Rome*: 89–125. Exeter.

—— (1991) 'Statius' *Thebaid*/Form Premade', *PCPS* 37: 30–80.

Henry, E. (1989) *The Vigour of Prophecy: A Study of Virgil's 'Aeneid'.* Bristol.

Heraeus, W. (1930) 'Ein makkaronisches Ovid-fragment bei Quintilian', *RhM* 79: 253–78.

Heydenreich, T. (1970) *Tadel und Lob der Seefahrt.* Heidelberg.

Hijmans, B. L. (1971–2) 'Aeneia Virtus: Vegio's *Supplementum* to the *Aeneid*', *CJ* 67: 144–55.

Hill, B. H. (1972) *Medieval Monarchy in Action: The German Empire from Henry I to Henry IV.* London. (Pp. 118–37 of this book contain an English translation of the *Gesta Ottonis* by Sister B. Bergman.)

Hill, C. (1989) *A Turbulent, Seditious and Factious People: John Bunyan and his Church.* Oxford.

Hinds, S. (1987) *The Metamorphosis of Persephone: Ovid and the Self-Conscious Muse.* Cambridge.

Hirsch, E. D. jr (1967) *Validity in Interpretation.* New Haven, CT.

Holland, R. (1932) *The Lost Generation.* London.

Hollis, A. S. (1990) *Callimachus: Hecale.* Oxford.

Hornsby, R. A. (1970) *Patterns of Action in the Aeneid.* Iowa City.

Hutchinson, G. O. (1988) *Hellenistic Poetry.* Oxford.

Jaeger, C. S. (1985) *The Origins of Courtliness: Civilizing Trends and the Formation of Courtly Ideals.* Philadelphia.

REFERENCES

James, A. W. (1978) 'Night and Day in Epic Narrative From Homer to Quintus of Smyrna', *Museum Philologum Londiniense* 3: 153–83.

Janko, R. (1986) 'The Shield of Heracles and the Legend of Cycnus', *CQ* 36: 38–59.

Jenkyns, R. (1982) *Three Classical Poets: Sappho, Catullus and Juvenal.* London.

Jocelyn, H. (1972) 'The Poems of Quintus Ennius', *ANRW* 1.2: 987–1026.

Johnson, W. R. (1976) *Darkness Visible: A Study of Vergil's Aeneid.* Berkeley/Los Angeles.

—— (1987) *Momentary Monsters: Lucan and his Heroes.* Ithaca/London.

Jones, F. L. (ed.) (1964) *P. B. Shelley, Letters.* Oxford.

Jones, J. W. and Jones, E. F. (eds) (1977) *The Commentary on the First Six Books of the Aeneid Commonly Attributed to Bernardus Sylvestris.* Lincoln, Nebraska.

Juhnke, H. (1972) *Homerisches in römischer Epik flavischer Zeit.* Munich.

Kallendorf, C. (1989) *In Praise of Aeneas: Virgil and Epideictic Rhetoric in the Early Italian Renaissance.* Hanover, NH/London.

Kambylis, A. (1965) *Die Dichterweihe und ihre Symbolik.* Heidelberg.

Kämpff-Dimitriadou, S. (1979) *Die Liebe der Götter in der attischen Kunst des 5. Jahrhunderts v. Chr.* Basel.

Katscher, R. (1973) '*Waltharius* – Dichtung und Dichter', *Mittellateinisches Jahrbuch* 9: 48–120.

Kenney, E. J. (1976) '*Ovidius Prooemians*', *PCPS* 22: 46–53.

Kessels, A. H. M. (1978) *Studies on the Dream in Greek Literature.* Utrecht.

Keuls, E. (1985) *The Reign of the Phallus: Sexual Politics in Ancient Athens.* New York.

Kinsey, T. E. (1965) 'Irony and Structure in Catullus 64', *Latomus* 24: 911–31.

Kirkconnell, W. (1952) *The Celestial Cycle. The Theme of Paradise Lost in World Literature.* Toronto.

Kissel, W. (1979) *Das Geschichtsbild des Silius Italicus.* Frankfurt am Main.

Klingner, F. (1956) 'Catulls Peleus-Epos', *SBAW* 6: 1–92.

Knopp, S. F. (1976) 'Catullus 64 and the Conflict Between *Amores* and *Virtutes*', *CP* 71: 207–13.

Knox, B. M. W. (1950) 'The Serpent and the Flame: The Imagery of the Second Book of the *Aeneid*', *AJP* 71: 379–400. Rpt Commager 1966: 124–42.

—— (1977) 'The *Medea* of Euripides', *YCS* 25: 193–225.

Knox, P. (1986) *Ovid's Metamorphoses and the Traditions of Augustan Poetry.* Cambridge.

Konstan, D. (1977) *Catullus' Indictment of Rome: The Meaning of Catullus 64.* Amsterdam.

Kovacs, D. (1987) 'Ovid, *Metamorphoses* 1.2', *CQ* 37: 458–65.

Kratz, D. M. (1977) 'Quid Waltharius Ruodliebque cum Christo?', in Scholler 1977: 126–49.

—— (1980) *Mocking Epic: Waltharius, Alexandreis and the Problem of Christian Heroism.* Madrid.

—— (ed. and tr.) (1984) *Waltharius and Ruodlieb.* New York.

—— (1987) 'The *Gesta Ottonis* in its Contexts', in Wilson 1987: 201–9.

Kroll, W. (1960) *C. Valerius Catullus.* Fourth edn, Stuttgart.

Küppers, J. (1986) *Tantarum Causas Irarum: Untersuchungen zur einleitenden Bücherdyade Der Punica des Silius Italicus.* Berlin/New York.

Kytzler, B. (1986) 'Zum Aufbau der statianischen "Thebais". Pius Coroebus, Theb. I 557–692', *ANRW* 2.32.5: 2913–24.

Lafaye, G. 1894. *Catulle et ses modèles.* Paris.

Latte, K. (1960) *Römische Religionsgeschichte.* Second edn, Munich.

Learned, M. (1970) *The Saga of Walther of Aquitaine.* Westport, CT. Rpt of 1892 edn.

REFERENCES

Lee, G. (tr.) (1990) *The Poems of Catullus.* Oxford.

Leeman, A. (1958) 'The Good Companion', *Mnem.* 11: 318–21.

Lefèvre, E. (1971) *Das Prooemium der Argonautica des Valerius Flaccus.* Wiesbaden.

Leo, F. (1913) *Geschichte der römische Literatur I.* Berlin.

Lesueur, R. (1990) *Stace, Thébaïde Livres I–IV.* Paris.

Lewalski, B. K. (1966) *Milton's Brief Epic.* Providence/London.

Leyser, K. J. (1979) *Rule and Conflict in an Early Medieval Society: Ottonian Saxony.* London.

Liebeschuetz, J. H. W. G. (1979) *Continuity and Change in Roman Religion.* Oxford.

Little, D. A. (1970) 'Richard Heinze: Ovids elegische Erzählung', in E. Zinn (ed.) *Ovids Ars amatoria und Remedia amoris: Untersuchungen zum Aufbau*: 64–105. Stuttgart.

—— (tr.) (1990) *Lucan. Pharsalia: The Civil War.* Dunedin.

Lloyd-Jones, H. and Parsons, P. (1983) *Supplementum Hellenisticum.* Berlin.

Luiselli, B. (1967) *Il verso saturnio.* Rome.

Lynch, K. L. (1988) *The High Medieval Dream Vision: Poetry, Philosophy and Literary Form.* Stanford.

Lyne, R. O. A. M. (1978) *Ciris: A Poem Attributed to Vergil.* Cambridge.

—— (1987) *Further Voices in Virgil's Aeneid.* Oxford.

—— (1989) *Words and the Poet.* Oxford.

Lynn-George, M. (1988) *Epos: Word, Narrative and the Iliad.* London.

McDermott, W. C. and Orentzel, A. E. (1977) 'Silius Italicus and Domitian', *AJP* 98: 24–34.

McGuire, D. T. jr (1990) 'Textual Strategies and Political Suicide in Flavian Epic', in Boyle 1990: 21–45.

McKay, K. J. (1972) 'Frustration of Anticipation in Vergil, *Eclogue* vi?', *Antichthon* 6: 53–9.

MacMullen, R. (1966) *Enemies of the Roman Order: Treason, Unrest, and Alienation in the Empire.* Cambridge, MA.

Magoun, F. P. and Smyser, H. M. (trs) (1950) *Walter of Aquitaine: Materials for the Study of his Legend.* New London, CT.

Mann, N. (1984) *Petrarch.* Oxford.

Marconi, G. (1961) 'Il proemio degli Annales di Ennio', *RCCM* 3: 224–45.

Marcovich, M. (ed.) (1989) *Silver and Late Latin Poetry, ICS* 14.

Mariotti, S. (1955) *Il Bellum Poenicum e l'arte di Nevio.* Rome.

—— (1985) *Livio Andronico e la traduzione artistica.* Urbino.

Martindale, C. (1986) *John Milton and the Transformation of Ancient Epic.* London.

Mason, H. A. (1963) 'Is Juvenal a Classic?', in J. P. Sullivan (ed.) *Critical Essays in Roman Literature: Satire*: 93–176. London.

Matier, K. O. (1981) 'Prejudice and the *Punica*: Silius Italicus – A Reassessment', *AC* 24: 141–51.

—— (1989) *Silius Italicus at Bay: Pliny, Prejudice and the Punica.* Durban.

Mayer, R. (1982) 'Neronian Classicism', *AJP* 103: 305–18.

Mendell, C. W. (1924) 'Silius the Reactionary', *PhQ* 3: 92–106.

—— (1967) *Latin Poetry: The Age of Rhetoric and Satire.* Hamden.

Merchant, P. (1971) *The Epic.* London.

Milton, J. (1642) *The Reason of Church-Government.* London.

Moles, J. (1990) 'The Kingship Orations of Dio Chrysostom', in *Papers of the Leeds International Latin Seminar* 6: 297–375.

Momigliano, A. (1957) 'Perizonius, Niebuhr and the Character of Early Roman Tradition', *JRS* 47: 104–14.

Mommsen, T. (1881) *Römische Geschichte*, vol. 1. Seventh edn, Berlin.

321

Morel, W. (1963) *Fragmenta Poetarum Latinorum.* Leipzig.

Morris, C. (1972) *The Discovery of the Individual 1050–1200.* London.

Murrin, M. (1980) *The Allegorical Epic: Essays in its Rise and Decline.* Chicago.

Nardo, D. (1973) *La sesta satira di Giovenale e la tradizione erotico-elegiaca latina.* Padua.

Narducci, E. (1979) *La Providenza crudele e la distruzione dei miti augustei.* Pisa.

Newman, J. K. (1986) *The Classical Epic Tradition.* Madison.

Nichol, J. (1936) *The Historical and Geographical Sources Used by Silius Italicus.* Oxford.

Niemann, K. (1975) *Die Darstellung der römischen Niederlagen in den Punica des Silius Italicus.* Bonn.

Nimis, S. A. (1987) *Narrative Semiotics in the Epic Tradition: The Simile.* Bloomington.

Nolhac, P. de (1907) *Pétrarque et l'humanisme.* Second edn, Paris.

Norden, E. (1915) *Ennius und Vergilius.* Leipzig.

Norman, F. (1969) 'The Old English *Waldere* and Some Problems in the Story of Walther and Hildegunde', in P. Valenin and G. Zink (eds) *Mélanges pour Jean Fourquet*: 261–71. Paris/Munich.

Northrup, M. D. (1978) 'Like Dreams that Delude the Sleeping Senses: Aeneas' Moral Failure and Vergil's Imagery of the Insubstantial', *Ramus* 7: 26–37.

Nugent, S. G. (1990a) 'The Sex which is Not One: De-constructing Ovid's Hermaphrodite', *Differences* 2: 160–85.

—— (1990b) 'Ausonius' "Late Antique" Poetics and "Post-Modern" Literary Theory', in Boyle 1990: 236–60.

O'Connell, M. (1977) 'Pictorialism and Meaning in Catullus 64', *Latomus* 36: 746–56.

O'Hara, J. J. (1990) *Death and the Optimistic Prophecy in Vergil's Aeneid.* Princeton.

Osmun, G. (1983) 'The Abduction of Hylas – Again', *CB* 59: 56–60.

Otis B. (1964) *Virgil. A Study in Civilized Poetry.* Oxford.

—— (1966) *Ovid as an Epic Poet.* Cambridge.

—— (1970) Second edn of above.

Page, T. E. (ed.) (1894) *Virgil's Aeneid I–VI.* London.

Palagia, O. (1986) 'Imitation of Herakles in Ruler Portraiture: A Survey from Alexander to Maximinus Daza', *Boreas* 9: 137–151.

Palmer, R. (1980) 'Allegorical, Philological, and Philosophical Hermeneutics: Three Modes in a Complex Heritage', *Revue de l'Université d'Ottawa* 50: 338–60.

Parry, H. (1964) 'Ovid's *Metamorphoses*: Violence in a Pastoral Landscape', *TAPA* 95: 268–82.

Pavlock, B. (1990) *Eros, Imitation and the Epic Tradition.* Ithaca/New York.

Perutelli, A. (1978) 'L'inversione speculare: per una retorica dell'ekphrasis', *MD* 1: 87–98

Plass, P. (1988) *Wit and the Writing of History.* Madison.

Pointon, M. (1990) *Naked Authority: The Body in Western Painting 1830–1908.* Cambridge.

Pollitt, J. J. (1972) *Art and Experience in Classical Greece.* Cambridge.

—— (1986) *Art in the Hellenistic Age.* Cambridge.

Pomeroy, A. J. (1990) 'Silius Italicus as "*Doctus Poeta*"', in Boyle 1990: 119–39.

Pöschl, V. (1950) *Die Dichtkunst Virgils.* Innsbruck. Tr. G. Seligson (1962) *The Art of Virgil.* Ann Arbor.

Putnam, M. C. J. (1961) 'The Art of Catullus 64', *HSCP* 65: 165–205.

—— (1966) *The Poetry of the Aeneid.* Cambridge, MA.

Quinn, K. (1968) *Virgil's Aeneid: A Critical Description.* London.

—— (1979) *Texts and Contexts: The Roman Writers and their Audience.* London.

Raby, F. J. E. (1934) *A History of Secular Latin Poetry in the Middle Ages.* Oxford.

—— (1957). Second edn of above.

Rambaux, C. (1985) *Trois analyses de l'amour: Catulle Poésies. Ovide Les Amours. Apulée Le conte de Psyché.* Paris.

Reggiani, R. (1979). *I proemi degli Annales di Ennio: Programma letterario e polemico.* Rome.

Reilly, J. F. (1953–4) 'Origins of the Word Epyllion', *CJ* 49: 111–14.

Reinsch-Werner, H. (1976) *Callimachus hesiodus: Die Rezeption der hesiodischen Dichtung durch Kallimachos von Kyrene.* Berlin.

Richardson, L. jr (1944) *Poetical Theory in Republican Rome.* New Haven.

Richardson, N. J. (1974) *The Homeric Hymn to Demeter.* Oxford.

Richlin, A. (1983) *The Garden of Priapus.* New Haven.

—— (1992) 'Reading Ovid's Rapes', in A. Richlin (ed.) *Pornography and Representation in Greece and Rome*: 158–79. New York.

Roberts, M. (1985) *Biblical Epic and Rhetorical Paraphrase in Late Antiquity.* Liverpool.

—— (1989) *The Jeweled Style: Poetry and Poetics in Late Antiquity.* Ithaca/London.

Rose, K. F. C. (1971) *The Date and Author of the Satyricon.* Leiden.

Ross, D. O. jr (1969) *Style and Tradition in Catullus.* Cambridge, MA.

Rostovtzeff, M. (1957) *The Social and Economic History of the Roman Empire.* Second edn, rev. P. M. Frazer, 2 vols. Oxford.

Rowell, H. T. (1947) 'The Original Form of Naevius' *Bellum Punicum*', *AJP* 68: 21–46.

Rudd, N. (1976) *Lines of Enquiry: Studies in Latin Poetry.* Cambridge.

Russo, C. F. (1965) *Hesiodi Scutum.* Florence.

Rutherford, R. B. (1985) 'At Home and Abroad: Aspects of the Structure of the *Odyssey*', *PCPS* 31: 133–50.

Saller, R. P. (1982) *Personal Patronage under the Empire.* Cambridge.

Sanford, E. M. (1931) 'Lucan and his Roman Critics', *CP* 26: 233–57.

Schaller, D. (1987) 'Vergil und die Wiederentdeckung des Epos im frühen Mittelalter', *Medioevo e Rinascimento* 1: 75–100.

Schetter, W. (1960) *Untersuchungen zur epischen Kunst des Statius.* Wiesbaden.

Schlam, C. (1984) 'Diana and Actaeon: Metamorphoses of a Myth', *CA* 3: 82–110.

Schmidt, P. L. (1975) 'Neoteriker', in K. Ziegler, W. Sontheimer, and H. Gartner (eds) *Der kleine Pauly* 5: 1630–1.

Schneider, B. (1985) *Das Aeneissupplement des Maffeo Vegio.* Heidelberg.

Scholler, H. (ed.) (1977) *The Epic in Medieval Society: Aesthetic and Moral Values.* Tübingen.

Schubert, W. (1984) *Jupiter in den Epen der Flavierzeit.* Frankfurt am Main.

Seagraves, R. W. A. (1976) 'The Influence of Vergil on Petrarch's *Africa*', Ph.D. Diss. University of Columbia.

Segal, C. P. (1965–6) '*Aeternum per saecula nomen*: The Golden Bough and the Tragedy of History', *Arion* 4: 617–57; *Arion* 5: 34–72.

—— (1969) *Landscape in Ovid's Metamorphoses: A Study in the Transformation of a Literary Symbol.* Wiesbaden.

—— (1971a) *The Theme of the Mutilation of the Corpse in the Iliad.* Leiden.

—— (1971b) 'The Song of Iopas in the *Aeneid*', *Hermes* 99: 336–49.

Sforza, F. (1935) 'The Problem of Virgil', *CR* 49: 97–108.

Shanzer, D. (1990) 'Rhetoric and Art, Art and Ceremony, Martyrs and History, Martyrs and Myth: Some Interdisciplinary Explorations of Late Antiquity', *Envoi* 2.2: 231–68.

Simon, B. (1987) 'Tragic Drama and the Family: The Killing of Children and the Killing of Story-telling', in S. Rimmon-Kenan (ed.) *Discourse in Psychoanalysis and Literature*: 152–75. London.

Skutsch, O. (1958) Rev. of Mariotti 1955, *CR* 72: 45–8.

—— (1968) *Studiana Enniana*. London.

—— (1985) *The Annals of Quintus Ennius*. Oxford.

Small, S. G. P. (1983) *Catullus: A Reader's Guide to the Poems*. Lanham, MD.

Smarr, J. (1982) 'Petrarch: A Vergil without a Rome', in P. A. Ramsay (ed.) *Rome in the Renaissance: The City and the Myth*: 133–140. Binghamton, NY.

Snyder, J. M. (1980) *Puns and Poetry in Lucretius' De Rerum Natura*. Amsterdam.

Solimano, G. (1988) *Epistula Didonis ad Aeneam*. Genoa.

Solodow, J. B. (1988) *The World of Ovid's Metamorphoses*. Chapel Hill.

Spaltenstein, F. (1986) *Commentaire des Punica de Silius Italicus (livres 1 à 8)*. Geneva.

Spencer, T. J. B. (1968) '*Paradise Lost*: The Anti-Epic', in C. A. Patrides (ed.) *Approaches to Paradise Lost*: 81–98. London.

Springer, C. P. E. (1988) *The Gospel as Epic in Late Antiquity*. Leiden.

Stahl, H. P. (1985) *Propertius: 'Love' and 'War'*. Berkeley.

Starr, R. J. (1987) 'The Circulation of Literary Texts in the Roman World', *CQ* 37: 213–23.

Stehle, E. (1990) 'Sappho's Gaze: Fantasies of a Goddess and Young Man', *Differences* 2: 88–125.

Steuart, E. (1925). *The Annals of Quintus Ennius*. Cambridge.

Strecker, K. (ed.) (1951) *Waltharius*. MGH, Poetae Latini Aevi Carolini 6 part 1: 1–81. Weimar.

Strzelecki, L. (1935) *De Naeviano Belli Punici Carmine Quaestiones Selectae*. Krakow.

—— (1964) *Cn. Naevii Belli Punici Carmen*. Leipzig.

Suerbaum, W. (1968) *Untersuchungen zur Selbstdarstellung alterer römischer Dichter*. Hildesheim.

—— (1972a) 'Ennius bei Petrarca: Betrachtungen zu literarischen Ennius-Bildern', *Ennius, Entretiens Hardt* 17: 293–352. Geneva.

—— (1972b) '*Poeta Laureatus Et Triumphans*. Die Dichterkrönung Petrarcas und sein Ennius-Bild', *Poetica* 5: 293–328.

Sullivan, J. P. (1968) *The Satyricon of Petronius: A Literary Study*. London.

—— (1976) *Propertius: A Critical Introduction*. Cambridge.

—— (1985) *Literature and Politics in the Age of Nero*. Ithaca/London.

Syme, R. (1939) *The Roman Revolution*. Oxford.

Tartaglini, C. (1986) 'Arianna e Andromaca: Da Hom. Il. XXII 460–72 a Catull. 64, 61–67', *A & R* 31: 152–7.

Thalmann, W. G. (1984) *Conventions of Form and Thought in Early Greek Epic Poetry*. Baltimore.

Thomas, R. F. (1982) 'Catullus and the Polemics of Poetic Reference (Poem 64.1–18)', *AJP* 103: 144–64.

—— (1983) 'Callimachus, The Victoria Berenices, and Roman Poetry', *CQ* 33: 92–113.

Thomson, D. F. S. (1961) 'Aspects of Unity in Catullus 64', *CJ* 57: 49–57.

Thornton, M. K. and R. L. (1989) *Julio-Claudian Building Programs: A Quantitative Study in Political Management*. Wauconda, Illinois.

Tieghem, P. van (1944) 'La littérature latine de la Renaissance', *Bibliothèque d'Humanisme et Renaissance* 4: 177–418.

Toohey, P. (1988) 'An [Hesiodic] Danse Macabre: The Shield of Heracles', *ICS* 13: 19–35.

Trendall, A. D. (1981) 'A Campanian Lekanis in Lugano with the Rape of Persephone', *Quaderni Ticinesi* 10: 165–95.

REFERENCES

Tylee, C. M. (1990) *The Great War and Woman's Consciousness: Images of Militarism and Womanhood in Women's Writings, 1914–64*. London.

Vahlen, J. (1928) *Ennianae Poesis Reliquiae*. Third edn, Leipzig.

Väisänen, M. (1988) *La Musa dalle molte voci*. Helsinki.

Velli, B. (1965) 'Il proemio dell *"Africa"'*, *Italia Medioevale e Umanistica* 8: 323–32.

—— (1976) 'La memoria poetica del Petrarca', *Italia Medioevale e Umanistica* 19: 171–207.

Vermeule, C. C. (1981) *Greek and Roman Sculpture in America*. Berkeley.

Vernant, J.-P. (1982) 'From Oedipus to Periander: Lameness, Tyranny, Incest in Legend and History', *Arethusa* 15: 19–38.

Vessey, D. W. T. C. (1970a) 'The Myth of Linus and Coroebus in Statius' *Thebaid* I, 557–672', *AJP* 91: 315–31.

—— (1970b) 'Thoughts on the Epyllion', *CJ* 66: 38–43.

—— (1973) *Statius and the Thebaid*. Cambridge.

—— (1974a) 'Pliny, Martial and Silius Italicus', *Hermes* 102: 109–16.

—— (1974b) 'Silius Italicus on the Fall of Saguntum', *CP* 69: 28–36.

—— (1975) 'Silius Italicus: The Shield of Hannibal', *AJP* 96: 391–405.

—— (1982) 'Flavian Epic', in E. J. Kenney and W. V. Clausen (eds) *The Cambridge History of Classical Literature*, vol. II: 558–96. Cambridge.

—— (1986) '*Pierius menti calor incidit*: Statius' Epic Style', *ANRW* 2.32.5: 2965–3019.

Vidal-Naquet, P. (1986) 'Les Boucliers des héros. Essai sur la scène centrale des Sept contre Thèbes, Oedipe entre deux cités. Essai sur l'Oedipe à Colone', in J. Vernant and P. Vidal-Naquet, *Mythe et Tragédie en Grèce Ancienne*, T. 2:115–47. Paris.

Vlastos, G. (1991) *Socrates: Ironist and Moral Philosopher*. Ithaca/London.

Vynckier, H. (1987) 'Arms-Talks in the Middle Ages: Hrotsvit, *Waltharius*, and the Heroic *Via*', in Wilson 1987: 183–200.

Wallace, M. T. V. (1968) 'Some Aspects of Time in the *Punica* of Silius Italicus', *CW* 62: 83–93.

Walsh, P. G. (1986) 'Virgil and Medieval Epic', in R. A. Cardwell and J. Hamilton (eds) *Virgil in a Cultural Tradition: Essays to Celebrate the Bimillennium*: 52–64. Nottingham.

Ward, J. O. (1979) 'Gothic Architecture, Universities and the Decline of the Humanities in Twelfth-century Europe', in L. O. Frappell (ed.) *Principalities, Powers and Estates: Studies in Medieval and Early Modern Government and Society*: 65–75. Adelaide.

—— (1990) 'Rhetoric, Truth and Literacy in the Renaissance of the Twelfth Century', in R. L. Enos (ed.) *Oral and Written Communication: Historical Approaches*: 126–57. London/New Delhi.

Warmington, E. H. (1957) *Remains of Old Latin*, vol. 2. Cambridge, MA.

—— (1973) *Remains of Old Latin*, vol. 1. Third edn, Cambridge, MA.

Waszink, J. (1962) 'Retractatio Enniana', *Mnem.* 15: 113–32.

—— (1964) 'Il proemio degli Annales Di Ennio', *Maia* 16: 327–40.

—— (1972) 'Zum Anfangsstadium der römischen Literatur,' *ANRW* 1.2: 869–927.

Watson, L. (1990) 'Rustic Suffenus (Catullus 22) and Literary Rusticity', *Papers of the Leeds International Latin Seminar* 6: 13–33.

Watson, P. A. (1984) 'The Case of the Murderous Father: Catullus 64.401–2', *LCM* 9: 114–16.

Weber, C. (1983) 'Two Chronological Contradictions in Catullus 64', *TAPA* 113: 263–71.

Weitzmann, K. (ed.) (1980) *Age of Spirituality: A Symposium*. New York.

325

Wemple, S. F. (1981) *Women in Frankish Society: Marriage and the Cloister 500 to 900*. Philadelphia.

West, M. L. (1985) *The Hesiodic Catalogue of Women: Its Nature, Structure, and Origins*. Oxford.

Westra, H. J. (1980) 'A Reinterpretation of *Waltharius* 215–59', *Mittellateinisches Jahrbuch* 15: 51–6.

White, P. (1982) 'Positions for Poets in Early Imperial Rome', in Gold 1982: 50–66.

Wigodsky, M. (1972) *Vergil and Early Latin Poetry*. Wiesbaden.

Wilkins, E. H. (1943) 'The Coronation of Petrarch', *Speculum* 18: 155–97.

Wilkinson, L. P. (1970) 'Pindar and the Proem to the Third Georgic', in W. Wimmel (ed.) *Forschungen zu römischen Literatur*. 286–90. Wiesbaden.

Williams, R. G. (ed.) (1976) *G. Vida: De Arte Poetica*. New York.

Wills, G. (1983) 'Critical Inquiry (Kritik) in Clausewitz', in W. J. T. Mitchell (ed.) *The Politics of Interpretation*: 159–80. Chicago.

Wilson, K. M. (1985) *The Dramas of Hrotsvit of Gandersheim*. Saskatoon.

—— (ed.) (1987) *Hrotsvit of Gandersheim: 'Rara Avis' in Saxonia*. Ann Arbor.

—— (1988) *Hrotsvit of Gandersheim: The Ethics of Authorial Stance*. Leiden.

Winkler, J. (1990) *The Constraints of Desire: the Anthropology of Sex and Gender in Ancient Greece*. New York.

Winterfeld, P. (ed.) (1965) *Hrotsvithae Opera* (*MGH, Scriptores Rerum Germanicarum...*). Berlin.

Wiseman, T. P. (1985) *Catullus and His World: A Reappraisal*. Cambridge.

Wittgenstein, L. (1958) *Philosophical Investigations*. Tr. G. E. M. Anscombe. Second edn, Oxford.

Woodhouse, W. J. (1930) *The Composition of Homer's Odyssey*. Oxford.

Zabughin, V. (1921) *Vergilio nel rinascimento* 1. Bologna.

—— (1923) *Vergilio nel rinascimento* 2. Bologna.

Zanker, P. (1988) *The Power of Images in the Ages of Augustus*. Ann Arbor.

Zeitlin, F. I. (1982) *Under the Sign of the Shield: Semiotics and Aeschylus' Seven Against Thebes*. Rome.

—— (1986) 'Thebes: Theater of Self and Society in Athenian Drama', in J. P. Euben (ed.) *Greek Tragedy and Political Theory*: 101–41. Berkeley/Los Angeles.

—— (1990) Rpt of Zeitlin 1986 in J. J. Winkler and F. Zeitlin (eds) *Nothing To Do with Dionysos? Athenian Drama in its Social Context*. Princeton.

Zetzel, J. E. G. (1983) 'Re-creating the Canon: Augustan Poetry and the Alexandrian Past', *Critical Inquiry* 10: 83–105.

Ziegler, K. (1966) *Das hellenistische Epos*. Second edn, Leipzig.

Zorzetti, N. (1990) 'The *Carmina Convivalia*', in O. Murray (ed.), *Sympotica*: 289–307. Oxford.

Zwierlein, O. (1988) 'Statius, Lucan, Curtius Rufus und das hellenistische Epos', *RhM* 13: 67–84.

GENERAL INDEX

Accius 97, 167

Achilles 49, 60, 72ff., 84, 94ff., 101f., 130, 144, 172, 177, 209f., 224, 229, 232, 246, 268

Actaeaon 118–23

Adelaide (widow of King Lothar) 287f.

Adrastus 170ff.

Aegeus 64ff., 75

Aegritudo Perdicae 13

Aelius Stilo 47

Aeneas 28ff., 42, 69f., 83–107, 113–18., 128ff., 134ff., 162, 173ff., 201f., 208–10, 218–20, 231f., 249ff., 268ff., 276–9, 281, 297ff., 301ff.; (analogy with Achilles) 84, 96f.; (analogy with Christ) 307–10; (analogy with Jason) 201f.; (analogy with Odysseus) 95f.; (*immemor*) 85; (medieval and Renaissance tradition of) 303; (Romanization of) 83, 86, 97, 99

Aeneidomastix 79, 155

Aeschylus 72

Aesop 150

aetiology 53, 59, 81, 83, 94, 220f., 254, 256, 308

Agrigentum (temple of Zeus) 29

Agrippa 6, 79, 88, 155

Alan of Lille 265, 290

Aldus Manutius 303

Alexander (the Great) 230, 264, 299

Alexandrianism 3, 59f., 66, 72, 74, 76, 80f., 112, 128f., 144–50, 155, 192, 210, 248

allegory (in Catullus) 63, 70; (in Lucan) 135, 142 n.36; (in medieval and Renaissance epic) 265f., 300f., 305–9; (in Virgil)

83, 156

Alpher 268ff.

amicitia 9

amplificatio 14, 182ff., 256

Anchises 30f., 83, 92f., 95f., 98, 295, 297

Antimachus 144f., 166

Antoninus Liberalis 197, 213

Antony (and Hercules) 212

Apollo 4, 30, 72, 238, 240, 249, 251; (temple of) 4

Apollonius Rhodius 7, 12, 39, 59ff., 63, 66, 69, 97, 126ff., 144f., 163, 192ff., 201–5, 213

Apuleius 63, 258

Ara Pacis 9, 83

Arator 13

Aratus 59, 74

Arbronius Silo 3

Argonauts 4, 61, 163, 192ff.

Argos 166ff.

Ariadne 64ff., 68ff., 195ff.

Aristotle 6, 89, 230

art 99–104, 230–3; *see also* ecphrasis

artes poetriae 263

Arvale Hymn 21

Ascanius 116f., 202, 208–10

Attila 267ff.

Augustine 302

Augustus (or Octavian) 4, 9, 80f., 83, 92, 98, 112, 126–34, 147f., 210, 212, 245, 299f.; (of Prima Porta) 9

Avitus 13, 265

Babrius 12, 151f.

Bacchus 64ff., 71, 116, 184, 220f., 227, 238

Bakhtin, Mikhail 3, 265, 292 n.24

Barthes, Roland 168f.
Basini, Basinio 302
Behn, Aphra 157
Bellum Actiacum 3
Beowulf 158
Berengar 287f.
Bergman, Ingmar 16
Bernardus Silvestris 290
Bertolucci, Bernardo 16
Boccaccio 295
Borges, Jorge Luis 192–4
Browning, Robert 16
Brunhilde 273
Brutus (Marcus) 136f., 140
Bunyan, John 157
Burgundians 267ff.
Byron, George Gordon 16, 125

Cadmus 114ff., 167ff., 219
Caecilius 80
Caesar (Julius) 9, 63, 83, 125ff.,
    144f., 156, 182, 219, 242, 295
Caesius Bassus 32
Calais 196
Caligula 155
callida iunctura 88
Callimachus 1, 41, 53, 59ff., 144–50,
    154, 164, 182f., 186, 279
Callisto 123
Calvus 59f., 80
Camenae 22, 39
Camerinus 3
Camoens 16, 294
Cannae 126, 220ff.
carmen heroum 2
carnival 264f., 275, 281–3
Carus 13
Cato (elder) 20, 50; (younger) 50,
    133ff.
Catullus 5, 8, 11f., 59–78, 80f., 86ff.,
    97, 99, 111, 116, 127, 145, 195f.,
    200; (as moralist) 67ff.
causality 219–22
Ceres 240ff., 246ff., 253ff., 288
Cervantes 193f.
Chanson de Roland 143
Christ 15, 300f., 303ff.
Churchill, Winston 132
Cicero 3, 15, 20, 45, 50, 60, 130,
    145, 233f., 295ff., 300; (*ad
    Herennium*) 263
Cid 261

Cinna 59f., 80
Claudian 9, 13f., 104, 155, 237–60,
    265f., 261, 300
Claudius Marius Victorius 13
Clemens 13
Cleophas 307
Clodia 63
Commodus 155
Cordus 13
Cornelius Severus 3
Corippus 13
Cornificius 80
Costner, Kevin 16
Cotta 137f.
Cowley, Abraham 16
Creon 168ff.
Creusa 95, 208–10
Croce, Benedetto 11, 110
Culex 143
Cyane 240, 249f., 253f.
Cynthia 146f., 149

Daedalus 100ff.
Dante 15, 126, 135, 137
David 300
death (in epic) 225–7
de Battaglia, O. F. 11, 132ff.
Defoe, Daniel 157
Diana 72, 118–23, 251
didactic 5f., 59, 74ff., 112, 145, 244,
    265
Dido 69f., 85, 88ff., 92f., 113, 128,
    130f., 173f., 177, 179, 183, 202,
    219f., 231f., 249ff., 268ff., 276–9,
    281, 301f., 304ff.
Dio 139
Diodorus Siculus 97
doctrina 192
Domitian 9, 13, 126, 139, 163, 165,
    210–12, 233f.; (and Earinus)
    210–12; (and Hercules) 210–12
Domitius Marsus 3
Don Quixote 157, 192–4
Dracontius 13
dreams (in epic) 39ff., 42, 55f., 96,
    222, 230f., 243, 246ff., 295, 297–9
Durrell, Lawrence 16

Earinus 210–12
ecphrasis 6, 9, 29, 60, 63ff., 81,
    99–102, 220, 228, 231f., 247–50,
    253, 303f.

Eisenstein, Sergei 16
elegy 5, 12, 14, 70, 109–12, 145ff.,
  153, 306
Eliot, T.S. 2
Embrico 265
Enceladus 240f., 257
Ennius 1ff., 6f., 9f., 15, 34, 37–58, 61,
  81, 86ff., 97, 129, 144, 176, 221,
  229, 295–300; (characterization
  in) 48ff.; (dream of) 39ff., 55f.,
  299; (theme) 48–53; (style) 53–55;
  (versification) 54f.
epic: ('bardic tradition') 19f.;
  ('canonic') 79ff.; (chronicle epic)
  302; (conventions of) 110–12,
  162f., 218ff., 247ff.; (criticism of)
  11, 143–61; (as duel) 172f.;
  (genre) 4ff., 79ff., 109ff., 289f.;
  (and history) 80ff., 218f., 221,
  234; (as lamentation) 185;
  (medieval) 14f., 261–93;
  (militarist ideology in) 176ff.,
  188f.; (as moral and political
  critique) 84–96, 125ff., 188f.,
  210–12; (mythological), 3f., 80ff.,
  86ff., 143ff., 218ff.; (as narration)
  182ff.; ('norms' of Roman epic)
  2f.; (politico-historical) 2ff., 80ff.,
  125ff., 143ff., 218ff., 302f.;
  ('primary'/'secondary') 143f.;
  (recuperable) 80–3; (religious)
  303ff.; (Renaissance of the) 15f.,
  294–313; (and scopic horror)
  177ff.; (style) 5f., 22ff., 29ff., 43f.,
  52–5, 60, 64ff., 75f., 86ff., 126,
  128, 255f.; ('subjective') 88ff.;
  ('tertiary') 158; see also genre
epigram 12, 60, 74, 152–5
epithalamium 61, 67, 72ff., 253
epyllion 11, 13, 59ff., 75f., 80f., 86–8,
  90, 111f., 264
Erectheum 29
Erkambold of Eichstätt 289
Ermold the Black 14
Eteocles 167ff.
Euhemerus 49
Euripides 61, 65, 69, 71, 115, 144,
  182f., 248

Fabius Maximus 221ff.
fable 150–2
fame 39, 45f., 48ff., 84–6, 95f.,

99–102, 227–30, 294, 297ff., 302
Fielding, Henry 157
figura etymologica 34, 54
Fulvius Nobilior 9, 50
Furius Antias 3
Furius Bibaculus 3, 9
furor 71, 82, 84, 90, 92ff., 98, 103,
  115–17, 292 n.19
Gautier de Chatillon 14
genre 2ff., 11f., 71ff., 80f., 89f.,
  110–12, 126ff., 143–61, 229ff.,
  234f., 244, 251, 263f., 289f., 302;
  ('Generic Fallacy') 11, 110;
  (generic mixture) 5ff., 71–6, 89f.,
  110–12, 263, 302; ('norms') 2f.
Germanic saga 267–85
Gesta Ottonis 285–90
gigantomachy (or Titanomachy) 29,
  227–9, 240–2, 257,
gods (in epic) 24f., 28, 71ff., 82, 105
  n.8, 106 n.34, 118–23, 128, 134–7,
  156, 219–22, 224f., 227–9, 243–5,
  295
golden age 74, 98, 126f., 134ff.
goliardic poets 266
Graz fragment 272–4
Gregory of Tours 270
Gui d'Amiens 14
Gunther 268ff.

Hagen 268ff.
Hannibal 49, 220ff., 295ff.
Hayley, William 1
Hector 94, 172, 174, 177, 247, 268,
  297
Heiric(us) 268ff.
Helen (of Troy) 147f.
Hellenization (of Rome) 8f.
Heptateuchos 13
Heracles/Hercules 60ff., 64, 69, 92,
  114, 183, 196ff., 210–12, 220f.,
  227–9; (and the princeps) 210–12;
  (Shield) 60ff.
Hermaphroditus 203–8
Hesiod 1, 38f., 41, 60ff., 69, 74
Hiltgunde 268ff.
Hincmar of Rheims 284
Homer 1ff., 6f., 12, 22ff., 34, 38–44,
  47ff., 55f., 60, 64, 69, 79f., 86f.,
  94ff., 101f., 125f., 143, 145ff.,
  156f., 162, 166, 172ff., 176f., 183,
  188, 192, 200f., 209f., 218, 223,

225, 229, 234, 238–40, 244ff., 252,
255f., 294ff., 300, 304f.
Honorius 9
Horace 4ff., 22, 34f., 80, 88, 111,
126, 129, 150ff., 154, 164f., 183,
238, 264, 268, 296f.
Hostius 3
Hrotsvit 14, 285–90
Huns 267ff.
Hylas 12, 194ff.
Hypsipyle (as narrator) 183ff.

Ilia (dream of) 42
imagery 23f., 44f., 93f., 98, 202f.,
205–8, 210–15, 225, 227–9, 299
imitatio 1, 12, 20, 22–8, 41f., 55f.,
183ff., 188, 192ff., 218, 239,
263–6, 283, 289, 291f. n.19, 294ff.,
303ff.
immemor 70, 85
intertextuality (*Aeneid*) 94–8; for
elsewhere *see* palimpsestic mode
intratextuality (*Aeneid*) 90–4
Iulus Antonius 3

Jason 61, 65ff., 201, 205
Jocasta 171, 182
Joseph (husband of Mary) 306
Joseph of Exeter 14
Joyce, James 16
Judas 305, 308
Julian 129, 139
Julius II 302
Julius Cerialis 13
Junius Bassus (sarcophagus of) 257
Juno 29, 72, 82, 91, 94, 118, 201–4,
219ff., 228, 243f.
Jupiter 30, 72, 83f., 92, 96, 118f.,
234, 237, 241, 243–6, 252, 302, 304
Juvenal 12f., 152f., 164
Juvencus 13, 303

Largus 3
Laura 299f.
Lausus 84, 86, 91f., 115, 292 n.19
Lemnos 184f., 196
Leo X 304
Lesbia 60, 63, 70f., 74, 200
libertas 131ff., 136ff.
Livius Andronicus 1ff., 5, 7, 9f., 15,
19–28, 35, 39, 43, 94f., 144
Livy 1, 9, 15, 19, 31f., 97, 218f., 221f.,

225, 229ff., 234, 242, 295ff., 300
Lothair II 284
Lucan 5ff., 9, 11, 12f., 15, 86,
99, 104, 125–42, 155–8, 162, 165f.,
173, 176, 182, 218ff., 225,
229–31, 233f., 290, 295, 300,
303; (criticism of) 156; (death
of) 138; (and liberty) 131ff.;
(style) 126
Lucilius 38, 111, 153
Lucretius 5, 16, 37, 86, 90, 97, 125,
303f., 306, 309
Lupus 3
Lynceus 3f.
lyric 5, 14, 71, 74ff., 111, 144, 149,
152f., 300, 302

Macaulay, T.B. 19f.
Macer 3, 9
Maecenas 9
Manilius (*Astronomica*) 5
Manilius Vopiscus 13
Marcellus 297
Martial 5, 12f., 126, 143, 152ff.,
211f., 218, 233, 235
Masinissa 301f.
Matthew of Vendôme 264
Medea 61, 65ff., 205
medieval epic 261–93;
(allegorical impulse in) 265f.;
(modes and styles) 262ff.;
(readership of) 261f., 283
Mezentius 84, 86, 91f., 115–17, 174,
281, 292 n.19
Milton, John 2, 16, 135, 157f., 294,
304f., 307, 309f.
minimalist criticism 127ff.
Mopsus 197ff., 201
Moschus (*Europa*) 69
Mussolini, Benito 132

Naevius 1ff., 5f., 9f., 21, 28–35, 39,
42f., 49, 80f., 97, 129, 144; (and
the 'chronicle style') 31ff.;
(content of *Bellum Punicum*) 28f.
Narcissus 200f., 203–8
Nemea (as poetic grove) 182f.
Nemesianus 13
neoterics 3ff., 11, 60, 80, 87f., 90, 99
Nero 9, 129f., 137ff., 155f., 166, 233
Nibelungenlied 158, 261, 273
Nicander 59, 197

Nicomachi (and Symmachi, diptych of) 257
Nivardus of Ghent 14
Nonnus 126
Novalician Chronicle 272

Odysseus 22ff., 69, 95f., 144, 176, 183, 297
Oedipus 163, 167ff.
Ovid 3ff., 7, 9, 11f., 70, 80, 83, 99, 104, 108–24, 127, 129f., 149f., 152, 155, 162, 200f., 203–8, 210, 218, 222, 225, 238–40, 244–6, 250, 252ff., 258; (exile of) 4, 127; (humanity of) 121ff.

Pacuvius 97
palimpsestic mode 1ff., 6ff., 10–15, 42, 94–8, 112–18, 188f., 192ff., 255, 263f., 268ff., 276–9, 290, 292f. n.19, 295ff., 303ff.
Palinurus 92, 308
Pallas (son of Evander) 93f., 174
Paris 220
Parthenon 8f., 129
Parthenopaeus 175, 182, 187
Particulo 150f.
pastoral 5, 12
patronage 9f., 101f., 233
Paul, St. 137, 140
Peleus 61ff., 97, 195ff.
Pentheus 114–18
Pergamum (Great Altar at) 241
Persius 12, 152ff.
Petrarch 15, 261, 294–302; (and *imitatio*) 295f.
Petronius 12, 156ff., 258
Phaedrus 12, 150ff.
Philomela 122f.
Piazza Armerina 255
Picasso, Pablo 127
pietas 40, 74, 82, 84, 93f., 103, 122f., 174, 208–12, 245, 286f., 292 n.19, 300f., 306
Pindar 81, 183, 240
Pisander 97
Plato 132ff.
Plautus 25, 31
Pliny 164, 218, 233ff.
Pluto (or Dis) 226, 238ff., 251
poeta cliens 3, 10
Polybius 97

Polynices 167ff.
Polyxena 73
Ponticus 3f., 9, 166f.
Pound, Ezra 16, 146–8
Procne 122f.
Prometheus 72
Propertius 4f., 12, 79f., 145–50, 167, 196f., 199–201, 203f., 206, 304
Proserpina 238ff., 246ff.
Prudentius 9, 13, 135, 266, 283

Quintilian 5, 125, 277, 305
Quintus Curtius 264

Rabelais 157
Rabirius 3, 9
Racine 167
recusatio 5, 163
Remus 42, 52ff., 92
Renaissance (epic of the) 294–313
Reposianus 13
rhetoric 130f.
Rhianos (*Messeniaca*) 49
Richardson, Samuel 157
Robert of Sicily 299f.
Romulus 38, 41, 49ff., 83, 92
Ruodlieb 14, 289

Saleius Bassus 9, 13
Sallust 68f., 74, 126
Salmacis 203–8
Sannazaro 303
Sappho 60, 63, 144f.
satire 5, 12, 60, 111f., 152–5, 265, 281–3
Saturnian verse 5, 9, 19–36; (caesura in) 21, 26–8, 29, 33f.; (epic decorum in) 24–8; (formal features of) 20f.; (hypotaxis in) 27f.; (later distaste for) 22, 34f.; (stylistic features) 22ff., 29ff.; (sub-literary) 21, 30
Scipio (Aemilianus) 9, 295; (Africanus) 38, 46, 49ff., 83, 144, 219ff., 295ff.; (Barbatus epitaph) 21
seafaring 63, 195f., 237
Sedulius 13, 265, 303
Sejanus 151
self-consciousness 6ff., 10, 15, 38–48, 55f., 60ff., 76, 101ff., 238, 295ff.
self-reflection 9ff., 42, 99–104, 183ff., 192, 212–15, 233, 300

Seneca 8, 129, 134, 137, 139, 154f., 167
Serranus 9, 13
Sextilius Ena 3, 9
Shelley, Percy Bysshe 125
Siegfried 273
Silius Italicus 8ff., 12f., 37, 104, 126, 129, 138, 156, 218–36, 266; (art in) 231–3; (causation in) 219–22; (death in) 225–7; (epic conventions in) 222–4, 229f., 234; (immortality in) 229, 234; (life of) 218, 233f.
Smollett, Tobias George 157
Socrates 134–6
Sophonisba 301f.
Spenser, Edmund 16
Statius 4, 7ff., 12f., 83, 104, 125ff., 130, 136, 139, 154f., 158, 162–91, 211, 233, 283
Sterne, Laurence 157
Stilicho 9
Stoicism 137ff., 156
structure (*Aeneid*) 90–4; (*Annales*) 37f.; (*Bellum Punicum*) 28f.
Symmachi *see* Nicomachi

Tabularium 8
Tacitus 126, 135, 138ff.
Tasso 16, 294
Tereus 122f.
Thebes 4, 12, 114–18, 162–91; (as cacotopia) 167ff.
Theocritus 12, 197–9, 203f., 243
Theseus 59, 64ff., 68ff., 166ff., 171ff., 195ff.
Thetis 61ff., 195ff.
Theutberga 284
Thidhreksaga 272
Thrasymachus 132ff.
Tibullus 149
time (in epic) 61f., 130f., 219, 229–34, 248
Titus 234
Tolstoy, Count Lev Nikolayevich 16
tragedy 5, 81, 89f., 143f., 150, 153, 158, 166f., 182
Trajan 139, 233
Troy 28f., 72ff., 86, 91, 145f., 208, 229, 268ff., 301
Turnus 89f., 92f., 97, 103, 172f., 176, 180, 303, 310

Tydeus 170ff., 176–9

umbra 85, 103, 207, 213, 295

Vacca 138f.
Valerius (consul of 263 BCE) 28f.
Valerius Cato 80
Valerius Flaccus 4, 9, 12, 82, 104, 126, 130, 155, 192–217, 233
Varro (Marcus Terentius) 54, 131
Varro Atacinus 3, 9, 80
Vegio, Maffeo 302
Venus 6, 82, 96, 202, 221f., 257, 306, 309
Vergina (tomb at) 251
Vespasian 135, 162f., 166, 218, 234
Vesuvius 13
Vibius Maximus 164
Vida, Girolamo; 15, 302–10; (and *amor*) 306; (*Christiad*) 303–10; (as 'Christian Virgil') 303; (*De Arte Poetica*) 304ff.; (and *imitatio*) 305ff.; (and the unrecognized god) 306f.; (Virgilian allusions in) 304ff.
Viking Sagas 261
Virgil 1ff., 4ff., 6, 9ff., 12f., 15f., 56, 79–107, 110ff., 125ff., 143, 147f., 154ff., 162ff., 172ff., 179, 182f., 188f., 192, 194, 197ff., 201–3, 208–10, 213, 218ff., 233f., 238, 243, 263f., 268ff., 294ff., 303ff.; (*Aeneid*) 79–107 and *passim*; (*Eclogues*) 2, 5, 80, 86, 92, 97ff., 102f., 148, 198, 213, 238, 242ff., 247ff., 255f., 261ff., 266, 268ff., 283, 289f., 300, 303; (*Georgics*) 4, 80f., 86, 97ff., 102f., 197f., 299; ('Virgil's Wheel') 6; (critics of) 79f., 147f., 155
Virgin Mary 301, 303, 306, 308
virtus 12, 68f., 71, 73ff., 145, 172–89, 227–30, 295, 299ff., 312 n.28; (*Virtus*) 227–9, 301
Visconti, Luchino 16
Vitellius 135
Volusius 3
Vulcan 6, 99

Waldere fragments 267
Walter of Aquitaine 268ff.
Walter of Chatillon 264, 290

Walter of Compiègne 265
Waltharius 14f., 267–93; (Carolingian context) 284f.; (concubinage in) 273; (lordship in) 269ff.; (patriarchal power in) 271f.; (vassalic loyalty in) 273; (Virgilian allusions in) 268–83
War (as duel) 172, 224; (transformed by epic) 222–7; (as struggle over meaning) 170ff.

Warrior (as brother) 173ff.; (as shield) 171ff.; (as wall) 176ff.
Women (in epic) 180ff., 271f., 282–5, 287–90; (voice of) 183–9
Wordsworth, William 16

Zama 220ff., 295ff.
Zeitlin, Froma 168
Zeno 137

INDEX OF MAIN PASSAGES DISCUSSED

Apollonius Rhodius
Argonautica 1.1228–33: 199
    1.1231–3: 204
    3.755–8: 205

Catullus *Carmen* 64.11–15: 195
    64.19–21: 62, 75
    64.47–52: 67
    64.348–51: 73
Cicero *Pro Archia* 22: 50
Claudian *De Raptu*
  Proserpinae 1. *Pref.* 2–3: 237
    1.4: 238
    1.32: 239
    1.274f., 282f.: 248f.
    2.2f., 20f.: 249
    2.34f., 42f., 94ff.: 250f.
    2.158ff.: 241
    2.204f., 244f.: 242f.
    2.269f., 272: 252
    2.317ff., 355f., 359f.: 253
    3.5, 13–17, 19f.: 244f.
    3.30ff.: 237
    3.57–62: 243f.
    3.78f.: 246
    3.106–8: 248
    3.181f., 196f.: 242
    3.189f., 249f.: 254
    3.269, 328f.: 255

Ennius *Annales* (Skutsch 1985) 1.
  fr.1: 38
    1. frr.2, 3, 5, 6f., 8: 40
    1. fr. 9: 41
    1. fr.11: 39
    1. fr.47 (72–91): 52f.
    1. fr.62: 50
    5. fr.1: 48

    7. frr. 1–1a: 6, 42f.
    7. fr.2: 41f.
    8. fr. 1 (247–53): 51f.
    8. fr. 12 (268–86): 46f.
    16. frr. 1, 3–5: 45
  incerta fr. 69: 45
  incerta fr. 487: 39
  Epigrams (Vahlen 1928) frr. 1, 2, 4
  (23f.): 15f.
    frr. 3 (19f.), 4 (21f.): 49f.
  Satirae (Vahlen 1928) 3. fr. 1: 42
  incerta fr. 5: 47

Homer *Iliad* 4.20–3: 244
  Odyssey 1.1: 22
    1.64: 23
    1.169: 25
    3.108–12: 25
    6.295–9: 27
    8.138f.: 25
    8.378–80: 24
Homeric *Hymn to Demeter* 16ff.: 239
Horace *Epistulae* 2.1.156f.: 8
    2.1.157–9: 34f.
Hrotsvit (of Gandersheim) *Gesta*
  Ottonis 1ff.: 286f.

Juvenal *Satira* 1.1–14: 153

Livius Andronicus *Odussia*
  (Büchner 1982) fr. 1: 7, 22
    fr. 3: 23
    fr. 7: 25
    fr. 10: 25
    fr. 12: 23
    fr. 13: 23
    fr. 15: 27
    fr. 18: 26

fr. 19: 23
fr. 20: 24
fr. 21: 23
fr. 30: 24
Livy *Ab Vrbe Condita* 21.1.2: 218
  40.52.5–7: 32
Lucan *Bellum Civile* or *Pharsalia* 1.1: 6
  1.4, 8: 165f.
  1.32–67: 139
  1.128: 133
  1.158–82: 131f.
  1.670: 133
  2.312: 137
  3.143–9: 137
  5.504–677: 6
  7.447: 135
  7.640: 133
  7.695f.: 132
  7.706: 135
  9.601–4: 134
Lucretius *De Rerum Natura* 1.117–18:
  16
  1.117–19: 37

Martial *Epigrammata* 9.65.1–14: 211f.
  10.4.1–12: 153f.

Naevius *Bellum Punicum*
(Strzelecki 1964) fr. 3: 33
  fr. 4: 29
  fr. 5: 30
  fr. 10: 30
  fr. 20: 30
  fr. 25: 31
  fr. 32: 33
  fr. 34: 34

Ovid *Amores* 1.15.25f.: 113
  Fasti: 4.445ff.: 239
  Metamorphoses 1.1–4: 108
  1.183–5: 245
  1.204f.: 245
  3.141f.: 119
  3.174–7: 119f.
  3.198–206: 29f.
  3.407–9: 203
  3.531–48: 115f.
  4.311f., 315f., 346–9: 206
  4.385f.: 207
  5.356ff.: 239
  5.420ff.: 240
  14.568–72: 117f.

Persius *Satira* 1.69f.: 153
Petrarch *Africa* 1.1f.: 15, 296f.
  9.133–8, 404–6: 298
  Seniles 4.5: 301
Phaedrus *Fabulae* 1. *Prolog.* 3f.: 151f.
  1.28.1f.: 152
  4.2.1–7: 150
  4.6.11–13: 152
  4.7.21f., 5f., 7–9:150f.
Propertius: *Elegiae* 1.7.1f.: 167
  1.20.33–42: 199f.
  1.20.47f.: 201
  2.1.13f.: 147
  2.1.149f.: 147
  2.34.59–66: 79
  2.34.65f.: 147f.
  2.34.81f.: 148
  3.1.31–4: 145f.
  3.1.7: 146
  3.1.35–8: 146

Silius Italicus: *Punica* 1.1–16: 218f.,
  227
  2.410–13: 37
  5.670–3: 226
  6.653–716: 232
  9.287–9: 224
  10.309–11: 223
  11.481f.: 232
  13.796f.: 229
  17.399f.: 223
  17.643f.: 233
  17.653f.: 221
Statius *Silvae* 4.7: 164
  Thebais 1.1–3: 7f.
  1.1–46: 163ff., 169
  1.426f.: 176
  1.589–612: 177
  2.505–15: 189
  2.642f.: 175
  3.126–32: 181
  3.165–8: 181
  5.210–462: 184f.
  6.513–17: 187f.
  8.751–6: 177f.
  8.760–2: 177
  8.764–6: 178
  9.340–402: 181f.
  11.119–35: 178
  11.407f.: 185
  11.524–33: 178
  11.599f.: 179

11.619–21, 624–6: 180f.
12.288–90, 316–20, 325–41: 186f.
12.429–32: 179
12.796–819: 163f.
12.816f.: 8
Valerius Flaccus *Argonautica* 1.1–4: 195f.
    1.218–20: 197
    3.549–57: 202f.
    3.551f.: 214
    3.558–61: 205
    3.560f.: 207
    3.570–2: 214
    3.596f.: 209, 213
    4.18f.: 209
    4.22–4: 214
    4.36f.: 209
Vida *Christiad* 1.1–7: 308
    1.811–14: 307
    2.649f.: 305
    6.520–3: 307
Virgil *Eclogae* 6.44f.: 213
    10.75–7: 103

Georgica 3.46–8: 4, 80f.
Aeneis 1.1: 6
    1.1–7: 82
    1.453–65: 99
    2.768–70: 208ff.
    6.1–8: 87
    6.30–3: 102
    6.719–21: 95f.
    6.791–5: 98
    6.851–3: 83
    8.370–406: 6
    8.608–731: 6
    8.617–25: 174
    10.907–11.16: 174
    12.665–80: 89f.
    12.945–52: 93f.
    12.950–2: 85, 103

Waltharius 223–6: 276
    857–75: 269
    1239–64: 270
    1280–96: 281ff.
    1393–1406: 271

336